India Studies in Business and Economics

Indian economy is one of the fastest growing economies of the world, entering the top 5 club in 2022. The country is an important G20 member and is also a founding member of BRICS. A significant player in the global market with a notable demographic advantage and an important geo-political and geo-trade position, India has a pivotal role to play in meeting global SDG goals. This makes research from the country of immense interest to the global community, especially to those trying to understand emerging developmental challenges through a developing economy and/or Global South perspective.

With this backdrop, this series aims to bring forth latest studies and research specific to India from all areas of economics, finance, business, trade, and management science, often with strong social science and political economy linkages. The titles featured in this series present rigorous research, both empirical and non-empirical in nature, usually accompanied by policy recommendations. They evoke and evaluate various aspects of the economical and/or the business and management landscape in India, with a special focus on India's relationship with the world. The series also tracks research on India's position on social issues, health, politics, agriculture, rights, and many such topics which directly or indirectly affect sustainable growth and SDG goals of the country.

Primarily publishing authored monographs and edited volumes, the series also considers collection of case studies, reports and proceedings of important national conferences. It welcomes contributions from the academic community, corporates, think tanks and/or non-governmental organizations, and also policymakers to publish their work. Proposals must contain a detailed concept note describing the book's content and its importance; academic CV of authors/editors; extended chapter abstracts that clearly define the chapter's content; and a sample chapter. Each proposal will undergo a double-blind peer review. Reviews can be more detailed if recommended by reviewers.

Guidelines for submission and our policies on ethics is found on the series homepage www.springer.com/series/11234.

Joy Deshmukh Ranadive • Samapti Guha
Editors

Building Pathways to Women's Empowerment

Three decades of India's Annapurna Pariwar

Springer

Editors
Joy Deshmukh Ranadive
Independent Consultant
Pune, Maharashtra, India

Samapti Guha
School of Management and Labour Studies
Centre for Social Entrepreneurship
Tata Institute of Social Sciences
Mumbai, Maharashtra, India

ISSN 2198-0012 ISSN 2198-0020 (electronic)
India Studies in Business and Economics
ISBN 978-981-95-7158-1 ISBN 978-981-95-7159-8 (eBook)
https://doi.org/10.1007/978-981-95-7159-8

This Springer imprint is published by the registered company Springer Nature Singapore Pte Ltd.
The registered company address is: 152 Beach Road, #21-01/04 Gateway East, Singapore 189721, Singapore

Foreword

This volume, *Three Decades of Annapurna Pariwar: Building Pathways to Women's Empowerment*, offers a deeply insightful and timely reflection on one of India's most enduring and innovative models of women-centred financial inclusion.

From its modest beginnings in 1993, when Dr. Medha Purao Samant lent Rs. 9000 from her personal savings to nine vegetable vendors in a Pune slum, Annapurna Pariwar has grown into a federation of six interlinked institutions. These include a cooperative credit society, a mutual insurance platform, a pension and social security initiative, an early childcare service, an education sponsorship programme, and a training and advocacy wing. Each component is an integral part of Dr. Samant's coherent vision of development that sees women not as passive recipients of welfare but as active architects of collective prosperity.

Of particular relevance to contemporary policy discourse, Annapurna Pariwar's pioneering work in the domain of community-based health and life insurance is important. Health shocks continue to be among the leading causes of impoverishment and indebtedness for low-income households in India. With the outreach and quality limitations associated with the public sector, a largely stagnant private insurance sector focused on the urban elite, and limited fund allocations to government-funded insurance schemes, financial protection and healthcare access among informal workers, especially urban slum dwellers, remain low, fragmented, and inadequate. The Annapurna model offers a compelling complementary proposition to fill the gaps left by government programmes.

Launched in 2003, Annapurna's mutual health insurance programme was conceived as a participatory risk-sharing mechanism grounded in solidarity and mutual trust. It was designed with the active involvement of women members, priced affordably, and administered transparently. Claims processes were simplified; exclusions were minimised; settlements were prompt. Over time, the scheme evolved to include additional coverage for life, disability, and hospitalisation, responding to emerging member needs. Crucially, the programme has sustained high enrolment, minimal dropout, robust claim ratios and an absence of fraud, which represents a model for building self-sustaining financial solutions that rely on community solidarity.

This innovation directly addresses a structural gap in India's health financing landscape: the absence of mechanisms that effectively cater to those excluded from both commercial insurance and fully funded public health systems. The Annapurna mutual insurance model stands as evidence that it is possible to design and sustain locally governed, financially viable, and socially responsive health protection mechanisms. It merits serious attention in ongoing debates on universal health coverage and community-based health financing in India.

Annapurna Pariwar's contribution extends well beyond financial and health services. It has built a 'microfinance-plus' architecture that integrates social protection, human development, and institutional ownership. The early childcare centres (*Vatsalya Purna*) support working women by providing safe and stimulating environments for their children. The educational sponsorship programme (*Vidya Purna*) supports the next generation with scholarships and mentoring. The pension and savings programme (*Aadhar Purna*) enables women to build security for old age, often their first experience with structured, long-term savings.

There is strong evidence that, to have maximum impact on the lives of the people they serve, local institutions will need to work towards offering comprehensive solutions, moving well beyond narrowly defined services. The value of effective day care, once again filling the gaps left by government programmes, on the long-term mental health of children and the opportunity it creates for women to lead more equal lives, has been well documented. It is also very clear that India is ageing rapidly. Given the severe shortage of family resources and the absence of a comprehensive government social security programme, the process of building up an old-age fund must begin early. The efforts of Annapurna in all these domains fill essential gaps and build models from which both government and non-government actors have a great deal to learn.

Under the consistent leadership and vision of Dr Samant, Annapurna has maintained a strong institutional coherence and has displayed confidence and exemplary courage in the face of the extreme turbulence of the last three decades. Where several institutions failed, Annapurna Pariwar continued to operate through economic liberalisation, urban expansion, regulatory shifts, demonetisation, and a global pandemic. Each posed formidable challenges to liquidity, outreach, and member well-being.

The institution responded to these challenges by embracing digital innovations, restructuring services, and deepening member engagement. That it did so while sustaining its independence and focus on community needs is a testament to the leadership of Dr. Samant and her team. It signals that building multiple organisations that stay focused on well-defined communities and serve them comprehensively is a superior development strategy relative to one in which each organisation attempts to scale nationally, taking a very narrow approach. This is also well borne out by the experiences of community-focused institutions around the world. A book like this can serve as a blueprint for those who want to serve and help communities in other parts of the country and the world to prosper in a similar manner.

From a policy perspective, this volume is especially important. As India continues to refine its approach to financial inclusion, gender-responsive budgeting, and health coverage, the lessons from Annapurna are of direct relevance. First, it demonstrates that meaningful inclusion is inextricably linked to community focus. Second, it indicates that cooperative and mutual models can be professionally managed and financially sound. Third, it affirms that gender-focused institutions can succeed at scale, provided they are designed with authenticity and respect.

For regulators, Annapurna's experience invites us to revisit how we assess institutional risk and viability. Current regulatory frameworks tend to favour conventional corporate forms and standardised metrics. Cooperative or mutual structures are often treated as legacy arrangements, subject to overregulation or under-support. Yet, as Annapurna shows, such entities can outperform more commercially structured organisations on key indicators of sustainability, repayment, and social impact. There is a strong case for developing enabling regulatory frameworks that recognise and support such entities. It is worth noting that several developed countries with sophisticated financial systems, such as Germany with its Sparkassen, Switzerland with its Raiffeisenbanken, and the United States with its thousands of credit unions, have continued to support and nurture their cooperative institutions. They have recognised that these institutions have to be at the core of any comprehensive development strategy.

For government agencies and ministries, particularly those focused on women and child development, health, and urban livelihoods, Annapurna's experience has much to offer. It shows how service delivery can be combined with capability building and institutional empowerment. It suggests that working with local, deeply embedded organisations in such sensitive yet critical service-oriented areas may be a more effective strategy than building large public sector behemoths.

For donors and development practitioners, this book offers a compelling case for grounded, locally governed solutions. In an era when global development finance is often channelled through large intermediaries or technocratic consortia, the long-term success of Annapurna suggests that sustained investment in community-owned platforms can yield deeper, more sustainable outcomes. The book's documentation, combining institutional analysis, case narratives, and field insights, offers rich material for learning, replication, and adaptation.

But perhaps the greatest value of this contribution lies in its reminder that real empowerment is not episodic or transactional; it is institutional. It takes time. Annapurna Pariwar did not simply offer services to poor women; it built an organisation with them, and, in many respects, through them. Its legacy is not only in the loans disbursed or the claims settled, but in the confidence and solidarity it fostered.

As this book makes clear, the future of inclusive finance and social protection in India will depend not just on new products or digital tools but on our ability to imagine and support institutions that are just, participatory, and resilient. Annapurna Pariwar is one such institution. This volume is both a celebration of its journey and a provocation to the broader ecosystem: to listen, to learn, and to lead with values. Edited by Dr. Joy Deshmukh Ranadive and Dr. Samapti Guha, it fills the gap in the literature on Annapurna Pariwar-led urban finance and gender issues of development.

It is my sincere hope that this book will find a wide readership, not only among academics and practitioners, but among regulators, legislators, civil servants, and public leaders. For in its pages lies not just a story of what has been achieved, but also a map for how development institutions can be reimagined—one community at a time.

June 11, 2025

Nachiket Mor PhD
Banyan Academy of Leadership in Mental Health
Reserve Bank of India (2013–2018)
National Bank for Agriculture and Rural Development (2013–2018)
ICICI (1987–2007)

Acknowledgements This book is the result of the sincere, untiring dedication of several people towards the goal of empowering marginalised, hardworking women. The book took shape after three webinars, organised by INHAF and Shri Kirti Bhai Shah, discussed various aspects of Annapurna Pariwar. The vision for the book, however, went beyond the webinars. The minute details of the journey of the organisation, its evolution and its stand on women's empowerment were documented. Academics and sector experts who were familiar with the work of Annapurna Pariwar were invited to discuss the organisation and its relevance in today's microfinance and microinsurance sector.

First, thank you to Dr. Medha Purao Samant, CMD and Founder of Annapurna Pariwar, for sparing the time during her very busy schedule of running Annapurna Pariwar to answer questions regarding the genesis of the organisation, its journey, the organisational evolution and her vision and views on women's empowerment. Thank you to Shri V.C. Joshi, a known expert in banking, for his guidance through discussions, given his long history with the organisation. Thank you to Shri Anand Awdhani for discussions while formulating the vision of the book. Gratitude to all the authors of the book: Ms. Girija Sirinivasan; Ms. Shraddha Kalani and Dr. Chandralekha Ghosh; Dr. Kanish Debnath; Dr. Archana Singh; Dr. K. Naveen Kumar; Dr. Tara Nair; Dr. Monica Nandan; Dr. Gokul Mandayam; Dr. Marissa Kaloga; and Ms. Simran Hatkar for drawing out insights on the relevance of Annapurna Pariwar in the microfinance and microinsurance sector today.

We are grateful to Dr. Nachiket Mor (Visiting Scientist, Banyan Academy of Leadership in Mental Health, and Visiting Professor at the Indian School of Business) for writing the foreword of the book.

As editors, thank you goes to our families for the support only they can give.

Dr. Joy Deshmukh Ranadive and Dr. Samapti Guha

Contents

Editors and Contributors

About the Editors

Dr. Joy Deshmukh Ranadive is an economist by training and a social scientist by practice. She brings with her over three decades of experience in the area of social development. She is an advisor and consultant to NGOs and corporates on issues of sustainability, CSR, gender and social programmes. Dr. Joy retired as the Global Head of CSR, Tata Consultancy Services. She has previously served as Director of the Indian School of Microfinance for Women in Ahmedabad and as Country Director of the International Centre for Research on Women, which is head quartered in Washington. A doctorate in Economics and a gold medallist at MA from the University of Mumbai, Dr. Joy has several books and papers to her credit in the areas of gender, development, microfinance, human rights and CSR.

Dr. Samapti Guha is a Professor, Centre for Social Entrepreneurship, School of Management and Labour Studies, Tata Institute of Social Sciences, Mumbai. She is a Development Economist and earned her Ph.D. in Economics from Jadavpur University in 2004. After completing her Ph.D., she worked at the Indian Institute of Dalit Studies, New Delhi and the Institute of Rural Management Anand (IRMA), Gujarat. In 2006, she was selected as a Sir Ratan Tata Fellow at the London School of Economics and Political Science, UK, for her post-doctoral study. In 2007, she joined the Tata Institute of Social Sciences and launched a new MA programme in Social Entrepreneurship, managing the Centre single-handedly for three years. She has mentored more than 50 social start-ups. Her areas of research include microfinance, women entrepreneurship, microenterprises, social entrepreneurship, financial inclusion and development economics. She has published articles in numerous national and international journals and books. She has attended and presented articles in several national and international conferences.

Contributors

Kanish Debnath MYRA School of Business, Mysuru, Karnataka, India

Chandralekha Ghosh Department of Economics, West Bengal State University, Barasat, India

Samapti Guha School of Management and Labour Studies, Centre for Social Entrepreneurship, Tata Institute of Social Sciences, Mumbai, Maharashtra, India

Simran Hatkar Community Based Insurance Programme, Pune, Maharashtra, India

Shraddha Kalani Livin' My Dream, Bangalore, Karnataka, India

Marissa Kaloga Management & International Business, University of Auckland, Auckland, New Zealand

Gokul Mandayam School of Social Work, Rhode Island College, Providence, RI, USA

K. Naveen Kumar National Institute of Bank Management, Pune, Maharashtra, India

Tara Nair Work Fair and Free Foundation, Bangalore, Karnataka, India

Monica Nandan Strategic Partnership and Social Impact, Department of Social Work and Human Services, Wellstar College of Health and Human Services, Kennesaw State University, Kennesaw, GA, USA

Joy Deshmukh Ranadive Independent Consultant, Pune, Maharashtra, India

Archana Singh National Insurance Academy, Pune, Maharashtra, India

Girija Srinivasan Community Institutions, Financial Services, and Enterprise Development Consultant, Pune, Maharashtra, India

Introduction

Joy Deshmukh Ranadive and Samapti Guha

Abstract The microcredit movement in India started with the initiation of the cooperative societies in 1905. After independence, several banking reforms had taken place in India such as Bank Nationalisation in 1969, introduction to priority sector lending in 1972, formation of Regional Rural Banks in 1975, creation of National Bank for Agriculture and Rural Development in 1982, etc.

1 Microfinance Movement in India and Sustainable Development Goals

The microcredit movement in India started with the initiation of the cooperative societies in 1905. After independence, several banking reforms had taken place in India, such as Bank Nationalisation in 1969, introduction to priority sector lending in 1972, formation of Regional Rural Banks in 1975, creation of National Bank for Agriculture and Rural Development in 1982, etc. The aim of such banking reforms was to promote social banking, which is inclusive in nature. Parallelly, in the 70s, the microcredit movement was initiated by the Self-Employed Women's Association (SEWA), a trade union, by setting up SEWA Urban Cooperative Bank in Ahmedabad, Gujarat. At the same time, self-help groups were nurtured

J. D. Ranadive
Independent Consultant, Pune, Maharashtra, India
e-mail: drjoydeshmukh@gmail.com

S. Guha (✉)
School of Management and Labour Studies, Centre for Social Entrepreneurship, Tata Institute of Social Sciences, Mumbai, Maharashtra, India
e-mail: samapti@tiss.ac.in

J. D. Ranadive, S. Guha (eds.), *Building Pathways to Women's Empowerment*, India Studies in Business and Economics,
https://doi.org/10.1007/978-981-95-7159-8_1

by national and international NGOs for financial inclusion in India. This movement was influenced by Dr. Md. Yunus of Bangladesh Grameen Bank, Bancosol Bolivia, Bank de Rakayat in Indonesia, etc. Women-led SHGs and Joint Liability Groups (JLGs) are at the centre of the microcredit movement in India. This lending structure positively impacted marginalised women's access to and usage of credit, and they were linked to the banking system. On the non-financial perspective, it increased their mobility, and they exercised their rights to freedom and were protected from violence. It also helped them to take up economic activities for their economic empowerment. In the 90s, along with the NGOs, Commercial Banks, and Cooperatives joined the microcredit movement. The success of NABARD led SHG Bank Linkage programme (SBLP) post 1995 accelerated this movement. It established the fact that the poor are bankable. By 2000, SBLP became the world's biggest microfinance programme. Other financial institutions also became interested in providing other financial services through Women Collectives such as SHGs and JLGs. Post 2000, economic transition of microcredit institutions took place. It transformed microfinance institutions. Several institutions transformed from non-profits to not for profits and for profits. These organisations started to deliver microcredit plus services such as micro savings, microinsurance, micro pension etc. They changed their legal status from NGOs to Non-Banking Financial Companies (NBFCs) (Guha & Ghosh, 2015). It helped them to mobilise the public savings and increase the outreach. Women-members of SHGs and JLGs got access to different microfinance products. Some of the products such as microinsurance and micro pension helped them to get social security. It also increased the collaboration between different financial institutions such as Microfinance Institutions, Insurance companies, Commercial Banks etc. The households of the women members also got the benefits from the microcredit plus services. Some households have built assets such as housing, some households created emergency funds through micro savings, some households engaged in productive activities by using microcredit etc. Microcredit was also used for repaying the past debts. Several members borrowed from the informal money-lenders, and they were caught into debt trap due to usurious rate of interest. MFIs helped these households to repay their past debts and later, they used the credit for productive activities. In the case of Cooperative Societies, members are the owners of the society. So, these marginalised women are entitled to the ownership of the democratic institution, and they are the decision makers. This empowered them economically, socially, and politically. In the context of feudal and patriarchal society, MFIs are facilitating the process of empowerment of women. It is a unique contribution of microfinance in India.

As the sector is growing, regulation of the institutions is required. These institutions are also working with public money. There is a regulatory transition in this sector. Post 2013, according to the Mor Committee report, the Reserve Bank of India accepted the application of 10 MFIs to become Small Finance Banks. These newly formed microbanks have experience of delivering micro financial services. They have gone through the previous economic transition. Majorly, they are offering all micro financial services to their old members but for the financial sustainability, they are offering banking services to the middle- and upper-income classes. There is a mandate that they will work on financial literacy for different sections of the society. These banks have helped the economically active people to start and scale up their business activities. The presence of different forms of MFIs is contributing towards financial inclusion, women empowerment and creating a financial ecosystem for small businesses. In this context, this book aims to explain the relevance of cooperative model of microfinance in the present context in terms of achieving women empowerment, several SDG goals such as SDG 5, SDG 8 and SDG 11.

2 Rationale of the Book

This book, **'Three decades of Annapurna Pariwar Building Pathways to Women's Empowerment'**, chronicles the 30-year journey of Annapurna Pariwar, a conglomerate of six organisations that organically evolved from meeting the needs of poor, productive women from the slums of Pune and Mumbai. It is the effort of Dr. Medha Purao Samant, who gave up her job at a bank to solve the financial problems of vegetable vendors in the area she visited to buy her necessities. Beginning with nine women, and financing loans from her own pocket of a sum of Rs. 1000, Medha Tai, as she is called, today has 40,000 active borrowers and a total loan disbursement of Rs. 3000 crore. From one location in a slum in Pune, it has spread to 650 slums and to 1250 slums in Mumbai. From one single person, Medha Tai, the organisation now has a staff of 300. As the needs of members grew and as Medha Tai and her team realised what the members needed, and services became a bouquet that were relevant to the community and the times. The organisations are women-founded, women-led, women-run, and women-owned. The uniqueness lies in the cooperative model, in mutual insurance, in democratic practices and in the voices of women flowing from not just above to below but vice versa.

Annapurna Pariwar is a group of six organisations that together are a social enterprise. Having come into being in 1993 at a time when there were major changes in the Indian economy in the form of globalisation and urbanisation Annapurna Pariwar sought to address issues of livelihood and poverty alleviation in the slums of Pune and Mumbai. As an organisation, Annapurna Pariwar adopted a path that was sustainable and did not depend upon grants. The journey is a fascinating account of learnings in organisational evolution and its impact upon the lives of poor women.

3 Women Empowerment and Sustainable Development Goals

For advancing women's rights, the Beijing Convention of the UN in 1995 played an important role as 189 countries attended to discuss gender inequality and how they can promote women's rights for gender equality and equal opportunities in the World. After two decades of the Beijing Convention and 15 years of the Millennium Development Goals, in 2015, a new set of global agreements emerged, the UN Sustainable Development Goals (SDGs). Among the 17 goals, SDG 5 focuses on 'Gender Equality and Empowerment of Women and Girls' (https://sdgs.un.org/goals/goal5). It is a new compact for women's rights and equality. It is also accepted by donors, civil society, and several national and international stakeholders (Dhar, 2018). SDGs are applicable to everyone universally, and each goal is based on human rights. SDG 5 is the outcome of the movement of women's collectives in different parts of the world. It has two aspects: Economic empowerment of women and stopping the discrimination, including violence against women, such as trafficking, female genital mutilation, forced marriage, unpaid work, etc. Dhar (2018) mentioned that women's collectives were critical of the government's negligence regarding women's human rights, and they demanded that states should work towards gender equality and women's empowerment. These activists also critically observed that SDGs require more commitment from the States so that the female workforce has collective bargaining for wage equality and to adjust macroeconomic policies by adopting a gender perspective.

In the context of India, Dhar (2018) mentioned that the feminist activists Vina Mazumdar and Lotika Sarkar came up with the first report of the Committee on the Status of Women in 1974. They pointed out the serious issue of socio-cultural gender discrimination, which was the reason for the disempowerment of women. They mentioned the problem of the declining sex ratio in India. After four decades, the second report was published in 2015. It discussed the gender gap through an intersectional lens. It also voiced the complexity of the women's lives in India. Though the government of India has taken several steps to empower women, the author mentioned that political will is required to address the problem of patriarchal, misogynist, and feudal mindset of the society.

Hirway (2018) analysed the disproportionate engagement of women in unpaid work. The author mentioned that the status of women in the labour market is inferior, as they are predominantly engaged in unpaid work. Due to patriarchal norms, women are less educated, less mobile, and educated women ended up with low-profile and stereotypical jobs such as teaching, nursing, clerical jobs, etc. Due to this fact, they lack upward mobility. So, in the labour market, they do not get the justice and equality. To address this issue of gender inequality, the author mentioned that SDGs recommended actions to protect the women's rights. These actions are, '(a) elimination of all forms of discrimination against women and girls, (b) elimination of all forms of violence against women, (c) ensuring sexual and reproductive health as well as rights to women, (d) elimination of all forms of patriarchal malpractices, such as child marriages, forced marriages and so on' (Hirway, 2018; pp. 104). Further she suggested to the policy makers to give the visibility to the unpaid work during the policymaking and time use surveys need to be conducted at the National level to understand the status and size of the unpaid work.

In the context of gender inequality, women's collectives have been playing a crucial role for several decades. These collectives are working against gender inequality, gender violence etc. Desouza (2012) analysed three collectives from Delhi, Mumbai, and Goa to understand the strength of the women's collectives. The author did the outcome analysis of these collectives and found three most important factors of the successes of these collectives: collective ideology, participation, and accountability. The collectives used democratic structure rather than hierarchical structure. The author found that after the short-lived actions of the collectives, the members-activists tried to pursue other goals with confidence and collective models emerged. These models also influence other organisations-participants. In such a way, these collectives have influence on public policy making. The author mentioned that even if it has an influence on policy making, it has not achieved its radical goals of mobilisation, broader cultural and personal outcomes. She opined that these goals need to be recognised. These goals also help the collectives to achieve SDG 5.

4 About the Book

Annapurna Pariwar, as a women's collective, tries to mobilise the women, and over almost three decades, women from the slums have been mobilised by Annapurna Pariwar. Dr. Medha Samant, CMD of Annapurna Pariwar, successfully created six social enterprises based on the complex issues related to the lives of the marginalised women in the slums of Pune and Mumbai. This organisation addressed the issues of gender inequality, women's empowerment (special focus on economic empowerment) to protect the rights of women, and it is trying to deliver justice to these marginalised women. The microfinance wing of Annapurna Pariwar, AMCCSL, a multi-state credit cooperative society owned by its member-borrowers, is an example of a women's collective that is empowering women economically. This book explains how Annapurna Pariwar has addressed the issues of women's rights, empowerment and worked towards SDG 5.

The book is divided into two parts. The first part has three chapters charting the journey of Annapurna Pariwar based on interviews with Medha Tai. Milestones, organisational evolution, and challenges, especially demonetisation and Covid are discussed. Chapter 2, **Annapurna Pariwar: Journey across Challenges** traces the historical journey of Annapurna Pariwar, its genesis and the challenges faced and overcome along the way. The response of Annapurna Pariwar to the turning points it faced, led to the evolution of six developmental organisations which organically evolved from meeting the needs of poor, productive women from the slums of Pune and Mumbai.

The Chap. 3, **A System that Works: Management of Annapurna Pariwar** focuses on the management model of Annapurna Pariwar. The model is unique since it was organic and evolved over time while catering to the needs of the community it served. A system has been built over the years that encourages staff to function in efficient ways and instil a loyalty toward the ideology on which the organisation was built. The succession plan, cadre of senior management are instrumental in the running of the organisation. The financial sustainability of the organisation and how it was achieved will be detailed out. The use of in-house technology has facilitated the smooth transactions of microfinance and microinsurance within Annapurna Pariwar. There is a two-way communication between the organisation and its members. Principles of democracy are adhered to. These systems will be highlighted in this chapter. The importance of voice, especially of the community, and how it influences and teaches the organisation how to move forward, shapes the model of Annapurna Pariwar. Financial stability and the link to digitisation is critical. Annapurna Pariwar has its own system of digitisation that facilitates the processes of loan disbursements, loan collection, insurance claims, etc. Both hardware and software are synergised to make the tasks of loan officers and band staff smooth. The digitisation organisation of Annapurna Pariwar and its role in managing an efficient system will be illustrated. The role of the Board of Annapurna Pariwar is central to the organisation. Regular, documented Board meetings and how they steer the organisation forward will be drawn out in this chapter.

The Chap. 4, **Empowering Women from One Milestone to Another**, locates the processes of empowerment using the framework of increased economic, socio-cultural, physical, and political spaces within the lives of women members.[1] (Deshmukh Ranadive, 2002). Women's empowerment is not a simple linear process of cause and effect. It entails a complex configuration of factors that affect economic, socio-cultural, political, physical, and mental spaces. These are seen at the individual micro level as well as at the meso level of communities. The cause can be activated in any space, and its effect is seen in all the other spaces. Economic space is determined by ownership of immovable and movable assets, both tangible and non-tangible, which enhance women's economic independence. Access and control over assets, over livelihoods, over savings, access to credit, to insurance, to pension schemes, enhance economic spaces. Socio-cultural spaces increase when women's position within kinship structures, such as family and communities, is enhanced. Caste, class, region, ethnicity, and religion play a significant role within socio-cultural spaces. Physical spaces are captured with mobility, access to transport, access, and ability to venture out of the limited domain of house and slum to access livelihood and other options. Physical space is also enhanced with increased safety and ability to move freely in geographical areas. Physical space is enhanced with control of women's bodies and reproductive decisions. Political spaces increase the decision-making ability of the women within the formal and informal institutions such as family, neighbourhood,

[1] This framework is an original contribution of the editor to empowerment studies.

common spaces, Political Institutions, other social and economic institutions where they express their agencies to take the decision and enable other women to take their decisions. Mental space is not an independent variable. It is connected to expansion in any one or several other spaces. Increased mental space allows women to take decisions which lead to their empowerment.

Microfinance and micro insurance services have enabled processes of empowerment to be activated. Further, the input of 'plus' services that Annapurna Pariwar has factored into microfinance and micro insurance has accelerated the empowerment processes. Case studies of select women members will be detailed to capture these processes. Women will be selected so that the juxta positioning of the life cycle of Annapurna Pariwar and the lifecycle positions will draw out various connections of the interventions and the commensurate empowerment impacts.

At the macro level, the book will investigate the policy and methods of Annapurna as an organisation. The deep impact of the macro and meso changes is felt at the micro level of individual women. In the first place, economic spaces have increased. sociocultural spaces, physical spaces, and political spaces in terms of leadership have increased. It is evident from the voice generated by Annapurna Pariwar that communication of ideas occurs from the macro to meso to micro levels. This is one of the stellar strengths of Annapurna Pariwar's empowerment model. Mental spaces shift on account of the shift in the other four spaces. The nine case studies are based on interviews conducted with nine women in the three decades of Annapurna Pariwar's journey. Juxtaposed with the lifecycle of the organisation itself, it sheds light on the evolution and hence ability of Annapurna Pariwar to expand different spaces of the nine women.

Part Two: is about **Locating the Relevance and Value of Annapurna Pariwar**. It contains analyses from well-known authors and academics who will contextualise the relevance of Annapurna Pariwar's work and future against, microfinance, microinsurance, plus services, social entrepreneurship, and digitisation. Authors in this book work on several social phenomena, such as social entrepreneurship, microfinance, cooperatives, women empowerment, and women entrepreneurship conceptually through the lenses of Annapurna Pariwar.

Within this part and in continuation of the chapters, Chap. 5 by Ms. Girija Srinivasan is titled **'Microfinance: The Relevance and Uniqueness of Annapurna Pariwar'**. This chapter discusses the history of micro finance in the country; SHG movement over three decades capturing the key factors that contributed to the success of SHG movement and missing services; emergence of lending by NGOs, key factors that made NGOs lenders and pros and cons; conversion to for profit NBFCs, growth; greed for return on capital, and crises, RBI and Government action; community owned financial institutions, their relevance. The chapter also delves into the role of MF and growth, challenges, and Annapurna Pariwar as a community-owned financial institution. The chapter examines the intention of initiating the organisation and the positioning of Annapurna Pariwar as a member-owned institution. It investigates the organisational form and factors guiding the governance and management structure. What are the key elements in organisational visioning to ensure double bottom growth (financial and social)?

Several questions are answered in this chapter -Did Annapurna Pariwar remain member-centric? What were the challenges? How were they faced? Issues such as meeting micro finance standards—which metrics were measured in terms of governance, management, HR, products and services, portfolio quality plethora of financial institutions and many choices available are investigated. Questions such as—what percentage of members continue and why? Did Annapurna Pariwar re-invent itself to meet competition, changes in external environment and changes in demographics of members? Which are the major partners to the growth of Annapurna Pariwar? How did they align with the intent of Annapurna Pariwar? Why is Annapurna Pariwar still relevant today? What do members appreciate about Annapurna Pariwar? What are the core factors for AMM to be relevant for another 20 years are discussed?

The Chap. 6 of the book by Dr. Samapti Guha, is **'Regulation in the Microfinance Sector: Challenges and Relevance for Annapurna Pariwar'**. This chapter discusses how the microfinance sector in India has transformed over the five decades. The regulatory structure of this sector has evolved. In India, initially, microfinance institutions adopted the oldest structure of cooperatives and non-profits such as Trust and Societies. In the nineties, when NABARD started the world's largest microfinance programme, SHG-Bank Linkage Programme, there was a transition in the sector. Several microfinance institutions transformed from non-profits to not-for-profits and for-profits. Regulatory structure of these MFIs has changed from Trust or Societies to Non-banking Financial Companies under Section 25 Companies Act and Section 8 Companies Act and later some of them have changed to small finance banks under RBI regulation. Annapurna Pariwar started its microfinance journey 30 years ago. It is a group of 6 non-profit organisations. Microfinance is delivered under Annapurna Mahila Multi State Co-op Credit Society Ltd. It is successfully empowering the marginalised section of women who are economically active in Maharashtra. Though there are several MFIs that have transformed into NBFCs and Small Finance Banks, Annapurna Pariwar did not change the regulatory structure from a Cooperative Society. This chapter studies the relevance of cooperative structure in microfinance sector and how Annapurna has addressed the challenges to retain this structure.

Chapter 7, by Dr. Samapti Guha, Ms. Shraddha Kalani and Dr. Chandralekha Ghosh, is, **'A Comparative Study on Financial Literacy Initiatives of Small Finance Bank and Cooperative Society in India: An Exploration'**. Financial exclusion and social exclusion co-exist in India. Due to this factor, several generations are facing financial hardship and lack of accessibility to education and employment, etc. Therefore, their financial and social status remain unchanged. Financial inclusion is required to break this barrier. Financial inclusion, financial literacy and financial stability are the different dimensions of the integral strategy of inclusive economic growth of any country. In India, several microfinance institutions such as Cooperative Societies, NBFC-MFIs, NGO-MFIs and small finance banks are operating. These institutions are promoting financial inclusion through financial literacy for the marginalised section of the population. The method of delivering financial literacy varies between the institutions. Sometimes customers are different for the different MFIs. It is important to understand how the oldest model of MFIs such as Credit Cooperative Society and the new model of MFIs such as Small Finance Bank (SFB) have been implementing financial literacy programmes and at what stage of the lending process these programmes are delivered. The difference between these two organisational structures is that a cooperative society is owned by the customers and Small Finance Bank is owned by the investors /shareholders. This chapter aims to do a comparative study on financial literacy initiatives taken by a credit cooperative society, Annapurna Mahila Credit Cooperative Society and a small finance bank, ESAF Small Finance Bank in order to address the goal of financial inclusion and financial stability. For this study, case study method is adopted to understand the process of delivery of financial literacy in studied organisations.

Chapter 8, Dr. Kanish Debnath, **'Building Social Safety Nets: Community Based Micro-Insurance at Annapurna Pariwar'**, provides a comprehensive overview of the global landscape of micro-insurance, with a particular focus on life and health insurance. Micro-insurance, designed to serve low-income populations, plays a crucial role in providing financial protection to vulnerable communities, especially in developing countries. The chapter will explore various models of micro-insurance across the globe, analysing how these models have evolved to meet the diverse needs of different regions. It will delve into the beneficial features of Annapurna's health insurance model, which has been recognised as an exemplary case in the micro-insurance industry. Annapurna's approach is unique in its ability to offer affordable and accessible health coverage to underserved populations, ensuring that even those with limited financial means can receive the care they need. The chapter will highlight the key attributes of this program, such as its premium structures, including family members of the beneficiary, comprehensive coverage, and community-driven approach. These characteristics contribute to the sustainability and long-term success of Annapurna's health insurance program, making it a valuable case study for other initiatives. Finally, the chapter will conclude by drawing important lessons from Annapurna's model, offering insights for future micro-insurance programs aiming to replicate its success.

Chapter 9, by Dr. Archana Singh, **'Regulation in the Microinsurance Sector: Challenges and Relevance for Annapurna Pariwar'** covers the evolution of the Microinsurance regulation of IRDAI and the corresponding journey of the Microinsurance sector in India. The Regulation of Social and Rural Obligation 2002 and the Microinsurance Regulation of 2005 kick-started a series of initiatives by insurance companies that were eager to collaborate with NGOs/MFIs to cover the space. Annapurna Pariwar faced challenges in these collaborations and started its sole journey of setting up mutual insurance to cover the health risks of its members. The chapter examines the position and contribution of Annapurna in offering risk management solutions and the challenges faced in this regulatory space. It also discusses how mutual insurance is placed in the current guidelines and its impact on organisations like Annapurna. It discusses other regulations like Point of Salespersons, IMF Regulation, and CPSC Regulation which were intended to increase the access to insurance for the masses. It touches upon the initiatives taken by the regulator to make insurance more inclusive for smaller organisations that are providing innovative alternatives to the low-income segment of society. It concludes with recommendations that will help Annapurna Pariwar to upscale and handhold other community-based organisations in offering insurance. These changes will be important in achieving the 'Insurance for All by 2047' targets set by IRDAI.

Chapter 10, by Dr. K. Naveen Kumar **'Digitisation and its role in Annapurna Pariwar'** discusses how digitalisation has emerged as a transformative force in enhancing the operational efficiency and outreach of microfinance institutions. This chapter investigates the impact of digitalisation on Annapurna Pariwar, a microfinance institution focused on financial inclusion and socio-economic development. As digitalisation reshapes industries, particularly in developing regions, Annapurna Pariwar leverages mobile technology and data analytics to enhance operational efficiency and customer engagement. The study analyses key digital initiatives, including mobile banking solutions and digital loan disbursement systems, highlighting how these tools improve client interactions and expand service reach. Through a framework assessing investments in data analytics, customer experience enhancements, and technological upgrades, the research identifies challenges such as infrastructure limitations and resistance to change. Strategies are proposed to address these issues, ensuring a holistic approach to digital transformation. By leveraging qualitative and quantitative data, the research highlights the benefits of digitalisation in increasing operational efficiency, enhancing customer satisfaction, and fostering financial inclusion. Further, the findings reveal that successful digitalisation is not merely a shift to technology but requires a cultural and organisational realignment, emphasising experimentation and risk-taking. Additionally, the paper underscores the importance of partnerships within the digital ecosystem to broaden the scope of digital financial inclusion and optimise service delivery. By drawing lessons from Annapurna Pariwar's experience, this research offers valuable insights for other financial service providers aiming to navigate the digital landscape effectively. Ultimately, it emphasises that a customer-centric approach, aligned leadership, and strategic partnerships are crucial for driving sustainable growth and impact in the evolving digital financial services sector.

Chapter 11, **'Augmenting the Value of Microfinance: 'Plus' Services of Annapurna Pariwar'** by Dr. Tara Nair analyses the value of Annapurna Pariwar's plus services. The organisational growth and diversification of Annapurna Pariwar since the mid-1970s bear testimony to the vision of its leadership that though access to credit is a foundational right of poor and resourceless women, they cannot move out of poverty just by availing credit. There are more acute constraints arising out of the structure of societal institutions embedded as they are with gender norms and social norms rooted in patriarchy. They severely constrain women's capabilities to build a life of value for themselves and their families. Absence of affordable and reliable childcare, access to children's education, and timely and affordable healthcare are the most critical human development deficits that burden poor households and push them back to chronic poverty. Annapurna Pariwar has systematically integrated services to address these constraints over the years and created a conglomeration of organisations consisting of cooperatives (micro credit, early childcare), non-profit companies (micro insurance/ old age security, digital solutions), and public charitable trusts (education, research). Annapurna Pariwar's impact on the community and women, hence, needs to be assessed by analysing how these various value-added interventions have interacted with each other and with the larger systemic shifts that occurred over a very critical phase in India's microcredit history. This chapter is an attempt to do such an analysis.

Chapter 12 is by Dr. Monica Nandan, Dr. Gokul Mandayam, Dr. Marissa Kaloga. It is titled **'Social Entrepreneurship and the Value of Annapurna Pariwar'**. This chapter describes the social and solidarity economy that contextualises the social entrepreneurial journey of Dr. Medha Purao Samant, founder of *Annapurna Pariwar.* Social and solidarity economy (SSE) is one of the pathways for accomplishing the United Nation's Sustainable Development Goals, and for framing diverse options for financial structures that make the world more just for populations that are often marginalised. This description contextualises the chapter. The chapter illustrates how Dr. Samant exemplified social entrepreneurial orientation and skills in the initiation and growth of Annapurna Pariwar. The chapter also incorporates relevant concepts from community social work and futurist practitioners that were exhibited by Dr. Samant during her social entrepreneurship journey. The chapter utilises the Effectuation Framework to illustrate her journey as a social entrepreneur. The evolution of the organisation is also described within the social entrepreneurial processes the founder adopted or deployed for the initiation and growth of the six distinct verticals (micro-finance, micro-insurance, day care, scholarship-based education support, research, and software development) within the cooperative social enterprise. Finally, how she recognised or created opportunities for structuring the first financial cooperative, how she was innovative in the process, how she was proactive in the financial and other sectors, while taking calculated risks to create sustainable impact in the lives of women living in poverty is described. Throughout the chapter, illustrations of fairness, equity, and empowerment are provided within the social and solidarity economy context.

5 Way Forward

This book aims to discuss the three decadal journey of Annapurna Pariwar. Authors have discussed Annapurna's contribution from different aspects, such as women empowerment, financial product innovation, regulatory structures, creation of social enterprises to solve the critical social problems of the members and the society. It was not a very smooth journey for Dr. Medha Samant. Her commendable work has created several scopes for the policy makers, researchers, practitioners and social entrepreneurs to take forward her work for bringing the positive social change in the society. It is established that the scientific implementation of the oldest model of microfinance, Cooperatives, has several positive impacts on the communities. This is the only model that offers ownership of the institutions to customers. So, members are the owners of the cooperatives and it is an empowering exercise for the leader like Dr. Samant. It has proved that the marginalised women not only are bankable, if they are given chance, they could be institute builders. Policy makers might take up this issue in consideration when they will develop the policies for the institute building for the marginalised communities. Practitioners and social entrepreneurs also consider this model of mission-centric enterprise for positive social change (Nicholls, 2006). Researchers will consider the aspect of new innovative product development for microfinance plus services such as insurance and pension. They will also consider longitudinal study of Cooperative models and impact of microfinance on the members of the cooperatives to understand the relevance of this model. It is also important to study why such a model is performing for so many years. All of these aspects are aligned with several SDGs, such as SDG 5, 8, and 11. As editors, we can assure you that this book will help the readers to find new dimensions of microfinance, social entrepreneurship and women empowerment through the lens of Annapurna Pariwar.

References

Desouza, S. (2012). The strength of collective processes: An 'outcome analysis' of women's collectives in India. *Indian Journal of Gender Studies*, *19*(3), 373–392, SAGE Publications. https://doi.org/10.1177/097152151201900302, https://ijg.sagepub.com

Deshmukh Ranadive, J. (2002). *Space for power: Women's work and family strategies in South and South-East Asia*. Rainbow Publications.

Dhar, S. (2018). Gender and sustainable development goals (SDGs). *Indian Journal of Gender Studies*, *25*(1), 47–78, Sage Publications. https://doi.org/10.1177/0971521517738451

Guha, S., & Ghosh, C. (2015). Institutional framework of MFIs economic benefit to clients in Mumbai Slums. *Economic and Political Weekly*, *50*, 151–159.

Hirway, I. (2018). Translating the SDG commitments into reality: Time use data for gender equality and women's empowerment in the global South. *Indian Journal of Human Development*, *12*(1), 93–108, SAGE Publications. https://doi.org/10.1177/0973703018778128, https://journals.sagepub.com/home/jhd

Nicholls, A. (2006). *Social entrepreneurship: New models of sustainable social change*. (Oxford, 2006; online edition, Oxford Academic, 31 Oct. 2023). https://doi.org/10.1093/oso/9780199283873.001.0001. Accessed 13 May 2025.

Part I
Interview with Dr. Medha Purao Samant by Dr. Joy Deshmukh Ranadive

Annapurna Pariwar: Journey Across Challenges

Joy Deshmukh Ranadive

Abstract This chapter traces the historical journey of Annapurna Pariwar, its genesis and the challenges faced and overcome along the way. The response of Annapurna Pariwar to the turning points it faced, led to the evolution of six developmental organisations which organically evolved from meeting the needs of poor, productive women from the slums of Pune and Mumbai. It is the effort of Medha Purao Samant who gave up her job at a bank to solve the financial problems of vegetable vendors in the area she visited for buying her necessities. Beginning with nine women, and financing loans from her own pocket of a sum of Rs. 1000, Medha Tai as she is called, today has 40,000 active borrowers and a total loan disbursement of Rs. 3000 crore. From one location in a slum in Pune, it has spread to 650 slums and to 1250 slums in Mumbai. From one single person Medha Tai, the organisation now has a staff of 300. As the needs of members grew and as Medha Tai and her team realised what the members needed, and services became a bouquet that were relevant to the community and the times. These grew into various savings schemes: micro mutual insurance for life, health, assets, etc; a pension scheme; childcare centres for children (these are self-sustaining enterprises) and educational support to the children of single mothers. Challenges such as demonetisation and Covid-19 pandemic, wreaked havoc on the likelihoods of Annapurna members and the functioning of the organisation. The organisation coped with these times in ways that are lessons for the future.

J. D. Ranadive (✉)
Independent Consultant, Pune, Maharashtra, India
e-mail: drjoydeshmukh@gmail.com

J. D. Ranadive, S. Guha (eds.), *Building Pathways to Women's Empowerment*, India Studies in Business and Economics,
https://doi.org/10.1007/978-981-95-7159-8_2

1 Introduction

This chapter is based on an in-depth interview with Dr. Medha Samant, CMD, Annapurna Pariwar, Medha Tai, about her journey with Annapurna Pariwar. The interview is conducted by Dr. Joy Deshmukh Ranadive, editor of this book. This chapter traces the historical journey of Annapurna Pariwar, its genesis and the challenges faced and overcome along the way. The response of Annapurna Pariwar to the turning points it faced, led to the evolution of six developmental organisations which organically evolved from meeting the needs of poor, productive women from the slums of Pune and Mumbai. It is the effort of Medha Purao Samant who gave up her job at a bank to solve the financial problems of vegetable vendors in the area she visited for buying her necessities. Beginning with nine women, and financing loans from her own pocket of a sum of Rs. 1000, Medha Tai, as she is called, today has 40,000 active borrowers and a total loan disbursement of Rs. 3000 crore.

2 Interview with Dr. Medha Purao Samant by Dr. Joy Deshmukh Ranadive

Dr. Joy: So, how did it all begin, when and why?

Medha Tai: It did not begin on one day. I completed my graduation in Statistics. In the first and second year, I studied Actuarial Science and Economics too. But in the last year, I studied Statistics.

I completed my graduation from Ruia college in Mumbai. Immediately after my graduation I joined Bank of India. I had passed the entrance exam of the banking service recruitment board a year earlier. It was 1981. The nationalisation of all banks in India was done in 1969. Hence, banks were spreading all over India, serving underserved areas, creating more jobs for youngsters like me. From 1981 to 1993, I worked for Bank of India. Those were 12 important years of my life.

A lot happened during these years. On my personal front, I got married. Then my father developed a cardiac problem and he was under treatment for many months before finally passing away untimely. Then I became pregnant, had my son. Immediately after my delivery, my father-in-law was sick for a long time. So, there were almost two years of sickness, child bearing and childbirth.

My residence in Mumbai was in Andheri, Lokhandwala complex. Whereas my office was initially at Opera House and later at Churchgate. So, I had to commute at least three hours a day. Further, there were other factors impacting my life of less resources and a lot of struggle. Hence, all these 12 years, especially 8 years in Mumbai, were very hectic, as a young wife, young mother, home maker, who was also a bank employee and trade union leader.

When I completed my graduation, I had plans to continue my education. I was studying German language at Max Muller Bhavan. I was also looking forward to learning German technical translation from a very senior translator, who was my colleague's father. My plan was to give up the bank job after a few years. But after my father's death I decided to continue with the bank job and also work for the All India Bank Employees Association. I had made up my mind to give up on any promotions and personal benefits. I rather wanted to devote my life for the Banking trade union movement, walking in the footsteps of my father.

Today when I look back that was a very emotional decision. But it changed the course of my life. My decision was welcomed by my father's comrades. They already started taking the initiative to groom me as a top trade union leader. I was contesting elections at my home Bank, that is, Bank of India. I had a very strong and popular opponent in the election. She was senior to me. Yet, I won three consecutive elections opposite her. I soon became popular with all the colleagues and comrades. I used to take up any small or big matters to the management and try my best to resolve them amicably. I was a women's representative. Hence, I took up especially women's issues because they were close to my heart - it be a separate toilet or day care centre or transfer or equal treatment with male colleagues.

In those 8 years in Mumbai, I was sent by the management to study the workers' teacher's training course, at Central Labour Institute. This was a three-month course, which taught me Labour law, handling cases of employee's grievances, International Trade union activities etc. I met and made friends with trade union activist and leaders from other banks too. After this course, I started working for Maharashtra State Bank Employees Federation. I soon became a popular woman leader amongst all bank employees. I had a lot of enthusiasm and vision which I had imbibed from my father. I used to think of the long-term issues of banking, Trade union and women's issues. Right from my childhood I was always mature and was a leader among my fellow students and friends. I was always helpful to needy friends. In my college days, I had joined NSS (National Social Service), which had a social mission as against the NCC (National Cadet Corps) which focussed on physical education. Through NSS I used to and would go to the orphanage or the slums to teach the children and women, basic literacy. At that time, I had joined All India students Federation and was very active in anti-fee rise movement. In the early eighties AISF was part of the joint committee (the student anti fee rise committee), I was a member of AISF and we got moderate success. All India Students Federation was linked with the progressive students' movement. We were active in several issues impacting college students.

Dr. Joy: Did you get a job satisfaction in the bank?

Medha Tai: The answer is yes and no. I was getting a good salary, good facilities. I could get a housing loan and loans for many other things like vehicle, home appliances etc, which help us to set up our home and family easily. On the other hand, though I had decided not to take any promotions, I was respected by my colleagues and seniors alike, due of my trade union leadership and sincere efforts to resolve the problems amicably by facilitating a dialogue between management and staff. I was popular among my colleagues.

However, I had started feeling that my job was not challenging enough. In Mumbai I worked in the Bank's Opera House Branch earlier and then the Bombay Main branch in the first eight years. Within the Bombay Main Branch, I was rotated within almost three departments. I tried to learn whatever I could, in whichever department I worked in. Which is why I know several things about banking. But I was also committed to my union work, focusing on women-related issues and overall trade union issues. The management of Bank of India wanted to invest in grooming young trade union leaders. I was sent for workers, teachers training courses. It was a three-month diploma. In Mumbai, at Kurla, there is a worker, teachers training college where these courses were conducted. I stood first among 25 students, who were all from different banks, and were young trade union leaders.

In 1993, there was a transition that took me from Mumbai to Pune. My husband started his own company in Pune. We decided to sell our flat in Andheri and buy another flat in Pune. Again, the entire haul of setting up house and getting established in another city was tremendous. My son was transferred from one school to another. On coming to Pune, for the first six months, I had to commute up and down between the cities of Mumbai and Pune since I did not immediately get a transfer to Pune. When we shifted to Pune in 1989, I was initially busy setting up a new home, a nuclear family with my 6-year-old son, for whom we had to find a new school and day care. I had to learn to drive a two-wheeler. There was a lot of hard work initially. It was multiplied in the first 6 months because I had to commute between Mumbai and Pune. Subsequently, I got a transfer to Pune, to the Karve Road Branch, which was just 4 km away from my home. Since I had learnt to drive a two-wheeler, the travelling time from home to office and office to home was altogether just half an hour. It was nothing compared to the travelling in Mumbai from Andheri to Churchgate and back. So, it saved a lot of time. I could read much more. I wanted to pursue studies. However, I was selected by the zonal office to work for the marketing team. This was a very unique experiment by our Bank management. 25 people were selected from all branches who were vocal and convincing. These were employees who could go to the customers, meet them in their offices and homes and convince them to deposit in our bank.

There were only two women in this team, which included me. I was happy to be a part of this unique experiment. We worked with all 25 branches in Pune. That also brought a lot of exposure in the geography of Pune. It also exposed me to the fact that everywhere there were plush housing complexes, but there were also lot of slums and poor localities. Soon I was promoted to a customer relations assistant. Hence, there was job satisfaction and interesting work; however, I had started feeling I should do more. I felt that I should not be spending all my life working for the bank.

As compared to Mumbai my life was much easier in Pune, I got time to read and observe around me. I was slowly beginning to understand that our country had started a new phase of globalisation, open economy and privatisation. The meaning of this slowly started capturing my mind, and it meant that the welfare schemes for the poor were going to be closed one after the other.

Pune was a smaller city than Mumbai. I had started noticing the issues of poor women who were very close to my bank branch. They were borrowing from private money lenders. And the banks were turning a blind eye and not financing them. I found these challenges more relevant to be addressed. From 1989 to 1993, I worked in the Pune zone in Bank of India. All was well. I worked in a branch that was just four kilometres away from where I lived, I would drop my son to school at Abhinav Vidyalaya and then report for duty at the bank. On my way home in the evening, I would buy vegetables from Paud Phata Vegetable Market. There I would see Shevantabai and Lakshmibai selling vegetables. They were hard-working women, and I built a rapport with them since I would not bargain regarding the prices. I used to see them taking loans from the money lenders. I would tell them that they should come to the bank and take loans from the bank. I tried convincing them that they were being fooled. But they thought that I was the one trying to fool. They didn't trust me at first because initially they had come across people who had tried to cheat them.

It was after two years of rapport, that they started trusting me. My colleagues at the bank would tell me not to get into any trouble. They said: 'You are very brave and committed. But don't bring this to the bank. We have a target of 2%. We manage that. Who will go through the trouble? You yourself have to work on it. You will have to recover the money borrowed. Who wants to get it take responsibility?' To add to that, Ms. Shevantabai and others also said that they did not want loans from the bank. So, for two years (1991–1993), I had a conversation with them. My bank, my home, everything was going well. I was writing a lot in those days. My stories and poems were very well received. I was awarded for them too. I was talking about different things. I was talking about women. I was writing about women too. I used to draw a lot of drawings. Yet, I felt that the bank and the union were not challenging at all. I wanted to work for those who are hungry. I was able to think in a lot of different ways. I was creative. It was a good time, those following four years (1989–1993).

Dr. Joy: What are the external influences in your life?

Medha Tai: My father was the most influential person in my life. His philosophy of life, his understanding of Marxism and economic problems of our nation always gave me a larger picture beyond me, my family and my personal life. I wanted to do something for society and the nation because of my father. My mother was also an activist, but she was a person working with her heart rather than her brain. She had compassion for the poor. She used to help a lot of people, especially poor women, but she could not think of larger issues and long-term solutions. Hence, I had developed compassion for poor people. I always wanted to help people. However, I was a person of both head and heart.

Hence, after settling down in Pune I had started thinking beyond myself my family. When I looked at the slums, I observed that the vegetable vendors in a market just a kilometre away from my bank were borrowing from private money lenders, whereas banks still had the priority sector lending scheme. I never thought of just helping poor vegetable vendors by giving them some little money or old clothes. I started thinking on the lines of a permanent long-term solution. I also started comparing the life of my friends from banks, especially women who had a very comfortable life to the poor women I saw. Due to a good, well paid bank job and high salary most of them had husbands who were well educated and earning well. So, their family life was comfortable. Yet, they wanted more comforts. Most often they would approach the union for transfers near their homes.

As compared to that I was looking at the poor vegetable vendors were deprived of even basic facilities like good home and education for their children. This comparison made me think more to do something for these poor women, which would be long term, which would help them change their lives.

Dr. Joy: What were the influences in your growing up years that shaped your world view of the society and its problems and issues?

Medha Tai: The most influential persons in my life were my father Com. Dada Purao, my school principal Dada Rege and to some extent, my mother at the young age but as I was growing, I could see that my mother was impulsive and she would act before thinking. Once I started realising this in my teenage years, I mostly did not follow her. But my father continued to be the tallest figure in my life.

His understanding about economics, the problems of our country and Marxism impacted my young mind the most. My school Bal Mohan Vidya Mandir was started and run by Dada Rege who was a man of wisdom.

He was a patriot and he frequently spoke about Lokmanya Tilak, Mahatma Gandhi and Sane Guruji. This influenced me with patriotic thoughts as well as kindness and love for the universe. Lokmanya Tilak was a leader of the Freedom Movement in India. Before Mohandas Gandhi, Tilak pronounced that freedom is our birth right and we shall fight to get it from the British rulers. Mahatma Gandhi then followed Tilak and became the tallest leader in the Indian freedom movement. Sane Guruji followed Gandhiji. He was a man with the kindness of a mother. He spoke, wrote and gave pure love to young students, sick people, and anyone he met. He has written a lot of literature for children. I read all his literature in my childhood.

Of course, both my parents were freedom fighters. My grandfather Shantaram Purao was a freedom fighter and a congressman. He had a great collection of books and all my uncles and aunts read voraciously, I read a lot in my childhood. I loved my universe. I was kind to the poor and also animals and trees. I used to write good essays and poems which were read openly to the classroom in school with a lot of praise.

Our house in Dadar Mumbai welcomed several well-known leaders and influential persons in society. This included Acharya Atre, Comrade Dange, Bhai SM Joshi, Shahir Amar Sheikh, Shaheer Annabhau Sathe and alike. All these famous people who came to our house were patriots, writers, poets, great orators, fearless freedom fighters. They were people who fought any kind of oppression. They were not rich with money, yet were still famous. All these were stalwarts in their field. They used to talk on different topics, mainly the problems of society and the solutions. As a young child and later as I grew, I used to listen to all their discussions. I did not understand it all but whatever I understood was very interesting. I never enjoyed small talk or playing with friends as much as I enjoyed listening to these discussions and reading a lot of books.

My father used to conduct a study circle for youth in Mumbai. He would come home after his bank and union duties, read a lot and write a lot of serious articles. Young people would flock into our house very late in the night. They would sit crowded in the small living room and listen to my father as he unfolded truth of Marxism while explaining minute details. I would sleep there keeping my head on the lap of my father, and would listen till I fell asleep.

I started believing that the society is unequal. There are rich and poor and because the poor do not have resources to produce wealth they are working for the rich, getting very small remuneration for their hard work but they had to do so for earning their bread and butter. Hence, they can be helped by controlling the resources to produce and having equitable distribution of wealth.

My childhood memories are of my grandparents (meaning my father's parents and his siblings). We lived together as a joint family. Later on, though we separated, all my uncles and aunts lived in proximity in the vicinity of Dadar, Prabhadevi, Bandra and Grant Road. My grandfather worked in the High court. He did not have a very big earning and had 8 children to look after. He used to tell them that he would not leave any property or assets for them but would give them education. He would educate as much as they wanted and he would pay for it. He maintained that only with high education can you rise in life.

My grandfather was himself a bibliograph. He was the chairperson of the first cooperative Bank, Dadar Nagri cooperative Bank, which won an award at the hands of British Queen or viceroy. He along with a few more like-minded people formed a cultural centre in Dadar named as Vanamali hall. Even today this place houses many cultural activities.

All my uncles and aunts would read a lot. Our house looked like a library where all would sit in the small living room, quietly reading. All became graduates or double graduates. They were employed in good jobs and had a very peaceful family life. My grandmother even within the limited means used to cook very tasty food for all the family. Several relatives who would visit us, praised her cooking.

When I started growing up, I would go with my parents to the textile mills area. They were both active in the Girni Kamgar Union., which was a textile workers union that was established and linked with the Communist party of India. It united mill workers and fought for their rights. Sometimes they used to address the gate-meetings of textile mill workers. I used to stand next to my father or mother and listen to them speak. Their speech was full of compassion, inspiration and was about fighting against oppression. My father's speech would be more learned, with data, with long term solutions. My mother was kind, she used to help people on the spot, but she never thought or spoke of long-term solutions. I could see poverty everywhere in the textile mill area. That area looked different than our residential society at Dadar, Prabhadevi.

Silently in my mind, I used to study my parents' behaviour. I observed a lot and thought of myself helping people. However, I was more inclined in working out long term solutions. So in my impressionable age, growing age I was being shaped as a studious person, reading a lot, observing people's problems, helping people and thinking of long-term solutions to poverty. Earning a lot of money never became my goal.

Dr. Joy: You have talked about the influence of your father particularly and how you learnt so much from him. What about his or your mother's influence on your other siblings?

Medha Tai: My mother's family was in Goa. They lived in a very small village. My maternal grandparents were not educated. They had a lot of land, agriculture. My grandmother used to carry out the deliveries of young women who could not deliver a child easily. She was known for handling difficult deliveries. My grandfather was known as a very kind gentleman who would give shelter to anyone who asked for it. We could not visit Goa very regularly, but once in two or three years we used to go and meet our grandparents there. They were all kind and loving.

My mother came from Goa as a freedom fighter trying to escape at the age of 12 from the Portuguese soldiers. Goa was ruled by the Portuguese until 1961. Even my father took part in the freedom moment against the British rulers. Hence in our family there was a strong feeling of patriotism in which I grew up.

My father was 32 years old and my mother was 25 years old when I was born. I was the eldest daughter. I have two younger sisters. They are 3 years and 7 years younger than me. Being the eldest sibling I was expected to take care of my sisters. I would do it lovingly, I would teach them, help them to complete their homework go to their class in school if there is any problem. Both of them were different from me. They were interested in playing with their friends, and like most other children they were enjoying their childhood. They rarely took interest in what our parents were doing. I don't remember them accompanying our parents to the textile mill area or to the various meetings. Also, they were too young to listen to the Study Circles which my father used to conduct for the young comrades in our house. Hence my sisters did not pick up the interest in social activities.

Dr. Joy: Please explain the transition in mind processes you went through when you were contemplating moving out of the bank. What was the opinion of your family friends colleagues?

Medha Tai: I did not discuss with many people. I definitely discussed with my husband first. I asked him whether he would support the family financially if I give up my Bank job. I of course explained to him what I wanted to do. He was most supportive. He said he could support our family financially and he assured me that he trusted that I will do anything successfully.

I spoke to my mother, she was very happy. As per her understanding she thought I am joining her work which was not the real case. In fact, I was going to take my own path. However, I did not discuss with many people. I informed my decision to my in-laws and my sisters as well as husband's sisters but, they had nothing much to say since all of them knew that I gave the matter great thought.

With my friends and colleagues, I did not have so many discussions though my Bank colleagues knew that I was thinking in that direction. Some friends who were close to me, thought that whatever I will do, will be well thought over. Several others thought that my husband is doing very well in his business, and hence I don't need to continue my bank job and that was why I was leaving. Only my branch manager and some seniors tried to convince me not to take such a big decision. They thought that I should wait till the bank offers voluntary retirement scheme. I humbly said no. I cannot wait.

As I have said earlier, we had shifted to Pune. I had comfortably settled down in my bank and union work. I had successfully found a good school and day care for my son and my husband's business was settling down So I could have easily, comfortably enjoyed a good family life in Pune. But there was a thought process going on in my mind, that I should do something more than bank job. Just working for the banking union meant helping the middle class, who did not require this help so much, as the poor women selling vegetables in the market. I was also thinking that I should have a larger goal in life. I did not want to spend all my energy in the banking industry and trade union.

There were two important triggers in the years from 1990 to 1993. It was the fall of Soviet Russia which aroused a lot of unrest in my mind (as well as in some young people) who had grown up following Marxism and looking at Soviet Russia as a successful example of implementation of the same. My mind was questioning the theory of Marxism, the establishment of Soviet Russia, the journey of the Indian state post-independence on the path of welfare state. The second trigger was globalisation, market economy and privatisation. I was trying to read and understand this new theory which was opposite of the hitherto welfare approach of the Indian state. Earlier there were welfare policies for the poor and the deprived which included women. We were a soft capitalist economy with welfare measures to uplift our 70% rural population and overall, 30 to 35% population below poverty line.

Now onwards there will no longer be welfare schemes. Even earlier the schemes of banks like priority sector lending were not implemented on a large scale. But at least these schemes existed. With privatisation and the market economy these schemes may not exist at all hence the poor will be left alone to fight their battle with poverty. The condition of the women population which was 50% was not good. They were left without education, without any assets, hence unable to contribute to the economy and earn for themselves. How was the capitalist globalised, privatised economy going to take care of these elements of society?

In such a scenario I meet Shevantabai, Lakshmibai and their likes. I could see them borrowing small loans from a private money lender at a very high interest rate. I thought of giving them a loan from the bank. My colleagues in the bank were not interested in such an experiment. Whereas Shevantabai and others were also not interested in going to a bank and getting treated like dirt.

Here I found purpose of my life. I felt inspired to do this experiment of lending to these women forming a small group of 10 such poor vegetable vendors.

Shevantabai had personified the plight of the poor women without any access to assets or resources and she was a challenge. She was right there in the educational capital of Maharashtra, a very much educated Pune where the first women's school was established. Pune boasted of the highest education rate amongst women. Right there was Shevantabai and others like her.

Dr. Joy: What were the fears if any, once you took the decision?

Medha Tai: There was no fear. My mind was so charged up. I thought of facing the challenge together with Shevantabai and her group of women—The challenge of poverty, the challenge of no access to bank credit, the challenge of designing a solution that was based on their needs, that was not depending on any grants or donations, that could be self-dependent, long term, and appealed to many women in similar situation.

Dr. Joy: Explaining the economy at National, State, Cities levels as well as the Slums and Community level.

Medha Tai: *When I took a decision to start giving collateral free loans to the poor vegetable vendors, at the national level, the then Congress government had taken a big policy decision to implement an open economy, push for the market economy and privatisation. At the global level, with the fall of Soviet Russia there was no power which would control the America-led capitalism. Even China was not seen as a superpower or as powerful as it is seen now. Hence the whole world was moving towards globalisation, a capitalist economy where no or little welfare measures would be taken for the poor.*

In India, at the state level there was a big rural to urban migration happening for over four decades. It was more or less the same ratio of migration in all Grade 1 cities like Mumbai, Delhi, Chennai Kolkata, and Grade 2 cities like Hyderabad, Pune etc. In the fifties immediately after independence, the rural population, was 70% and urban population was 30%. Over the years, this ratio changed to 60% 40% respectively mainly since there was no development and no job opportunities in the rural areas. The problem of landless labourers was huge in the rural areas. Also because of skewed urban development, desperate rural families were migrating in the hope of survival. They were living in filthy slums, without any amenities or social support. Access to credit was unimaginable because they had no assets in their names. Hence, their situation was—once poor, always poor.

I had seen some chawls of textile mill workers in Mumbai, with my parents. I had visited some slums in Mumbai because I went to conduct adult literacy classes under the NSS. However, after shifting to Pune I had not visited any slum. In fact because of my job in Bank of India, in order to do deposit mobilisation, I got an access to plush housing societies and offices where the elite classes lived. **I could see glimpses of slums behind most of those elite societies. These always grabbed my attention.**

I started going to a few slums after I made friends with Shevantabai, Lakshmi Bai and their friends and relatives. In the early years of 90s, I visited Gosavi Vasti in Kothrud Shastri Nagar, Gujarat colony, Jay Bhawani Nagar, Ramnagar, Kishkinda Nagar, Vadar wadi, all around Kothrud, Warje. Later I went to Taljai Mata Vasahat, Market yard Vasahat on Satara road. Then I started visiting Aundh ITI slum Indiranagar slum Kasturba Nagar slum Sanjay Nagar slum etc. Some of these were very small slums, whereas some were huge slums.

Some of these slums consisted of a single community like Vadar, Banjara, Matang Navbouddha etc. However, several of these slums consisted of a heterogeneous community mixed with Lower caste Hindus, Muslims, Navbouddha, Mang and Matang. All of these communities were on the lower most rungs of society. Most of them were engaged in lower end jobs, earning a daily wage and just being able to make a survival. No upper caste people lived in the slums.

Dr. Joy: What were the challenges when you began?

Medha Tai: For me, the situation of these slum dwellers was very pathetic. I felt challenged to find solutions to this situation. The challenges were many. First of all, raising funds to be able to supply credit on a continuous basis to be able to pull these poor women out from poverty. Secondly, there was no office, no human resources, no infrastructure. Thirdly, winning the trust of these women, so that they leave the private money lender *Anna* and walk with me.

Then due to the heterogeneous structure of the slums, it was very difficult to form groups of like-minded people from these asset-less poor families had, who had the same requirement of credit.

I had known very little about NABARD self-help groups or Grameen Bank. My mother under the guidance of my father had implemented the Bank linkage program for the poor from 1975. However, they were not small groups. Under one area leader, hundreds of women were linked to the bank credit. But where I stood, this whole road ahead was a blur.

Hence every single step had to be paved carefully. It had to be thought out a 100 times by talking to hundreds of women. I had to figure out what they wanted, what would help them, what were they ready to do. The legal registration, choosing the right option was another big challenge. My mother thought I am going to join her Annapurna Mahila Mandal.

Which I was not going to do, because I knew our functioning styles would have been totally different. Earlier I had tried to work with her, but had always found it difficult since she preferred short term solutions which were more grant-dependent. I wanted to search for a long-term solution without any grant. Hence, I just took the name Annapurna and started working without any registration. **It was a big risk, yet I took it. Leaving the bank job without any promise ahead, was another big risk which I took.**

Dr Joy: Please tell us about the name 'Annapurna'.

I will explain about the name Annapurna what it means to me and to the organisation. I go back to memory lane. I was hardly 15 years old. My mother was beginning to work with the khanavalvalis (women who ran food mess services) in Mumbai. My father was guiding her to form an NGO which will connect the mess runners to the DRI (Differential Rate of Interest) schemes of the nationalised banks. They would spend nights discussing this what the name of the NGO should be. They thought Khanavalvalis is a derogatory word. Instead, the women should be recognised in a respectable way. Hence, they chose the name of the goddess of food, Annapurna. Annapurna was also the name of my grandmother, my father's mother. Again, the building in which I was born and my grandparents lived, was Annapurna Nivas. So, with all the discussion, they decided to name the NGO that is the trust as Annapurna Mahila Mandal.

This name was so carved in my mind that when I decided to work with the poor vegetable vendors, by giving them small collateral free loans, I thought of the name Annapurna.

Though I had not decided to work with my mother, in the same organisation Annapurna Mahila Mandal, I took the name Annapurna and attached Pariwar to it. I understood that I could not work with only women I will have to cater to the needs of their families too. Hence, Pariwar.

Dr. Joy: Did you plan the trajectory? Or did it evolve organically?

Medha Tai: I did not and could not have planned the trajectory. Since I had not experienced poverty, I did not understand what poor women expected from me or from the would-be NGO. However, I kept the dialogue with the women ongoing, regularly, frequently and openly, without fixing any goals. That's how I understood what they were thinking, what they were aspiring for, what they could do, what they could not do. Hence, I would say the trajectory evolved organically. Initially we started the collateral-free loan program with very small doses of loans. Then we started saving, because the women expressed that they wanted to save something for the future and they did not want to depend on loans only. The next need was not expressed orally but could be sensed from their situation was related to health. Quite a few of our members were facing health problems, which were, say minor, could be treated easily. But because they were uneducated, ignorant and did not have any insurance coverage the doctors or quacks took them for a ride. They did unnecessary tests to extract money from them, gave them wrong medicine/treatment, and they lost lives to very minor diseases which were curable. Observing this situation made me think of and search for health and life insurance. I didn't find any affordable, accessible health insurance for the poor. So, I started a community based health insurance and then eventually life insurance after trying the life insurance program of LIC. No insurance company was offering any affordable health insurance package for the poor, hence we had to start our own program in- house.

Soon in 2003, another situation in the community was observed which I then discussed with the members. This was a rape case of a 6 years old girl child by a few boys from the same community. This girl was left alone at home by her single mother, who had to provide for herself and the girl. This got me thinking about the safety and security of the children of single mothers. Hence, I raised funds from Times Foundation to start the first day care centre in a slum called

Karve Nagar. Around the same time, I realised that around 10% of our borrowers were single mothers. They were borrowing from us to pay the school fees of their children to educate them. They could not have possibly repaid these loans, because that was not adding to their earnings. Hence, I thought of starting an educational sponsorship program for the children of single mothers. This started in 2003, with money from donors. Today this program has completed 22 years. We can support this program from the profits of Annapurna Mahila co-operative credit society.

Dr. Joy: What were the achievements that helped to move forward and what were the setbacks that pushed you backwards.

Medha Tai: These synchronise with the evolution of the organisation as also learnings and resolutions, what worked what did not work. If I have to break my journey and also the journey of Annapurna Pariwar into important milestones then these would be:

The beginning of the Micro Finance program in 1993 was the first big milestone. This led to micro savings in the next few years to come. These micro savings are financing today 50% of our loan portfolio. Then in 2003, I started health mutual fund, the in-house insurance program, which was the first of its kind in India. A very unique program in the absence of any affordable insurance for the poor in this country.

In the same year in 2003, we started Vatsalya Purna, the Day Care centres program in the slums, after the incidence of rape of a 6 years old girl child. in Karvenagar slum. This was very unique, need based, not giving any freebies, offering a service for which the slum women paid. Hence, we had to keep this affordable. This is another important milestone. Within a year we started Vidyapurna the educational sponsorship program for the children of single mothers, who were the borrowers of Annapurna cooperative credit society. This was another important milestone. Though Vidya Purna, Vatsalya Purna were both not our core business, they added value to our comprehensive development program. These programmes added a social safety network for the poor women who missed social support system.

Now, I will come to what did not work: We had started a vocational training and placement program named as Sandhi Tantra Purna. We started this in 2000 and closed it in 2011. This was need-based but nobody was ready to pay for the training since they wanted the trainings free. Hence, we had to always raise funds to organise vocational trainings. On the other hand, the employers who wanted us to supply human resource, never wanted to pay for this service because they thought, anyway human resource is cheap. Hence this was a 'perpetual grant dependent program', unlike all the other programs. I was not self-sustaining. Hence after implementing it for 11 years, I had to take a tough decision to close it.

There were other programs like my mother's catering services and working women's hostel. These were losing money, and not helping many women. I tried to run them after my mother retired, but ultimately had to take a decision to close these. There was Shantipurna, a programme for giving free service to the slum dwellers which included guidance in documentation and counselling in family matters. This was never going to be self-sustainable, hence we implemented it from 2003–2006 and then closed it. There was also a programme called 'Early Childhood Development'. It was introduced by InterAid our then funding partner. I did not even give it a local name though I had liked the concept. I knew it would not work in the long term. The programme invited young mothers with their children into our slum office day care centre of half hour and give them toys and explain the importance of mother and child playing together. I knew it was not need based and members would not pay for it. I would remain grant dependant. I ran form 2004–2005.

What and why worked in the chain of programs? Micro credit, micro insurance, micro pension are need-based financial empowerment programmes and they received a great response and became sustainable very soon. The programs like Vidyapurna and Vatsalya Purna are not sustainable, but they are useful and we were able to support them from the profits of credit society.

What and why didn't work—the training and placement program, catering services and working women's hostel the counselling programmes, ECD programme were never sustainable, did not enjoy client support and were a drain on funds. Hence, they had to be closed.

Dr. Joy: What is the relevance of Annapurna Pariwar and uniqueness of Annapurna Pariwar within micro finance and micro insurance; poverty alleviation, livelihoods, women's empowerment, community wellbeing, peace and harmony within slums?

Medha Tai: First of all, Annapurna Pariwar is a group of six organisations that is unique and relevant in many ways. It has evolved organically on the basis of needs of poor women. It's not a bundle of services being sold off the shelf by some service providers or commercial company with a goal to make profit. The services are designed by its users, based on their needs. The evolution of these services was through a constant top to bottom and bottom to top line of communication. And most importantly, the users not only design the product.

But they decide the price and pay the price too. And last but not least, they are the owners of all six organisations. They share the profits and they keep contributing to modifications of the services, products and prices.

Annapurna Pariwar is the only multi state co-op credit society in India. Of the other 200 + MFIs in India, these are mostly NBFCs or Section 8 companies or Trusts, Federations etc.

More recently there are Small Finance Banks. Being a co-op credit society, Annapurna Pariwar collects savings, which finance the loan portfolio. This facilitates the controlled cost of loanable funds, and reduces dependence on external borrowing. It increases profits and shares the profits with the users by way of dividend. Hence the users do not only pay the interest on loans, but also earn interest on their savings, and dividend on their shares.

The more they invest in shares and voluntary saving products like Fixed Deposit, Recurring Deposit, Aadhar Purna pension Deposit, the more they earn.

Further, they participate in the decision making processes by attending various meeting platforms created by Annapurna Pariwar, like community meetings, community representative meetings, AGMs and Board meetings. Following is the beautiful principal of cooperation—One share, one vote. Many shares, still one vote only.

The insurance programme was developed in 2003, when there was a complete absence of any affordable insurance for the poor in India. It was designed by the members of Annapurna cooperative credit society who own this section 8 company which houses the insurance services. One by one all the insurance services like—Health insurance, Life insurance, Family insurance, Asset insurance were developed. The users are designers and buyers too. They participate in the decision making. They do not fall sick and take claims, rather they are incentivised to have better and better health awareness, prevent falling sick, go the network hospitals when sick, save money from their own pocket as well as Annapurna's claim fund. They get better benefits each year. Premium increase is infrequent—after minimum three to four years. There is almost zero rejection of claims, minimum turnaround time, highest client satisfaction and support, resulting into more than 70% renewal each year.

Regarding women's political empowerment in Annapurna Pariwar, First of all women's empowerment is ensured here as more than 95% clients, staff and board members are women. They control all decisions, enjoy the profits. The decisions are always women centric or family centric. Women mostly do not think of themselves first, but they think about the family first. Hence, the wealth creation is distributed fairly within the family.

Due to Annapurna Pariwar's planned approach and financial literacy program, most of the members are well aware about the next loan cycle. They are aware of how much money they will get in hand, how much they have to pay as the processing fee, how much saving they have to put in. Hence, they plan and go on expanding their business and assets with each loan cycle. They bring more family members in their business.

Due to our Joint Liability group model (actually our original name was Common Goals Group), every group which sticks to each other for all loan cycles (we call them A type groups). They are incentivised even more and this ensures that all group members and their families prosper. This is how the community prospers. Prosperity with strong bonding within the group and community naturally brings peace and harmony within the community.

Dr. Joy: Do you think Annapurna Pariwar will remain relevant in the years to come? For how long? And why?

Medha Tai: Annapurna Pariwar model may remain relevant for a long time to come. Mainly because of the following factors. It is a cooperative. The Cooperative Act is prevalent in India since the last one and half century. Cooperatives are still relevant in all Europe and parts of Africa.

There are very big cooperatives there serving large groups of people, delivering various products and services successfully. In India there have been examples of successful cooperatives like Amul, SEWA and Annapurna. The failure of several cooperatives is mainly due to factors like politicisation of the cooperative, unprofessional management, control of the cooperative in the hands of a few. From this perspective Annapurna Pariwar is very different. It is sticking to the original principles of cooperation. *Control of the members through AGM; Members designing the products; Members buying the products; Members sharing the profits.*

Annapurna Pariwar's micro finance program and micro insurance program are both self-sustainable, professionally managed, politically detached, having in house software and data control and community control on the field activities. So, they can remain relevant and keep serving the community.

The other four organisations under Annapurna Pariwar are subsidiary organisations. They offer social support programs like Day Care centres for toddlers in slums and educational sponsorship program for the children of single mothers. They are financially partially sustainable, yet they are supported by the microfinance and micro insurance wing of Annapurna Pariwar, because they help bring social sustainability for the members of these programs.

Hence, Annapurna Pariwar as a group of 6 organisations, working for and with the poor women in a given geographical area Pune and Mumbai, the two biggest cities in Maharashtra is very impactful, relevant and it can be replicated anywhere in India, after some alterations and modifications

Dr. Joy: Whether Regulation in Micro Finance and Micro Insurance sector remain relevant for Annapurna Pariwar?

Medha Tai: Actually NO, because Annapurna Pariwar has paved it's way in the absence of any regulation in these two sectors. This is so since, the founder is completely focused and dedicated to bringing the financial services to the poor, underprivileged women and she worked out several solutions which were not exactly available in the legal framework. However, a different interpretation and some modifications in the organisation structure facilitated the existence, survival, sustenance of AMCCS, APVS. Hence Annapurna Pariwar by itself really is not dependent on any major legal modification.

Yet being a cooperative MFI, it cannot get a membership of any credit bureau, since the CICRA Act doesn't support it. Membership of a credit bureau is applicable and essential for all the microfinance institutions in India since 2012 post Andhra Crisis. Annapurna Pariwar has written to the RBI many times in the last few years that it is using public money by raising deposits as a cooperative and it is operating in the 'collateral free loans to the poor' space (micro finance) hence it cannot work with CIBIL membership alone. Annapurna Pariwar requires to be a member of a credit bureau, but this has fallen on deaf ears.

Annapurna Pariwar has worked out an alternative to take membership through its section 8 company instead of its cooperative credit society. yet the CICRA Act has to be modified. That will make the life simpler for Annapurna management and staff. Recently, they banned even not -for -profit companies from credit Bureau membership. Hence, forcing us to make credit inquiries to another Fintech company, thereby adding to the costs and credit risks. Hence, I say, we existed, 'in spite of' the poor legal framework.

The regulation of micro insurance companies, by reducing the solvency capital requirement, will pave the way for an extension of Annapurna insurance services to the millions of poor in this country. They will get micro insurance providers with a clear mandate to serve the poor.

If Annapurna Pariwar or VIMO SEWA can get regulated, that will also ensure that with the extension of operations in different geographical regions where poor clients can avail of affordable insurance services from tried and tested insurance providers. Vimo Sawa is a cooperative established by Padma Bhushan Elaben Bhat to offer insurance services to the poor. This will also facilitate the goal of IRDA to extend the insurance services to every nook and corner in India

Dr. Joy: Is the micro insurance sector a mode of ensuring loan repayment of micro loans?

Medha Tai: I do not endorse that vision. That's a very short-sighted perspective about micro insurance. I know that many microfinance institutions look at micro insurance services from that perspective. But I never look with that perspective. The proof of this is Annapurna Pariwar Vikas Samvardhan started its first insurance service with health insurance and not with loan linked Life insurance in 2003. That's because we were designing the most required insurance service by our women members. We had linked to the group insurance scheme of LIC already a little earlier in 1997, and we continued with LIC until 2009. This scheme was covering the death of the borrowers, by reimbursement of the loan amount to us. This scheme by LIC gave higher compensation for accidental deaths. (The frequency of accidental deaths is very low, this secret we know by now. The accidental death ratio is less than 1% of the total members covered.) Later in 2009 we started our own life insurance which was designed in consultation with our members. This scheme covers the borrower's death. No difference between natural and accidental deaths.

Our life insurance service went much beyond just writing off the loan amount. We started giving good financial assistance to the family of the deceased borrowers. This scheme was well modified since then to cover even high amount loans as well as continues to give financial assistance to the family of the deceased borrowers. In spite of almost zero rejection, we have settled thousands of claims and have yet saved a good amount which stays in the reserve funds. Every year the body of Community representatives can and decide how to utilise the reserve funds for giving better services to our members. I am explaining this elaborately so that it becomes absolutely clear that our scheme is not designed just to cover our loan portfolio but it aims at helping our members in all kinds of unfortunate, unforeseen events. Even today the group insurance scheme of LIC exists, many MFIs are selling the same vanilla product to its client who have no control on this decision.

Dr. Joy: Over time, how have the various models of microfinance within the areas that you operate in, affected the operations of Annapurna Pariwar? Is there room for all or are there consequences of competition?

Medha Tai: The competition in microfinance is said to help the members get a better range of services with lesser interest rate. Due to high competition the rates would come down, as it is advocated. However, it has not happened. The interest rates in MF sector are defined by RBI. Most MFI's are Non Bank Finance Corporations which keep getting investments from private investors as well as loans from banks. They clearly work for profit and the profits are going to the private investors, equity holders and board members. Hence the poor do not get any benefit of the competition. At the most we can say that access to credit has become easy, but many MFIs take interest at the highest applicable interest rate as per RBI mandate. They do take higher processing fees and load hidden costs on poor clients.

Over-borrowed status has increased in the last so many years. The Andhra crisis was the tip of the iceberg, wherein many farmers and women committed suicide, due to their inability to repay the loans. Even today so many MFIs are seen operating in the same geographical regions, which are green pastures. Rarely these profiteering MFIs are seen going to difficult terrains. They poach members, staff of other MFIs who are known to be successful there. This is leading to an over-borrowed status of clients.

Annapurna Pariwar has faced the consequence of this kind of competition. However, we have a lot of thrust upon client education, financial literacy. Our members have completely trust us. Even with so much competition around in both Pune and Mumbai, 40% of our members do not borrow from anyone other than us. This is mainly due to our comprehensive development approach.

A System that Works

Joy Deshmukh Ranadive

Abstract The management model of Annapurna Pariwar is unique since it was organic and evolved over time while catering to the needs of the community it served. A system has been built over the years that encourages staff to function in efficient ways and instill a loyalty toward the ideology on which the organisation was built. The succession plan and cadre of senior management are instrumental in the running of the organisation. The financial sustainability of the organisation and how it was achieved will be detailed out. The use of in-house technology has facilitated the smooth transactions of microfinance and microinsurance within Annapurna Pariwar. There is a two-way communication between the organisation and its members. Principles of democracy are adhered to. These systems will be highlighted in this chapter. The importance of voice, especially of the community, and how it influences and teaches the organisation how to move forward, shapes the model of Annapurna Pariwar. Financial stability and the link to digitisation are critical. Annapurna Pariwar has its own system of digitisation that facilitates the processes of loan disbursements, loan collection, insurance claims, etc. Both hardware and software are synergised to make the tasks of loan officers smooth. The digitisation organisation of Annapurna Pariwar and its role in managing an efficient system will be illustrated. The role of the Board of Annapurna Pariwar is central to the organisation. Regular, documented Board meetings and how they steer the organisation forward will be drawn out in this chapter.

J. D. Ranadive (✉)
Independent Consultant, Pune, Maharashtra, India
e-mail: drjoydeshmukh@gmail.com

J. D. Ranadive, S. Guha (eds.), *Building Pathways to Women's Empowerment*, India Studies in Business and Economics,
https://doi.org/10.1007/978-981-95-7159-8_3

1 Introduction

This chapter is based on the conversation between Dr. Medha Samant, CMD of Annapurna Pariwar whom we call Medha Tai and Dr. Joy Deshmukh Ranadive. The management model of Annapurna Pariwar is unique since it was organic and evolved over time while catering to the needs of the community it served. A system has been built over the years that encourages staff to function in efficient ways and instill a loyalty towards the ideology on which the organisation was built. The succession plan and cadre of senior management are instrumental in the running of the organisation. The financial sustainability of the organisation and how it was achieved will be detailed. The use of in-house technology has facilitated the smooth transactions of microfinance and microinsurance within Annapurna Pariwar. There is a two-way communication between the organisation and its members. Principles of democracy are adhered to. These systems will be highlighted in this chapter.

2 Interview with Dr. Medha Purao Samant by Dr. Joy Deshmukh Ranadive

Dr. Joy: If you were to describe the model you adopted for Annapurna Pariwar, how would you describe it?

Medha Tai: The model that I adopted for Annapurna Pariwar is not a model that I have copied and pasted from elsewhere. This model has been worked out brick by brick, inch by inch, with my members and staff over the past 32 years. This model is cooperative yet very professional. That means there is complete transparency and democracy in the operations. I have kept no secret from anyone. I give every reason for taking a particular decision. Each stakeholder has been provided with a meeting platform wherein they express their views on every decision, every process, and every step of the working.

However, any decision once taken after discussions and deliberations cannot be changed by a single individual just because he or she thinks otherwise about it later on. In case the decision has to be changed, it can be changed again, going through the same process of discussion through the same platforms of meetings. Each time the data has to be reviewed, checking whether the data supports the viewpoint that we are endorsing through our decision.

Hence, I can say, our model has top-to-bottom and bottom-to-top communication. There is definitely strong leadership at the top, which is supported by an equally qualified and experienced managing committee. Yet there is communication with each stakeholder. All the decisions are transparent yet strongly followed in practice once taken.

Dr. Joy: What could you say is/are the reasons for the sustainability of your organisation?

Medha Tai: Sustainability of the organisation comes through (a) financial sustainability; (b) members' support leading to a sustainable institution; (c) consistency and involvement of staff, and (d) consistency and involvement of the board. Last but not the least has been sustainability through all the difficult times like (a) Andhra crisis, (b) demonetisation, (c) Covid-19 Pandemic. Annapurna Pariwar has sustained and evolved stronger with each crisis. The reason for this is mainly due to strong leadership. I have to mention here, taking the risk of self-praise, that I never give up. I work tirelessly. I am completely dedicated. I follow ethical principles.

I don't break a promise or turn my back on any commitments, no matter how difficult they are. The board and staff have complete trust in me, which I have earned. Hence, they follow me whenever it's a war-like situation. In a normal situation, the sustainability comes from taking financially wise decisions, equally focussing on the welfare of members and staff.

Another important factor is that though I never started this as a profiteering business, I never underestimate the competition. In all the decision-making process, I make it a point to involve every stakeholder, but once decisions are taken, I do not allow anyone not to follow those.

Dr. Joy: Would you say that you are financially sustainable? And why?

Medha Tai: Of the unique features of Annapurna Pariwar leading to its sustainability is the consciously chosen cooperative model. Due to this, we were never dependent on investments from private investors and equity holders. We could build our retail investors' portfolio, as well as various voluntary and non-voluntary saving products for our borrowers. This was difficult but not impossible. Hence, we are financially sustainable. Members always continued to support us because we never sold-off-the-shelf products, for our profits. The products were always need-based, designed by discussions with members.

The field staff, key staff, all staff for that matter were and are happy to work with Annapurna Pariwar because of the following factors—a good salary package; an increment every year; opportunities for promotion; clear rules and structure for increments and promotions, incentive for field staff; very good superannuation benefits; several welfare schemes for staff like health insurance, life insurance, home loan, bachat gat loans; and above all, job satisfaction due to social goals of the organisation, transparency and democracy. All board members are satisfied in contributing, supporting Annapurna Pariwar because of the same reasons.

I started with zero capital, no resources, including human resources, office place, etc. Today, with a clear vision, dedicated hard work, we have a Rs. 200 + Cr savings portfolio, which is financing our Rs. 200 Cr loan portfolio. We don't even require any external finance as of now. Yet to provide for the future growth, I have made sure that we have sanction from IOB, A CC for Rs. 50 Cr without my personal guarantee, from BOB A CC for Rs. 10 Cr without my personal guarantee, NCDC credit sanction for Rs. 30 Cr. So, all in all, we have a credit cover of Rs. 90

Cr. for future growth. In addition, we have a very good system to raise social investors' deposits if we have a requirement. Aadhar Purna pension deposit is another area which keeps financing our loan portfolio. With good profits and assets created we can humbly but proudly say that we are financially sustainable.

Dr. Joy: What are the steps you took to become financially sustainable?

Medha Tai: More than steps, the clear vision and philosophy helped more towards financial sustainability. For example, not taking money and equity from private investors was the absolutely clear vision from day one. Similarly, not taking any profits for my (founder's) home, board members' homes was absolutely clear vision from day one. Hence, the path of cooperation was chosen rather than choosing the NBFC form, though both were recommended by RBI. This was akin to swimming against the mainstream, for which I was never scared because of my goals. Hence, the self-financed portfolio and assets, profits followed.

The road was very narrow, unused and difficult. There was a period during the years 2011 to 2020 when most micro finance institutions were non-bank finance corporations. They were getting equity, a lot of investment and loans. Being a cooperative, we were getting nothing. Our retail investor's portfolio was not created in a day. It took almost 7 to 8 years of hard work, dedication and sticking to the goals. During this period, almost the whole world, including the regulatory authorities, rating agencies and our bankers, financers were pushing us towards becoming non-bank finance corporation. We were growing steadily during this period, however, we were not getting enough loanable funds. In spite of giving my personal guarantee, banks did not give any enhancement after the Andhra crisis. So, we were operating within the same sanctioned limits as 2012 till 2022.

During this period, there was demonetisation. We lost almost 2 crores due to default by members. Still, no help came our way. We kept borrowing from smaller Business-to-Business (B2B) lending financial institutions at much higher rates of interest. Still, we kept following all the RBI mandates. The most difficult to follow was keeping the highest lending rate below 25%. We got a small margin, had a shoestring budget, it was only due to our principals and not-for-profit nature that we survived. Then there came Covid, and we lost another 5/6 crores.

In the meantime, the small finance bank structure evolved. RBI gave licences to 11 entities who converted themselves into SFB. Then, senior colleagues from the microfinance industry started advising me to become an SFB. I studied the structure, and I realised that we could easily float an SFB. Yet I evaluated and realised that converting into SFB will not be gainful. First of all, we will become taxable. Secondly, we will be directly governed by the RBI, and we will not be able to give more than 15% unsecured loans as compared to our 100% unsecured loan portfolio today. This clearly means deviation from our goals.

So, I stayed away from that decision. However, during the Covid, our situation changed to a great extent. We lost more than 5 crores, but due to our cooperative and group structure, the group members contributed to the bad debts which could not be repaid by their group members. Hence, unlike other MFIs, we didn't burn only our money.

During Covid, our members were repaying slowly, but they were not ready to borrow more. So, we did not require loanable funds to the extent which we required before Covid. Hence, we invested into property, which came handy to borrow more later. In addition, we slowly and steadily built the retail investors portfolio, which now comes handy to lend out to our members, who are borrowing as per their usual requirements before Covid. Hence, our financial sustainability improved drastically.

Dr. Joy: What is the importance of Regulation in MF sector and MI sector in order to make Annapurna Pariwar sustainable?

Medha Tai: There was and still is a complete absence of any suitable legal framework. We are operating in the field of MF since 1993 since the past 32 years. RBI has set up a task force which has been issuing circulars since 1998 for MFIs. These are very general guidelines and have many contradictions. Recently, they have banned any NGO s from becoming members of any credit bureaus. After the Andhra crisis, the RBI made it mandatory for MFIs to become members of credit bureaus. These included trusts, federations, co-op credit societies, section 8 companies. Today all of these are banned from becoming members of any credit bureaus. We have to keep writing to Sa Dhan, RBI, and we have to keep finding some way out because it takes ages before they do take cognizance of our presence and problems.

RBI does not regulate the co-operative sector. However, they, as per their circular in 1998, have advised that trusts, federations, co-op credit societies, and section 8 companies can do micro finance. I have been getting their circular since 1998, reading and following them. In the last 10 years or so, we can find their circulars on their website. All banks that finance us, rating agencies that rate us and credit bureaus are following the RBI. Hence, they look at us from the same perspective as per the RBI mandate.

It mostly applies to NBFCs, best suitable for their operations. We are operating on a biased playing ground.

The co-operative registrar office is in Delhi. They never monitored/audited us. We had to file returns, AGM proceeding, resolutions, etc. annually. That's it. They have got converted into a ministry during 2022–23. During this period, all requests from us fell on deaf ears.

Now again we have established some contact, a connection with the ministry. We are getting our bye-laws, etc. rephrased as per the new CRCS (Central Registrar of Coperative Societies) act.

Hence, so far, our sustainability has zero contribution from regulators. It's mainly our ethical principles that kept us in line with what is good, ethical, and hence sustainable.

Dr. Joy: What is the importance of management cadres in order to make Annapurna Pariwar sustainable?

Medha Tai: Actually, our management cadres are very simple. They are not trained in the MF sector. I have groomed them in-house. But the best part is they take ownership. They are dedicated to Annapurna Pariwar. Sustainability in a stable, dedicated team is what we have in Annapurna Pariwar.

Our Human Resources (HR) manual explains in detail about the rules & facilities given to staff as per statutory requirements. Whereas the Welfare manual explains in detail about the rules & facilities given to staff voluntarily by the management. These are available in soft copies too. Before writing these, I of course had studied Labour law, various HR practices and manuals, and had met with consulted labour consultants. Around 12/13 years ago, SIDBI had undertaken a study of HR practices in MFIs. They had selected Annapurna Pariwar in the 10 MFIs sample. I am happy to mention here that in their study report, which is in the public domain, they have mentioned Annapurna Pariwar and appreciated our HR practices.

Having said this, I go to the common attributes that I have looked for, right from the time of selecting my first staff some 28 years ago, when I was responsible for it alone. I always looked for 'Will rather than Skill'. Skilled staffs were unavailable then, and even now, we don't get exactly well-trained, skilled staff who are trained to work for a co-op MFI. Hence, I started taking simple housewives during the late nineties, and trained them in-house, by teaching them everything including credit—debit to doorstep delivery as well as recovery of collateral-free loans. It wasn't an easy job at all. However, it was the only option. After having built a 'strong woman force' in the field who actually work in the slums, I think it is the biggest strength of Annapurna Pariwar. Most other MFIs have men and boys for recovery, which makes the implementation difficult since the husbands of members don't appreciate men interacting with their wives.

The other attributes which I look for while hiring staff are—compassion for the poor; seeing the importance of the need to empower women; honesty, hardworking; ownership feeling for the organisation. Of course, these have to be built in-house.

Dr. Joy: How were you building leadership in-house?

Medha Tai: Initially, I was directly leading the field staff who were simple young women, educated up to 10/12th grade, to work in slums. Slowly, the need emerged to have leaders in the field (slums, branch offices in different slums) as well as back office departments like Accounts, Admin, Management Information System, Software development, etc. Here, after a lot of experimentation, I came to a conclusion, and thereafter I have written in the HR manual—'whom', how to recruit and 'whom', when to promote, etc.

So, for field work, the branch manager is the first leadership level. This person is promoted from loan and saving officers, service executives (women, field staff). Then there are different management levels for field monitoring. After trying various educational qualifications and training, I have come to a conclusion, and thereafter I have written in the HR manual that we should hire—Master's in Social work (MSW), mostly with specialisation in urban and rural community development, or Women and Child Welfare. Are the best candidates to groom for managerial-level staff for field monitoring. Hence, we recruit from various colleges MSW freshers, hire them as system auditors, and if they are good, promote them to service managers (micro insurance wing) or portfolio managers (micro finance wing). Thereafter, they can move upward as deputy managers. Our CEO Ujwala, joined 22 years ago as a field coordinator and rose up to this level. Our COO Ad. Arati joined 20 years ago as a branch manager and rose up to this level.

We have groomed a team of 6/7 deputy managers, 8/10 PM SMs, and 4/6 system auditors who are always there in the team under training. For the back office team leaders, we hire staff by giving advertisements in local newspapers and social media platforms. We also circulate the recruitment information among existing staff and members through flyers and WhatsApp messages. We hire 12th grade pass to graduate/post-graduates with computer skills as back office operators.

From this level, leaders are promoted by internal promotions and exams. The software team was groomed in-house, too. However, my husband convinced three of his old colleagues to join Annapurna Pariwar, namely Manjiri, who is the team leader of the MFMS team. In this way, most of the team members and leaders are built in-house. The key to build a strong team and leadership is—Good salary and employment benefits; Transparency in all processes like increment, promotion; Giving appropriate power with responsibility; No internal politics or interference.

Dr. Joy: Do you hire men?

Medha Tai: We do hire men. There are men at specific levels—Field monitoring, (MSW Trained); IT persons for hardware, software; doctor, driver; courier boys, office assistant; security. However, 100% field staffs are women, who go to the houses of members. 100% back office operators are women, who sit team by team in each department. The ease and comfort of work are more in this way. Our teams are well-gelled, cohesive. We have observed some mishaps like affairs, financial cheating by male staff in the past 20 years. This experience has endorsed today's system of staff recruitment and positioning.

Dr. Joy: Tell us about the organic building of cadres, knowledge technology?

Medha Tai: Yes, I do believe in organically building cadres, knowledge, and technology. My experience supports my belief. Being a unique MFI with co-op culture, we don't have similar organisations like us. Hence, we could not hire staff from other MFIs. We do not believe in the culture of poaching other MFIs staff.

There is some past experience when we gave newspaper advertisements, as a response, we came across staff, mainly men, from other MFIs. We soon experienced cultural and goals shifting. We could not continue with those hired from other MFIs. Currently, the staff from top-to-bottom are groomed in-house. The knowledge and technology are also acquired, built in house. Being a co-op MFI, we had a unique experience walking on a completely raw, new path. Hence, nothing could be copied and pasted.

Even our software had to be developed in-house. We had tried five different software before settling up our own MFMS (Micro Finance Management System) team in 2011. But since our requirement was unique, we had to set up our own software team. We required share capital, saving products which were not required by NBFC MFIs, hence were not developed by any software company. Plus, we had a loan-linked insurance program, which was not required by most NBFC MFIs, hence was not developed by any software company. So, all in all, it was the team, knowledge, technology—everything is built in house.

Dr. Joy: How did your software come into being?

Medha Tai: Being a unique MFI with co-op (co-operative) culture, we don't have similar organisations like us. Hence, we could not buy software from other MFIs. The knowledge and technology had to be acquired, built in house. Being a co-op MFI, we had a unique software requirement. It had to be developed in-house. We had tried five different software before settling up our own MFMS team in 2011. But since our requirement was unique, we had to set up our own software team.

We required share capital and saving products which were not required by NBFC MFIs, hence were not developed by any software company. Plus, we had a loan-linked insurance program, which was not required by most NBFC MFIs, hence was not developed by any software company. So all in all.

It was the team, knowledge, and technology. Everything is built in-house. The software team was groomed in-house too, however, my husband convinced three of his old colleagues to join Annapurna Pariwar, namely Manjiri, who is the team leader of MFMS team.

From 2011 till 2024, i.e. in the last 13 years, our MFMS Team has developed many modules based on our requirements. So, it has a share capital module, various saving products, as well as loan linked health, life, asset insurance program and above all pension program. All of these are unique.

Our MFMS Team discusses the requirements with me (founder CMD) or Ujwala, CEO, based on which they develop modules. They release version after version every alternate month. All the team leaders of the user departments are testing the screens and reports after the release of each version and reporting whether the development is as per the requirement.

Dr. Joy: How does your software keep pace with the changing technology in market?

Medha Tai: The new products, services or processes are developed due to mainly three reasons.

1. Regulatory changes by RBI or co-op ministry asking MFIs/co-ops to make changes in rules/products/process.
2. Credit bureau/Rating agencies changed requirements about data/data quality/process

3. It's us, the leadership of Annapurna Pariwar, who see and feel the need of our members, based on which we develop products and services. We have a top-to-bottom and bottom-to-top communication system in Annapurna Pariwar, which brings in information based on which we at the top management decide to change the products/services. Based on these new products and services, we give requirements to our software team. After some discussion through monthly meetings with the software team, they define the parameters, specify the time span required and come up with the next module with new requirements.

We had digitised the field operations to a much higher level even before the Covid-19 Pandemic. However, during Covid, we carried out a further automation. We outsourced the android-based solutions, to Sahyadri Electromech company, which is my husband's sister concern. They are experts in ECG (through telephone), which is based on Android technology. They developed a tab-based collection and disbursement system, which are more easy to operate for our field staff. We have named it as 'App Purna'. Our LSO (Loan ans Savings Officers), BMs (Branch Managers) are doing group formation to Group Recognition Test from App Purna. Also, they do recovery using App Purna tab-based technology. Our MFMS Team has developed an interface, so data from App Purna flows into MFMS software and vice versa smoothly, on a daily basis.

Same is the case with our micro insurance operations. Our SE (Service Executive) opens all health claims using App Purna tab-based technology. This has reduced the turnaround time in all field operations as well as reduced the cost of operations. This was required to enhance client experience, satisfaction as well as ease of operations.

During Covid-19 Pandemic, we increased the use of all types of technology:

1. We set up many WhatsApp groups for various types of reporting by staff. This made the back and forth communication easier, faster, and paperless.
2. We bought many Zoom licences and gave them to each team leader. We set up many Zoom meeting platforms for various types of reporting by staff. Everyday Zoom meetings between Pune and Mumbai teams made the daily operations more efficient, reducing the cost of travelling, printing and stationary.
3. We outsourced the automation of the accounts department to another company. Through the process development by them, all the credit and debit entries flow from our MFMS software into Tally accounting software. This has reduced turnaround time in Tally entries, reconciliation, and balance sheets preparation, and we require less staff in the account team.
4. We outsourced the automation of Admin department to Sahyadri Electromech company. They have developed an ERP software system which efficiently gives us data about staff attendance, recruitment, joining, resignation, salaries and increments.

For all of these systems and processes, I was 100% involved. Admin systems were developed by me in Excel many years ago, and the same were transferred into the new ERP system. The accounts manager and MFMS Team had to coordinate with the external software agency for MFMS and Tally automation. Our CEO Ujwala is equally involved as I am in field automation. Beyond doubt, my husband's support and guidance were important for various software initiatives. We also have an external IT consultant, Mr. Balbir, who keeps bringing information about outside technology. All this has helped us to be a techno-savvy MFI more than most others.

Dr. Joy: What are your plans to update the software & technology to keep pace with changing products and services?

Medha Tai: We can't 100% predict what changes will have to be done in future, still we have to keep gathering information about what's happening in the MF industry, MI sector, what the RBI and IRDA are thinking/doing. What co-op ministry is thinking/doing. (As an example, you may look at the recent changes due to credit bureau rules that impacted co-op MFIs and not for profit section 8 MFIs). Yet, we are planning and slowly doing changes to make our technology better every day, every month.

For bringing external information, we have experts from various sectors connected to Annapurna Pariwar, and we arrange periodic meetings with them. They include Actuaries like FX (Francois -Xavier Hay) and Paulami, Sector leader Sa Dhan, Sector expert Ranjani, technical experts like Mr Balbir, Mr. Samant.

We are continuing our software and technology development.

1. MF field App Purna still has to develop planning sheets, planning schedule of LSO, BM.
2. MI field App Purna still has to develop Life, Asset claims.
3. ERP software system will be used for the purchase of asset, asset schedule maintenance.
4. Tally automation will be done for all six organisations.
5. Tying up with Wingsure company, based in the USA, with which FX is connected as one of the founders and shareholders, we are trying to develop claim opening and claim information tracking by direct clients from their smart phones.

Dr. Joy: Whether the technical/software team leader is included in the senior leadership?

Medha Tai: Yes and No. By default, we have not decided who can be in the top team. In fact, I keep telling all team leaders—There is a lot of space at the top. But the teams/team leaders have to have the aptitude and desire to be in the top management. You can't force anyone to be a leader. So far, we have not come across any technical/software experts who desire to be in the top management. However, they all play very important and crucial role in the existence of Annapurna Pariwar. Hence, all are appropriately rewarded.

Dr. Joy: Do you plan retirement? When? What is your succession plan? How do you plan to stay connected to Annapurna Pariwar which you have founded and built brick by brick?

Medha Tai: From day one, when I started Annapurna Pariwar, it was very clear in my mind that

1. I was going to build a public institution and not a proprietary company.
2. An individual's life is limited, but an institution has to live longer. The best-founded and relevant institutions live longer, two/three generations.
3. I will retire one day and my successor wasn't going to be my relative necessarily.

With the above three things being absolutely at the core of all my thoughts, I have always imagined that I will retire someday.

I actually would have loved to be on the boards of all six organisations. And be just involved in decision-making process. However, I had to literally build everything from scratch, brick by brick. There was no guide, no ready question answers. The road was completely new, what my members were demanding was worth trying, but with exploration, experimentation and experience sharing.

This was a very interesting journey from 1993 till 2003, until I was just developing a need-based program for my members in Pune. After 2003, my journey became complex, because I had to take care of my mother's organisation with all the challenges and continue to do my own work. Until 2011, it was complex yet interesting. I could set up all MF and MI services in Pune and Mumbai.

After 2011, the Andhra crisis and its impact on the MF industry, my journey became really very difficult. With lot of regulatory requirements like giving personal guarantee, membership of credit bureau, getting rating done, whereas the rating agencies and credit bureaus still do not have proper guidelines for co-op MFI s like us. To guide my simple, home-groomed team to respond to all these new requirements, daily demanding something new was very tiring for me. This was the situation from 2011 till 2014.

By 2014, we somehow settled with the changed scenario of many competitors, ratings, credit bureau compliances, etc. After 2014, many laws and regulations changed. These included PFRDA (Pension Fund Regulatory and Development Authority), FCRA (Foreign Contribution Regulation Act), PMLA (Prevention of Money Laundering Act), and charitable trust requirement, everyday keeping me on my toes. Finding solutions to new problems daily, changed requirements was a challenge. Until 2016, when we faced demonetisation. It was a big blow to the poor, hence the MF industry. Many MFIs got destroyed.

To keep Annapurna Pariwar living and growing again, I literally slogged for those two years. Ujwala and Arati, in fact, emerged as leaders during this period. They supported me, though they didn't understand all intricacies of the situation. The Income tax department started harassing us for accepting old notes, which we had to do out of compulsion. We are still fighting a case against them.

And in March 2020, we strode back into a good position as a group of institutions.

Then Covid came. Again, four years of sleepless nights, slogging there was a new crisis. I got completely exhausted. Annapurna Pariwar rose again from the ashes, but I got burnt out. I was thinking of retirement in 2020, at the age of 60. But Covid forced me to stay put, else Annapurna Pariwar would not have survived. I never wanted to retire when Annapurna Pariwar was bleeding. I always wanted to handover a healthy (financially, culturally) organisation to my successors. Not a bleeding organisation. Hence, I slogged. Solutions that I worked out could not be easily thought of by anyone.

I have burnt out, but Annapurna Pariwar has come out of Covid with shining colours. Now I really and finally want to retire from day-to-day operations. I will be on all boards of Annapurna Pariwar, as long as they want me.

Dr. Joy: Will future leadership be rotational?

Medha Tai: No. The CEO will lead the organisation. COO will lead field operations. They both are groomed by me, are devoted, and own the organisational responsibility. They have very good communication and coordination. There are good teams and team leaders to support them, and the Board, including me, to guide them.

Dr. Joy: How do we ensure Democracy and Voice within our management?

Medha Tai: In simple words, we have platforms for meeting at every level. We have WhatsApp groups through which the everyday reporting of smallest to the most important tasks is done. Hence, there are no communication gaps. Plus, there is an opportunity for every stakeholder to speak in the meeting, express their opinions and experience in front of other stakeholders. Hence, all the opinions and experience are gathered in order to take further decisions and actions. The meeting platforms are created for ordinary members, their elected representatives, who are called community representatives. All the levels of staff members, as well as board members, on the six organisations of Annapurna Pariwar. Also on each of the board, there are member representatives and staff representatives as well as independent experts. So, every board is a combination of sector experts, clients who buy and experience the products/services, and staff at the implementation level. Hence, the decisions are taken by combining the opinions and experiences of each stakeholder. The periodicity of every meeting is maintained, no matter whatever difficulties are faced. During Covid, we shifted to virtual meetings by buying a number of Zoom licences. We had bought Zoom licences on 19th March 2020, just before there was a lock-down declared for the whole Nation.

Hence, our communication never stopped, even during Covid. We kept on the meetings on the Zoom platform through WhatsApp groups. Due to this, top-to-bottom and bottom-to-top communication, all the voices are heard democratically, and all the decisions are taken transparently, however once the decisions are passed by majority vote, everyone has to abide by that decision.

Dr. Joy: What are the essential elements for efficiency and effectiveness in Annapurna Pariwar?

Medha Tai: Efficiency means to me is as follows-

1. That every staff member and every single process is efficiently performing within the promised turn around time,

2. Minimum number of mistakes and maximum accuracy in result,
3. The cost of all operations is kept to minimum, and it is as per the promised cost.

May it be the interest rate charged on loans, the interest rate given on savings, the service charges on the insurance services, or day care centres, etc.

Effectiveness means to me as follows—that the products & services of Annapurna Pariwar are relevant, effective in the sense that they address the needs of the clients appropriately.

For the efficiency, we have written all the processes and systems. They are defined in our in-house software. So, turnaround time and cost of every service are well defined. There is no ambiguity in this.

The members are given receipts and books or cards for every service on which it is printed in black and white. For efficiency, we have trained every staff member in hard skills and soft skills. Hard skill is given in-house by the seniors using the software reports, forms, formats, processes and manuals. Whereas as soft skills like teamwork, communication, time management, team leadership are imparted by external management trainers.

We have engaged management experts as trainers for our teams for many years, we have formed batches of all staff and periodically arranged trainings. Hence, we have a trained team that understands the meaning of professionalism. There are parameters to check whether every service is delivered within time, at a defined cost and with zero mistakes.

Every staff member is evaluated monthly and annually on the basis of their job description, their work compliance within TAT and without mistakes. Plus, organisation undergoes an annual credit rating and code of conduct audit, besides a financial audit. We strive to get best grades always. In order to test, check the effectiveness of our service, the best measure is client satisfaction and client continuation.

In spite of a lot of competition in the field of micro finance and recently most microfinance institutions offering a shelf-ready Vanilla product in life and health insurance, buying them from commercial insurance companies, unlike us. Still, our client satisfaction is at the highest level. Even today, 40% of our members borrow only from Annapurna Pariwar. Most of our members are in the 7th and above loan cycle, so continuing with us for the last 15 to 20 years. Though we are a cooperative MFI, having a portfolio of only 200 crores, as against there are small finance banks with 20,000 crores portfolio and NBFCs too having more than 10,000 crores portfolio. We are still considered one of the most relevant microfinance institutions in India.

Dr. Joy: Where do you think Micro Finance field is going?

Medha Tai: I think the micro finance field is going nowhere. It started as an experiment, which was a response to the need for finance without any guarantee or collateral security. It started in many parts of the world where there were people, mostly women with less resources. It developed as a need based financial service and evolved over the last five decades. It was not regulated until 15 years ago.

Until it was not regulated, it was not widely spread. They were in the form of Thrift and internal ending groups, which were informal. RBI took cognizance of these informal groups in early eighties.

RBI through NABARD tried to formalise the self-help groups by extending bank finance to these groups. SHG movement got boosted in the late eighties and early nineties. Later on, they added subsidies in these groups if they included reserved categories of members. After this, the movement slowly deteriorated. Many elements like groups control going into the hands of group leaders, losing the focus on empowerment killed this movement.

Then, the RBI created SIDBI, which tried to finance small industries and also micro-finance institutions. This has been helpful in developing micro-finance institutions. Many of them got equity from SIDBI, which helped bringing stability for the micro-finance industry in the late nineties. We can even consider FWWBs contribution in building the small MFIs by giving them training, exposure, seed capital. However, SIDBI changed their focus many times after 2000. RBI, through its rural and priority sector lending department, started issuing guidelines for micro financing from late nineties.

Micro finance industry further got developed during 2000 to 2010 because most nationalised banks were given target to finance the Priority sector at a lower rate of interest. It was a big boost to the MF industry when the RBI created an institution, namely NBFCs, and the RBI regulated this new baby after 2005.

It was a lame baby with only power to lend and not to collect thrift and savings. So, this lame baby namely NBFC was perpetually dependent on investors' money, equity and bank loans.

In order to attract investments, MF industry stalwarts and experts promoted that this industry is profitable. After this we saw a decade filled with hundreds of new NBFCs, which were attracting millions of investor's funds, banks were completing their priority sector lending targets by tying up with big NBFCs, and everybody was making money in the name of poverty alleviation and empowering women.

And then came the Andhra Crisis. Due to over lending, multiple lending, many poor farmers in Andhra Pradesh committed suicides. This was an eye-opener. RBI, the sleeping tiger that was supposed to regulate the MF industry woke up after the Andhra crisis. They set up a committee called Malegham Committee to study what went wrong in Andhra Pradesh. On the basis of Malegham Committee report, RBI made it mandatory to get credit rating and code of conduct audit done every year for all MFIs from 2012, post Andhra crisis. They introduced new terms, norms like ethical financing, responsible financing. We must recognise the role of Sa Dhan in guiding, shaping new MFIs as well as in voicing the issues faced by MF Industry with RBI, Finance Ministry, etc. RBI had earlier recommended who can do MF as per their consolidated circular in 2009. It included co-op credit societies, section 8 not-for-profit companies, Nidhi companies NBFCs, etc.

However, the RBI didn't regulate any of these institutions except for NBFCs. Hence, mostly after 2005, the MF sector is dominated by NBFCs. Sa Dhan has more than 200 MFIs, out of which majority are NBFCs. Later on, RBI discovered that NBFCs remain weak due to no savings portfolio. Hence, RBI introduced small finance bank structure about 12 years ago. They issued only 11 SFB licences so far, and governed them. So, RBI recommends co-op credit societies, section 8 companies to do micro financing. However, it governs only NBFCs and SFBs.

There is no wholistic view point on micro finance institutions, who will regulate them, who will protect the investors' and loaned funds by controlling multiple lending, over borrowed status of the poor clients. Three years ago, RBI lifted the cap on the maximum loan number as well as maximum loan amount. They changed their guidelines to check the income and expenses and fifty percent to be kept for loan repayment, fifty percent to be kept for other domestic expenses. This was a disastrous move, according to me. Currently, many borrowers are carrying more than 10 loans at a time. Many are borrowing because many are lending irresponsibly. Many are borrowing to repay. The credit bureau check has become all the more essential for real ethical, responsible financing. And at such a juncture

RBI has wef 30.4.2025, banned section 8 companies from becoming members of credit bureau.

RBI had earlier banned co-op credit societies from becoming members of credit bureau in 2016. There are 12 Co-op MFIs including Annapurna, who are members of Sa Dhan. There are more than 70 section 8 companies who are members of Sa Dhan. All these are having about Rs. 2500 crores portfolio.

Yet RBI has banned them from becoming members of credit bureau retrospectively. So, we are in the MF business and RBI doesn't want to protect our money and our clients. We did pursue it with RBI on our own, as well as asked Sa Dhan to take it up with RBI. We have already taken this up with RBI, CO-OP ministry, Sa Dhan. I have been talking, convincing all policymakers to allow not-for-profit entities to become members of credit bureau. Yet no resolution.

Empowering Women from One Milestone to Another

Joy Deshmukh Ranadive and Simran Hatkar

Abstract This chapter locates the processes of empowerment using the framework of increased economic, socio-cultural, physical, and political spaces within the lives of women members. This framework is an original contribution of the editor to empowerment studies. Economic spaces are about the ability of women to have access to and control over economic resources. Socio-cultural spaces are about women's increased status and power within the household and the repositioning of familial hierarchies. Physical spaces are about increased mobility within the community and beyond. Political spaces focus on women's roles in external groups, organisations, etc. Ultimately, empowerment leads to an increased ability to make decisions, take responsibility for those decisions, and finally see the decisions through to yield positive results that improve the quality of life. This framework allows for connecting the different spaces with each other and to micro and macro changes in the social environment. Microfinance and microinsurance services have enabled processes of empowerment to be activated. Furthermore, the input of 'plus' services that Annapurna Pariwar has factored into microfinance and microinsurance has accelerated the empowerment processes. It has also contributed to SDG 5: achieving gender equality and the empowerment of all women and girls. Case studies of select women members will be detailed to capture these processes. There are women who were part of the group of nine women that Medha Tai had initially helped. Some of the case studies will focus on them. Other case studies will feature women who joined the journey along the way. Women will be selected so that there is a variety of lifecycle milestones of both the women and Annapurna

J. D. Ranadive (✉)
Independent Consultant, Pune, Maharashtra, India
e-mail: drjoydeshmukh@gmail.com

S. Hatkar
Community Based Insurance Programme, Pune, Maharashtra, India
e-mail: smrnhatkar06@gmail.com

J. D. Ranadive, S. Guha (eds.), *Building Pathways to Women's Empowerment*, India Studies in Business and Economics,
https://doi.org/10.1007/978-981-95-7159-8_4

Pariwar. This juxtapositioning will draw out various connections between the interventions and the commensurate empowerment impacts that led to achieving SDG 5.

1 Introduction

Across time, among the real and potential clients of microcredit, women are seen as the most appropriate targeted beneficiaries since it is argued that, in contrast to men, the entire household benefits when the loans are given to women. Women are also reputed to be more reliable than men when it comes to repayments. It is further claimed that microcredit empowers women since it accords economic independence and instils confidence by virtue of their participation in groups as well as their undertaking and expanding economic activities. Before conceiving the SDGs, the work of Annapurna Pariwar (AP) tried to focus on a goal similar to the present SDG 5: achieving gender equality and empowerment of all women and girls.

Group-based microcredit interventions targeted at poor women offer a greater potential to expand the endowments of women, exchange outcomes for women's labour and produce, and consumption outcomes for women than the groups focused on the poor in general. This is because group-based microcredit interventions with women offer the space to break women's isolation, expand their access to credit, assets, and income independent of men, and increase their bargaining power within the family and outside. The realisation of this potential seems to depend on whether addressing women's poverty is part of the goals of the organisation, the extent to which the goals are shared at different levels of the organisation and among different associated stakeholders, the gender and social relations (age, caste, headship, etc.) sensitivity of the leadership, the extent to which the organisation is process-driven and staffed accordingly, and whether the orientation of the organisation stretches beyond profit maximisation (Burra et al., 2005).

Empowerment is not a new concept. Every society has local terms for autonomy, self-direction, self-confidence, and self-worth. What is new is the attempt to measure empowerment in a systematic way. One of the biggest challenges in measuring empowerment is that it is a latent phenomenon. Its presence can only be deduced through its actions or results. Hence, most behaviours are proxies for the underlying phenomenon (Narayan Deepa, 2005). This chapter, '**Empowering women from one milestone to another**' is divided into two parts. The first part is an interview with Dr. Medha Samant, referred to as Medha Tai, which brings out her vision and views on women's empowerment and highlights how her organisation AP, addresses women's empowerment and contributes to SDG 5. The second part locates the processes of empowerment using the framework of increased economic, socio-cultural, physical, and political spaces within the lives of women members. This framework is an original contribution of the editor to empowerment studies. Economic spaces are about the ability of women to have access to and control over economic resources. Socio-cultural spaces are about women's increased status and power within the household and the repositioning of familial hierarchies. Physical spaces are about increased mobility within the community and beyond. Political spaces focus on women's roles in external groups, organisations, etc. Ultimately, empowerment leads to an increased ability to make decisions, take responsibility for those decisions, and finally see the decisions through to yield positive results that improve the quality of life. This framework allows for connecting the different spaces with each other and linking them to micro and macro changes in the social environment. Microfinance and microinsurance services have enabled processes of empowerment to be activated. Furthermore, the input of 'plus' services that AP has factored into microfinance and microinsurance has accelerated the empowerment processes. Case studies of select women members will be detailed to capture these processes. There are women who were part of the group of nine women that Medha Tai initially helped. Some of the case studies will focus on them. Other case studies will feature women who joined the journey along the way. Women will be selected to ensure there is a variety of lifecycle milestones of both the women and AP. This juxtaposition will draw out various connections between the interventions and the corresponding empowerment impacts.

2 Part One

2.1 Interview with Medha Tai

Dr. Joy: What is your understanding of the empowerment of women?

Medha Tai: In my opinion, empowerment of women is a very encompassing word. In today's times, with so much advancement in Science and Technology, the girl child is killed in the womb. So, the right to take birth is the first point of women's empowerment. Then, good medical treatment, good education, equal social treatment without gender biases, economic freedom, and political rights—all of the above components are involved in the empowerment of women.

Given the focus of AP (Annapurna Pariwar), the first felt need observed by me in the 1990s, coming from my banking background, was the need for credit. Without any asset or collateral security, the women wanted loans at affordable costs, and that is where we began. Going forward, we understood their need for health, life, asset insurance, and pension for old age security. They did not want to depend on anyone in such vulnerable situations. So, we went on developing services around their needs. Even the day care centres were aimed at mother and daughter empowerment, where poor mothers have to earn and the daughters suffer in education because they have to help their mothers in cooking and taking care of younger siblings.

Our Vidyapurna project also aims at helping poor single mothers educate their children. So, all in all, most of our projects are aimed at empowering women economically and socially. Their right to education is protected, their right to good medical treatment is protected, and old age security is protected. We also give them the right to participate in decisions at all levels in AP, so they influence every single decision that will impact them. This is how we have practically become the catalyst in the empowerment of women members of AP.

Dr. Joy: How do you think the empowerment of women is connected to the men and boys in their lives?

Medha Tai: The empowerment of women is always connected with the men and boys in their lives. As home makers, they are concerned about the well-being of their husbands, children, and family. I realised this much earlier. I had heard that the bachat gat programmes were not supported by the men in the villages. These were savings and internal lending groups by poor women, given the name of self-help groups by NABARD in the 1980s. They thought that these people (NGOs or Bachat gat federations) were instigating women to fight with the men. So, from day one, I used to invite the husband or the grown-up children in the case of single women to our office, and I used to talk to them about why we are giving them the loan. I used to ask them whether they agree that they want this loan and whether they appreciate that their wife/mother is taking responsibility for four other women because none of them have any asset to offer as collateral security. I think this particular action has played a very big role in the 100% recovery of Annapurna loans. Because most husbands appreciated that I was giving them respect, explaining everything to them, and that's how they participated whole heartedly in all our initiatives. I used this strategy of involving men and boys from the beginning when I began work in 1993. Involving men and boys has not only helped the women members in the groups but also the entire community.

Later on, I went to Insisute of Development Studies (IDS) at Sussex University. I learnt from none other than Naila Kabir the most important sentence in the empowerment of women: 'If you wish to empower women you have to engage men in the dialogue'. After this, I very consciously involved the men folk in the families of our members. Even in our pension program, a choice is given to the member to opt for the pension with husband or without husband. Most women opt for the pension with their husbands. That's how so many women, viz. 34,000, could become members of our Aadharpurna pension programme. If we had not involved men in the programme, they would have thought AP was offering pensions only to women and not to men. In that case, they wouldn't have allowed their wives to contribute in such large numbers to this pension programme.

Also, in our health and life insurance, all the men and women in the families of our members are covered. So, they get benefit from coverage for all illnesses as well as death. Even in our day care centres Vatsalya Purna, or our educational sponsorship program, Vidya Purna, we have maintained no bias between boys and girls. Everyone gets admission, everyone gets sponsorship, irrespective of gender.

Hence, I state here that we understand the importance of empowering men along with women. We have incorporated that in all our programmes, and this has contributed to the success of all our programmes. Moreover, our name is not Annapurna Mahila Program, but it is AP, addressing the families of the members.

Dr. Joy: Have you made conscious effort to involve men and boys in your programmes? If yes, how, and why?

Medha Tai: Yes, we have made a very conscious effort to involve men and boys in all our interventions. We have ensured that each programme of AP has an impact on the empowerment of our members, 95% of whom are women. Right from the selection of the community to the selection of the members, to their involvement in each intervention, and the decisions about the same, it is ensured through all our systems.

Dr. Joy: Have you tried to measure the empowerment impact on Annapurna members?

Medha Tai: Yes, we have measured the impact time and again. We have actually conducted surveys with the help of MCrill and Microsave around 15–20 years ago to measure the impact. The results were good. Thereafter, we programmed our software to be able to measure empowerment. There are 28 parameters in the software, namely the increase in income, the educational status of the growing children, the asset creation of the family, the assets in the name of the women, the condition of house improvement, the power given to women to take family decisions, etc. However, due to continuously changing priorities because of regulatory changes and market turbulence, we could not develop the reports from our software.

But sometime in the future, we will be able to print the reports and show that, on all these parameters, our women have a much better status as compared to the women of other communities. As of now, we can say that most of our members continue to be members of AP up to the 10th or 12th loan cycle, and each loan cycle takes them to better financial stability. By helping them in cases of medical emergencies, death, or asset loss, our members have built assets like houses in their names, they will get pensions in their old age, and they are very vocal on Annapurna platforms. Through the health mutual fund, life mutual fund, family mutual fund, and asset loss mutual fund, we have protected them from all kinds of shocks that hamper their progress towards sustainability. It is possible that, sometime, a comparative sample of Annapurna members and non-members can be studied for empowerment.

Dr. Joy: In Annapurna Pariwar would you say that it is empowerment by default (i.e., due to the products and services you offer) or empowerment by design (i.e., a deliberate programme design that shifts factors in women's lives that leads to empowerment).

Medha Tai: I will say it is both because I was very clearly inclined to empower poor women by linking them with bank credit. So, as a starting point, the empowerment of women in AP was clearly in design. Also, involving men in the process was very much a part of it from the beginning. I gained a much better theoretical understanding of this from my gender and empowerment training at IDS, just four years after starting AP.

So, I would say it was by design. But it was also by default because every intervention was based on the needs expressed by the women. The products and services were designed to empower the women and their families.

Dr. Joy: What will you say is/are the biggest indicator/s of women's empowerment of Annapurna members?

Medha Tai: Most of our projects are aimed at empowering women economically and socially; their right to education is protected, their right to good medical treatment is safeguarded, and old age security is ensured. We also give them the right to participate in decisions at all levels in AP so they can influence every single decision that will impact them.

We have measured the impact time and again. We have programmed our software to be able to measure empowerment. There are 28 parameters in the software, namely: the increase in income, the educational status of growing children, the asset creation of the family, the assets in the name of women, the condition of house improvement, and the power given to women to make family decisions.

As of now, we can say that most of our members continue to be members of AP up to the 10th or 12th loan cycle, and each loan cycle takes them to better financial stability, helping them in cases of medical emergencies, death, or asset loss, our members have built assets like houses in their names, they will receive pensions in their old age, and they are very vocal on Annapurna platforms. This is how we have practically become the catalyst in the empowerment of women members of AP.

Dr. Joy: What does the sense of belonging to Annapurna mean to the women members?

Medha Tai: It really means a lot. It means support. It means financial stability. It means financial literacy. It means that they can plan with each loan cycle—what they will do, how they will grow, how they will educate their children, and how they will build their assets. It means that they will not be left high and dry when there is a medical emergency in their family, and it also means a lot of emotional support.

They are all bonded emotionally to me, and I too am bonded with them. Also, they have a very strong emotional connection with our staff at the top and the staff at the grassroots. Above all, they know they are shareholders and the owners of AP. They feel very happy to receive dividends on their share capital because we have taught them that it comes out of the profits made by AP. They take pride in saying this.

Dr. Joy: What made you include plus services into your model?

Medha Tai: All our plus services were based on the needs of the members. Some were felt needs, whereas others were strategic needs. For example, loans and day care were the felt needs. However, they knew that they had to pay interest on the loans. In fact, they were paying much higher interest to private money lenders. Hence, I did not have to convince them about paying the interest on loans. But I had to convince them about saving in different ways. Once they started saving, and it was built into the programme, today, through all their thrift, savings, and pension funds, they are financing half of our loan portfolio. This brings sustainability to both our members and us as an institution. The members build their savings and thus secure their future. We get assured funds at comparatively lower costs (11%) than banks (13%).

Though day care centres were their felt need, they had never experienced them. Hence, they were not ready to pay for the same. They expected that it should be a free service. Through a lot of dialogue, negotiation, and practically showing them how good the day care centres could be with their participatory, co-operative model, they have started willingly paying for the same.

About services like insurance and pension, these were their strategic needs. The members did not initially ask for these, but whenever they had a medical emergency or a death in the family, I took that opportunity to discuss these events with them. Discussions were about what to do and how to bring a solution in such emergencies. This resulted in them being ready to design these services by defining the cost & benefit and being ready to pay for the same. So, every service was designed out of their need. This is an example of a mission-centric social enterprise where solving the problem is the mission of the enterprise.

However, as a leader, I had to be very clear and focused about not listening to such needs that were expressed when they were not directly linked to economic empowerment and could not be self-financed. For example, we implemented the service of training and placement with them for more than 10 years and then stopped. The need was expressed, but they were never ready to pay for the same because the employers did not respect or pay for their skills learned through classroom training. Another service, which we did not even offer, was taking them to pilgrimage (a felt and demanded need).

Dr. Joy: Are there more plans for adding more plus services?

Medha Tai: No. First of all, I do not plan what they will need. The need should surface through a very organic procedure. In the past, when I was 100% responsible and involved, I only had a good, patient listening ear. Hence, I heard their needs, which they expressed verbally, and which I learned through the situation and their body language. I developed that into a dialogue, design, and then delivery. Now, I have retired from field operations, and I will be on the decision-making bodies of AP. So, I will not take such an initiative on my own.

I have set up platforms for meetings, through which the implementing staff or senior-level staff hear about various needs that they feel are umbilically linked to the full platter of services we offer. These could be sustainable, and they should bring them to the board. Then we can discuss and decide whether we would like to take them up and add them as another plus service.

Dr. Joy: Do you see plus services as enabling member retention?

Medha Tai: Yes and No. It is a double-edged sword. A plain, simple microfinance vanilla product is very easy to deliver in today's times. Any additional service could be helpful for member retention if it is really good, based on the needs of clients, correctly priced, and appropriately delivered; then it could be an asset for the organisation. However, if any additional service is not need-based, not correctly priced, not properly delivered, or if you try to cheat the client, promise something different, and deliver something different, then it could be the biggest liability. Members will run away from the organisation. Just for a loan vanilla microfinance product, members have hundreds of options. They don't need to come to you for plus services unless you are really good to them, which AP is.

Dr. Joy: What are the goals your staff members oriented towards, especially those in operations, e.g., repayments, disbursements, etc., or are there larger goals of empowerment also factored in? If yes, how is this done?

Medha Tai: See, the answer is a bit complex. All the teams do not have the same goals. For example, the microfinance implementation team has to ensure loan delivery and loan recovery on time. They cannot wait for empowerment to happen or factor in the different parameters of empowerment, which are measured independently. The microinsurance implementing team is more of a service-giving team. This team delivers five services—health insurance, life insurance, asset insurance, pension, and Vidyapurna sponsorship—during June, July, and August every year. Even this team does not directly do anything about empowerment; however, due to the social security programs, empowerment happens automatically, as it is designed in the programme irrespective of the delivery mechanism of the team. In the same way, the implementing team has a different goal. Back-office teams do not have any such social goals, except that they have to provide correct and timely data with zero mistakes and within the defined turnaround time. We have to understand that these team members have taken up the job at AP not because of their social goals but in order to earn a good living for their families. Side by side, if they are motivated and inspired by the good work being done by AP for empowering poor women, they take pride in what they are doing.

We have displayed our vision, mission, and goal for each project. Putting it together becomes the goal of AP. The staff reads this frequently because it is displayed in all common places. Irrespective of their personal goals, the organisation goals are interwoven into the programmes and services. These are measured through defined parameters in the software. Hence, it is not person-dependent; it is system-dependent.

Dr. Joy: Within your operations have you entered household dynamics? If yes, please explain?

Medha Tai: See, in the beginning, when I was solely responsible for all field operations and was active in the slums, I encountered so many issues within the families of the members. To mention a few: husband and wife fights; husband having an affair outside; husband being alcoholic; husband having two wives; fights between two members or their families.

However, I had basic common sense, and since I was earlier working with middle-class women in the banking trade union, plus I was trained as a social worker in handling human dynamics, I could handle these dynamics without entangling with the AP credit and savings programme.

It is a very risky path because if members get angry with you, they can straight away declare that they are not going to repay your loan. This is a big risk to carry. I have personally experienced all of these reactions. Hence, after I engaged teams in different projects at the field level, including the field monitoring and back office support team, I decided not to involve them in handling psychological or household issues. For a few years, I implemented the Shantipurna program, wherein we had trained social workers/field workers who visited the homes of our members and checked if they needed counselling or administrative support, such as obtaining ration cards securing admission for their children, etc. However, since these services were free of cost, financial sustainability could not be achieved. So, as long as we received some grants from InterAid for this programme, we were able to implement it.

We have been free from any overt household dynamics for the last 15 years. Though I believe that with the economic empowerment of women, their position in the family changes to a much better status. Many members express during meetings that their husbands have stopped beating them because they are AP members. It is the same generation that initially took loans and has witnessed the change brought about by economic stability. The entire family stabilises. The husbands, who were initially stressed, are calmer now. Money comes into the family. Small doses of loans build their economic stability. Future plans can be made. Children also learn to respect their mothers, who are our members. They ensure that their fathers treat their mothers better.

Dr. Joy: How do you see women members becoming leaders in the public space? Are there pathways that you have built for this to happen? If yes, please explain.

Medha Tai: No, in fact, I am against our members becoming public leaders. Though I myself come from a political family and have my own political ideas, I have stayed away from electoral politics all my life. I wanted to implement this credit + programme professionally, without bringing any electoral or party politics into it. The knowledge of politics and having clear political ideas is something different from getting into electoral politics. As we give financial literacy and health awareness to our members, we also talk about politics with them. I personally do it through my samajik vishay circulars earlier and now through videos. I try to bring about awareness regarding who should be our choice as good states persons? What are the real issues of people, like inflation, unemployment? And from what kind of religious or communal issues we should keep a distance, because they will be detrimental to our development, etc.

However, it has been my experience that our community representatives, who are elected from their groups and community to be on AP decision-making bodies, are sometimes picked up by some political parties, clearly using them as vehicles for cashing votes of the community.

Actually, alone, these community-leaders have not done anything to deliver services like credit, insurance, sponsorship, etc. They are a part of AP's system and mechanism. However, they try to encash their popularity in the community by joining some party, which is actually detrimental to Annapurna's programme. Hence, we have made resolutions that if any community representative wants to join any political party, they have to resign as a community member from AP.

Dr. Joy: Have any Annapurna members stood for elections in local government?

Medha Tai: Yes, a few, but not with our backing; rather, after resigning from the Annapurna community representative body.

Dr. Joy: Have you encountered caste or religious dynamics within Annapurna members? If yes, please explain. Do the socio-political dynamics within the slums where you operate, ever interfere with your goals?

Medha Tai: There are caste and religious dynamics in all the slums, which also impact the socio-political dynamics within the slums. I particularly know that in Pune, there are many slums with a majority of people belonging to the same religion or caste. Also, there are some slums where many different castes and religions live mostly peacefully, but occasionally, triggered by some politicians or builders, there are fights. In Mumbai, most of the slums are mixed with people from different religions, castes, states, etc.

Actually, the local slum dynamics don't get in our way if we don't get in their way. That has been my experience. We observe all dynamics and politics, but we do not get involved in them. Very consciously, I have trained all the staff and created systems to ensure that we do not interact with or take any help from local politicians. There have been occasions when local politicians have requested me to allow them to felicitate me on their platform, but I have made it a rule that I don't go on any party platform. There are clear written instructions in our manual stating that when we look for a rented branch office, we don't take it near any political party office, liquor bar, Matka adda, etc. I think because of this very clear stand, our work has never been hampered by local dynamics or politics.

Dr. Joy: What are the lessons that you have learnt from your women members and from the communities?

Medha Tai: There are many lessons learnt; it is very difficult to list them all, but I will narrate a few very important lessons learnt. The most important lesson is—'We should not think that we know it all'. Just because we are educated, most of us think that we are going to change their lives. I never had this disillusion. In the beginning itself, had I not known what Shevanta Bai had faced, what life these women had experienced, I would not have realised that the real solutions are not something that we have studied in books. It is not taught in any school or college. Hence, walking with them a few steps, trying to understand them and their life, which was my normal, natural way of working, has helped me to come all this way. I never offered them any readymade programme. I said, 'we will try it out', 'we will work it out', 'are you ready to walk with me?' This was my most important communication, which I think helped me to win the trust of our members.

Secondly, I said, 'it our money, it's not my money', that has also been very important communication. Because of this, they always protected the money. They always made sure that everybody repaid. So, we have to give ownership to people and should not give them the impression that 'I am the owner' and 'you are my subordinate'.

The most important lesson learned from the women and communities is that wisdom is not taught in school and college; it is acquired in the university called life.

3 Part Two

3.1 Tracing Empowerment

3.1.1 Spaces and Nine Interviews

Women's empowerment is not a simple linear process of cause and effect. It entails a complex configuration of factors that affect economic, socio-cultural, political, physical, and mental spaces. These are seen at the individual microlevel as well as at the meso level of communities. The cause can be activated in any space, and its effect is seen in all the other spaces. (Deshmukh Ranadive Joy, 2002, 2005).[1]

Economic space is determined by the ownership of immovable and movable assets, both tangible and non-tangible which enhance women's economic independence. Access to and control over assets, livelihoods, savings, credit, insurance, and pension schemes enhance economic spaces.

Socio-cultural spaces increase when women's positions within kinship structures, such as family and communities, are enhanced. Caste, class, region, ethnicity, and religion play a significant role within socio-cultural spaces.

Physical spaces are captured with mobility, access to transport, access, and the ability to venture out of the limited domain of the house and slum to access livelihood and other options. Physical space is also enhanced with increased safety

[1] The framework of 'Spaces'—Economic, Socio-cultural, Political, Physical and Mental was first introduced in Deshmukh Ranadive Joy, Space for Power Women's Work and Family Strategies in South and South-East Asia, Rainbow Publishers, in collaboration with Centre for Women's Development Studies 2002.

And subsequently elaborated in Deshmukh Ranadive Joy, "Gender, Power and Empowerment: An Analysis of Household and Family Dynamics" in Narayan Deepa (ed) Measuring Empowerment Cross Disciplinary Perspectives, The International Bank for Reconstruction and Development, The World Bank. Washington DC, 2005. It was applied to UNDP projects in (Burra et al, 2005). Microcredit, poverty and empowerment. Linking the triad. Sage Publications.

and the ability to move freely in geographical areas. Physical space is further enhanced with control over women's bodies and reproductive decisions.

Political spaces increase the decision-making ability of women within formal and informal institutions such as family, neighbourhood, common spaces, political institutions, and other social and economic institutions, where they express their agency to make decisions and enable other women to make their own decisions.

Mental space is not an independent variable. It is connected to expansion in one or several other spaces. Increased mental space allows women to make decisions that lead to their empowerment.

We will be using the framework below to ascertain the empowerment effects of nine Annapurna members. The framework extends from macro to meso to micro-effects. Shifts in the macro affect the meso and, hence, the micro (Fig. 1).

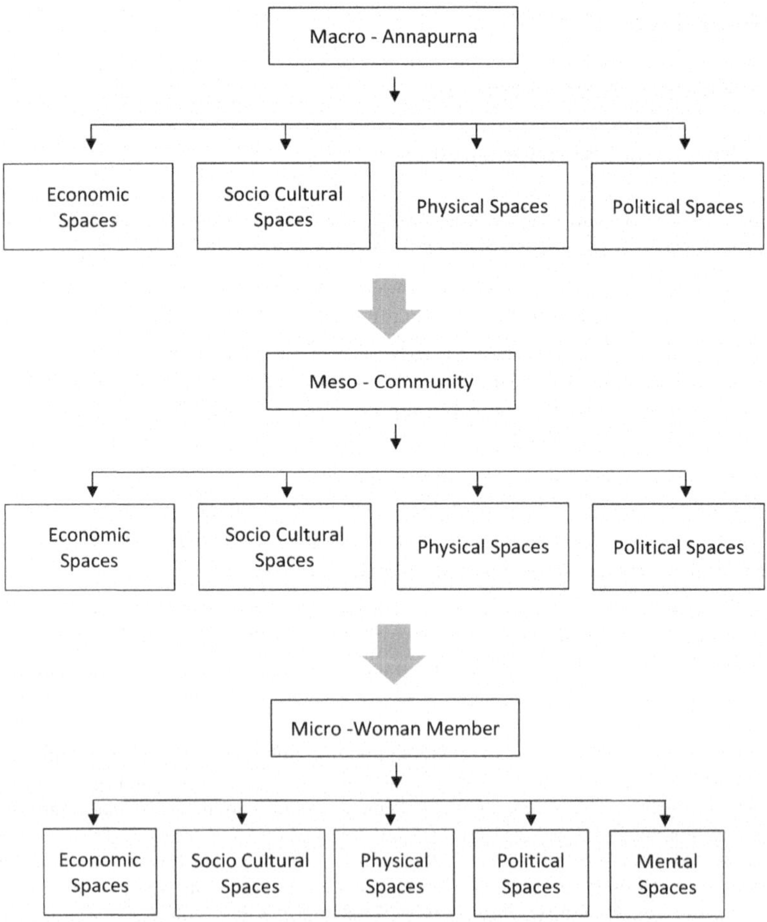

Fig. 1 Framework to ascertain the empowerment effects of Annapurna members

At the macro level, we will investigate the policy and methods of Annapurna as an organisation. This has been covered in Chaps. 1 and 2 of this first section through the interviews with Medha Tai. Primarily, AP has moved economic spaces through its microfinance, microinsurance, and pension programmes. Simultaneously, through its plus programmes of Adharpurna and Vatsalyapurna, it has expanded socio-cultural and physical spaces.

At the meso level, the community feeling of being a member of AP has bonded women together. Being a part of a savings group and being responsible for each other's financial discipline has fostered an expansion of all the four spaces.

The deep impact of the macro and meso changes is felt at the microlevel of individual women. In the first place, economic spaces have increased. Socio-cultural spaces, physical spaces, and political spaces in terms of leadership have also increased. This is evident from the voice generated by AP, where the communication of ideas flows from the macro to meso to microlevels. This is one of the stellar strengths of AP's empowerment model. Mental spaces shift on account of the shift in the other four spaces.

The nine case studies are based on interviews conducted with nine women across three decades of AP's journey: first from 1993–2003, then from 2004–2014, and lastly from 2015–2024. Each of the three women in the three decades has been selected at three lifecycle points in their lives: (1) within the reproductive age and under 35 years of age; (2) post-reproductive age, between 35 and 55 years of age; and (3) post the age of 55. This approach provides insight into how AP's programme

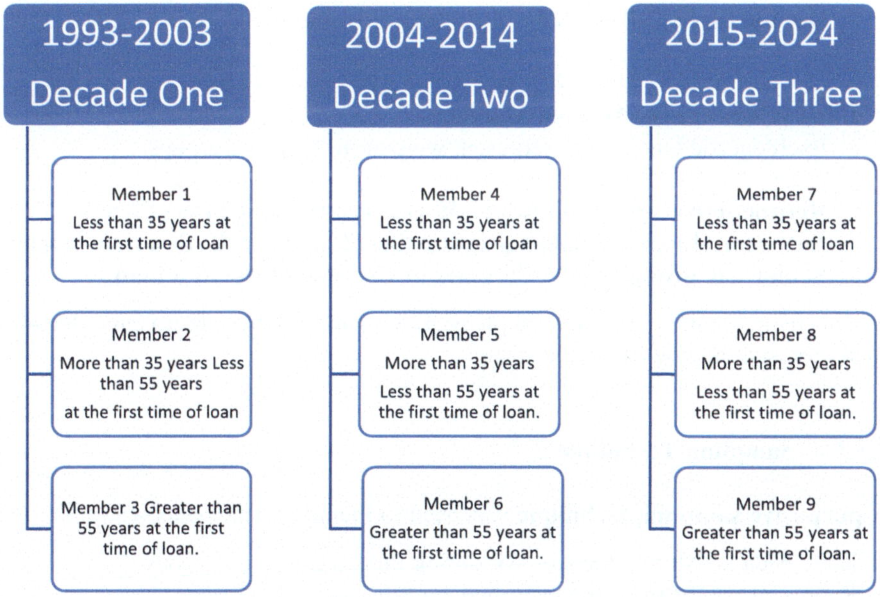

Fig. 2 Description of sample participants

addresses the empowerment needs of women. Juxtaposed with the lifecycle of the organisation itself, it sheds light on the evolution and, consequently, the ability of AP to expand different spaces for the nine women. The lifecycle of the organisation has been intertwined with the lifecycle of the women respondents. This has been done to highlight the relevance of AP at different points in the lifecycle of its women members (Fig. 2).

3.1.2 Sampling Method

1. **Sampling Frame**

The population includes women members of AP who have been associated with its programmes over the last 30 years. The sample was drawn from the Pune and Mumbai branches, which were the main centres of the organisation's activity during different periods.

2. **Stratification Criteria**

To ensure temporal and developmental representation, the sample was stratified across the following dimensions:

- **Time-based Cohorts (Decades)**
  - **Decade one (1993–2003):** early phase of organisational development.
  - **Decade two (2004–2014):** expansion and institutional strengthening.
  - **Decade three (2015–2024):** digital maturity and social security integration.

- **Life-cycle Stages of Women Members**
  Each decade has tried to represent women in three age groups:
  - **Reproductive age group (up to 35 years at the first time of loan)**
  - **Post-reproductive middle-age group (35–55 years at the first time of loan)**
  - **Senior age group (Above 55 years at the time of the first loan)**

This matrix results in a total sample of **nine women—three from each decade**, each representing one life-cycle stage.

3.1.3 Sampling Technique

A **purposive sampling technique** was used to identify participants who:

- Have been active members of AP during their respective decades.
- Represent one of the three identified age/life cycle categories.
- Can reflect on their experiences over time.

3.1.4 Rationale

This sampling design allows:

- A **comparative cross-temporal analysis** of empowerment outcomes.
- Examination of **intersections between age, time, and programme evolution**.
- Understanding how empowerment processes unfold over different phases of a woman's life and the organisation's growth.

3.1.5 Sample Size Justification

Given the **in-depth qualitative nature** of the research, a small but information-rich sample was deemed appropriate. The focus is on **depth over breadth**, capturing nuanced shifts in the five empowerment spaces—**economic, socio-cultural, physical, political, and mental**.

The interview questions delved into each of the five spaces for each woman member. As mentioned earlier, the macro and meso spaces have been illuminated through Chaps. 1 and 2 via the interviews with Medha Tai. Since we are asking questions now and asking the women to recall events from the past, the questions will be similar, but the reference and context will pertain to a specific decade. Interviews were conducted for over an hour per respondent.

3.2 *Case Description: 1993–2003 Decade One: Early Phase of Organisational Development*

3.2.1 Participant 1

Participant 1 is a 60 year old woman and a member of AP. She came to know about AP through Medha Tai. She mentioned,

'I used to see her come to the market and meet other women. She had also visited our small fruit shop which we had near Paud road. I had taken the loan in 1993'.

When she got married, her husband was an auto driver, and she was a homemaker. After two to three years, they started a fruit-selling business, and she stated,

'I had taken the loan for stocking up fresh fruits in the shop. Medha Tai might remember it. It was a very different experience as this was the first time, I was doing work and taking a loan. I had my husband's support all throughout which helped me too. That time Medha Tai used to personally be present while giving the loans'.

She used to keep taking loans from AP—Rs. 1000 to Rs. 2000—and eventually, she got help for up to Rs. 7000. Then she stopped in between. They managed to handle inventory and cover things themselves. She had taken a Rs. 1000 loan initially, and since then, she has taken Rs. 1,70,000 in loans. She also has savings with them, which she has not withdrawn.

She initially took loans for productive purposes, and later, after having children, she used loans for their education. She mentioned,

'Because of the education, my son is an electrician, and my daughter works as an interior designer. I was able to contribute to their growth and success today'.

Microcredit also helped her to improve the financial condition of the household, she remembered.

'As I told you we had the opportunity to stock up more products on our stall. Also, before my husband used to drive a rented rickshaw like it was someone else's and we used to pay them. Now he has his own rickshaw. We could slowly and steadily by our own throughout the years'.

AP also provides non-loan-tied savings facilities. The participant mentioned,

'I have my Adharpurna going on since quite a few years. I used to deposit ₹200 monthly, now I'm depositing ₹1500 monthly. It should at least help with the basic monthly medicine that I require. If Medha Tai has said we will get pension we will get it like she always says "Adharpurna hi tumchi mathar pan chi kathi ahe" Adharpurna is like the stick that supports you in old age'.

In the context of microinsurance, the respondent received help from AP. She explained,

'Over the years I have got several claims. When my daughter delivered a baby, we got a claim. My husband had thyroid surgery; we got a claim. And then when I got cancer, I got a third claim. Even though I wasn't admitted in the network hospital I still got a claim. They helped with ₹7500. Even though I wasn't admitted in their listed hospital for many days, they still said since surgery happened and it was an emergency, they would give the claim. The claims really helped in a time of need. I got cancer, and the place where I get treatment doesn't give medicines. They told me to get them from outside, so I bought them myself using that money. So yes, it was useful. I am currently taking my treatment at Vishranti Hospital. It's free for women. Chemotherapy and all are free. Outside, they said each chemo costs ₹30,000–₹40,000. How could poor people like us afford that? My husband drives a rickshaw, and my son is an electrician. Now I'm okay, by Allah's grace. But when I was diagnosed with cancer, I completely collapsed. I used to wonder whether I would even survive. It was really hard. I had six rounds of chemotherapy, and they were very hard. They used to inject 3.5 bottles into me. One of my injections costs ₹61,000. That's the one they used. Yes, that injection was very expensive. My relatives gave me money, and through Vishranti Hospital—which helps women—I got the first injection for ₹15,000. Then for the second injection, I applied for admission under the urban poor scheme. I got from the Corporation. Till now, I've taken 12 injections. Five are remaining. They had prescribed 17 total'.

She was asked whether she had suffered during the COVID-19 pandemic or not. She responded that she did not. She mentioned that whatever she had, she spent. She took care of the weddings of her children, and she also did sewing work, hemming, putting falls on sarees, and many small things. After her shop was lost due to the road expansion, she stayed at home and did many kinds of work.

Joining AP also gave her mobility, respect in the community, and in the households. The respondent mentioned that as a community representative, she interacted with a number of members, and it increased her knowledge. She also got lots of information from AP and Medha Tai. She mentioned,

'Medha Tai taught us so well—no bank person talks the way she does. She helps poor people rise. She always says, "A family must unite." Even in Mumbai and Pune, everyone knows her. When we were CRs, she visited our homes and took photos. My photo was sent everywhere—Mumbai and other places. I was acknowledged and respected everywhere. Yes, definitely. I feel great at meetings. When Medha Tai calls me on stage and stands beside me, puts her arm around me and says, "She's been with us since the start, from the ₹1000 loan days"—I feel proud. Everyone sees and hears that. It really boosts my confidence'.

She said that her family is supportive, and she has always brought income to the family. She has not received support under Vidyapurna, as it is meant for children of single mothers. She also knows about Vatsalyapurna, the day care centres. She thinks it is a very good initiative and helpful for the parents in the community. It is a very dangerous world out there; we can't leave children anywhere now a days, but the day care centre gives a feeling of security.

She mentioned that after joining the group of AP, it increased her mobility and also her communication power as she felt capable of guiding other young women. It is also a politically empowering process, she mentioned,

'after leaving the old house near Paud Fata, I formed a new group. I made a group of five members and many others learned about Annapurna because of it. I helped people understand that forming a group and taking loans can be very helpful. Then many groups were formed in Kelwadi, Hanuman Nagar, etc. *I introduced Annapurna's name here. I told people, "Take a loan, form a group of five, it helps with medicine, everything." Many members from my group got sick and received claims. They were very happy. During meetings, when we gathered and shared our experiences, the other group members used to ask me, "Will we get a claim? If someone has a heart problem, will they get money? Will we get money after an operation? Or only at billing time?" I used to explain everything to them'.*

She also took part in the Annual General Meeting (AGM) of Annapurna Pariwar to decide the interest rate, but this year she could not attend due to her illness. Regarding the decision-making process for the electoral process, she mentioned that she cast her vote for the person who has already helped the marginalised people like her. She received help during her daughter's marriage, her illness, etc. Joining Annapurna helped her build her social, financial, and political life.

She expressed that Annapurna membership increased her confidence. The support of Annapurna made her stronger. I started to take all family decisions along with her family members. She mentioned that during the family crisis, her family supported her in solving the problems. She also stated that she has learned a lot from Medha Tai of Annapurna. All team members of Annapurna supported her during her crisis. She said,

'I have learnt a lot from Annapurna Medha Tai and everyone have stood behind us like a strong support and gave us loans when no one was ready. 'Annapurna is for poor people. Whatever their needs are, Annapurna is there to help them. And Medha Tai—she never leaves our side. She stands strong for the poor. And I'll never leave her side either. Annapurna belongs to the members, and the members belong to Annapurna. I pray that Allah blesses them with more growth and success and keeps them with us'.

3.2.2 Participant 2

Participant 2 is 54 years old, and she was introduced to Annapurna by her mother, Laxmi Mohite. She mentioned that she did not get any loan from any source, so she approached Annapurna, and she got her first loan of Rs. 1000. She mentioned,

'That time Medha Tai use to personally give loans and come to take the instalment. She used to teach us a lot about saving and how to use finances properly. Annapurna has always stood strong behind us and supported us because of it and have given us loans when no one did. Because of this as a single mother I could educate my children, support house and family. Now my family has grown, and all my children are educated and independent'.

She mentioned that after joining Annapurna, she started a better job. As her husband left her, membership with Annapurna helped her access loans, which supported her in taking care of her children. She built her house and supported her children's education and marriage. She kept a recurring deposit (RD) with Annapurna, and under ADHP, she utilised the facilities, which were helpful in times of need. She mentioned,

'I am filling my monthly payments and looking forward to the pension that I will be getting. If you look at it it's not a lot of money but if you save a little monthly it comes in handy at the time of need.With the help of Annapurna we could build our house and stabilize as a family. I could provide for my children's education due to which they are independent now that is the biggest investment a parent can ever make for their family'.

She explained the impact of her membership with Annapurna. She availed the insurance facility. She has received a lot of claims throughout the years. She got help when her son met with an accident, and her daughter-in-law was pregnant. It helped her to meet the hospital expenses. She said,

'It supported us financially now the benefit has also increased and now you also get 500 rupees per day for the hospitalization (Hospiwage Product) additional to the benefit for the claim. So, it is really helpful'.

She was asked how she managed crises during demonetisation and the COVID-19 pandemic. She mentioned that she did not face any problems during demonetisation but during COVID, she became jobless and went to her village. However, she managed to pay the instalments by borrowing from relatives and her son. Later, she started working with the bureau.

Joining AP also gave her a platform to earn dignity and respect in the community and within her family. She mentioned,

'Since I'm an old member, people recognize me. I may not know much, but they listen to me. Even during AGM when Tai calls us on the stage as old members, I felt very nice Tai has done a lot for us. In my house all my children respect me because they have all seen the struggles. They acknowledge all the hard work done to be where they are today'.

Her children also feel very happy to see her success. As she took the help of Vidyapurna to raise her children, they are grateful to Annapurna, as both of them are working now. Since she was a single mother, she became the sole bread earner. This situation forced her to make a lot of tough decisions. It increased her mobility outside the home. It also increased her knowledge. She explained,

'There are so many things that you do not know about when you stay at home but when you start going out for work or to such big programs like the AGM or community meeting you learn and understand a lot of things. Medha Tai and Annapurna's staff really tries their best to explain and educate the members properly. Now I took my decision and I am not afraid of anything'.

In the decision-making process of Annapurna, she took part from the beginning as a group leader. She did not miss any AGM, as she learned from Medha Tai that it is important to take part in decision-making. She also guided her peers in the community about the process and several services of Annapurna, such as the RD scheme, the process of claim settlement, the names of the network hospitals, etc. Regarding the electoral process, she mentioned,

'Yes, I vote after thinking. We don't just follow others. We think on our own. We gather and decide together. Women don't get much attention during elections, but we come together. It is important to vote for the people who actually do the work for people and are current. The Men try to influence our decisions but we don't listen'.

Joining as a member of Annapurna gave her the confidence to make decisions, and she has undergone psychological changes. For example, she narrated,

'When my son was 15, I needed his signature for a document that required the person to be 18. I didn't ask anyone. I just made him sign. That was a big moment for me. That was my first personal decision. Later in 2005, the issue came again, and my son signed again. No one could question me about not having a husband. It needs a lot of courage to be able to manage stuff alone especially in those days'.

She, along with her son and daughter-in-law, takes the decisions, and they are very friendly. She mentioned that she speaks freely and keeps sharing information. During her son's marriage, everything was well-planned. If anything wrong happens in the neighbourhood, she protests as a senior. Everybody listens to her as she is the senior, and she is respected. She expressed her happiness about this treatment by the juniors.

She also spoke about her learnings from the Annapurna membership. She stated,

'Through all the years with Annapurna I have understood the importance of savings and for being there for each other. Without Medha Tai's support I would

have never been where I am today, Annapurna has grown because of Medha Tai. I wish they continue this forever and many more women benefit from them'.

3.2.3 Participant 3

Participant 3 is a 65 year-old woman who joined AP around 30 years ago after her husband, who worked in a company, lost his job when the company closed. She was part of a group of 15–16 women that was created. Several dropped out, but she sustained. They contributed Rs. 100 per month initially, and by the third month, she got a loan of Rs. 1000. This gradually increased until it reached Rs. 200,000 over time. With the loans, she set up her sewing business, bought a sewing machine and material, and was able to earn. The participant recounted her experience of how, at the time of the first loan, Medha Tai took them to Mumbai on an exposure visit to see Prema Tai's work. Through AP, the participant learned a lot about savings and did not have to mortgage gold or assets. When asked about how she built capital, she spoke of how, from one small room, they have built a three-storied house. Her son works in a Maruti showroom, and her daughter is married. In terms of non-loan-tied savings, she saves Rs. 1500 in Adharpurna, has a recurring deposit of Rs. 8500, and has other savings too. As she says:

I proudly always say that you don't join any bank to get a loan, just formed a group. Create a trustworthy group and take a loan, you will benefit from it and after you give your instalment timely, no one comes to you. In other banks they require so many documentations etc.

The participant is respected by her family and community since she has been supporting them with help from Annapurna. Since she is now old, she has started a puffed rice business that is easier. Her family and husband support her attempts. In her words:

I feel like a responsible citizen now. I have confidence that I can handle any business and any crisis in life now. When you start bringing money in the house you learn about a lot of new things and issues around and also learn to find solutions.

Regarding insurance services, the participant said that since her son has a job, she got Rs. 70,000 for her eye operation from his insurance benefits. Hence, she did not apply to Annapurna. However, her daughter, who is in a group, got a claim for her son. The claim was met very quickly by the staff of Annapurna.

Regarding COVID and demonetisation, the participant said that initially, she thought they would not have to pay their instalments, but when they got a notice, they paid. In 2020, she took a loan of one lakh. Health-wise, her family did not have problems since they were vaccinated.

She recounted how all the women in her group would travel together to attend the meeting.

The meeting used to be at 12 all of us used to leave together at 11 and travel talking and laughing with each other. The participants learned about Vidyapurna and Vatsalyapurna by attending AGMs and listening to the information shared there.

When asked about who she votes for, she said that she votes for those who do work and if that candidate is useful to her and her community. She thought that all communities lived in harmony, supported each other, and celebrated festivals together.

The participant used to be a group leader and would mobilise other women to join AP. She travelled with Medha Tai to round up defaulters and have them repay loans. Since she has aged, she now focuses on her own loan repayment. It is significant when the participant says:

My confidence has surely increased. Because now I always have money in my bank account, I have a balance I do not need to ask any family member or friends/neighbours. If today I want to do something or go somewhere I can do it because I have the money and I have the savings in my account and I could only do this because of the support from Annapurna family.

When asked about her role in decision-making, the participant said that she runs the household expenses. Her husband and sons give her their salaries, and she manages the finances.

Because I have the capabilities of financial discipling and planning. Because of my saving habits with Annapurna, we have saving as it is said "पैशाला पैसे लागत." *(Money follows Money).*

When asked about her role in the community, the participant said, 'whenever the ladies sit together, they discuss and talk about various issues'. She said that they should be brave and take decisions in the house; they should step out and see the world. They should not limit themselves to children, the kitchen, and cooking; there is so much outside that can be seen and done.

When asked about what her learnings from her association with AP were, the participant said:

The new generation, which is there must keep growing the organization, like till now Medha Tai has got the organization for the poor women so that. Even though she is a woman she can very well manage finance working and run a home she doesn't only need to be in the kitchen or just take care of the family. She needs to understand that by doing so we are also burdening ourselves we should stand on our feet independently and earn for ourselves.

3.3 Case Description: 2004–2014 Decade Two: Early phase of Organisational Development: Expansion and Institutional Strengthening

3.3.1 Participant 4

Participant 4 is 59 years old. She got to know about AP earlier and has been taking loans for over 10 years. She knew people who were taking loans before she did, and hence, when the LSO officer came for promotions, she was already aware.

Her group started with Rs. 8000, and the group consisted of 15 members; then it became 9, and now it is 5. Now she has received Rs. 75,000. During COVID, she hadn't taken a loan. She was in the village, and there was no work; they stayed in the tent. She thought that the interest and all doesn't cause much trouble like other banks. It happens easily; it's a good experience. They took the loan, and there was no burden; it didn't feel troubling. In her words, '*You don't realize when it starts and ends*'

They had a bit of trouble in the group in 2014–2015, but no issues after that.

When asked about her financial goals, the participant said that both her daughters were already grown up, and the loan she took from Annapurna helped her in setting up her clothes business and make household improvements. She doesn't need to borrow from anyone. Since she was a single mother, the loan from Annapurna helped her build her business and bring income into her household. It also helped her set up a parlour for her daughter. She did not use Annapurna's insurance services since, for illnesses, they went to private doctors and did not have major illnesses that required hospitalisation.

It was a struggle during COVID and demonetisation. They went to their village, mortgaged gold, and took half a year to recover some of it back. When asked about the increase in her social status, the participant said,

'*my daughters respect me because after their father separated from us, I took the complete responsibility of the house and took care of them. Even in the community we were given the award of good group during the AGM so that's why everyone respects me in the community also*'.

It was with Annapurna's support that a single mother like her could tide over the situation. Loans from Annapurna can be trusted.

The participant could not benefit from the Vidyapurna scheme since, by the time she took her first loan, her children were too old to avail of the scheme. She was aware of Vatsalyapurna and thought that it was a very good scheme for working mothers. She said that it is a safe space, and children learn a lot; plus, value education is inculcated.

About her and her family's evolution, the participant said,

'*Earlier times were hard for us, but since I have started earning it has become a bit easier for us. I won't say we are rich, but we are at the medium level and happy with what we have*'.

The participant is from a slum in Mumbai and does not travel out much since she finds train travel confusing and difficult. She also chose not to become a group leader since she was not confident about being able to recover from anyone who defaulted. She prefers to focus on her own loan repayment. She does not herself mobilise women, but if someone asks for help, she directs them to the LSO Tai. She finds the loan application process earlier with LSO Tai's using tabs. At banks, they are asked to come with different documents all the time. The participant votes for candidates who work for the community and not for those who ask for money.

When asked about how AP has helped to increase her confidence, the participant said,

'I am self-confident that I can stand on my own feet and support myself and my family. It gave us support. I now believe if I get 1 lakh, I can take 2 lakhs more and do something'.

In her family, decisions are taken together. She lives with her daughters, one of whom is married, and also her daughter's mother-in-law, who is a single mother. She mentioned,

'we all sit together and take the decisions. It is better that way as there can be many perspectives to one situation and discussion always helps'.

She believes that she is respected in the community, and people do listen to what she has to say.

Regarding what she learned from her association with AP, the participant said,

'The biggest lesson I learnt from Annapurna was, A person with no support can stand on her feet, manage a family, and move ahead. That gives joy. I want to continue and support my children's future. Use well what I have. The pension and health scheme are very useful. No fraud. Documents come every year. They even inform by phone. Even if we deduct some amount, we don't feel bad. The benefits are there. This is a path for women to rise from poverty. Grow your business, grow your work, be strong on your feet. That's the purpose'.

3.3.2 Participant 5

The participant is 34 years old and got to know about AP since then. The LSO Tai would come to her area for the promotion of the organisation. It has been 10 years since she first took the loan, and she was newly married at that point in time. She had first taken the loan from the office that was in Nehrunagar.

'We were a group of 15 first and now they are 5. It felt good to work with other women'.

She feels that now the process is a bit better than before. When she started, it was difficult because both her husband and she were working, and her children were small. Hence, it was difficult to attend meetings or even the loan process meetings. Currently, she has an ongoing loan of Rs. 1,40,000. She finds it easy to pay the EMI. There are benefits too, like coverage for medical expenses after hospitalisation.

Regarding her financial goals, the participant said,

'The first loan that, I had taken was for my children's education. Now I need it for household expenses etc, one needs money for everything. My children are in nursing. I needed money to pay their fees'.

The participant and her husband work as sanitation workers. Her husband's job is to clean the drainage systems of all the big societies in Mumbai. Annapurna's loan helped increase their income and improve their household status slightly. She does not take loans from banks and does not need to either.

When asked about non-loan tied products, the participant said that she has a pension and an RD (recurring deposit) ongoing. The RD has just started, so it is not yet matured. Regarding the pension, she has been putting in money for the past two to three years. She pays Rs. 150 to the pension and Rs. 100 to the RD. When it matures, she plans to keep them as her savings. Other than this, she has been unable to make other investments or purchases. She uses the money for basic needs.

The participant has not yet used the insurance facility but wants to because she has a big dental surgery coming up. She consulted the medical officers and took their guidance. They told her about all the hospitals she can use—government, trust, or even private—and they also explained to her how she can submit the claim at the branch. So, once her operation is done, she will be doing that.

Regarding COVID and demonetisation, their work had stopped since people would not allow sanitation workers to enter the societies to clean the spaces. At that time, her husband took up a part-time job as an office boy, which is what helped them during COVID. Plus, they had some of the money left from the loan they had taken from Annapurna, which is what they survived on.

Regarding feeling respected in her household, the participant felt:

'I feel that because I can support my family more financially my role has changed in the family. In my maternal home my mother was a housewife that's why she was never respected therefore I know how it feels'.

Her husband and children support her, seeing the value that Annapurna brings. She is aware of Vidyapurna from the information provided during AGMs. She also shared that she goes out with the group for meetings, and it is important since there is learning when that happens. However, she cannot go anywhere without permission, except for work. She can wear whatever she can afford and what she is comfortable in.

The participant was a group leader for some years and then took a break for two years. She was able to mobilise several women and brought them in touch with LSO Tai. About voting, the participant said she voted for those who worked for the community and fulfilled the promises they made. She highlighted that within the community there was harmony. In her words,

'all of Annapurna's staff also puts in a lot of efforts to educate us and bring us awareness through various topics. Even Medha Tai does it through her Samajik Vishay videos'.

When asked about how she felt about her confidence, the participant said that Annapurna is like a family, and through their support, she surely does feel that she can achieve any goal that she wants to obtain. Within her family, all decisions are taken by sitting together. She freely expresses her opinions within her family and community. She said,

'I do not worry about anything, if you fear in life, you will not be able to do half the things you want and hold yourself back'.

The participant feels that Annapurna is a very beneficial organisation.

'We should do our repayments properly and take complete benefit of the schemes that are provided by Annapurna.

3.3.3 Participant 6

Participant 6 is 45 years old. She got to know about AP because a distant relative was taking loans. When she first took the loan, she was trying to start a business and needed finance to pay off her other loans. So, she took a loan from Annapurna. Then she stopped borrowing for some years because she shifted from her old house, but she started again once she settled into the house that she is currently staying in.

When asked about her experience of taking a loan for the first time from AP, she said that the experience was much better than other places. At that time in 2007, she had taken loans from a lot of places. She was able to invest in various businesses and pay off all her loans from other organisations.

When asked about the impact that access to credit through Annapurna had on her livelihood, she said that it had a huge impact since they were able to buy machinery and supplies with the help of Annapurna's loan. She used her first loan to pay off the other organisation's loans, and then, with the second loan, she used it to start a shop—plaster and lighting fittings. Before the lockdown, she took a loan for the shop again and bought a printer, a Xerox machine, etc.

Regarding non-loan tied products, the participant talked about Adharpurna. She used to pay monthly money for Adharpurna, but during the lockdown period, she had to stop because she did not have the money to pay for it. She might restart it soon after she feels better and starts earning more money. She was unable to make any investments since the money is used for household needs and their business.

The participant recently had open-heart surgery, and she received an insurance claim of Rs. 40,000 and a Hospi Wage benefit of Rs. 5000. It helped her pay off the money she borrowed from her relatives for the operation. It was a very big surgery, and she is glad that she got support from Annapurna.

The participant discussed her situation during demonetisation and COVID. She said she usually has always paid her instalments on time. During demonetisation, people did not pay money as they were not accepting the banned notes, even though the government had given some time to exchange them. She had lost her business for 2–3 months. Similarly, during COVID, she took the loan in February 2020, and in March 2020, there was a lock down. That year, for one year, they had no money to pay and barely had money to eat. We had a stationery shop that was working well, but during COVID, it shut down, and then she started her own clothing business. Now that too is gone because she had open-heart surgery.

Regarding respect in the family, the participant said,

'I do feel respected in the house as I am always trying to bring money in the house some way or the other to support my family and my children. People see me as an old member since I have taken a loan since 2007'.

Her family doesn't say much about her involvement with Annapurna. All that matters is that they have finances for various services. She thinks that after the current loan, she will mostly be stopping and withdrawing her savings.

The participant did not benefit from Vidyapurna since she is not a single mother. She was not aware of Vatsalyapurna. Regarding mobility, the participant felt that she gets the chance to go out more. Usually, they don't get to go out unless it's for some family function or work, so she used to like going to meetings. This year, she hasn't been able to attend any of the meetings because of her illness. As it is, she is not confident about travelling alone and is not allowed to do so. Before marriage, she travelled with her parents or aunt, and after marriage, with her husband or children. She wears a burka out of choice and is comfortable in it.

The participant was never interested in being a group leader. Although, at one time, when the leader of the group she was in defaulted and ran away, she helped the group. Since she is not an outgoing person, she has not mobilised other women but helps when and if needed by sharing the name and number of Annapurna staff. She has, however, participated in meetings about choosing the rate of interest and dividends.

While she was asked, 'have you ever participated in choosing interest rates or dividends during the AGM?' she responded,

'It feels good to see someone women taking the decisions together. It makes me feel good'.

When asked about voting, she said she goes by what her family tells her. She is also disillusioned since political candidates just make promises to gain votes and later forget it all.

The participant felt that her confidence has increased compared to what it was earlier. Even after struggling financially, she is always trying different ways of earning money, and in that, she has always had AP as her support. While she expresses her opinions in her family, mostly it is what her husband or father-in-law says that is carried out. She said,

'I mean I do express them, but I don't think they are acknowledged, but at least I get to express them'.

When asked what the biggest lessons are that she has learned through her association with AP, the participant said,

'The biggest lesson I have learned is to only take loan when in need and not to take multiple loans otherwise you struggle financially, and it is very difficult to come above it. In Annapurna they do not force you to take loans even though we have higher eligible amount they always say to take only the amount that is required and needed. Salute to the Annapurna team and all the Tais are doing a good job and are very supportive for the members'.

3.4 2015–2024 Decade Three

Case Description: Decade Three (2015–2024): Digital Maturity and Social Security Integration

3.4.1 Participant 7

Participant 7 is a 62 years old member of AP. She learned about Annapurna from her friend, who has been a member for some years. She never took a loan as it was not needed. However, when she mortgaged her gold asset for her son's business, she mentioned,

'I took a loan from Annapurna it is a loan of Rs. 55,000 but this with some additional money helped me in getting my gold back. It was an easy process. In banks, a lot of documents are required for loan application but here the LSO Tai came to our house and uploaded our documents through tab, I was so astonished and happy. Even for the loan I had taken my son to the branch as my loan guarantor as my husband was past the age limit and the complete system felt different and trusted. Also, my son lost the job and needed money to support his family'.

She joined Annapurna at the age of 61 years. She did not apply for the pension scheme as she did not know about it. Presently, she started an RD of Rs. 500, and later she wants to keep the savings as an FD. She also did not buy insurance; however, she mentioned that,

'I haven't availed of it, but I will soon be planning a cataract operation for myself, so the SE Tai has asked me to call the medical officer and to take proper guidance from them so that I am able to get maximum benefit'.

During the COVID-19 pandemic, she suffered a lot as she could not run her vegetable business for three to four months during the lockdown. As a result, she did not have money for a good three to four months. Since she joined Annapurna, she is well respected in the family, though her husband and son did not like her taking a loan at this age. She responded,

'I explained to them that we had to do what we have to do to survive in difficult times and use whatever resource we have'.

She did not take benefit from Vidyapurna (scholarship for children of widows) and Vatsalyapurna childcare services as she did not know about these schemes of Annapurna. She also mentioned that she joined Annapurna much later.

'I was a housewife for many years, my husband was a labourer, and he had a paralysis attack on the left side due to which he was bed ridden. It was a tough time. But that's when I started to go out and earn money for my family'.

After joining Annapurna, she started attending community meetings. As she is the eldest in the group, peers are very kind to her, and the group leader is very supportive. She is mobile, and she is not at all scared whenever she goes out. As she is a new member, she has not got any leadership role at Annapurna, and she did not attend any AGM. When she was asked whether she could convince any woman to join Annapurna, she stated,

'I have not done any of that but, if someone does ask me, I will surely tell them that one should take loan from Annapurna it is like a blessing for poor women in need and looking for a support'.

When she was asked whether she took part in the electoral process or not, she mentioned,

'For many years I did not vote because I did not have all my documents to make my voting card. But then when I turned 50 with the help of my son, I got my voting card done and I am voting now. I usually discuss with the ladies in the community and give the vote because I don't understand much'.

Joining Annapurna increased her confidence, and she was happy when she got her gold asset back. However, she expressed her discomfort when she was not included in decision-making in the family during her daughter's marriage. She mentioned,

'we make all the decisions together. Only during my daughter's wedding, the elders in the family and my husband had taken the decision which I was not happy with. Sometimes, I really feel that I am more of a listener than speaker'.

She is very positive about the contribution of Annapurna in her life. She said,

'I love that with financial support we can always save money. I always had a dream to have savings which I could not fulfil because I did not have the resources. Now with Annapurna at least I can save little by little for my old age and future'.

3.4.2 Participant 8

Participant 8 is 44 years old and an Annapurna member. She learned about Annapurna from her sister-in-law, who lives in Kondhwa. One day, she visited their house, and LSO Tai had come home to collect the monthly instalment from there. She asked her sister-in-law about it, and her sister-in-law explained everything about Annapurna. She even provided her with the contact numbers of several staff members who work in her area. She also shared her experience with Annapurna.

'It was a nice experience nice we had the LSO Tai come and collect our documents for the application. First all documents use to be collected in hard copy now everything is done through tab which is even faster'.

She is a Mehndi artist and takes orders for weddings and functions. So, when it is wedding season, she earns well enough, but when it is not Mehndi season, during that time, she makes handmade agarbattis, etc., but that doesn't help her earn enough to sustain. She still has to pay the kids' education fees, their bus fees, etc., so she mostly takes loans to support her household chores and her children's education, and if any is remaining, she invests it in her business.

Explaining how credit from Annapurna helped her, she mentioned,

'Truthfully, I would have not been able to survive if I did not have support from Annapurna. My husband is a plumber, but he works independently and therefore if we only depend on him then our house would have not survived. We have 4 children who all go to private school because in government school they do not teach properly. That's why I took the loan to help us out'.

She is also availing the facilities of pension and other savings at Annapurna.

'Yes, initially I was not doing any other savings than the one with the instalment but then the SE (Service Executive) Tai did the promotion about Adharpurna and

even spoke to my husband about it. I have started my pension 4 years ago I was paying Rs. 100 per month but then now I have decided to put in Rs. 500 to get a better pension. I have heard that the interest rates are also good for the Recurring Deposits so maybe when the season starts, I will start that too'.

She also bought consumer durable goods such as a refrigerator by availing a loan from Annapurna. She purchased an insurance product, and when she was asked about the impact, she said,

'*Yes, my youngest daughter has epilepsy, and it was just recently diagnosed so when it first happened, we were so scared, but we spoke to the medical officer in Annapurna, and she told us to go to Deenath Mangeshkar hospital who has a special department only for Epilepsy patient where we could give her proper treatment and she is much better now*'.

COVID-19 pandemic affected her badly. She said that she and her husband did not have any income for six months, and somebody had spread false news about their community, so they did not get business even after the lockdown was lifted. She mentioned,

'*I had to start from scratch and create a new client circle. Why would the government encourage this? I have no idea but due to that our community suffered a lot. I had taken a loan in Jan 2020 for some housework but because of COVID it did not start so we survived on that till we could earn money*'.

Initially, she faced a lot of issues after joining Annapurna. People misguided her husband about her behaviour but slowly, when she was able to help in the house and bring money, everyone started respecting her, and her husband also started respecting her. She said,

'*initially my mother had come to sign as a loan guarantor but after the first loan when I paid it, my husband supported me and came as my guarantor. ... because I am able to share the financial responsibility of the children, he does respect me*'.

She did not take help under Vidyapurna as it is not applicable to her. She thought of taking Vatsalyapurna childcare services, but because of her daughter's health condition, her family told her not to put her in the day care centre. She also agreed that membership in Annapurna made her confident and changed her behaviour as she mentioned,

'*before I had to ask my husband before going out anywhere but now I just say that I have to go for the meeting of Annapurna and he doesn't ask much because he knows that only if I attend these meetings will I get more increased loan amount*'.

Regarding her mobility, she mentioned that earlier her husband did not allow her to go alone; as a result, she lost some orders because her husband was not free to drop her. Later, she convinced her husband, and he allowed her to go by an autorickshaw belonging to her relatives. She can at least travel independently, but she has to wear a burkha, and she cannot have any choice.

She is still facing obstacles in taking the leadership role and holding meetings at her home, as her husband does not want to see her in this role. Though she has attended the AGM and other meetings of Annapurna, she is sharing information about Annapurna among other needy women in her locality. Regarding casting a vote, she mentioned,

'Yes, I do vote, in my house they tell me who to vote for I just say yes and then go and vote for the person I want to. Why should I vote for someone just because my family told me to?'

Though she is facing problems at home, she understands the importance of decision-making. She does not like any pressure imposed on her by her husband. She mentioned,

'I feel more confident, and I feel that I can fight back to things that my husband forces on me. Most of the decisions are taken by the family head and then told to us. I didn't have a say during the family planning process too. I don't feel confident enough to share my opinion, but I am going to start to, slowly I will get there'.

She perceived that she had built up a lot of confidence because of the support she got from Annapurna. She said,

'being independent is very important so that people don't misuse and take you for granted. It is important to earn money to for yourself'.

3.4.3 Participant 9

Participant 9 is a 34 year old Annapurna member. She had come along to one of the AGMs with her aunt. Her aunt had told her about it, but she was sceptical, so her aunt suggested she come with her to the AGM, and then she saw it. She was shocked to see such a huge crowd of women coming together.

Regarding her experience with Annapurna, she said,

'It was my first time taking a loan, so I was very much anxious and excited also. I had taken the loan to start my clothing business. My husband was very supportive of me and always wanted me to earn. I really miss him sometimes. I became financially independent; I was able to shift us to a better house and also support our children'.

Credit from Annapurna helped her to buy good quality materials, which attracted customers, and she was able to put up a stall. Earlier, she used to work from home or go to customers' houses; now they come to her stall. Her husband encouraged her to invest in the pension programme and also made her do RD. In her words,

'So, I pay rupees 1000 for my pension since 2019 and make fixed deposits so that I can have a secure future'.

She also invested in her business, which helped her stabilise her family and earn money. The COVID-19 pandemic impacted her very badly. She mentioned Annapurna's help during that time.

'In 2021 during the second wave of COVID I lost my husband he was a sanitation worker, he got COVID and he already had diabetes and other complications. We were not able to admit in the hospital. That time Annapurna had helped us with 20,000 rupees and also given us food and ration in 2020 lockdown'.

Since joining Annapurna, her husband and relatives have respected her a lot. She has received a lot of support from them. In her words,

'As I was able to shift us to a better house and community my husband and our relatives always supported us and are proud of me. My husband was always happy that I was doing some other work rather than being a sanitation worker, so he always supported me and with this work I was able to concentrate at home and at work'.

She benefited from Vidypurna for both her son and daughter after her husband passed away. It really helped her take care of the whole house, manage the business, and bring up her children. Regarding Vatsalyapurna childcare services, she said,

'My younger one does go to the day care centre it is a wonderful service. As a mother I have a lot of concerns about my child, his safety and surrounding but in the day care centre they take care of the children so nicely and also teach them such beautiful things that I don't have to worry about anything. I just take him there with his food and leave without worry'.

She mentioned that after her husband, she has become the family head; it is a very heavy and difficult role. She stated,

'You have to make tough choices everyday alone'.

Joining Annapurna as a member improved her knowledge about the outside world. She mentioned,

'I get to step out and forget about my family and work for some time the focus is completely on us. I get time to talk to other women and just gossip and understand what is happening around'.

She is also quite mobile after joining Annapurna. She travels alone, and she does not have any fear. She thinks that if she gets scared now, she will not be able to do anything for herself or her children. She has control over her dress and the way she wants to present herself in public.

She has leadership qualities. She is a group leader in Annapurna, and she said,

'I am always in contact with my group and help them in the time of needs. My group supported me a lot when I lost my husband and also gave me a lot of strength. I have convinced many women to take loan from Annapurna and also guided them for claims document submission. I also helped one member submit their claims by taking their documents and submitting them in the branch office as they were still recovering. I attend all the AGM's and participate in all the meetings'.

She cast her vote for the person who does not discriminate and does equal work for all. In Annapurna, there is no discrimination or differentiation; that is why they are treated equally everywhere and receive proper treatment. In her words,

'Even Medha Tai always makes us aware about social causes and financial education through her videos'.

Several times, she reiterated the support of Annapurna and her peers when her husband passed away. Membership gives her lots of strength. In her words,

'I was able to gain back my confidence I feel stronger with all the support that I get. I take all the decisions now and even before my opinions were always heard. If I feel that something is wrong, I speak up against that no matter if that person feels bad or not it is important to speak up and share your opinions'.

While she was asked about the lessons she has learned from the Annapurna journey, she stated,

'Without the support from Annapurna I would have been lost after my husband passed away. They have supported me in all aspects that I can think of, and it shields me like a mother does to her child. It has taught me that if you want to you can do anything and nobody can stop you or say anything'.

3.5 Analysis

When we see Medha Tai's views on empowerment, we observe that she has placed economic spaces at the forefront as the primary leaver for activating empowerment. The products and services are reaching women and supporting them as they need. Since these products and services are designed in consultation with men, they fit their needs well. However, since her methods include involving men and boys, social mobilisation through the formation of groups of five, encouraging women to lead those groups, engaging primarily women officers in operations, and encouraging the movement of voice from the top to the bottom and vice versa, Medha Tai has triggered all the other four spaces too. If a large study with a large sample size were conducted, one could expect positive results on shifts in all five spaces. However, since we have selected nine women to study them in their lifecycle needs within AP's lifecycles, we find interesting positive results too.

Annapurna Pariwar is seen as a family. Medha Tai is regarded as a mother figure. Having money and savings in the bank has contributed hugely to self-confidence. Dependence on relatives and friends is seen negatively. The women do not perceive relying on Annapurna as dependence; it is more like family support. This sense of belonging builds social capital, which is one of the most significant contributors to empowerment. This sense of belonging also promotes gender equality and the empowerment of women, which aligns with SDG 5. In the words of Participant 9 from Decade 3, *Without the support from Annapurna I would have been lost after my husband passed away. They have supported me in all aspects that I can think of, and it shields me like a mother does to her child. It has taught me that if you want to you can do anything and nobody can stop you or say anything.* Annapurna Pariwar's influence is intergenerational. Participant 2, for example, got connected to the organisation because her mother was a member. Participant 1, who is 60 years old today, has had a relationship with Annapurna since the time she was young, newly married, and starting life. AP has been with her throughout, lending a hand with her children's upbringing, their marriages, and more. Over time, she was able to build her family's growth.

Evidently, the value of being with Annapurna also stems from going through life and lifecycles with the support of the organisation. Participant 7, who entered at the age of 61 in Decade 3, expresses regret. There was resistance from the male members of her family about taking a loan at 61, but circumstances required her to do so, and she did. Being a new member within Decade 3, it looks like Participant 7 will take some time before other spaces in her life, shift.

Single women, like Participant 2, have particularly benefited from AP's microfinance, microinsurance, and plus programmes. The fulcrum of stress is narrow and heavy for single women. When an organisation like AP provides support, there is a sense of family. Since Annapurna largely employs women to operate their programmes the connection is easier for members. Participant 4's account also reflects how, as a single mother, she was able to manage on her own. However, women with husbands and families also report receiving support and respect due to their association with AP. Participant 3's interview sheds light on this. She reports that all family decisions are run through her, and she is the one who manages the money.

The value of insurance in times of illness cannot be understated. Cancer in the case of Participant 1, son's accident, daughter's pregnancy, and dental treatment in the case of Participant 5. The guidance that the organisation offers is particularly helpful. Participant 8's daughter, who has epilepsy, was helped by Annapurna's medical office to get the right treatment at the right hospital. Participant 6's heart surgery is another case in point.

The leadership positions, such as community representative, have proved significant for women like Participant 1 in gaining confidence. The recognition and exposure they receive from their role contribute towards them feeling worthy and validated. Older members, particularly those who have been part of the organisation since its inception in 1993, are accorded special recognition and respect. This has been highlighted by the three respondents from the first decade. Medha Tai validating them in AGMs has a powerful effect on their social status and sense of self-worth, and family support is thereby enhanced. This is evident in Participant 2's case as well. Participating in AGMs and being a part of AP's decision-making processes is seen as important and fulfiling.

Information is powerful. Women like Participant 1, who have a role within the AP's system, are more aware of issues. Voice is important. The ability to speak and have people listen has been seen in all the respondents. Social collectivisation, for the purpose of microfinance, has led the respondents to see the efficiency and efficacy of gaining access to credit. Participant 3's account corroborates this. The AGM is a powerful forum that AP uses effectively to reinforce the empowerment processes it has activated in the lives of its members. It is also promoting gender equality through this platform so that women can access democratic power for collective decision-making. Empowerment through decision-making is also articulated in SDG 5.

Decision-making is a family matter. Single women seem to have more of a say than married women. Families have been supportive of the women's participation in AP's programmes since they too see the value it brings on all fronts. The interface between women members and Annapurna staff is instrumental in relationship building. Participant 1 is a case in point. Respect particularly comes from the fact that the women members, as Participant 5 says, *'put food on the table'*.

The loss of fear regarding physical mobility, since women were able to travel, attend meetings, and be more visible, has contributed to their empowerment. Participant 2 clearly states that an increase in physical mobility has contributed to increased information and awareness. It has facilitated women meeting and sharing a sense of sisterhood. Participant 3's account sheds light on this. Participant 3's words—*I always say that they should be brave and take decisions in the house they should step out and see the world. They should not limit themselves to children, kitchen and cooking, there is so much outside that can be seen done etc.* Participant 4's fear of travelling alone or going to meetings due to distance only reinforces how physical mobility can decrease spaces that are empowering. Participant 4 is a case that shows how her resistance to becoming a leader within Annapurna has kept her at a mere functional level, where she manages her loan. Participation in the system, leading to a necessity of travel, has been empowering for the women who opted for it. Participant 4 has used her participation in the pension scheme and her access to credit for livelihood as her primary levers of empowerment. Not all women can travel alone, but even being able to go in a group, as mentioned by Participant 5, makes a difference to exposure and awareness. Annapurna facilitates this on occasion.

Information and awareness of social issues through videos have been used by Annapurna staff, which has been effective, as pointed out by Participant 5. There are women members like Firoza who are more in the background and focus on the repayment of their loans. They do not opt for leadership positions. Yet, it seems like through observations, there are lessons that are learned. As Participant 6 said about the AGM and decisions regarding interest rates and dividends, '*It feels good to see someone women taking the decisions together. It makes me feel good*'. Participant 6's empowerment lies in the realm of financial literacy and knowing the principles of when and why a loan is taken. The use of tabs and technology seems to have registered in the minds of women members like Participant 7, who see its value in being transparent and trustworthy. This aspect was also brought out by her when she spoke of the Adharpurna pension scheme. Participant 8 from Decade 3 also remarked on the same.

There was resistance from Participant 8's husband, who was influenced by societal opinions, and she had to rely on the support of her mother. It highlights the effectiveness of access to credit in later changing the behaviour of unsupportive family members, particularly men. Even permission to attend meetings is tied to the fact that these meetings bring more money into the household, as seen in cases like Participant 8's. Social norms, as dictated by religion, could be stricter for women from certain communities. Despite such odds, it is heartening to hear Participant 8 say—*I feel more confident, and I feel that I can fight back to things that my husband forces on me.* A shift in economic spaces has definitely influenced mental and socio-economic spaces as well. This phenomenon has been observed in other studies on microfinance. Although she is not yet consulted by her family, it seems that the process of gaining confidence has begun. In contrast, Participant 9, who is younger, had a supportive husband who, unfortunately, passed away during the second wave of COVID. The support of the group and the fact that she is a group leader have shifted political spaces and allowed her to gain courage and confidence.

In these nine accounts, we can see that what Medha Tai has said about empowerment in her interview holds true. The organisational culture, which was brought out in Chap. 2, runs through its operations, and the benefits are reaped by women members, resulting in empowerment shifts. Further, through macromovement within AP, the meso spaces are affected. Women members can avail themselves of the created community-level social capital, and it is not just access to loans that works; it is an entire scaffolding of support that is put into place.

References

Burra, N., Deshmukh Ranadive, J., & Murthy, R. (2005). *Micro-credit, poverty and empowerment. Linking the triad.* Sage Publications.

Deshmukh Ranadive, J. (2002). *Space for power women's work and family strategies in South and South-East Asia.* Rainbow Publishers, in collaboration with Centre for Women's Development Studies 2002.

Deshmukh Ranadive, J. (2005). Gender, power and empowerment: An analysis of household and family dynamics. In D Narayan (Ed.), *Measuring empowerment cross disciplinary perspectives.* The International Bank for Reconstruction and Development, The World Bank.

Narayan, D. (2005). *Measuring empowerment cross disciplinary perspectives, "Introduction".* The International Bank for Reconstruction and Development, The World Bank.

Part II
Locating the Relevance and Value of Annapurna Pariwar

Microfinance: The Relevance and Uniqueness of Annapurna Pariwar

Girija Srinivasan

Abstract This chapter covers a brief history of microfinance in the country; the self-help groups (SHG) movement over three decades, capturing the key factors that contributed to the success of the SHG movement and the missing services, the emergence of lending by NGOs, the key factors that made NGOs lenders and their pros and cons, the conversion to for-profit NBFCs, growth, greed for return on capital, and crises, RBI and Government action, and community-owned financial institutions and their relevance. In Section B, Annapurna Pariwar (AP) as a community-owned financial institution is explained. The research questions addressed in this chapter are: What was the intention of initiating the organisation? The positioning of AP as a member-owned institution. Which organisational form was chosen and why? What factors guided the governance and management structure? What are the key elements in organisational visioning to ensure double-bottom growth (financial and social)? Did it remain member-centric? What were the challenges, and how were they faced? Meeting microfinance standards—which metrics were measured in terms of governance, management, HR, products and services, and portfolio quality. With a plethora of financial institutions and many choices available now—what percentage of members still continue and why? Did AP re-invent itself to meet competition, changes in the external environment, and changes in the demographics of members? Who are the major partners contributing to the growth of AP, and how did they align with the intent of AP? Why is Annapurna Mahila Mandal (AMM) still relevant today? What do members appreciate about AMM? What are the core factors that will keep AMM relevant for another 20 years?

G. Srinivasan (✉)
Community Institutions, Financial Services, and Enterprise Development Consultant, Pune, Maharashtra, India
e-mail: girija41@yahoo.com

J. D. Ranadive, S. Guha (eds.), *Building Pathways to Women's Empowerment*, India Studies in Business and Economics,
https://doi.org/10.1007/978-981-95-7159-8_5

1 Introduction

Annapurna Pariwar (AP) is a Maharashtra-based group of six organisations promoting the empowerment of urban slum women through financial services and social development support services. Annapurna Mahila Co-operative Credit Society (AMCCSL) is the microfinance arm of AP. AMCCSL is a multi-state co-operative providing microfinance services in the urban slums of Maharashtra, Goa, and Karnataka for the past three decades. AMCCSL is a member-centric, member-owned, and member-governed financial institution offering a full suite of financial services—microsavings, micro and enterprise credit, mutual micro-insurance, and micropension to its members. To appreciate what sets AMCCSL apart from other microfinance initiatives requires a deeper understanding of the evolution of the microfinance movement in the country.

India has a long history of microfinance; over the centuries, many ways to deliver financial services to the masses—for both charity and profit—have been devised. However, the term 'microcredit' was coined in the 1970s to describe small amounts of credit provided to poor and very poor entrepreneurs. In the early 1980s, the term was expanded to 'microfinance' to indicate the type of banking service provided to low-income individuals or groups who otherwise wouldn't have access to financial services.

In the illustrious record of microfinance, the three decades from the 1970s to the 1990s have been significant in the Indian context, which saw increased involvement of formal institutions. The 1970s saw the establishment of new formal and semi-formal institutions such as SEWA Bank and the Working Women's Forum in India.[1] Another significant initiative was the establishment of the Grameen Bank of Bangladesh, which influenced many Indian NGOs to adopt the Grameen methodology and transform into microfinance institutions (MFIs) during the 1980s and 1990s. The 1980s also saw keen interest from policymakers, governments, and central banks in finding new solutions to address the financial service needs of the poor. This period also led to the introduction of new microfinance programmes by the government, often subsidy-oriented and aimed at poverty reduction; an example is the Integrated Rural Development Programme (IRDP).[2]

The 1990s in India saw the foray of formal institutions into microfinance through linkage programmes with semiformal entities of different types; the world's largest microfinance and bank linkage programme—self-help group (SHG) bank linkage—was launched in India. National Bank for Agriculture and Rural Development (NABARD) played a pioneering role in piloting and then scaling up the model by working with the Reserve Bank of India (RBI) for policy direction to banks, capacity building of stakeholders including banks, government officials, NGOs, and the SHGs. The 1990s also saw many development-focused NGOs that had transformed their developmental mandate to include financial intermediation to ensure that the

---

[1] Shetty (2012) Micro Finance in India, Academic Foundation, New Delhi.

[2] The Government of India launched the Integrated Rural Development Program (IRDP) in 1978 and implemented it in 1980.

poor received affordable services. Many NGO-MFIs built their microfinance operations predominantly through donor funding, which was either grants or loans on soft terms. Though many initially ran experimental projects to prove the poor were bankable, they found it difficult to graduate the clients to the banking system and thus had to continue their financial services over longer periods of time.

Thus, the 1970s to 1990s saw some experiments, a few path-breaking innovations, and many successful sustainable initiatives which paved the way for scaling up microfinance services to millions of poor, especially women. Those with organisational capability turned ideas into action. Overall, there was much hope and hype in the promise of microfinance to lift people out of poverty.

Box 1

Microfinance has deep historical roots. Around 1500, affluent Englishmen started putting charitable loan funds in their wills. In the 1720s, Jonathan Swift lent 5 or 10 pounds at a time to 'industrious tradesmen' in Dublin while exploiting the joint liability technique associated with today's group-based microcredit. Much of modern microfinance traces back to the European co-operative movement of the nineteenth century, which arose as a response to the problems and possibilities of rapid industrialisation. Just over 200 years ago, an Englishwoman named Priscilla Wakefield pioneered savings banks for the poor. Just over 100 years ago, the British introduced credit co-operatives into what are today India, Bangladesh, and Burma. This is not to suggest that modern microfinance is not an achievement. As in the history of any important idea, each new generation introduced innovations.

Source: David Roodman[3] 2010.

Two predominant models emerged in the country—the bank-led approach, Groups-Bank Linkage Programme and the MFI-led approach. Both models depended on group methodology and relied on the social capital of the members as an effective lending collateral. While NABARD provided the stewardship to ensure that the eco system development for SHG bank linkage was well developed and different stakeholders were well capacitated, Small Industries Development Bank of India (SIDBI) played a very crucial role in the development of MFIs in the country, providing loans, equity, and also technical support to MFIs. SIDBI also ensured that other actors in the ecosystem, such as rating agencies, audit firms, training establishments, and software developers, were duly supported. There are three different categories into which we can classify MFIs—for-profits, non-profits, and community-owned mutual benefits. As a subset of the MFI are the member-owned, member-governed community financial institutions (usually co-operatives) such as AMCCSL, which have not received that much policy and eco system development support.

[3] https://www.cgdev.org/article/microfinance-open-book-blog-qa-david-roodman.

2 Groups Bank Linkage Programme

While chit funds and other similar informal group/village-based savings and credit operations have been in existence in India for several centuries, the SHGs have been operational since the early 1980s.

SHGs are small informal groups of 10–20 individuals, usually women, who are homogeneous with respect to social and economic background. They come together voluntarily to promote savings among members, which are placed in a group common fund and lent out to its members for purposes and loan terms as decided by the group. The rules for the savings and lending operations are set by the groups themselves.

In 1987, NABARD approved an Action Research Project for MYRADA to create what were then called Credit Management Groups, aiming to understand how to include the vulnerable poor financially through group mechanisms.[4] The project, funded by NABARD, showed promising results, and by 1992, the RBI supported NABARD in launching a pilot project to link 500 SHGs to banks over two years. These groups, initially known as neighbourhood groups, self-affinity groups, and credit management groups, were officially termed SHGs with the launch of this pilot project, a name that has endured. The methodology and the initial results caught the fancy of several donors. The community bonding and vulnerable women seemed a potent combination from a development point of view. Most donors supported the SHG movement in some way or another.[5]

The pilot project was successful, and the realisation that assetless poor women could connect with banks, save regularly, borrow, repay loans, and manage their savings with significant benefits was a major lesson for the policymakers. This understanding led to broader thinking at the RBI level. In 1996, the RBI declared that loans to SHGs would be treated as normal mainstream lending activity and would be included under priority sector lending. The RBI recommended that banks first open savings accounts for SHGs and, after a period of consistent saving, offer loans up to a multiple of the savings amount. These savings demonstrated to banks the financial discipline of women, proving that they could set aside money despite limited resources and reassuring banks of their ability to repay loans when due.

NABARD, in partnership with various voluntary organisations, particularly MYRADA, launched a major awareness and skill-building campaign for commercial bankers, voluntary agencies, and government officials in 1992. This initiative involved several banks in a capacity-building effort that combined conceptual training with practical exposure, where bankers were encouraged to visit and

[4] SDC, DFID, KFW, GIZ and many other international NGOs such as CRS, NOVIB, HIVOS and CARE funded SHG formation.

[5] Around the same time, Tamil Nadu formed and sustained SHGs under the IFAD-funded Women Empowerment Project. Andhra Pradesh also reported a few credit groups similar to SHGs in the late 80s. Karnataka with MYRADA's involvement had a few hundred groups under different pilots.

observe actual groups in action. The tangible evidence of these groups' success, alongside a solid understanding of the concepts behind group financing, fostered a supportive environment among banks. As a result, many banks prioritised linking with these groups, with a few even going as far as to assist NGOs in forming new groups.

The Union Budget for 1998–99, for the first time, took serious note of the utility of SHGs and set up a national target. NABARD was tasked with promoting 200,000 SHGs over the next five years. Successive budgets that followed in the subsequent years mentioned performance and set fresh targets. At its peak, more than 5000 Self-help Promoting Institutions (SHPIs) were mobilising SHGs. NABARD, led by the then Chairman Y. C. Nanda, announced in 1998 an ambitious target of linking a million SHGs to the banking sector by the year 2007; this target was achieved three years ahead of schedule. Most of the SHGs were based in rural and semi-urban areas. Kudumbashree, the SHG movement in Kerala, started as an urban poverty reduction programme given that the distinction between rural and urban areas in Kerala is very minimal.

There were some constraints being faced. Till 2010, the progress made in the SHG movement was confined to the southern states: Tamil Nadu, Karnataka, Andhra Pradesh, and Kerala. The presence of good-quality NGOs, a reasonably good banking infrastructure, higher levels of literacy even in rural areas, a higher level of trust among members in the community, trust between banks and the public at large, and significant support by the governments contributed to making the programme a success. The SHG growth was skewed, with the four southern states cornering more than 70% of SHG bank loans. The poorer states saw indifferent quality of group mobilisation and lukewarm bank response.[6]

Moreover, the SHG bank linkage programme depended on three key institutions to provide sustained financial services to SHG members—self-help promoting institutions, banks, and the SHGs. All three performing sustainably at high efficiency has been an issue. The job of setting up groups and ensuring they continued to perform well was both time-consuming and expensive. This needed a sustained capacity-building protocol to be adopted by SHPIs, who could not mobilise adequate resources[7] and their levying of service fees was frowned upon. This had repercussions on bank linkages. SHGs were federated at the village and cluster levels to ensure the sustainability of SHGs. This was experimented with by World Bank-funded projects in Andhra Pradesh.[8]

[6] Devaprakash (2005), Balancing quality and quantity of SHGs in India, https://www.findevgateway.org/sites/default/files/publications/files/mfg-en-paper-balancing-quality-and-quantity-in-shgs-in-india-aug-2005.pdf.

[7] NABARD started providing financial support to SHPI. However, the amount of money given was not covering all the costs as had been pointed out by different researchers in their studies from time to time.

[8] Girija Srinivasan and Ajay Tankha (2010), SHG federations—development costs and sustainability, Access Development Services, New Delhi.

The bankers' trust in SHGs was growing, with a good repayment track record. Overall, the loan sizes remained small compared to MFI loans, making it possible for MFIs to make in roads and grow exponentially where SHGs were already mobilised.

3 Central Government's Foray Into SHGs

While many state governments were initiating programmes for SHG mobilisation, in 1999, the Central Government announced a major self-employment programme Swarnjayanti Gram Swarozgar Yojana (SGSY), to be based on the SHG model. Some of the states used the SGSY to build confidence within government schemes to undertake poverty reduction initiatives. However, the quality of these groups varied widely across states, and the goal of self-employment was largely unmet due to limited access to bank credit—only about 20% of SHGs secured financing.[9] Repayment performance was poor because many groups lacked financial guidance. Despite low engagement from banks, SGSY remained popular due to subsidies, but the programme's execution suffered due to inadequate expertise from District Rural Development Agencies, affecting the quality of the groups.

The Radhakrishna Committee, set up to examine the credit-related issues of SGSY in 2009, found that the earnings of beneficiaries under the programme, even in Andhra Pradesh and Kerala, which were the better-performing states, were poor. The committee emphasised building the capacity of SHGs to absorb and apply credit in a functional manner. The committee made a significant recommendation to set up the National Rural Livelihoods Mission to accelerate the pace of coverage of rural households and take them towards remunerative self-employment.

4 Government Taking Over the Role of Mobilisation and Facilitation

In 2011, the National Rural Livelihood Mission (NRLM) was launched at the national level, though effective implementation started in 2013.[10] World Bank's technical assistance and funding to develop proof of concept in select blocks in 13 states enabled NRLM to ground the programme well in all the states and union territories (Ibid). The initial strategy was a staggered implementation of different components in a block, with institution building, financial services, and livelihoods intensification in a linear

[9] https://www.findevgateway.org/sites/default/files/publications/files/mfg-en-paper-shg-federations-development-costs-and-sustainability-2010.pdf.

[10] Girija Srinivasan and Srinivasan (2023), Spring board for powering women, Three decades of the SHG movement, Access Knowledge series, Access Development Services, New Delhi.

manner. However, in 2015, it was decided that the financial services and livelihoods services would be almost simultaneously implemented along with institution building, thus giving scope for quicker implementation, improved efficiencies, and longer time for engagement in livelihoods. NRLM's expansion was methodical, spearheaded by community resource persons (CRPs) carefully chosen and trained to spread the movement. The CRPs were experienced women. The strategy of SHG formation followed a saturation approach of mobilising as many poor women as possible in a village, which resulted in operational efficiency and reduced transaction costs. The groups are federated into three-tier structures of village organisations at the village level and cluster-level federations for a group of villages, and are capacitated to ensure the long-term sustainability of the institutions.

Several challenges were being faced by the bank linkage programme when NRLM was launched. There were a large number of groups that were only saving and were not linked to the bank for credit, and the credit multiplier on savings also had great scope for improvement. There was uneven and inadequate outreach in many regions. There were operational issues being faced, such as delays in the opening of SHG accounts and disbursement of loans; bad practices of impounding group savings by banks as collateral; and non-approval or inordinate delays in repeat loans, even when the loans were repaid promptly. Moreover, under SGSY, the overdues were very high. NRLM, as well as State Rural Livelihood Missions, worked intensively with bankers to ensure credit linkages. The improvement in the quality of groups vis-à-vis the earlier government programmes is providing confidence to bankers. NRLM took the support of IBA to adopt a more uniform system and procedures, including a common loan application form. There has been a very conscious effort in ensuring good repayment to the banks, keeping the non-performing assets very low. As of 31 March 2023, as per the Management Information Systems (MIS) report of NRLM, 76,93,710 groups have bank credit with a loan outstanding of INR 195,391 crore. The noteworthy feature is the loan performance of SHGs under NRLM, where the NPA rate is also low at 1.85%, making it a lower-risk asset class.

To conclude, in the early stages of the 1980s, the movement was nurtured by the voluntary sector, but it gained legitimacy and momentum through policy support from NABARD, a leading development bank, and the RBI. The government's involvement, particularly at the state level, began on the periphery but gradually expanded as it integrated its poverty reduction and self-employment programmes into the group-based model, eventually taking over the movement. Today, the movement is largely driven by government policies and protocols across various states and is heavily funded by public resources, a significant shift from its original focus. Moreover, the group's strength and cohesion have weakened due to changing local contexts, the advent of Jan Dhan Yojana,[11] and the rise of other financial

[11] **Pradhan Mantri Jan Dhan Yojana** launched in 2014 is a financial inclusion programme of the Government of India open to Indian citizens, that aims to provide affordable access to financial services such as bank accounts, remittances, credit, insurance and pensions.

schemes and digitisation efforts, making some of the group-based processes redundant. The key concern is also whether the institutions are autonomous or if they have become pipelines for delivering government programmes.

The other issues are lagging savings mobilisation and very little effort in other financial services. Though started as a savings-led model, today credit from banks at subsidised rates drives the financial services. There has been little innovation in offering need-based insurance services and old-age pensions. Enterprising women who need larger loans than what a typical group loan can offer find it difficult to graduate, though some initiatives have been taken in 2024. The sustainability of the federations is a work in progress.

5 Microfinance Institutions

The MFIs initially comprised largely of NGOs and semi-formal institutions. Since mainstream financial institutions were finding it difficult to reach poorer households, especially women, the involvement of these specialised institutions was important to reach the unreached. They were funded by donors and special credit projects, who also supported the MFIs to become increasingly professional. The innovations of microfinance,[12] especially group lending with joint responsibility instead of traditional collateral, door step delivery of services, and instalment payments taking into account household cash flows, were developed by these institutions. They designed systems and processes to ensure high loan recovery rates, which defied conventional wisdom about financing the poor. MFIs considered microfinance as an essential and repeat service that the poor needed to deal with poverty.

5.1 Emergence of For-Profit Micro Finance Institutions

The NGO—MFIs initiated microfinance for its development potential. However, the major concern about MFIs was that most of them became subsidy-dependent and did not attach importance to their sustainability within a reasonable period. This made continued funding difficult for donors and funders since financial viability was seen as a critical requirement to reach a larger number of the poor and to have a significant impact on poverty reduction.[13] Moreover, since donor funding is limited, financial viability assumes more importance because only

[12] Armendariz de Aghion, B. and J. Morduch. *The Economics of Microfinance*. The MIT Press: Cambridge, MA (2005).

[13] Asian Development Bank, Finance for the poor, Micro finance development strategy, http://www.adb.org/documents/policies/microfinance/financepolicy.pdf.

viable institutions can leverage funds in the market to increase scale. Thus, from development-oriented financing, a clear shift towards a financial systems approach for dealing with the poor was seen in the last decade of the last millennium. As NGO-MFIs' operations scaled up to reach more poor households, linking MFIs with commercial capital became necessary.[14] This shift led to many NGOs transforming into for-profit entities to attract equity. Commercialisation scaled up microfinance, but the shift from poverty lending to a financial systems approach resulted in changes in client targeting. The ability to handle loans became a key criterion in client selection and led MFIs towards the higher strata of poor clients and the near-poor.

The effort to formalise and professionalise MFIs successfully proved their potential for profitability, leading to the creation of sustainable institutions. Recognising the need to expand and serve millions of poor, stakeholders saw the necessity of scaling up. Few MFIs were seeking growth for the pride and power of being the largest, biggest MFI. Providing credit on such a large scale required substantial resources in equity and loan funds, which exceeded the capacity of major donors and was only accessible through mainstream financial systems and capital markets. Consequently, connecting MFIs to commercial capital providers became inevitable, leading to the unavoidable commercialisation of microfinance.[15]

As some MFIs aimed for rapid expansion, they attracted commercial investors who prioritised efficiency and profitability over social goals. Strategic equity investors often expect to have a seat on the board, advising on the direction of the institution and, as such, have the potential to alter the behaviour of management or the strategic priorities of the institution. As microsave observed, nascent businesses and markets necessarily attract high-risk, high-gain investors with a focus on quick profit. Investors in mainstream banks do not look for 30% per annum returns, but venture capital/PE investors do, since they perceive the risk of losing their investment as high (ibid). With external equity, MFIs faced pressure to demonstrate consistent profitability, sometimes at the cost of their social mission.[16] Venture capital and private equity investors drove MFIs to prioritise profit, leading to increased costs to clients and a shift away from the original social values. This shift resulted in compromised practices, higher interest rates, additional fees, and a focus on quantitative growth, ultimately marginalising clients and turning MFIs into profit-driven organisations.

The products and processes that were supposed to meet customer needs no longer reflected a genuine concern for them. Despite achieving cost efficiencies with a growing number of clients, the benefits didn't translate into lower interest

[14] Girija Srinivasan (2012) Microfinance India The Social Performance Report 2012, Sage Publications, New Delhi.

[15] Manoj K. Sharma and Graham A.N. Wright, May (2010) Commercialisation of Micro finance in India; is it all bad?, Micro Save India briefing note; 43.

[16] http://microfinance.cgap.org/2011/10/12/commercialization-can-the-dual-social-and-financial-missions-of-microfinance-coexist/#more-2812.

rates for the customers. Products remained largely unchanged, with rigid weekly instalments and short loan terms. The MFIs have been charged with not passing on the benefits of scaling up and increased efficiencies to the clients. The urge to grow big had become compulsive, and the pursuit of fancy valuations of equity and enterprise had become a competitive exercise.[17]

Community-owned institutions were routinely being asked to change form. MFIs adopting the SHG methodology, which offered members flexibility to accumulate their savings and decide the loan terms, were advised to shift to the Joint Liability Group methodology. Products that were long-term, with sensibly structured lumpy repayment instalments to suit the cash flows of client households, were changed to weekly one-year loans on the advice of expert consultants.[18]

5.2 *The Crisis*

The increasing competition among MFIs in India raised concerns about multiple loans and client over-indebtedness, prompting fears that vulnerable clients needed protection from unethical providers and unsuitable products. In southern India, where microfinance penetration was high, MFIs competed with the state-promoted SHG bank linkage programme. Despite two major incidents in 2006 and 2009, where MFIs were accused of unethical practices, no significant changes were made to improve their sensitivity towards vulnerable clients. In 2010, the Andhra Pradesh government passed an ordinance restricting MFI lending due to concerns about over-indebtedness, high interest rates, and coercive collection practices. Andhra Pradesh, where all the large MFI players were active, also had the largest number of SHG, which were nurtured by the state-run programme 'Indira Kranthi Patham', under which low-cost credit through interest subsidy was offered to SHG. The number of loans of SHG members and MFI customers, when put together, was more than 10 times the number of poor households in the state.[19] Overall, in the state, while one-third of microfinance loans were given out by MFIs, the remaining two-thirds were given through the SHG, which loan was the last straw in the debt crisis is not clear.[20] The crisis in Andhra Pradesh, where MFIs and SHGs both lent extensively, led to a repayment crisis that disrupted financial services for millions of households.

[17] N. Srinivasan, State of the sector report (2010), Access Development Services.

[18] N. Srinivasan, in blog on the CGAP microfinance blog series on responsible finance—September 2011.

[19] N. Srinivasan, http://microfinance.cgap.org/2010/11/19/crisis-by-invitation/.

[20] N. Srinivasan, http://microfinance.cgap.org/2010/11/19/crisis-by-invitation/.

5.3 *Focus on Responsible Finance*[21]

Globally, there were serious concerns about the performance of MFIs. The social performance/responsible finance movement came alive globally to address some of the undesirable trends in microfinance due to commercialisation and to put the clients back at the core of the business. Policy makers, donors, investors, practitioners, support agencies, and MFIs have been working on how to better balance MFIs' social and financial objectives.

Reserve Bank of India issued policy guidance to MFIs on fair practices code, client protection, and responsible lending practices. Sa-Dhan[22] and Microfinance institutions network,[23] (MFIN) had developed codes of conduct[24] for the network members (both for-profit and not-for-profit MFIs), encompassing client protection and ethical behaviour of staff, incorporating the social values of microfinance. SIDBI, the major lender to the sector, carried out a code of conduct compliance assessment in India. Technical service providers have been promoting social performance management through social performance audits and ratings, providing technical assistance to MFIs to adopt responsible financing practices.

Strategies, practices, and actions necessary to accomplish social performance, including revisiting the mission of the institutions and aligning the objectives and activities of the institution to achieve the mission, adopting responsible lending, listening to clients, being sensitive to staff, training and aligning staff behaviour for responsible financing, and aligning systems and monitoring social indicators alongside financial ones for making strategic decisions, have been promoted among MFIs.

There is an increasing realisation and acceptance that (a) ensuring clients are not over-indebted and that they clearly understand prices and terms will not only assist an MFI's clients but also help it maintain portfolio quality, (b) listening to clients and adapting products and services can likewise lead to improved client retention, and (c) hiring and retaining the right staff, putting in place strong internal controls, and even reaching out to the community help mitigate risks.

---

[21] CGAP in 2010 brought forth issues in responsible financing. It defines responsible finance as the delivery of retail financial services in a transparent and equitable fashion. The focus is on products, processes, and policies that avoid harmful or unfair treatment, appropriately balance customers' interests with those of providers, and achieve the social mission of microfinance.

[22] Sa-Dhan is the largest association of micro finance institutions of all legal forms. Sa-Dhan has been recognised by the RBI as a Self—Regulatory Organization (SRO) for the microfinance sector in the year 2015.

[23] Microfinance Industry Network (MFIN) was established in 2009 as an Association for NBFC-MFIs. In 2014, MFIN was recognised by the Reserve Bank of India (RBI) as India's first Self-Regulatory Organization (SRO) for the NBFC-MFIs.

[24] Social performance is the largest domain encompassing responsible finance and Code of Conduct as inner components deserving higher priority in the client protection standpoint. Sa-dhan, 2010, client protection and code of conduct of India MFIs.

MFIs have made steady progress since the AP crisis. The sector has been responding to the large crisis by adopting rules set by the RBI and the code of conduct established by industry associations. The sector has been witnessing a structural change over the last decade. The major change occurred about 10 years ago, in 2015, when leading MFIs became banks and small finance banks, thereby reducing the footprint of MFIs. Another major shift is the interest of banks in having a larger direct exposure to the sector; banks, in addition to providing bulk funding, have sought to create portfolios in their own books. Banks realised that microfinance assets could be taken onto their own books rather than being passed down to an MFI. The introduction of business correspondents provided the space and the instruments required by banks to take direct exposures in microfinance. So, today, there are different players and different channels through which microfinance flows to the end borrowers.

6 Current MF Portfolio

As per SIDBI,[25] the major microfinance purveyors in the country now include non-banking finance company—microfinance institutions (NBFC-MFIs), banks, small finance banks, NBFCs, and not-for-profit MFIs. The portfolio outstanding of the microfinance industry as of 31st March 2024, as per SIDBI data (ibid), is INR 3,77,706 crore, with 12.38 lakh active loans and 6.6 crore unique live borrowers. NBFC-MFIs are contributing the highest to the portfolio outstanding and disbursement amount (about 42%).

6.1 Community Owned Institutions

The microfinance landscape hosts various types of institutions,[26] many of which are highly efficient, rapidly growing, and profitable, offering valuable financial services and delivering strong returns to investors. While their performance is commendable, they do not always inspire us. In contrast, there are smaller, local institutions where members take immense pride in their work and invest significant energy in managing their operations, which is truly inspiring. Microfinance isn't just about efficiency and returns; it's about empowering people to manage their finances and tailor services to their needs. Even in a landscape dominated by large organisations, smaller institutions such as AMCCSL have an important role and

[25] https://www.sidbi.in/en/microfinance-pulse-edition/March-2024; viewed on 14 August 2024.

[26] There are three different categories into which we can classify MFIs—for—profits, non-profits and mutual benefit. All the mutual benefits are community-owned while some of the for-profit and non-profit companies are also community-owned.

deserve recognition. These institutions embody the spirit of social mobilisation and mutual support found in many local communities. The NGOs and individuals contributing to their ongoing development deserve praise.

Some institutions, particularly those owned by the customers themselves, deliver services with a strong focus on customer needs. Community-Owned Microfinance Institutions (COMFIs) have the potential to provide quality financial services to customers without compromising on their social mission and customer concerns. While profits are targeted, the surpluses made by such institutions revert to the community. Since the community is involved in governance, member-users are prioritised in the design of products and delivery processes. Such institutions do not feel the need for aggressive growth—but concentrate on fulfiling customer expectations regarding service quality and deepening of services. While most non-profits do not function effectively, community-owned institutions have been performing well and making a significant difference in the lives of their members (Srinivasan. G. & Srinivasan. N 2010).

This raises several questions about community involvement in financial institutions: can the community invest in and manage the institutions effectively? Will borrowers unduly influence policies, potentially compromising the institution's integrity? Can community-owned institutions be both profitable and financially disciplined? How can such institutions attract quality leadership and professional management? These are complex issues that require careful consideration, including initial mobilisation, appropriate organisational structure, leadership, management, governance, professionalisation, external partnerships, and sustainability.

Community-Owned Microfinance Institutions (COMFIs) have the potential to deliver quality financial services without sacrificing social missions or customer concerns. While they aim for profitability, any surpluses are returned to the community. With the community involved in governance, member-users are prioritised in product design and service delivery. These institutions tend to focus less on aggressive growth and more on meeting customer expectations. Community ownership plays a significant role in managing and governing these institutions. Mission drift is least likely to occur in community-governed institutions.

But community ownership and governance might not be an unadulterated blessing. There are several failed community institutions, especially in the financial sector, which serve as examples of how not to create such institutions without the initial involvement of people. Even financially successful ones were not always inclusive; the democratic nature lent itself to elite capture of such institutions. In some cases, such institutions became political, and their fortunes swung from one extreme to another depending on the political climate.

But there are some institutions in the community space that have done exceedingly well. These have designed their institutions and organisational processes to meet the local needs and the promoters' hypotheses of how best to gain community participation. One such exemplary institution is AMCCSL, operational in the slums of Pune and Mumbai.

7 Annapurna Mahila Co-operative Credit Society Limited

7.1 The Foundation

Dr. Medha Purao Samant is the inspirational leader who founded the AMCCSL. Her illustrious parents had instilled the values of an equitable society in her. Her father, Com. Dada Purao, a well-known banker and banking trade union leader, instilled the ideas of sustainable financial services and also taught the differences between class banking and mass banking. Her mother, Padmashri Prematai Purao, under her father's guidance, initiated the bank linkage programme for the poor in Mumbai slums. Loans were facilitated for economically active poor women from different banks. Though small, this initiative provided valuable lessons in sustainable services for the poor.

Dr. Medha, after her graduation, joined the Bank of India Head Office in Mumbai and, after 12 years, moved to Pune. She shopped for her vegetables in a nearby market, where she saw women vendors dealing with a private money lender, Anna. Over two years of transacting with them, the women trusted her and shared their financial details. They used to buy stocks of potatoes and onions, and since they did not have working capital, they borrowed from Anna, the private money lender. Anna gave Rs. 1000 as a loan after deducting Rs. 50 upfront and paid them Rs. 950. The loan was repaid on a daily basis, with an equal instalment of Rs. 25 for 50 days, amounting to Rs. 1250. Thus, the interest charged was Rs. 300 for 50 days on a Rs. 1000 loan. The women earned limited profits because of the high interest rate.

Though the banks had schemes to lend collateral-free, low-interest loans to the poor, the banks did not fully participate in these since they did not believe that the poor were bankable. Dr. Medha tried to convince her banker colleagues to lend to the women under the differential rate of interest scheme;[27] however, there was reluctance since the women resided in slums where they had no clear titles to their residences, and there was apprehension that they could migrate quickly, even before completing repayment.

Simultaneously, Dr. Medha was trying to convince the women vendors to borrow from the bank. The women said, 'we don't have the documents the bank asks for, we don't have any one with a salary slip to offer guarantee and moreover the bank will lock up and take possession of our houses if we miss even one instalment'. Thus, both the banks and vegetable vendors were not comfortable dealing with each other, and there was mutual distrust.

[27] The objective is to improve the economic conditions of the weakest of the weaker sections of community by providing financial assistance at concessional rate of interest (usually 4% rate of interest) for engaging in productive activities.

7.2 Commencing the Lending Operations

Dr. Medha then decided to lend to the women out of her own resources in 1993. Having heard of NABARD's group programme in rural areas since 1992, she wanted to try out the innovative concept of the social collateral of the group to extend loans to poor women. What was not clear to her was how the group dynamics would work in the urban setting. She encouraged the two vegetable vendors to make a group of 10 with other women they could trust for repayment and offered to lend them Rs. 1000 each. The operations were started in a small room in Dr. Medha's house, where she held meetings with the women and explained that they were starting a poor women's bank. She visited the homes of the nine members who came together and were ready to borrow, spoke to their spouses, and answered all their queries. The product of Anna, the moneylender, was reproduced; each woman was sanctioned a loan of Rs. 1000, after deducting Rs. 50, Rs. 950 was handed over. However, the interest rate charged was not usurious.

Dr. Medha visited the vegetable market every day and made a daily collection of the repayments. She also had personal interactions with them every other day and thus understood their business, their needs, etc. Dr. Medha played the roles of lending officer, accountant, cashier, etc. Most of the women wanted to have houses of their own. They wanted to educate their children.

After 50 days, the women were informed that their loans had been repaid in full, and the women also had savings of Rs. 250 after the service charge of Rs. 50 (the term 'interest' was not used). The women were overjoyed, calling the loan from Dr. Medha magical. Dr. Medha explained how the savings were generated and how Anna was charging high rates and taking away their profits; coming together as a group had made this financial service possible, and there was a need to multiply the savings. The difference between the loan from Anna and the loan from Medha Tai was crystal clear to the members at the end of the loan cycle. The word was spread by these women about their positive experience, and within a week, about 20 women came knocking on her doors for loans. Dr. Medha, after due processes, lent to them from her personal resources, and quickly, friends and relatives of these women were coming forward to form groups. Dr. Medha says, 'The demand was so high I decided to leave my job and fully plunge into this and do it full time. I think that was the best moment of my life. I got the purpose of my life, and I'm still happy with that moment'.

7.3 Bank for the Poor

The Annapurna Multi-state Credit Co-operative Society was registered earlier, but it obtained a multi-state licence in 1997. Until then, the growth was at a pace consistent with the resources raised for lending. Dr. Medha studied different legal forms, understood the implications of providing a full range of services to the members, and assessed the potential for raising resources without a mission drift. While many NGO MFIs were registered as a society or trust, this legal form was not suitable for providing full financial services, was unsuitable for business, and did not facilitate loans from banks. Though the NBFC–MFI legal form was much preferred, an NBFC would need to permanently depend on external resources from investors and financial institutions since NBFC MFIs are not allowed to mobilise savings. It was finally decided to register under the Multi-state Co-operative Society Act.

The co-operative, as a legal form, is not a preferred option due to fears of political interference, the potential for weak governance, and the lack of a profit motive. However, the advantages are that the institution will be community-owned, can offer a full bouquet of financial services, and mission drift is not easy. Moreover, the administrative and financial control of the multipurpose co-operative society lies with the central registrar, with the law making it clear that no state government official can wield any control over them. Dr. Medha and her team put in place the necessary systems to address the perceived weaknesses of weak governance and low profits. In the country, there are only about 900 multi-state co-operative societies, with only a handful of them in the microfinance space and probably none other than AP offering a full bouquet of financial services—savings, loans, insurance, and pension—to their members.

7.4 Ensuring Compliances to the Rules of Micro Finance Industry

Micro finance institutions have been functioning under different regulatory regimes. Considering that co-operatives are not rated highly on regulatory standards, Dr. Medha decided to follow the RBI's guidelines on microfinance issued to the banks and MFIs. Dr. Medha has been clear that AMCCSL belongs to the financial sector and not the co-operative sector. In designing AMCCSL, she has drawn upon the strengths of co-operatives, microfinance, and banking and diligently avoided the pitfalls in co-operatives. The co-operative spirit, thus, has been combined with the rigour of the financial system.

She accessed the RBI guidelines and adopted them voluntarily from the very first year of operation. Though AMCCSL is a co-operative and member-owned institution, the board has adopted and followed the core customer protection norms set by the Reserve Bank for the microfinance sector. This sets AMCCSL apart from other players in the sector, which often have come under the scrutiny of regulators and state governments. AMCCSL is also a member of Sa-Dhan, a network of MFIs, and has adopted the unified code of conduct for MFIs. AMCCSL has undergone periodical ratings to measure and benchmark its performance.

7.5 Setting Governance Standards

The other area of concern in co-operatives is weak governance. Balancing member interests and institutional requirements, managing borrower-dominated boards, negative perceptions of such institutions among funding organisations, unrealistic expectations of members, failure to make the distinction between customer friendliness and lack of disciplinary standards, disregard for prudential requirements, and tolerance of inefficiency are some of the problems that these institutions face to a lesser or greater degree. The manner in which ownership and governance structures were engineered holds the key to whether such organisations deliver on the mandate of community inclusion and participation.

Not that privately-owned MFIs are better in governance; in privately-owned institutions where a stake sale brings in new owners, the organisational ethos could change. Evidence on hand shows that some such institutions have become more commercial in their approach and prioritised returns over customer concerns.

While setting up the governance structure in AMCCSL, the governance standards have been set high. Delineation of roles and powers of the Board and CEO has been ensured so that there is no capture of either governance or management by the other. AMCCSL has a well-balanced board with representation from external banking experts, core staff, and members. Ms K.C. Ranjani, a veteran in microfinance and ex-SIDBI, is the Chair, while Dr. Medha is the Secretary-cum-CEO. The external experts on the board bring independent views and serve as a valuable source of knowledge for the members on the board regarding macro trends.

The Board is also very clear that, while dealing with poor people's money, management must be prudent and cautious. Each financial transaction is not a mere transaction, but it concerns a woman's life, and the bank must consider the lives of the women and create a positive impact; this thinking is in-built in the key decisions of the Board and staff. On account of the participative processes and the involvement of members in governance through their representatives, grievances are better handled.

As per Medha Tai, the governance structure has evolved over time. While all the group institutions have independent boards, three to four ex-bankers are common members to all. The Boards meet every quarter and, if needed, more frequently. A joint meeting of all the boards is conducted with the agenda and minutes for each of the boards kept separate. Apart from board members, actuarial advisors from France and chartered accountants of the different institutions, company secretary, and GST advisor also attend the meetings. The board gets expert opinions on issues such as investment strategy, systems, legal matters, and dealing with the Regulators. This brings in jointness, transparency, idea generation, and the CEO gets inputs on how to improve as well. The quality of information presented and the process of decision-making are transparent. The agenda and issues are presented in a simple and easily understandable manner, discussed thoroughly, and usually unanimous decisions are taken. While the management makes use of sophisticated financial analysis, the items in the financial statement are presented in simple terms for the Board, where member representatives also attend.[28]

The business planning process is organised bottom-up, with the Loan and Savings Officers (LSOs) and branch managers indicating the targets for the next year; this is refined by the management, and the overall plan is presented to the Board. The Board discusses strategies for achieving growth in business. Expansion has been in the local areas where identified customer potential exists. The Board has always followed appropriate interest-setting practices for both savings and loans. While one pathway to benefit members is to charge lower interest, the Board has been clear that market interest rates will be charged to ensure adequate profits and sustainable operations. There is no pressure from the grassroots leaders, who are elected representatives of the members of AMCCSL, to decrease the interest rate. They are also very intent on profitability and ensuring that services reach members on a sustainable basis.

All the important decisions are taken in the Annual General Meeting of AMCCSL. The board follows the double bottom line of financial self-sufficiency with social impact. Five percent of AMCCSL's profit is allocated to other sister organisations for their development work. Moreover, a portion of the profit also supports the activities of other NGOs in Pune/Mumbai. Thus, the profits benefit society in general as well, and the grassroots leaders support this initiative. Mission drift has not been an issue in AMCCSL.

8 Operations

8.1 Group Methodology for Urban Poor

AMCCSL adopts a group approach to mobilise poor women; while in the initial years, the SHG concept was the model that was drawn upon, in later years, features of the Joint Liability Group of MFIs were adopted.

While the group methodology was gaining momentum in the 1990s, when financial services were commenced, the groups were being promoted in rural areas. These groups were formed by drawing strength from the affinity the members shared, the in-depth information they had about each other as residents of villages for several decades, and the trust they had developed. Since resource-poor individual women with limited savings were not bankable, the financial resources of banks were leveraged using the social capital of group strength and cohesion. The group-bank linkage programme under the policy direction of RBI and NABARD, brought in path-breaking flexibility in lending to unregistered groups of poor individuals without collateral. Bankers were sensitised, trained, and given targets to lend to rural SHGs. However, there was no such initiative for urban areas.

[28] Interview with Dr. Medha Samant.

AMCCSL had to innovate and adjust the group methodology to the urban setting. While the first group consisted of nine women, the second group had fewer members. The slum dwellers are largely landless migrants who have settled in the slums for a few years in pursuit of their livelihoods. Unlike rural areas, they do not know each other for generations. Women who knew each other were limited in number. So, in the initial years, the groups were formed with any number of members but usually below 10. Even three-member groups were formed since AP was determined to give collateral-free loans to women who were willing to stand as guarantors for each other. They were called common goal groups because AP wanted the women to have a larger goal and vision for themselves. Moreover, they were meant for accessing many services and facilities beyond just taking credit. When the co-operative society got a multi-state licence in 1997, a simultaneous effort was made to develop accounting software and a management information system for the operations. There was a need to standardise the group size, and based on the experience gained, it was decided to establish the norm of five members per group.

These groups saved with AP, unlike SHGs, which rotate the savings among themselves. The credit is need-based, like that of the group, and hence different members can take different loan amounts for different purposes. While AP experimented with the centre concept of the Grameen methodology—three groups meeting together—this has been changed to meetings with only a five-member group due to difficulties in gathering groups in urban slums. Unlike other groups, where spouses are usually not informed of the loans, AP orients both husband and wife about the credit, thus creating joint responsibility to manage and repay the loan.

Moreover, to make operations efficient, the five-member group consists of only those members who avail credit; members not interested in loans move out of the group but continue to attend the meetings to avail other financial products. This resonates with joint liability groups of MFIs. Thus, the AP group methodology has evolved over a period of time and resembles joint liability groups now but with unique features of its own (Table 1).

8.2 Operational Area and Outreach

AMCCSL is operational in all 650 slum pockets of Pune and in about 1250 slums of Mumbai. As of March 2024, all 22 branches are functional, servicing about 25,050 groups with 125,254 members. The active loanees are 36,976 members (Fig. 1).

8.2.1 Branch Offices

There are a total of 22 branches. The operations take into account member comfort, the easy case load of LSOs for providing satisfactory services, and at the same time, maximising efficiency. Each branch has four to five LSOs and one service

Table 1 Comparison of Annapurna Groups, SHGs, and JLGs

Annapurna groups	SHGs	JLGs
5-member stand-alone group	10–20 member groups	Smaller groups, typically 5, are clustered to make transactions easier, and these groups come together to form a centre
Focus on a range of services, including insurance and pension	Focus on thrift first, then credit	Objective is credit, and most groups do not have any thrift. Insurance covers outstanding credit
Annapurna finances the group members with a group guarantee	Bank linkage for savings and credit is ensured. Credit linkage is typically with a bank	MFIs have financed the group members
Loans are given to individual group members, and repayment is collected monthly. The group guarantees the loans	The loans from banks are given to the group, and the group decides which member will receive the loan and on what terms	Loans are given to individual group members, typically with weekly, fortnightly, or monthly repayment instalments. The group provides an implicit group guarantee for repayment, even though loans are given to individual members of the group
Groups continue for the longer term but with only borrowing members; members not interested in loans in a cycle drop out of the group but avail other financial services, like RD, FD, Adharpurna pension	Groups are long-term, and the savings and interest margin from lending to members create a corpus. The surplus of the corpus is divided among members from time to time	These groups have much shorter lifespans and can re-form after each loan cycle with new members Members not interested in a loan drop out of the JLG
The groups are largely for availing financial services but also avail other select services offered by group institutions. The thrust of the financial services is especially insurance[a] and pension	Groups have other agendas such as social inclusion, skill upgradation, health, sanitation, education-related activities, and, at times, village development, including environmental protection	Most of these groups are transactional, borrowing and repaying. Incidental to credit, financial literacy is bundled into the operations

[a]While Annapurna Mahila Co-op Credit Society gives micro loans to members, Annapurna Pariwar Vikas Samvardhan company does the enrolment of community based insurance from the families of the members.

executive in charge of insurance; all are women who have usually risen from the ranks of group members themselves. Branch Managers are promoted from the cadre of Loan and Savings Officers and are all women. Doorstep banking is provided by these staff with very limited need for the members to visit a branch.

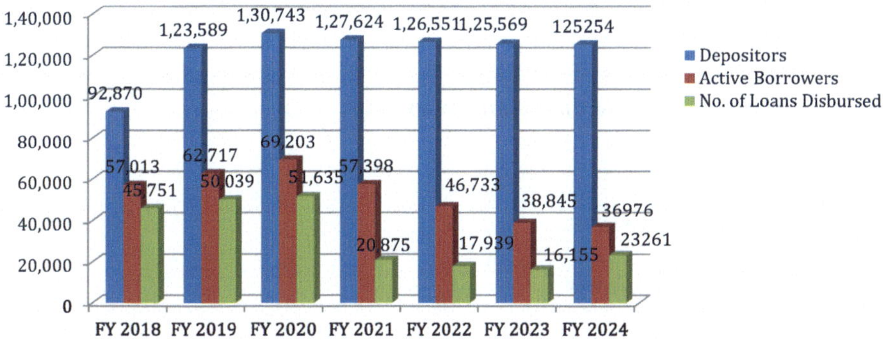

Fig. 1 Depositors, active borrowers, and number of loans disbursed

There is negligible turnover of staff due to the mission orientation and the benefits provided by the institution, with a satisfactory salary structure, incentives, and other benefits such as provident fund, gratuity, insurance, etc.

A branch usually covers slums within a radius of 7–10 km. The branch manager and LSOs are responsible for member mobilisation and group nurturing. While there are monthly targets set for group mobilisation, these are not aggressive targets and are set in consultation with the branch managers. The LSO shares all the information regarding AMCCSL, financial services offered, group responsibility, and there after the loan forms are filled in; the branch manager then visits the group and verifies all data. The average case load per loan and savings officer is currently at 350, which has almost halved post-COVID. Monthly repayment collection is set for fixed days, and loan sanctions and disbursements are set for other days, thus streamlining the work of the branch and the LSOs. The staff are groomed to listen to members; harsh talk or ill-treatment of members is not tolerated. The staff are fully aware that their pay checks signed by staff on behalf of the members who own the institution.

8.2.2 Member Retention

Member retention ratio is high, and members who leave usually do so in the first loan cycle. While there is increased competition from other MFIs, small finance banks, and private sector commercial banks, member education and their product experience enable the retention of members. Member satisfaction is assessed in meetings at all levels. If older members plan to leave, the branch staff contact them, ascertain reasons, and address grievances, if any. Moreover, the CEO holds monthly meetings through the web with select members in branches and gets first-hand feedback from staff and members.

AMCCSL was disbursing loans in cash and recovering them in cash until 2016. KYC documents were largely ration cards or voter IDs. Once Aadhaar cards came into vogue, AMCCSL linked the cards to the accounts of its members. When demonetisation affected cash flows, AMCCSL enabled all members to open accounts with mainstream banks, after which loans were disbursed to bank accounts, while recoveries are still made in cash since the members work in the informal sector and receive their earnings in cash.

9 Financial Services

9.1 Savings Products

For the poor, entrusting hard-earned savings to an institution is the ultimate act of faith. The ownership and visible participation in governance improve the credibility of the institution in the eyes of the members. The provision of savings services holds more value for many members than the other financial services on offer. Due to regulatory forbearance for mobilising savings from members, savings services are not easily available from other institutions in the sector. Savings services help members convert small seasonal surpluses into a capital fund over time. Through innovative design, these savings are transformed into old-age security. Meeting the higher-order aspirations of people becomes possible for AMCCSL. The savings products available are recurring deposits and fixed deposits, apart from compulsory savings along with loan repayments. AMCCSL also mobilises long-term savings to offer a pension product to women members. The savings are offered at competitive interest rates, which members find attractive. As of 31 March 2024, out of the total funds of Rs. 278.29 crore, 76%—Rs. 208 crore—are member savings. Fixed deposits constitute Rs. 91.23 crore, JLG savings amount to Rs. 79 crore, recurring deposits total Rs. 8.38 crore, and Adharpurna pension deposits stand at Rs. 26.23 crore.

9.2 Range of Loan Products

Unlike the typical MFIs, AMCCSL offers a variety of loan products; the member specificity is clearly discernible. Loans up to Rs. 150,000 are given for business creation or expansion, education, housing, asset creation, and repayment of old debts. SME and housing loans are given up to Rs. 20,00,000. The products differ in features based on the purpose and the expected cash flow. The term of loans varies from a few months to three years. After a one-month moratorium, loan repayment is initiated. Members' expectations have been gathered through active listening to clients, generating feedback from field staff, and representations by board members, and fed into designs that have ensured the products are closely aligned to livelihood requirements and consumption needs.

In a marked departure from the state of practice prevalent in the sector, AMCCSL has resisted the temptation to offer prefabricated products designed around highly replicable field processes and IT solutions to facilitate monitoring. Member comfort and acceptance have been core concerns. Designing the institutional processes and systems around member requirements has been a significant feature that stands out compared to other MFIs. The loan sizes are appropriate. The range of products and the customisation to local requirements came about with clear intent. The members have the freedom to borrow the amount they need. In case they do not want to borrow, they continue to avail themselves of other financial services such as savings, insurance, and pension.

The rates of interest and the manner of application of interest are transparent and clear. The rates were never expressed as flat rates in order to underplay the cost of loans. The pricing was done with utmost concern for the member and also with care not to distort the market. The current interest rates are set slightly lower than those of the sector. The focus of pricing is on cost recovery, reasonable profits, and not on high returns on capital or assets.

AMCCSL diligently follows RBI guidelines for microfinance loans. Since a co-operative society cannot be part of a credit bureau, Annapurna Pariwar Vikas Samvardhan[29] the Section 8 company, has become a member and furnishes data while also availing credit score reports before AMCCSL provides credit to its members. When, in 2013–14, there were rejections of loans to some members due to the RBI norm regarding the maximum number of loans a borrower can have, they were deeply distressed; ‘we are Annapurna members first and then we took loan from others, and we would like to continue to borrow from Annapurna’ was their refrain. AMCCSL communicated with all the members and educated them about the RBI norms and also about the perils of over-indebtedness. Despite so many access points for credit, about 40% of the members borrow only from AMCCSL.

The institution has a goal of 100% on-time recovery, and hence the LSO tries her level best to make full recoveries. AMCCSL has had negligible overdue accounts until 2016. However, demonetisation in 2016 and COVID-related disruptions in 2019–20 affected the portfolio quality since the livelihoods of the members were impacted. AMCCSL had made provisions for loan loss in the earlier years, which helped in writing off non-wilful defaults. After demonetisation, efforts were made to build the confidence of members to revive their businesses, and by 2020 the portfolio was doing very well, with nearly 70,000 active borrowers and a loan outstanding of Rs. 202 crores.

Then COVID struck. All staff and community representatives were in touch with the members. Since AMCCSL had provided a SIM card and mobile connectivity to all staff before COVID, the top management was able to communicate

[29] Vikas Samvardhan is a not-for-profit company, owned and run by the members of Annapurna Mahila Multi State Co-op Credit Society Ltd. Vikas Samvardhan insures them against death, accidents and health hazards.

with the members. When some members mentioned they had no food, community representatives identified the very poor, and AMCCSL transferred Rs. 1500 to these families to tide over the difficulties. Some others were supported in kind. The reserves of AMCCSL were utilised and AMCCSL dealt with the situation with utmost empathy.

AMCCSL adopted the RBI guidelines for financial institutions and NBFC MFIs in dealing with COVID-related repayment issues and offered a moratorium till September 2020. Without adequate cash flows, the members could not repay their loans, and AMCCSL had to write off Rs. 11 crore, largely out of the loan loss reserves. AMCCSL has declared an 8% dividend even in that year out of the profits generated. However, some members are yet to fully recover from the shock and revive their livelihoods. The active borrowers as of March 2024 have been 36,976 (Fig. 2).

9.3 *Insurance*

Risk mitigation for members has been a priority for AMCCSL, and it has tried to bring in the best-fitting off-the-shelf insurance products or, where feasible, custom-design a product to closely fit members' needs. The insurance products cover health, life, assets, and accidents. The actuarial expertise is provided by Inter

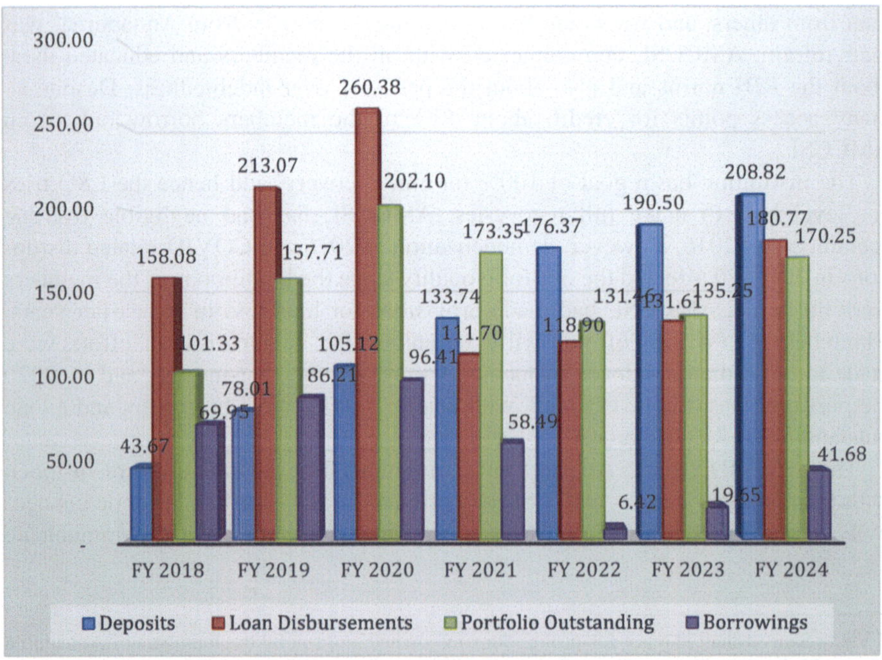

Fig. 2 AMCCSL—operational highlights of the past six years (Rs. in crores)

Aide, French actuaries. The mutual operates under Annapurna Pariwar Vikas Samvardhan, which is registered as a Section-8 company (not-for-profit). This is owned by the borrowers of AP, whose representatives are on the managing committee of this company, while the service executive is part of the branch network of AMCCSL. (Please refer to the chapter on insurance services of AMCCSL for more details).

Launched in 2003, health insurance is offered as a mutual insurance. AP ensures compliance and has benchmarked the programme to the requirements issued by the Insurance Regulatory and Development Authority (IRDA), though IRDA does not have any guidelines for mutual insurance. The health mutual is owned, designed, and managed by its members, who make decisions on product design and claims without engaging a third party in the underwriting process. The community-based health insurance programme covers 1,46,000 members as of March 2024. A minimum of Rs. 220/- per person to a maximum of Rs. 480/- per person is charged per year as premium. For any sickness and hospitalisation, a maximum of Rs. 40,000 is given to the member or household member who is insured.

In June 2009, a community-based life insurance scheme was started by AP, and the members were covered under this initiative. This is a self-owned and self-managed scheme run by the members of AMCCSL. The community-based life insurance scheme has 40,000 members as of March 2024. In case of a member's death, the outstanding loan is written off, and Rs. 20,000 is given to the nominee of the borrower, who is the main policy holder.

In 2006, asset insurance was offered to borrower members to cover the perils of fire, accident, etc., to protect business and house assets. A minimum premium of Rs. 25 to a maximum of Rs. 2500 is charged, for which a minimum benefit of Rs. 3000 to a maximum of Rs. 50,000 is provided to the insured.

What sets AMCCSL apart from other MFIs and small finance banks are the risk mitigation measures taken up by AP for its members. Microinsurance that covers the major risks faced by poor households is very rare. Most of them offer only credit life insurance, where if a client dies, the loan is written off, but the family does not receive much, not even for funeral expenses.

9.4 Adharpurna—Pension Product

This is offered as a long-term savings scheme, which is meant for the borrower members of AMCCSL. Pension at the time of old age has been an aspirational need for many of the AP members. Initially, in 2012, the Government of India (GOI) announced Swalamban, an old-age pension scheme, which was managed by the Pension Fund Regulatory and Development Authority (PFRDA).[30] After studying

[30] Pension Fund Regulatory and Development Authority is the regulatory body for overall supervision and regulation of pensions in India.

the details, it was decided to participate in this scheme; about 15,000 members were enrolled, and the women were depositing regularly for two years. However, in 2015, the tenets of the scheme, particularly the eligibility criteria, were changed, and it was not beneficial for members. About Rs. 2.5 crore had been deposited with PFRDA, which continues to be with them. Meanwhile, with the support of actuaries, AP designed their own pension programme named Adharpurna, which means an empowered woman. The women were educated about the need to shift from Swalamban to Adharpurna.

Depending on the age at which they join the programme and the targeted pension amount, members contribute every month, and these contributions are collected at their doorstep by SEs and LSOs. Members continue to save for their pension even if they drop out of a loan cycle. Members can continue paying in as long as they have not reached the age of 65 years. After reaching 65 years of age, members start receiving payouts on a monthly or quarterly basis, allowing them to secure their old age. This is considered a dream product for the members.

9.5 Dividend Declared

AMCCSL has declared a dividend on share capital, and thus the members have benefited from profit distribution. In the last ten years, AMCCSL has distributed Rs. 5.32 crore as a dividend. While the percentage of the dividend was high at 15% till 2016, demonetisation and COVID-related disruptions brought the dividend to 10% till 2019 and thereafter to 8% till 2023. In 2024, the dividend has been increased to 10%.

10 Software Based Management Information System

In 2011, AMCCSL developed in-house software named Microfinance Management System. Every quarter, the software was updated based on the emerging requirements of members and staff. However, this did not capture real-time data from the field, and the management did not get timely information. Purna E-Solutions Foundation, a company, was launched to provide software services to AMCCSL. The all-women software professionals of the company have developed tablet-based customised software for AMCCSL. The software team took up the challenge of tablet use by LSOs, who are only 10th-standard pass. The technology is simplified for users, with input fields in Marathi. The new software fully complies with the requirements of the RBI and also the Multi-purpose Co-operative Society. The new software has an interface with the earlier developed Microfinance Management System. The typical issue faced in the industry has been finding the right software. Since IT professionals did not know about microfinance, there were many failures in software adoption in MFIs. The banking professionals in AMCCSL worked closely with the IT team to get the software right.

SEs and LSOs were intensely trained in tablet usage. SEs and LSOs take the tablets to the slums, and paperless real-time data is captured; members receive printed receipts for amounts paid and also receive SMS notifications for balances. AMCCSL has fully utilised the opportunity provided by internet facilities to transition to data capture and generate useful reports for management.

11 Innovation in Fund Mobilisation

Since the savings of members alone are not sufficient to extend loans to borrowers, AMCCSL raised loans from banks. Indian Overseas Bank has been very supportive, as have other financial institutions. However, Dr. Medha had to provide her personal guarantee for each loan. Moreover, financial institutions required a credit rating for AMCCSL. The rating agencies do not differentiate between NBFC MFIs and co-operatives. Their observation was that AMCCSL is not as profitable as other MFIs. Senior management had to explain how AMCCSL is different, the clear policy intent of profit sharing with members, and also showcase the field activities to bring in the right perspective. The straight jacketed norms based on what NBFC MFIs do have been a deterrent to well-run co-operatives. Recently, AMCCSL acquired a 12-storey building in Pune to house the group institutions. The building reserve created over the years was used to acquire the building. This asset, in the future, can be mortgaged to raise resources.

Dr. Medha, to ensure the long-term sustainability of funds for AMCCSL, designed impact deposits for raising resources from the larger community in 2019. The key message has been 'valuable contribution for the empowerment of poor working women'. A very heartwarming response has been received from about 2000 socially oriented investors who have invested in fixed deposits. After studying prevailing interest rates, the board fixed an attractive rate, earning a maximum of 9.75% as the rate of interest (with 0.5% more for senior citizens). AMCCSL has created a win-win eco system for raising resources from the larger society to target poor households. It is to the credit of AMCCSL to have established a high level of credibility in raising finances.

12 Replicating AMCCSL

AMCCSL is a well-designed and well-tested model that can be replicated in other slum areas. The AMCCSL board decided not to expand their operations to other cities since it is a comprehensive model and cannot be simply expanded without adequate local presence and knowledge. Hence, AMCCSL offers a franchisee programme for NGOs/institutions interested in replication. Finding resources for the start-up has been a challenge since there is limited funding available for urban-based programmes. When Dr. Medha was appointed as a consultant in Marathwada to the DFID-funded Poorest Area Civil Society (PACS) programme, there was an opportunity to replicate the model with four small NGOs in the Marathwada region. Many of them followed the self-group methodology, and a few undertook an insurance programme. Later, with assured funding from IOB in 2010, the replication was taken up in other cities like Beed and Kolhapur, where AMCCSL provided handholding, systems including software support, as well as funds for lending in the initial years until the NGOs could borrow on their own. However, demonetisation and COVID-related disruptions did not provide a conducive ground for further replication. AMCCSL has plans to expand the franchisee model further in the near future.

13 Conclusions

Annapurna provides holistic financial services. The operations are automated and on par with any other Microfinance institution in the country. What sets apart Annapurna from other MFIs is that AMCCSL provides services with more empathy and a clear intention to listen to its members. The staff are trained to listen to the members and address any grievances, which are monitored by the CEO. Annapurna has also established turnaround times for different types of financial services, and these are strictly monitored. In the annual general body meetings, the members are asked, 'what can we do for you?' Annapurna firmly believes that the institution exists for the members and navigates its course along with the member clients.

The key differentiators of AMCCSL, as compared to other microfinance players, are:

- The poor do find resources to invest in the equity of their own institutions. External equity is not a dire requirement, nor does it help in structuring the organisation closer to the members' requirements.
- Savings schemes designed to capture income, build assets, and provide pensions.
- Different types of loans for different purposes.
- Longer loan repayment periods, taking into account the purpose and cash flows.
- Insurance products of a kind not available in the market.
- AMCCSL can counter competition and retain its character.
- AMCCSL has been able to focus on its mission over long periods of time. Growth and profits are incidental, and hence the operations concentrate on providing effective services to customers.

The learnings from AMCCSL could be used to educate others in the sector on how to build responsible finance practices into institutions, instead of treating them as options to be exercised in times of need. With very strong member ownership, AMCCSL has shown greater resilience in difficult times on account of its customer centricity, effective management of customer protection, and socially responsible behaviour. These principles, along with visionary leadership, make AMCCSL stand tall among microfinance institutions.

References

Aghion, B. A., & Morduch, J . (2005). *The economics of microfinance*. The MIT Press.
Devaprakash, R. (2005). Balancing quality and quantity of SHGs in India, https://www.findevgateway.org/sites/default/files/publications/files/mfg-en-paper-balancing-quality-and-quantity-in-shgs-in-india-aug-2005.pdf seen on 25 January 2025.
Sharma, M. K., & May, G. A. N. W. (2010). *Commercialization of Micro finance in India; is it all bad?* Micro save India briefing note; 43 http://microfinance.cgap.org/2011/10/12/commercialization-can-the-dual-social-and-financial-missions-of-microfinance-coexist/#more-2812
Shetty, S. L. (2012). *Micro Finance in India*. Academic Foundation.
Srinivasan, G. (2012). *Microfinance India, the social performance report 2012*. Sage Publications.
Srinivasan, G., & Srinivasan, N. (2010). *Community owned micro finance institutions—enabling double bottom line impact*. Rabo Bank and Access Development Services.
Srinivasan, G., & Srinivasan, N. (2023). *Spring board for powering women, three decades of the SHG movement, access knowledge series*. Access Development Services.
Srinivasan, G., & Tankha, A. (2010). SHG federations—development costs and sustainability, Access Development Services. https://www.findevgateway.org/sites/default/files/publications/files/mfg-en-paper-shg-federations-development-costs-and-sustainability-2010.pdf
Srinivasan, N. (2010). Micro Finance State of the sector report, Access Development Services.

Regulation in the Microfinance Sector: Challenges and Relevance for Annapurna Pariwar

Samapti Guha

Abstract The microfinance sector in India has transformed over the last five decades. The regulatory structure of this sector has evolved significantly. In India, microfinance institutions initially adopted the oldest structures of cooperatives and non-profits, such as trusts and societies. In the nineties, when NABARD started the world's largest microfinance programme, the SHG-bank linkage programme, there was a transition in the sector. Several microfinance institutions transformed from non-profits to **not-for-profits** and for-profits. The regulatory structure of these MFIs has changed from trusts or societies to non-banking financial companies under the Section 25 Companies Act and Section 8 Companies Act, and later on, some of them transitioned to small finance banks under RBI regulation. Annapurna Pariwar started its microfinance journey 32 years ago. It is a group of six non-profit organisations. Microfinance is delivered under Annapurna Mahila Multi-State Co-op Credit Society Ltd. It is successfully empowering the marginalised section of women who are economically active in Maharashtra. Though several MFIs have transformed into NBFCs and small finance banks, Annapurna Pariwar, being a cooperative society, did not change its regulatory structure. It is worth studying the relevance of the cooperative (multi-state) structure in the microfinance sector and how Annapurna has addressed the challenges to retain this structure.

S. Guha (✉)
School of Management and Labour Studies, Centre for Social Entrepreneurship, Tata Institute of Social Sciences, Mumbai, Maharashtra, India
e-mail: samapti@tiss.ac.in

J. D. Ranadive, S. Guha (eds.), *Building Pathways to Women's Empowerment*, India Studies in Business and Economics,
https://doi.org/10.1007/978-981-95-7159-8_6

1 Introduction

Microfinance in India has emerged as a movement. It started as a development activity and was supported by non-government organisations in India initially. As it was considered as a development programme, several national and international NGOs such as GTZ, Care International, etc., funded microfinance programmes in this country. The success of these programmes proved that the poor are bankable. Later on, it attracted the banking sector and graduated from a poverty-lending activity to a profit-lending activity. This sector has transformed over the past five decades, and the regulatory structure of this sector has evolved over time. In India, microfinance institutions adopted the oldest structure of cooperatives[1] and non-profits such as trusts and societies initially. From 1970s to 1990s, several countries such as Bolivia, Indonesia, Egypt, Mexico, Bangladesh, etc., experimented different delivery models of microfinance. For example, village banks, microfinance companies, cooperatives, joint liability groups, rural banks, etc. The success of Bancosol Bolivia in 1990s attracted major banks of the world, such as NABARD in India, Compartamos in Mexico, etc. During this period, the Indian banking sector innovated several banking institutions such as regional rural banks, cooperative banks, and the National Bank for Agriculture and Rural Development (NABARD), etc., to provide banking facilities to the marginalised sections. In the 1990s, NABARD started a pilot programme of 255 self help groups (SHGs) with the help of the Mysore Resettlement and Development Agency (MYRADA) in Karnataka in order to link these SHGs to the bank. It was the first attempt to link formal banks with informal SHGs, as in India, there is a strong presence of the informal credit market, which includes informal moneylenders, informal credit associations, etc. It was very successful, and in 1995–96, when NABARD started the world's largest microfinance programme, the SHG-bank linkage programme, there was a transition in the sector. Several commercial banks perceived the SHG-bank linkage programme as a priority sector lending programme. It helped the commercial banks to tap the untapped credit market and also created a demand for microfinance. MFIs, which were non-profits, started facing resource scarcity to cope with the high demand for microfinance. As they were non-profits, they could mobilise public savings or raise equities. For this reason, several microfinance institutions transformed from non-profits to not-for-profits and for-profits. The regulatory structure of these MFIs changed from trusts or societies to non-banking financial companies under Section 25 of the Companies Act and Section 8 of the Companies Act. From 2015, some of them transitioned to small finance banks under RBI regulation as per the Mor Committee's recommendation. This created a parallel banking system for microfinance customers. These banks also focused on the financial literacy of the customers for better financial inclusion.

[1] 'A cooperative is an autonomous association of persons united voluntarily to meet their common economic, social and cultural needs and aspirations through a jointly owned and democratically controlled enterprise' (National Policy on Cooperatives, GOI, 2002).

As the institutional framework is changed, the regulatory framework has also changed. Due to this transition, the MFI sector is facing several instances of regulatory non-compliance processes. Sometimes, these are not performed intentionally. There are several dilemmas among the loan officers, officers at the head offices, and the customers regarding loan size, interest rates, loan delivery, etc. Some frameworks demand a high level of portfolio performance along with extensive outreach to marginalised customers. This has created confusion among the loan officers. In the pursuit of achieving the best portfolio performance, they have disbursed the loans to economically better-off customers; however, this does not allow them to increase the outreach to poorer customers. Consequently, there are several instances of mission drift. Apart from mission drift, the problem of double-dipping has also arisen due to the pressure of meeting the target for SHG bank linkages per bank branch. For example, each of these commercial bank-branches needs to link at least five SHGs for credit to the branch, as per RBI norms. If the number of SHGs is fewer in a particular village, one SHG is approached by several banks for linkage without assessing their loan capacity. This increases the indebtedness of SHG members.

Among all the models, cooperatives are the oldest model of microfinance in India, which is a membership-based organisation. Members are the owners of the cooperatives. A democratic governance structure is at the core of the cooperatives. This structure allows them to address the concerns of the member-clients of the cooperatives. In the 1970s, it started its journey with the foundation of the SEWA Urban Cooperative Bank in Ahmedabad, founded by Dr. Elaben Bhat. After witnessing the success of the SEWA Bank, several cooperative societies began their microfinance journey in different parts of India. These institutions have promoted social capital, economic empowerment, and political decision-making among the members. The unique feature of these institutions is their ability to promote social and economic development simultaneously. Furthermore, these institutions operate on the principle of cooperation, which fosters ethical values among the members. This model is also perceived as a mission-centric social enterprise model. It is interesting to learn about the regulatory framework of the credit cooperative society and its impact on their performance. Credit cooperative societies were initially governed by the Cooperative Society Act, 1956. Later, they were registered under the Mutually Aided Cooperative Society Act, 1995, and presently, they are governed by the Ministry of Cooperation. Additionally, credit cooperative societies are governed by the state under its Cooperative Act. Only if they are registered as multi state then they are governed by the Central Ministry of Cooperation.

Annapurna Pariwar started its microfinance journey 32 years ago. It is a group of six non-profit organisations. Microfinance is delivered under Annapurna Mahila Multi-State Co-op Credit Society Ltd. It is successfully empowering marginalised section of women who are economically active in the slums of Pune and Mumbai in Maharashtra. Though, several MFIs have transformed into NBFCs and small finance banks, Annapurna Pariwar did not change the regulatory structure of the multi-state cooperative society. This legal status enabled Annapurna to provide ownership of the cooperatives to its members and distribute a share of the profit as a dividend among these poor members. It is worth studying the relevance of the cooperative structure in the microfinance sector and how Annapurna has addressed the challenges to retain this structure. Further, it is important to understand how this structure has helped Annapurna to avoid the problem of mission drift and continue to serve the marginalised section of people in the urban slums of Pune and Mumbai.

2 Literature Review

In this section, a brief literature review on the regulation of microfinance institutions, cooperative movements, and the role of cooperatives in social development is discussed. The major aim is to understand the existing research studies on cooperatives and the transition in regulations of the microfinance sector and to try to analyse why existing cooperatives want to retain the cooperative structure during the phases of regulatory transition.

2.1 Regulation of Microfinance Institutions

Microfinance institutions are playing a major role in the financial inclusion of vulnerable sections of the population. They are an important part of the financial market (SIDBI, 2013). Since the 1970s, the regulatory framework of these institutions has evolved to serve clients in the changing scenario of the financial market. India started its banking journey as social banking, and due to liberalisation it has transformed into corporate banking with a social inclination in terms of priority sector lending, micro-lending, zero-balance account opening, etc.

In this report by SIDBI, the institutional framework of MFIs was discussed, followed by the regulatory framework. In the initial period, NGOs were offering micro-financial services to bring about equitable development. During the nineties, mutually aided cooperative societies also provided microfinance to cater to many members. Later, several MFIs were transformed into NBFCs or Section 8 companies[2] to serve the investors better and assist the lenders in expansion. From 2013 to 2023, 10 MFIs were converted into small finance banks to serve different sections of customers and were regulated by the RBI (ibid).

The regulation of microfinance institutions was taken seriously by the Reserve Bank of India (RBI) after the Andhra Pradesh (AP) crisis[3] in 2010, and the

---

[2] NBFCs are for profits and Section 8 companies are not for profits.

[3] Microfinance institutions were mushrooming in Andhra Pradesh after 2004. Most of them depended on grants and debt. As most of them were NGOs and NBFCs, they were unable to

Malegam Committee was formed to address such crises in 2010–11. As per the recommendations of the committee report, RBI introduced a regulatory framework for NBFC-MFIs (RBI, 2021). It suggested the eligibility criteria for microfinance loans, which are linked to the core features of microfinance, such as lending small amounts to borrowers from low-income groups and flexible repayment schedules. It emphasised the protection of borrowers in terms of transparency in charges, ceiling on interest rates, etc. Every NBFC-MFI is not allowed to take public savings. As per the RBI regulations, an NBFC-MFI needs to be a member of at least one self-regulatory organisation recognised by RBI and is 'required to comply with the code of conduct prescribed by the SRO' (RBI, 2021, p. 9).

When we consider the regulation in the microfinance sector, there is a difference between old regulations and new regulations. Pravallika et al. (2023) compared these two regulatory frameworks. They identified several problems related to old regulations, such as defining microfinance loans, limited applicability of regulations, issues of loan pricing, and assessment of household income, etc. Such challenges of the old regulations created obstructions for the organisations to reach the target population. The authors analysed that the new regulations focused more on customer protection in the microfinance sector. In the new regulatory framework, tools are adopted to address the problem of over-indebtedness. They also mentioned that in the old regulatory framework, there was a lack of focus on governance and risk management. In the new regulations, a strong governance structure, risk assessment processes, and a method of monitoring the risks are incorporated. Further, old regulations were not suitable for digital innovation. New regulations introduced digital financial services provided by MFIs, and they also suggested several processes for maintaining cyber security and data protection. While old regulations were meant for the expansion of the MFIs, new regulations are meant for prudential regulations to mitigate systemic risks and bring stability to the sector.

In this context, Iqbal et al. (2019) analysed the relationship between corporate governance and the financial performance of MFIs in Asia. They considered 173 MFIs from 18 countries in Asia for the analysis. Based on the seven variables related to corporate governance, the authors developed a corporate governance index, and they found there is a two-way causal relationship between CGI and financial performance. It implies that strong corporate governance affects financial

---

accumulate savings. As a result, debt bubbles were generated due to lack of strong regulation. In coastal part of AP, several customers of MFIs committed suicide as they faced indebtedness. Repayment problem was high. AP government shut down several offices of SPANDANA and SHARE microfinance Institutions. This is called Krishna Crisis. Later, SKS microfinance and others who became NBFCs started depending on foreign equities. The investors were happy to earn profits from this industry. Interest rates were quite high. Investment dependency was too high. SKS microfinance went for IPO. The founder of SKS sold his shares to earn the profit. In the same time, Borrowers were facing harsh repayment criteria and several social evils emerged. AP government passed an ordnance to regulate the Microfinance sector. While all MFIs agreed to reduce the interest rates, it disappointed the foreign investors. So, there was a crisis due to withdrawal of investors (Mader, 2013).

performance, and MFIs that are performing financially well can have better corporate governance. It is also found that MFIs that are providing individual loans perform financially better, and they have good governance. It also raised a question that, to have a good governance structure, MFIs are diverted from group lending to individual lending. As we know, group lending techniques are well-suited for targeting poor customers, and MFIs achieved success in terms of poverty reduction among poor women borrowers. However, good corporate governance is not enabling the MFIs to perform socially well.

Jamaluddin et al. (2023) analysed the corporate governance of cooperatives. They found that the corporate governance of cooperatives outperformed that of corporations in some aspects. For example, a member CEO in a cooperative has more incentive and is more efficient, resulting in lower agency costs compared to outside CEOs. Board composition and gender diversity were also analysed. It was found from a bibliometric analysis by these authors that the size of the board is inversely related to asset utilisations. Considering gender diversity, it was found that women-led boards have a greater social orientation, and their social performance is better than that of male-led boards. Regarding financial performance, there is mixed evidence on the performance of women-led cooperatives where the majority of the board members are women. Some women-led boards contributed to successful performance, whereas others did not perform well financially (ibid).

Neo-liberal reforms[4] have several impacts on cooperative banking in the country (Sonker, 2019). The author mentioned that due to the neoliberal reforms, homogeneous legislation and supervisory norms were imposed on cooperative banks, similar to commercial banks. This changed the special character of the cooperatives, as meeting the core objective of rural and community development was substituted by generating quick profits. This regulation also changed the pattern of lending by the cooperatives, pushing the cooperative banks to diversify their operations beyond the mission of the cooperatives to bring rural development. Cooperatives needed to think about investment in government securities, non-SLR securities, and other speculative businesses.

Regarding the performance of cooperatives, Rath (2016) made a comparative analysis between the sugar cooperatives of Maharashtra and Amul of Gujarat. He mentioned that, to attract government funds, corporate boards of most of the sugar cooperatives in Maharashtra consisted of politicians, and they did not follow the bye-laws. Later on, these cooperatives' performances deteriorated. Whereas, under the leadership of Mr. Tribhuvan Das Patel and Dr. Kurien, bye-laws at Amul were followed strictly, and they are still performing well. Thus, following bye-laws and board constitution are important parts of corporate governance for the cooperatives' performance.

[4] Neo-liberal reforms mean the market-oriented reforms which emerged in nineties. Organisations started to operate on the principles of financial soundness and be driven by parameters of profitability and efficiency.

There are several microfinance institutions where regulatory non-compliance practices exist. Sangwan et al. (2023) analysed these practices carried out by the loan officers of MFIs during loan disbursement in the field. The authors did not attempt to study the effect of regulations on the performance of MFIs; instead, they sought to understand how the orientation of MFIs towards financial performance affected the loan officer's behaviour which led to regulatory non-compliance practices adopted by the loan officers. They further studied the dilemmas faced by the loan officers and customers during loan delivery. They found that in a particular geographical area, there is competition among loan officers, and at the branch level, portfolio performance influenced the loan officers to aggressively choose wealthier customers, as their credit records are better, so the target of choosing poor customers is not met. The pressure for better performance and competition pushed the loan officers to adopt regulatory non-compliance practices. Misreporting of clients' indebtedness is done by the loan officers to meet the target. In this context, the authors suggested that constant evaluation of objectives, forms, and types of government regulatory intervention is required to be modified on a regular basis. Sometimes, regulatory pressure forces the loan officers to deviate from the social mission of the MFIs.

2.2 *Cooperative Movements*

The cooperative movement in India started to mobilise agricultural farmers, particularly those engaged in allied activities. The purpose was to organise them to pool their meagre resources and provide economies of scale (GOI, 2002). Initially, cooperatives were institutionalised in 1904 when the Credit Cooperative Societies Act was enacted. Later, in 1912, a more comprehensive Cooperative Societies Act was passed. In 1919, under the Government of India Act, the subject of cooperatives was shifted to the Provinces. In 1942, the Multi-Unit Cooperative Societies Act was passed, and in 1984, the Multi-State Cooperative Societies Act was enacted. In British India, cooperatives were not actively promoted. It was considered as a Laissez-faire[5] activity, and the government did not take an active role. However, after independence, 'Cooperation was emerged as a planned development instrument and it received importance as a distinct sector of the National Economy' (GOI, 2002, pp. 2). In 1995, the Mutually Aided Cooperative Societies Act was passed to promote the cooperative movement, as it allowed the voluntary formation of cooperatives. In 2021, the Ministry of Cooperation was formed to advance the cooperative movement, and in 2023, the Multi-State Cooperative Societies Amendment Act was passed (https://www.cooperation.gov.in).

---

[5] A doctrine opposing governmental interference in economic affairs beyond the minimum necessary for the maintenance of peace and property rights.

In the early stages, the cooperative movement was aimed at helping farmers avoid exploitation by informal money lenders and middle men. Later, due to the exploitation by Polson Dairy, the dairy farmers' cooperative movement emerged under the leadership of Dr. Varghese Kurien, the Father of the White Revolution. This movement led to the creation of Amul, the National Dairy Development Board (NDDB), and the Gujarat Cooperative Milk Marketing Federation (GCMMF). Industrialisation of rural society occurred as a result of cooperative movements in India (Anandaram & Dubhashi, 1999). There are several cooperatives, such as sugar cooperatives, fishermen cooperatives, handloom cooperatives, and coir cooperatives, which are outcomes of cooperative movements in India. Rath (2016) mentioned that cooperatives are financed by the share capital of their members, and that's why the regulations and repayment rules are strict. Although cooperatives perform financially well in their initial years, later on, there was political pressure to keep the interest rates on loans very low, as it was considered public funding.

Cooperatives or collectives are sources of promoting social capital formation (Bharti, 2021). Cooperative members are able to access different resources and services and build networks through their organisational structures. These collectives have the unique feature of fostering social and economic development. They can be used for poverty alleviation, livelihood generation, and rural development. Furthermore, these organisations are also entrepreneurial in nature and improve the self-esteem and self-reliance of the members.

In the context of Australian Credit Unions, Unda (2023) mentioned that the credit union movement transformed societal conditions regarding the operation of financial institutions from 1940s to 1990s. This movement worked towards social justice based on democratic principles and values such as fairness, integrity, and so on. The author stated that understanding how values were manifested in cooperative movement-business interactions is not only required for the old credit unions but also for new organisations that will adopt the ethos of cooperation. The Australian credit union movement has contributed to establish fairness, customer centricity, and community engagement within credit cooperative unions. Post-1990s, the author noticed that demutualisation agenda took centre stage, and the conversion from credit union to mutual bank occurred. She recommended that, because of the cooperative ethos and other positive potential of credit unions, it is necessary to bring credit unions back in Australian society.

In times of uncertainty and risk, the resilience of a region is important. In Italy, Costa and Delbono (2023) explored the association between the presence of cooperatives in a region and the resilience for GDP per capita growth and employment from 2008 to 2019. The authors, using regional statistics, developed indices for both GDP per capita and employment. They analysed how these regional indices performed differently during various business cycles, such as recession and recovery. Furthermore, they analysed that the size of cooperative employment plays a positive role in the overall resilience of employment during recovery periods. In this context, it was found that workers' cooperatives enjoy a comparative advantage in managing the effects of macroeconomic crises. Members' engagement in governance democratically and their interaction with the local environment help cooperatives manage such situations. Here, the local environment refers to the interdependency between local communities and cooperative organisations. During crises, these cooperatives reduce the profit shares of member-workers to retain workers' employment. The authors pointed out the OECD's viewpoint that, post-pandemic, cooperatives help the economy move towards inclusiveness and sustainability. The authors recommend that a strong cooperative movement is required for inclusive growth and that it is a powerful tool for 'implementing the EU recovery and resilience programme' (p. 452).

2.3 Role of Cooperatives in Social Development

Cooperatives are self-governing associations of people who voluntarily come together to meet their common social, economic, and cultural goals through collectively owned and democratically governed enterprises (International Cooperative Alliance, 2022, cited in Jamaluddin et al., 2023). Around the world, cooperatives offer employment to 10% of the total workforce and contribute to long-term economic growth. Sonker (2019) explained that cooperatives are based on the principles of self-help, mutual aid, and cooperation. They were established to promote the growth and development of rural communities. Their primary mandate was to increase the flow of credit to agrarian communities and weaker sections of the rural population. The author further mentioned that neo-liberal economic reforms curtailed the importance of this democratic institution, leading to a sharp reduction in cooperatives as they became financially unviable. Additionally, the new governance system pushed cooperatives to invest in government securities, non-SLR securities, and other speculative markets, which obstructed their major focus on rural development and the development of the marginalised sections.

In the Indian context, to alleviate poverty, to create gainful employment, to address the issue of rural-urban migration, and to provide dignity to a large section of the population, Anandaram and Dubhashi (1999) suggested that a planned intervention is required. In this context, cooperatives have emerged as an alternative and meaningful activity. In rural areas, a rise in dairy cooperatives helped women take part in the labour market, and it empowered rural women. Cooperative societies for farmers helped them obtain financial assistance for procuring inputs for cultivation. It is a source of transformation. The authors also mentioned that there is a need to strengthen the cooperative movements in India, as the benefits of such collectives are enormous in the context of the rural population.

In the Indonesian context, cooperatives are the basis of the economic structure. Kusmiati et al. (2023) explained that for a just, progressive, and wealthy society, cooperatives need to function as economic movements and corporate organisations. The authors analysed that in Indonesia, the contribution of cooperatives to Gross Domestic Product (GDP) is decreasing. The number of active cooperatives decreased by 60% in 2018. They mentioned that the success of cooperatives is measured by the Ministry of Cooperatives and SMEs in the Republic of Indonesia by adopting five aspects of cooperatives: institutional, business, financial, member benefits, and societal benefits. They found from their exploratory factor analysis and regression analysis that member participation is the prime determinant of the success of the Indonesian cooperatives. Their participation in decision-making and policy formulation has strengthened the cooperatives. Apart from this, the governance structure, in terms of board constitution and vertical integration, has contributed to the success of Indonesian cooperatives. The authors mentioned that the number of board members, the board's ability and efficiency, the board's independence, and tenure have a positive impact on the success of the cooperatives. Vertical integration has helped reduce market risk and increase the bargaining power of the cooperatives. Lastly, collective activities have a positive impact on the success of cooperatives in Indonesia. Here, collective action demands the commitment of the stakeholders of the cooperatives and the motivation of the management.

Cooperatives have an enormous impact on women's empowerment. Most of the women in the world are not empowered due to a lack of access to resources. Bharati (2021) mentioned that women's empowerment is crucial for the integration and inclusion of women into development. Cooperatives organise women and engage them in economic activities to help them achieve autonomy, economic freedom, and livelihoods, which empower them. For the last four decades, self-help groups, as informal solidarity groups, have evolved as an informal form of cooperatives and played an important role in women's economic empowerment.

In social development, the role of consumers' cooperatives in America is crucial. Pencavel (2020) mentioned that these cooperatives have a history of 175 years. Based on a literature review, the author described that for these cooperatives, membership should be open to all; interest on capital should be invested modestly; members of the cooperative society govern, and each member has one vote, which does not depend on the amount of capital he or she has invested; the net earnings should be shared among the members, and no goods will be sold on credit. The authors found that consumers' cooperatives have not only survived but also thrived. In the context of America, consumers' cooperatives and the government collaborated to improve the rural economy and connected the rural economy to the national economy. The author analysed that within the U.S. Department of Agriculture, the Rural Business-Cooperative Service and the Rural Utilities Service are working with cooperatives to implement water and wash programmes and to provide telecommunication services in rural areas. Further, it is important to inquire whether working with cooperatives could help the government provide services in underserved urban areas or not.

The author mentioned that consumers' cooperatives provide economic advantages in terms of reasonable prices, dividends, fair wages, etc. They are creating economic growth along with social development. In the present scenario, the author noticed that departmental grocery stores in America, which are not cooperatives, have adopted some principles of cooperatives, such as paying dividends to customers and fair wages. So, they are imitating the age-old cooperative structure, and it is a good signal for capital-owned stores to create social values in society. It can be considered a success of the long-lasting cooperative movement in the United States of America.

3 Urban Cooperatives and Present Status

The cooperative movement in India is the outcome of the non-cooperative movement led by Mahatma Gandhi and Sardar Patel. In urban areas, the cooperative banking sector is part of a broader cooperative movement. Suhrud (2003) studied the urban cooperative banking sector in Gujarat. The author explained that, initially, cooperative banks played an important role in the social, economic, and political mobilisation of communities. He mentioned, 'In Gujarati, "Mandalis" or cooperatives was an important process of democratisation of non-political forms of association and institutions' (pp. 3354).

Later on, dominant groups started to prefer milk cooperatives and cooperative banks as an important source of finance. As the cooperatives were unable to add several economic activities to their ambit, they were unable to offer economic gain to their members. Further, mandalis were also associated with an inadequate level of technological and managerial innovation, which reduced their importance in the transition. The author also mentioned that urban people started investing in the stock market, and this also reduced the importance of urban cooperative banks. Furthermore, due to politicisation, cooperative banks became crisis-driven entities. This closed the opportunity for wealth creation among the marginalised section.

The success of SEWA in India depended on its focus towards the economic independence of women (Bharti, 2021). The cooperative engagement also improves their self-esteem and decision-making ability, which leads to an increase in their power to access different types of resources. The author also mentioned that women producers or entrepreneurs are socially and economically empowered because of their membership in SHGs, cooperatives, farmers' producer companies, etc. It increases their participation in self-employment, society, asset creation, etc., which boosts their self-confidence. The author further noted that the cooperative engagement of women increases the women's participation in electoral politics in Rajasthan. Though there are several benefits of women cooperatives, she also mentioned that mixed-gender cooperatives helped more in terms of empowerment than women cooperatives, based on her extensive literature review.

Rosa-Jiménez et al. (2023) studied urban neighbourhood cooperatives for self-management and self-financing of citizen-based regeneration of mass areas housing initiatives. These cooperatives also created a social economy where members were capable of reducing costs and generating additional resources for rehabilitation. The author analysed that these cooperatives created multiple social, physical, and environmental benefits for the members, along with financial benefits. As it is a mass housing construction-led cooperative, the benefit of economies of scale was exercised by the members.

In the context of the United States of America, Pencavel (2020) studied the downfall of housing cooperatives as there has been a transition from housing cooperatives to condominiums. Cooperative apartment buildings constructed by private builders were sold to individual buyers, with ownership of those apartments residing with the cooperative association. Presently, condominiums, which have similar features to housing cooperatives except for the ownership pattern, are popular. Any individual owns the condominium upon purchase, so ownership does not reside in an association. Furthermore, many condominiums do not follow the government rule of 'one individual member, one vote,' as they are sponsored by real estate developers.

4 Objectives and Research Methodology

In this study, an attempt is made to understand the transition of the regulatory framework on urban cooperative-led microfinance institutions in India. The objectives of this study are:

- To understand the existing regulatory frameworks of the microfinance sector in India.
- To understand how an urban Credit Cooperative Society, AMCCSL, perceived the transition of the regulatory framework in the microfinance sector.
- To understand why AMCCSL successfully retains its status as a Credit Co-operative Society during this period of regulatory transition.

As the study explored several subjective issues related to the regulatory framework perceived by a credit cooperative society, a single case study of the oldest credit cooperative society in Mumbai, Annapurna Mahila Multi-State Co-operative Society Limited, is considered. In-depth interviews with the CMD, Dr. Medha Purao Samant, and officials of AMCCSL were conducted to collect the primary data. We also collected the data from slum-dwellers who are taking micro-financial services from AMCCSL through focus group discussions. Later, the data were transcribed and manually coded. From the coding, a thematic analysis is performed. The findings are compared with the existing literature.

5 Case of Annapurna Mahila Multi-State Co-operative Credit Society Limited (AMCCSL)

5.1 Genesis of AMCCSL

In 1986, Annapurna Cooperative Society was registered as the State Cooperative Society in Maharashtra. In 1997, it was renamed as Annapurna Mahila Multi State

Co-operative Credit Society Limited (AMCCSL) under the leadership of Dr. Medha Purao Samant and was registered under the Multi-State Cooperative Act, 1984. The RBI recommended charitable trusts and Section 8 companies for microfinance activities as per their circular in 1998. Later, they recommended non-banking financial companies (NBFCs) after 2002 and small finance banks (SFBs) after 2015. Dr. Samant, CMD of Annapurna Pariwar, stated,

'I have tried first two structures and rejected NBFC structure as it has no power to accumulate the savings from the borrowers and also share of profit cannot be shared with the borrowers. I stuck up to Cooperative structure and thought AMCCSL does not need to convert into a small finance bank (SFB) later on'.

Later, Dr. Medha Purao Samant shifted microfinance activities from a Section 8 company to this cooperative society. The main objective to adopt this legal structure was that it allowed members of the cooperative society to be the owners of the cooperative, which led to the economic empowerment of the marginalised section of women in the slums of Pune and Mumbai. It is one of the oldest models of microfinance in India. As the members are the owners of the institution, dividends are distributed among the members. It is quite evident that more than 80% of MFIs in India are non-banking financial companies. When the finance coordinator of Annapurna Pariwar, under which AMCCSL is operating, was asked, why did AMCCSL not register as an NBFC? She responded,

'AMCCSL is the customer of three nationalised banks. Indian Overseas Bank (IOB) is one of them. In 2007, IOB approached AMCCSL and offered fund for transforming to NBFC. IOB had offered to issue a sweet equity to Medha Tai of Rs. 2 Crores. Our leader Medha Tai refused this offer. She wanted to stick to cooperative model as it is a membership-based and the aim of this organisation is to empower marginalised women'.

She mentioned that in a cooperative structure, dividends are distributed among the members; however, in the case of any other form of MFIs, the share of profit is not owned by the clients. In the case of non-banking financial companies (NBFCs), she mentioned these challenges,

'NBFCs cannot raise public savings. So, they need to borrow from external sources or they take investor's funds and investor demands return on investment. They charge a higher interest rate than the cooperative society'.

Further, the CMD of Annapurna Pariwar mentioned,

'NBFCs do not have permission to accumulate savings from the customers, they need to borrow from external sources and take investor's money and equity. In the case of AMCCSL, savings are raised from the members yet there is a need to raise a retail investor's portfolio because the borrower members are very poor. Their investment cannot be sufficient to lend them as per their need. As a result, the target group of customers is the same but the source of fund is different. Social investors who are mainly educated senior citizens, retired from good jobs invest in AMCCSL for good return on investment (ROI) and satisfaction to invest for cause'.

5.2 Choice of Cooperative Structure Over Small Finance Banking Structure

The new form of microfinance institutions is small finance banks (SFBs). In 2013–15, around 11 NBFC-MFIs became small finance banks, and they are regulated by the Reserve Bank of India. It was asked why AMCCSL did not apply for the transition to an SFB?

Finance coordinator of AMCCSL responded,

'Cooperative Societies can offer collateral free loans to its members. In the case of SFBs, only 15% loan of total loan portfolios can be offered as unsecured loans or collateral free loans. The social mission of Annapurna Pariwar might be deviated from, if AMCCSL becomes an SFB. Members are AMCCSL are coming from lower income groups and are slum dwellers. The main aim is to empower the members economically so that they can have better livelihoods and well-being.

Further, Banks need to maintain the protocol of selecting its managers. They need to have higher academic qualification such as MBA/Post Graduation in Management, Social Sciences etc. *In case of AMCCSL, we build the capacity of our members. Our most of the field staff are coming from the slums and with lower academic qualification such as 10th or 12th pass. We train them before sending them to the clients. We cannot afford people with high qualification. Our management staff are from Social Work background. In case of Cooperative Societies, such stringent conditions are not applied. Therefore, Cooperative model is suitable for our mission*'.

5.3 Relationship of AMCCSL with State Politics

It is found that credit cooperative societies are highly politicised and several political leaders are at the board of the societies. Sometimes, it affects the smooth performance of the cooperative societies. It was asked, how does AMCCSL address the political issues during its implementation? The financial coordinator responded,

'AMCCSL leadership, under Dr. Samant, purposefully keeps a distance from political parties. We do not take any benefit from them. In our executive board, independent directors are from Social Work and Banking field. Two of managing committee members are the members of AMCCSL. Senior staff members have representation in the managing committee'.

Further, the CMD of Annapurna Pariwar mentioned,

'For raising finance, AMCCSL is not approaching any political party. It is raising fund by offering fixed deposit facilities to the social investors. They are wealthy citizens who do not want loans from AMCCSL but wish to invest in AMCCSL for its social goal and good interest rate. So, we do not have any dependency on any political leadership'.

5.4 Reasons for Success of AMCCSL

Most of the credit cooperative societies in India are not performing successfully. It was asked, what are the factors contributing to the success of AMCCSL? The AMCCSL staff mentioned,

'Our leader Dr. Medha Purao Samant is a visionary. She gave personal guarantee to bank till now to raise loans. We are self-sustainable now under her guidance. Under her leadership, we managed the situation during Covid-19 Pandemic from 2020 to 2022, demonetisation from 2016 to 2018, though we have gone through several challenges. We have taken need-based actions. We also facilitated to open the savings account with the banks for 60,000 members. For raising funds, we have developed financial products such as Recurring Deposits, Fixed Deposits and Adharpurna long term deposits (giving payouts as pension) offered to the social investors. We have raised Rs. 90 Crores from social investment (non-borrowers) and Rs. 100 Crores from savings by borrower-members. Total Rs.200 crores investor's portfolio. As against this, we have our loan portfolio almost equal. For fund we do not depend on external sources. It helps us to maintain the sustainability of the business and the communities'.

The success of any enterprise depends on technology adoption. AMCCSL has also adopted digital technology over the past 20 years. It has been continuously upgraded, and one of the respondents mentioned,

'AMCCSL has digitalised its every operation. Our journey from issuing manual receipt to digitalised receipt to the members is noteworthy. We have started using tabs for loan disbursement and collection. We will soon be shifting to App. Presently 12 Software Engineers are on regular Payroll at Annapurna Pariwar. So, we are managing the digitalisation of our activities in-house. AMCCSL is also using the software for the operations in the slums. In case of digitalisation, research is important and there is immense requirement of training and development'.

5.5 Problems and Challenges

The Ministry of Cooperation was formed in 2021 to promote multi-state cooperative societies. If AMCCSL wants to modify in Bye-Laws or enhancement of share capital, they need to submit the changes within 15 days to the Ministry of Cooperation. Sometimes they face challenges, the staff of AMCCSL stated,

'We submitted the proposal for modification in bye-laws and share capital enhancement to the Ministry of Cooperation on time but we received the order after three year's follow up. We relentlessly tried to sort out how to get the order quickly'.

Annapurna Pariwar is also offering insurance products. For the insurance products, AMCCSL floated a Section 8 company (not-for-profit) 22 years ago, in 2003. As a credit cooperative society, they can not have membership with the Credit Bureau. They are still following this up with the RBI. For floating an insurance company, as per IRDA, they need Rs.100 crores as solvency capital. After a lot of lobbying with IRDA, it is expected to be reduced to Rs. 20 crores. However, this is still a large amount for AMCCSL to float an insurance company. This has been a challenge for them for a long time.

AMCCSL is also facing the challenge of competition from other microfinance institutions. The finance coordinator of AMCCSL mentioned,

'A lot of NBFCs are operating and they are designing different credit products. As per RBI regulation, interest cap is removed and as a result members are paying various charges. Also, overborrowing is increased. We are following all the recommendation from Sa-Dhan as well as RBI guidelines. We develop innovative products, have two-way communication with members hence we are surviving and growing'.

5.6 Perception of the Member-Customers of AMCCSL

In M East Ward in Chembur, there are several slums. In each slum, the sources of financial services are AMCCSL, Bandhan Bank, Community-led Rotating Savings and Credit Associations (ROSCAs), and SHGs linked with commercial banks. During the research study in 2022 on the financial health of the slum dwellers, 4–5 focus group discussions were conducted to understand the perception of the member-customers about the role of AMCCSL in their lives. They mentioned that,

'AMCCSL is not only providing credit but we can get insurance from them. Other institutions are not providing the insurance. We realised the importance of the insurance during the COVID-19 Pandemic. There are several families who lost their loved one. However, some of us are survived well as they have access to insurance product and after the death of bread earners, the families got the money'.

As cooperatives are democratic institutions and owned by the customers, some of the respondents during the FGDs mentioned,

'other banks treated us as poor customers but AMCCSL is owned by us and we get the dividend. This is extra income for us. This made us happy. During COVID-19, Bandhan Bank stopped giving us loans however, AMCCSL offered us pension and insurance and other services and loans are rescheduled. That gave us a relief. As we did not have the income source during the lockdown, rescheduling of loans and insurance services provided by AMCCSL helped us to survive. In this time, we also

did not continue our Bishi (ROSCA) as we did not have the money to continue it. Also some Bishi Owners stole the money and returned to their native place as it is informal arrangement, we did not lodge a complaint with the police'.

About other services of Annapurna Pariwar, respondents mentioned,

'*we are not only getting the business loans from AMCCSL, we also get loan for repair work at the residence, some of us also get financial help for education of the children. These services give us relief and make our lives easy*'.

To understand their perception of the regulatory framework of microfinance institutions, they were asked which institution is more beneficial in uncertain times. Some of them responded,

'*During normal time when we are having regular income, Bandhan Bank and Bishi (ROSCA) are good for credit, however, during the health emergency and uncertainty, AMCCSL is good as we have the access to insurance and pension along with credit*'.

6 Analytical Findings and Discussion

Based on the in-depth interviews, several themes are constructed. AMCCSL is one of the oldest micro finance institutions in India, and it is performing continuously for the poor women in the slums of Pune and Mumbai.

6.1 Cooperative Design Best Suited for Catering to the Marginalised Women in the Urban Slums

In this study, it is found that AMCCSL retained the cooperative structure from its inception. According to the requirement to transform into a small finance bank, any microfinance institution is allowed to disburse only 15% collateral-free loans as per the RBI, whereas in the cooperative structure, they can provide 100% collateral-free loans. So, it is easy for AMCCSL to serve the marginalised section in the urban slums. As a NBFC, any MFI is not allowed to mobilise the savings from the public, so it cannot offer micro-savings or create its own fund. These MFIs need to depend on external funds. The founder CMD of AMCCSL mentioned that it will not allow achieving financial sustainability, so if she wants to cater to the marginalised section of the people, the cooperative structure is the best-suited structure for urban micro-financial services. In this context, Rath (2016) mentioned that cooperatives are financed by the share capital of the members, and strict rules are required to maintain financial sustainability as it has a component to achieve self-sustainability.

6.2 *Creation of Social Investment Market Stops the Politicisation of Cooperatives*

Existing literature on cooperatives and the cooperative movement analysed that the performance of these institutions has deteriorated due to politicisation of the power, which has also affected the governance structure. These governance issues have led to inefficient financial performance and financial instability (Rath, 2016; Sangwan et al., 2023). One of the reasons for the financial stability of AMCCSL is that it never allows political leadership to run the institution. Instead of depending on political power, they created a space for social investment. The founder CMD of AMCCSL mentioned that, to raise funds, AMCCSL is offering FD facilities, and several socially sensitive investors have kept FDs with AMCCSL. This has created financial independence, as AMCCSL is building a corpus to serve its member-borrowers. This FD programme offers a very good interest rate, better than those provided by banks and other cooperative societies. Hence, retired senior citizens from well-paid private or government jobs are finding it attractive for two reasons—1. Good return on investment, and 2. Satisfaction due to a social cause. Therefore, the creation of a social investment market helps AMCCSL to stop the politicisation and this made AMCCSL different from other cooperative societies.

6.3 *Cooperative Structure Creating Bottlenecks for Expansion of Financial Services and Credit Monitoring*

During Covid-19, AMCCSL proved that insurance products are necessary for the members in the slums. To get the Section 8 company regulated as an insurance company by the IRDA, AMCCSL needs Rs. 100 crores as solvency capital, which is a significant amount for a credit cooperative society. The founder CMD of AMCCSL stated that it is expected to be reduced to Rs. 20 crores after lobbying; however, it is still a large amount. This created a barrier for AMCCSL to get the mutual insurance company regulated. Though Annapurna Pariwar has already formed a Section 8 company that serves mutual insurance products like health, life, family, and asset loss for the members of AMCCSL, many times the correct problem is identified by this cooperative society, but the regulatory structure obstructed to deliver the solution to such problems.

Further, the cooperative structure obstructs AMCCSL from being a member of the Credit Bureau. It is difficult to get credit data from them about the customers and potential customers. This has created the problem of double dipping, which has also led to the issue of high indebtedness among the member-borrowers. Being a cooperative society, the main aim of AMCCSL is to cater to marginalised women in the slums of Pune and Mumbai. If the RBI allows these societies to be part of the Credit Bureau, credit cooperative societies might achieve financial sustainability more easily and make informed decisions about loan disbursement to the member-borrowers.

6.4 Technology Adoption Helps AMCCSL to Bring Efficiency in the Process of Delivery

Most of the cooperative societies are old-fashioned, and they lack in adopting new technologies. One of the success factors of AMCCSL is technology adoption. For the last 20 years, they have been adopting new digital technologies. The respondents mentioned that they have had a fruitful journey from providing physical to digital services to the members. The staff of AMCCSL stated that adopting technology works as an enabler and brings efficiency to the processes of delivery. It helps the loan officers to record the data about the members digitally. They have an efficient data management system. As a result, 12 software engineers were recruited full-time in AMCCSL. The staffs are using technology devices such as tabs for loan disbursement, and members are issued digital receipts instead of physical receipts. It is found that technology adoption helped AMCCSL to standardise each and every process of delivery.

6.5 Regulations Need to be Reframed on Time

AMCCSL started as a State Cooperative Society and later, it was registered as a Multi-State Cooperative Society. Presently, it is regulated by the Ministry of Cooperation. So, credit cooperative societies have also been going through a regulatory transition. The founder CMD of AMCCSL mentioned that for modifying the bye-laws or enhancing the share capital in a cooperative, they need to take permission from the Ministry. However, this time, it has been delayed by 2–3 years due to the transition of the co-op department to the Co-Op Ministry. Continuous follow-up is required. It also requires a lot of time and leads to delays in delivery. Sometimes, it creates a lot of dilemmas about the processes among the staff. Unknowingly, loan officers might engage in regulatory non-compliance actions. This finding is supported by Sangwan (Sangwan et al., 2023). It is suggested that the Ministry needs to help the credit cooperative societies in reframing the policies on time for their further progress and timely delivery. This also helps the societies to adhere to the compliances.

7 Conclusions

AMCCSL has been delivering micro-financial services in the urban slums of Pune and Mumbai for more than three decades. The cooperative structure has helped this organisation serve marginalised women in the slums by offering 100% uncollateralised loans. This legal structure enables them to create financial assets for these poor women, as it allows them to receive dividends every financial year. Thus, the cooperative structure allows members to own the cooperative societies. It is evident that the success of AMCCSL depends on several process innovations. For example, to achieve financial self-sufficiency, it created a space for social investors who invest in the FD product from AMCCSL. This has helped AMCCSL become financially independent.

They also adopted digitalisation of their services. Here, technology enabled them to bring the efficiency in the processes of delivery of the financial services. As one of the objectives of microfinance is financial inclusion, retaining the structure of a cooperative society enabled AMCCSL to contribute to this aspect. The staff of AMCCSL helped marginalised women by providing credit. If we compare it with other structures such as NBFC-MFIs or small finance banks, it is found that the cooperative structure can offer a lower interest rate than NBFC-MFIs and an equal interest rate as SFBs. Even cooperative societies reach a greater number of marginalised customers than the other two MFIs, as banking law permits SFBs only 15% uncollateralised loans, and NBFC-MFIs cannot offer micro-savings as they are not allowed to accumulate public savings. If we consider the social performance and financial sustainability of MFIs through the journey of AMCCSL, a credit cooperative society is the best-suited model of microfinance in India.

References

Anandaram, K. S., & Dubhashi, M. (1999). Role of cooperatives in social development. *Indian Journal of Industrial Relations*, *35*(1) 108–113. Published by Shri Ram Centre for Industrial Relations and Human Resources.

Bharti, N. (2021). Role of cooperatives in economic empowerment of women: A review of Indian experiences. *World Journal of Entrepreneurship, Management and Sustainable Development*, *17*(4), 617–631. https://doi.org/10.1108/WJEMSD-07-2020-0095

Costa, M., & Delbono, F. (2023). Regional resilience and the role of cooperative firms. *Social Enterprise Journal*, *19*(5), 435–458. https://doi.org/10.1108/SEJ-07-2022-0064

Government of India. (2002, March). *National policy on cooperatives, department of agriculture & cooperation ministry of agriculture government of India*. Viewed at https://www.cooperation.gov.in/policies-guidelines on 11.11.2024 at 12.36pm.

International Cooperative Alliance. (2022). *Facts and figures*. ICP, Belgium. Viewed on https://www.ica.coop/en/cooperatives/facts-andfigures on 2.11.2024 at 7pm.

Iqbal, S., Nawaz, A., & Ehsan, S. (2019). Financial performance and corporate governance in microfinance: Evidence from Asia. *Journal of Asian Economics (2018)*, *60*, 1–13. https://doi.org/10.1016/j.asieco.2018.10.002

Jamaluddin, F., Saleh, N. M., Abdullah, A., Hassan, M. S., Hamzah, N., Jaffar, R., Aziz, S. A. A. G., & Embong, Z. (2023). Cooperative governance and cooperative performance: A systematic literature review. *Sage Open*, 1–21. https://doi.org/10.1177/21582440231192944

Kusmiati, E., Bisnis, F. E. D., Masyita, D., Febrian, E., & Cahyandito, M. F. (2023). A study on the determinants of successful performance of Indonesian cooperatives. *International Journal of Social Economics*, *50*(9), 1285–1301. https://doi.org/10.1108/IJSE-02-2022-0078

Mader, P. (2013). Rise and fall of microfinance in India: The Andhra Pradesh crisis in perspective. *Strategic Change*, *22*, 47–66. https://doi.org/10.1002/jsc.192

Pencavel, J. (2020). The performance of consumers' cooperatives in America. *Journal of Participation and Employee Ownership, 3*(1), 1–27. Emerald Publishing Limited. https://doi.org/10.1108/JPEO-07-2020-0019

Pravallika, P. J. L., Teki, S., & Udaya Bhaskar, N. (2023). How new regulations of micro finance sector transform the old ones and its impact. *World Journal of Business and Management, 9*(1), 22–32. Microthink Institute.

Rath, N. (2016). Cooperative Movements in India. *Economic and Political Weekly, 51*(40), 23–25.

Reserve Bank of India (2021). *Consultive document on regulation of microfinance* (pp. 1–31). Department of Regulation. Viewed at https://www.rbi.org.in/Scripts/PublicationsView.aspx?id=20377 on 12.12.2023 at 10am.

Rosa-Jiménez, C., Márquez-Ballesteros, M. J., García-Moreno, A. E., & Navas-Carrillo, D. (2023). Neighbourhood cooperatives for the integrated urban regeneration of mass housing areas: Speculations on a proposed model. *Social Enterprise Journal, 19*(5), 575–597. https://doi.org/10.1108/SEJ-01-2023-0010

Sangwan, S., Nayak, N. C., & Sangwan, V. (2023). Regulatory non-compliances in microfinance operations: A survey of Indian microfinance institutions. *Journal of Financial Regulation and Compliance, 31*(5), 714–728. https://doi.org/10.1108/JFRC-01-2023-0001

SIDBI. (2013, August) Legal & regulatory framework for micro finance institutions in India. *1* (2), prepared by Sa-Dhan, MFIN and SIDBI viewed at http://www.sidbi.in>assets>front>pdf>legal& …. on 12.10.2024at8am.

Sonker, A. P. (2019, November–December). Cooperative credit institutions and rural credit in India under neoliberalism. *Social Scientist, 47*(11/12 (558–559)), 37–62.

Suhrud, T. (2003, August 9–15). Collapse of urban cooperative banking sector. *Economic and Political Weekly, 38*(32), 3354–3355.

Unda, L. (2023). Cooperative values and the development of the credit union movement in Australia. *Journal of Management History, 29*(2), 232–251. Emerald Publishing Limited. https://doi.org/10.1108/JMH-04-2022-0012

A Comparative Study on Financial Literacy Initiatives of Small Finance Bank and Cooperative Society in India: An Exploration

Samapti Guha, Shraddha Kalani, and Chandralekha Ghosh

Abstract Financial exclusion and social exclusion co-exist in India. Due to this factor, several generations are facing financial hardship and a lack of accessibility to education, employment, etc. Therefore, their financial and social status remains unchanged. Financial inclusion is required to break this barrier. Financial inclusion, financial literacy, and financial stability are the different dimensions of the integral strategy for inclusive economic growth in any country. In India, several microfinance institutions such as cooperative society, NBFC-MFIs, NGO-MFIs, and small finance banks are operating. These institutions are promoting financial inclusion through financial literacy for the marginalised sections of the population. The way of delivering financial literacy varies across different institutions. There is a variation in customers across different MFIs. It is important to understand how the oldest model of MFIs, such as credit cooperative society and the new model of MFIs, namely small finance banks (SFBs), have been implementing financial literacy programmes and at what stage of lending, these programmes are being delivered. The difference between these two organisational structures is that cooperative society is being owned by the customers, while SFB is owned by the investors/shareholders. This chapter aims to conduct a comparative study on financial literacy initiatives taken by a multistate credit cooperative society,

S. Guha (✉)
School of Management and Labour Studies, Centre for Social Entrepreneurship, Tata Institute of Social Sciences, Mumbai, Maharashtra, India
e-mail: samapti@tiss.ac.in

S. Kalani
Livin' My Dream, Bangalore, Karnataka, India
e-mail: shraddha.kalani@gmail.com

C. Ghosh
Department of Economics, West Bengal State University, Barasat, India
e-mail: ghoshchandralekha@wbsu.ac.in

J. D. Ranadive, S. Guha (eds.), *Building Pathways to Women's Empowerment*, India Studies in Business and Economics,
https://doi.org/10.1007/978-981-95-7159-8_7

Annapurna Mahila Credit Cooperative Society, and a small finance bank, ESAF Small Finance Bank, to address the goal of financial inclusion and financial stability. For this study, a case study method is adopted to understand the process of delivery of financial literacy in the studied organisations.

1 Introduction

Financial exclusion and social exclusion co-exist in India. It results in the suffering of generations due to the non-accessibility of education, employment opportunities, etc. Thus, the social as well as financial status of these generations remains unchanged. To change this status, there is a need for the financial inclusion of these communities to be integrated with the formal financial sector. In this context, the Reserve Bank of India defines financial inclusion as '*providing access to financial services including credit and deposit facilities to marginalised groups at reasonable cost by mainstream institutional players*' (Chakrabarty, 2012).

Although financial inclusion has been discussed since the time of Independence, financial literacy, which is imperative for financial inclusion, came in very late, only after the global financial crisis of 2008. RBI Deputy Governor, Mr. D. K. Chakrabarty, in 2012 mentioned that '*Financial Literacy is imperative to financial inclusion and needs to go hand in hand which would ultimately lead to financial stability*' (Chakrabarty, 2012). Financial inclusion, financial literacy, and financial stability are part of an integral strategy.

The Standard & Poor's (S&P) Ratings Services Global Financial Literacy survey by the Global Financial Literacy Excellence Centre in November 2015 states that about 76% of India's grown-up population does not understand the basics of financial literacy, leading to poor and ineffective financial decisions, which burden the nation with the high cost of providing monetary security and low success. It is also very critical for the weaker and marginalised sections of society. The reasons for the lack of demand (financial literacy) for financial services are unawareness about financial products and services, lack of financial knowledge, attitude, and skill, meagre earnings, nil savings, high opportunity costs to travel to banks, the established informal system of finance in society, etc. From the supply (financial inclusion) side, the reasons are stringent procedures for bank account opening, unavailability of bank branches, ATMs in proximity, non-tailored products and services, asymmetric information about probable clients, the adverse selection problem, and the moral hazard problem.

To overcome the challenges on the supply side, following the success of Grameen Bank in Bangladesh, India also witnessed a surge in microfinance institutions (MFIs) lending to the poor at affordable interest rates without the need for financial collateral. Many MFIs have also been registered as cooperative credit societies and non-banking financial companies-microfinance institutions (NBFC-MFIs), which are regulated by the RBI.

Credit cooperative societies are the oldest model of microfinance institutions in India. They started in 1905. The uniqueness of such societies is that all members are owners of the society. It is a value-based collective organisation based on cohesiveness. The main aim of these societies is to provide livelihoods and welfare to the members. During the 1970s, when the microfinance movement started in India, several cooperative credit societies and cooperative banks joined the movement. This movement started with the inception of the SEWA Urban Cooperative Bank in Ahmedabad under the leadership of Mrs. Elaben Bhat, a lawyer, social activist, trade unionist, and founder member of the Self-Employed Women's Association (SEWA). Capacity building of the marginalised section was the motto of the microfinance movement. Providing financial services along with financial knowledge was at the centre of the movement. Several NGOs and cooperative societies led this movement. Microfinance has become an industry due to this movement in India.

In the year 2015, with its aim to advance financial inclusion, RBI granted in-principle licences to ten institutions to open small finance banks (SFBs). These are known as Differentiated Banks as they aim at providing specific banking products. These SFBs would primarily cater to the unorganised sector customers, micro-entrepreneurs, migrant labourers and other marginalised populations by offering them an affordable range of financial products and services to promote financial inclusion. Eight out of ten institutions which received the licence are NBFC-MFIs. Since they directly cater to the needs of the marginalised section and now would be offering them complete financial services, it becomes the responsibility of the SFBs to impart financial literacy to enable their customers to make sound financial decisions (Government of India. RBI, 2015).[1]

There is a dearth of literature on financial literacy models adopted by different microfinance institutions in India. Even so, there is a lack of information available about the financial literacy initiatives of the newly formed SFBs. It is important to know the financial literacy modules used, their challenges, outcomes, and goals practised by the old model of cooperative society and the new model of SFBs. In this context, the present study has made an attempt to examine the financial literacy initiatives of a cooperative society and an SFB in India to understand how they

[1] The minimum paid-up equity capital for small finance banks shall be Rs. 100 crore. The promoter's minimum initial contribution to the paid-up equity capital of such small finance bank shall at least be 40% and gradually brought down to 26% within 12 years from the date of commencement of business of the bank. The small finance banks will be required to extend 75% of its Adjusted Net Bank Credit (ANBC) to the sectors eligible for classification as priority sector lending (PSL) by the Reserve Bank. At least 50% of its loan portfolio should constitute loans and advances of upto Rs. 25 lakh.

The main advantage of small finance banks is low operating cost which gives them an advantage to survive in the market with minimal profit. They also get assistance from the government in case of bad debts. The small finance banks are more active in rural areas and are acquainted with the needs of the people. This may also lead to new products and services in order to meet the evolving customer needs. These banks are also capable of lending at low cost to small businesses (Dangi & Kumar, 2013).

provide financial literacy. Are they different? At which stage of the financial services do they provide financial literacy?

2 Literature Review

In this section, a thematic representation of the literature review on financial literacy in the context of financial inclusion, different initiatives taken by various agencies, initiatives undertaken by cooperative societies, justification for small finance banks and why they are likely to succeed in spreading financial literacy, steps to promote financial inclusion and small finance banks, and research on small finance banks in India has been provided.

2.1 Financial Literacy and Financial Inclusion

Financial literacy has multiple definitions. The most referred definition is given by the Organisation for Economic Co–operation and Development (OECD), which states that financial literacy as *'A combination of awareness, knowledge, skill, attitude and behaviour required to make effective financial decisions to achieve financial wellbeing'* (OECD, 2011).

Financial inclusion, financial literacy, and financial stability all three are part of an integral strategy (Kamboj, 2014). Agarwalla et al. (2015) state that if people believe that they do not have access to financial products, they might perceive low benefits from financial education programs, even if these are provided free of cost. Financial inclusion is a supply-side factor, and financial literacy is a demand-side factor. When both are in sync, financial stability is achieved. In this context, Chakrabarty (2013) mentioned that no major headway could be made in financial inclusion without financial literacy. Financial literacy can broadly be defined as the capacity to have familiarity with and understanding of financial market products, especially rewards and risks, to make informed choices. It refers to the ability to make informed judgements and to take effective decisions regarding the use and management of money. It is regarded as an important requirement for functioning effectively in modern society. Trends in retirement income policies, work patterns, and demography suggest its importance can only increase in the years ahead. Raising financial literacy supports social inclusion and enhances the wellbeing of the community.

There is a set of literature on the factors affecting financial literacy. These factors are important as they help various institutions formulate custom-made financial literacy programmes for financially excluded people. Bhargava (2016) suggested various determinants like sex, qualifications, earnings, location, age of the customers, and occupation as determinants of financial literacy. Agarwalla et al. (2013) have thrown light on the factors used to measure the influence of different socio-demographic variables, such as financial knowledge,[2] financial behaviour[3] and financial attitude.[4] The study suggests that financial knowledge is higher in families with high income. Men possess higher financial knowledge and have a higher propensity for affordability compared to women. The absence of college education has a negative impact on financial behaviour. In the case of financial attitude, women have a high positive attitude compared to men. Different channels have been identified by Kumari and Viz (2013) for the dissemination of financial literacy, such as through elementary education, social media, seminars for adults, SHGs, microfinance institutions, etc.

2.2 *Initiatives Taken by Different Agencies to Promote Financial Literacy*

The above literature shows that financial literacy is very important, and various socioeconomic and demographic factors have an impact on it. Various institutions have undertaken different policies. The OECD initiated and spearheaded the International Network on Financial Education (INFE) in 2008 for the promotion and facilitation of international cooperation between various stakeholders on financial education issues globally (OECD, 2008). To tackle this issue in India, the government, in 2010, constituted the Financial Stability and Development Council (FSDC) to deal with financial literacy along with various other financial inclusion-related issues. FSDC also prepared the draft National Strategy for Financial Education (NSFE) for India in 2012 (Indian Economy.Net, 2016).

Further, the National Centre for Financial Education (NCFE) was promoted by the Reserve Bank of India (RBI) and other regulatory bodies like SEBI, IRDAI, and PFRDA for promoting financial education to all sections of the population as per the NSFE (National Centre for Financial Education, 2015). Srinivasan (2013) mentioned different initiatives taken by various regulatory bodies in India. Project Financial Literacy is undertaken by the RBI to create awareness of basic banking concepts. Commercial banks create awareness through Financial Literacy and Counselling Centres (FLCC) on financial literacy. Other players like SEBI, IRDA, NABARD, the National Stock Exchange, brokers, and mutual funds have also played a role in financial literacy and inclusion in various arenas of the economy. In June 2012, as

[2] It is defined by numeracy skills and understanding of concepts of macroeconomics.

[3] It means making household budgets and a sense of timeliness of repayments and possession of savings habits.

[4] 'The Basic Savings Bank Deposit Account or BSBDA is a Savings Account that does not have a minimum balance. In contrast, a BSBDA has a maximum account balance that has to be maintained. The BSBDA holder will get an ATM cum Debit Card as a part of the account opening formalities. The holder will also get passbook services for free and not be charged for a non operative account. The bank allows a certain number of deposits and withdrawals in the month that are free of cost', http://www.hdfcbank.com.

per the revised guidelines on Financial Literacy Centres (FLCs), FLCs and all the rural branches of scheduled commercial banks were advised by the RBI to scale up financial literacy programme by conducting financial literacy camps at least once a month, which would facilitate financial inclusion through financial literacy and financial access. The major aim behind the setting up of small finance banks is to promote financial inclusion through financial literacy. There is a strong literature that provides a theoretical understanding of why small finance banks are better suited for a particular set of clients. Moreover, there is theoretical evidence that they will be better able to transmit financial literacy among their clients. In the next subsection, we will present some important studies on this aspect. So, we find that various agencies are working to promote financial literacy programmes.

2.3 Literature on Cooperatives and Financial Literacy

Cooperative societies are collectives of marginalised people such as agricultural farmers, labourers, artisans, etc. They help them access credit to improve their wellbeing. Cooperatives are based on the cohesiveness and joint ownership of the members. In India, the cooperative movement was organised for the socio-economic development of rural communities. Mitra (2014) mentioned that cooperatives are the outcome of the workers' class movement. They helped small and marginal farmers and dairy farmers to be included in the financial system. It started with the agro communities for their upliftment (Anandaram & Dubhashi, 1999). Later, the dairy cooperative movement under the leadership of Dr. Kurien started in the 1940s. The outcome was the creation of Amul, the National Dairy Development Board, etc. The cooperatives empowered rural women as they did not have any access to finance. These cooperatives helped women improve their social mobility along with economic empowerment. There are several cooperatives in India, such as sugar cooperatives, handloom cooperatives, etc. The authors recommended that the cooperative movement needs to be strengthened as both rural and urban areas need to have a strong cooperative movement in the context of liberalisation where inequality is rising. This movement needs to adapt to the present social and business environment.

In the context of Sri Lanka, Hulme and Montgomery (1994) analysed that cooperatives are not anti-poor and they have a role 'in a pluralist institutional development approach that is an essential component of strategies to improve livelihoods' (pp. 378). This organisation imparts financial knowledge to its members and executives. The authors suggested that these cooperatives should keep a distance from the state by managing political relationships and avoiding subsidy disbursement activities, as it attracts elite groups for manipulation. These institutions prepare themselves to adopt marketing mechanisms and cover the costs. The authors also suggested that donors assist in strengthening of organisational systems and personnel for community development. If the organisation is strong and personnel, well-versed in financial knowledge and financial planning, providing financial inclusion would be easier (ibid).

In the context of Nepal, Aryal and Panta (2015) explored the status of financial knowledge among the executive members of agri-based credit cooperatives. In these cooperatives, most of the executive members are financially illiterate and are supported by non-profit organisations. It was found that the executives of the cooperatives were unable to manage finances when the non-profit organisations withdrew their technical support. As they have limited access to financial literacy, these executives cannot identify the most profitable financial products. Most of them are unaware of the various modern financial products. They possess only basic knowledge of finance, and most of the executives deposit the savings into fixed deposit products. To better manage the cooperatives, the authors recommended implementing policies for financial literacy programmes targeted at the cooperative executives. This would enable these executives to make business decisions efficiently for the cooperatives, which might lead to higher income for the cooperatives. Ultimately, this would translate into improved welfare for the cooperative members.

It is a well-known fact that cooperative credit societies provide financial literacy, which has an impact on the savings behaviours of their members. Godar (2024) analyses the relationship between savings behaviour and financial literacy in Butwal sub-metropolitan city. The author found that financial literacy has a positive impact on economic growth through savings and the development of the financial sector. At the individual level, financial literacy and savings improve well-being in terms of children's education, consumption smoothing, etc. A high level of financial literacy helps a person understand banking processes and improves savings behaviour. Not only savings behaviour, but financial literacy also helps a person make appropriate financial decisions.

Financial literacy also improves the empowerment of women entrepreneurs in cooperatives (Nayituliki & Munene, 2022). The authors mentioned that budgeting practices, savings practices, and investment practices under the financial literacy programme of the cooperatives increase the financial capabilities of women entrepreneurs in the Gasabo district of Rwanda. They also concluded that financial literacy has improved the business capabilities of women entrepreneurs in cooperatives, but they need to improve their skills so that they become more competitive.

Mitra (2014) also analysed the problems of cooperatives in the face of liberalisations such as lack of democratic operation due to political pressure, wrong financial decisions taken by the Board, etc. Even so, the author reminded readers of the history of the cooperative movement and its role in the financial inclusion of marginalised communities, and how, under this organisational structure, communities became financially literate. In this context, the author suggested that the state needs to strengthen cooperatives for the upliftment of marginalised communities.

2.4 Literature on Financial Literacy and Small Finance Banks in India

Abijith and Raghavendra (2018) presented the introduction, functions, challenges, and role of small finance banks and examined the awareness level of customers.

Mohanty (2018) focused on the need for and importance of small finance banks. In his study, he analysed that small financial banks have huge potential in unbanked and underserved areas and play a major role in the development of the micro, small, and medium enterprises sector. Viswan (2017) focused on the awareness level of rural people about small financial banks and the operation of small financial banks in Kerala. Most of the respondents knew about ESAF for its easy process of sanctioning loans and repayment schedule. They perceived that the transition from an MFI into an SFB might help them access more financial services. The author found that the overall satisfaction level with SFBs is moderate.

Jayadev et al. (2017) presented that, due to mandatory norms and statutory requirements of CRR, SFBs are facing many challenges. Ray (2016) focused on the need for financial inclusion, issues, challenges, and RBI guidelines for small finance banks, and also presented the case study of Ujjivan Financial Services Limited. In the study, he also highlighted that small finance banks have great potential for financial inclusion, but the performance of these institutions has not been satisfactory.

The success of financial inclusion highly depends on financial literacy. The support of small finance banks can help the government to organise workshops to financially educate people. As a financial intermediary, the small bank can bring the financially excluded sections of the economy under the organised financial system of the economy. It is a win-win situation for both counterparts, small finance banks and the government. It creates new opportunities to expand their operations and grow their brand value in unserved sectors and target niche sectors. On the other hand, the government is also able to implement its policies successfully.

It is found that there is literature on SFBs and cooperative societies separately; however, there is a dearth of literature on which model is more successful in delivering financial literacy for financial inclusion in the Indian context. The main focus of this chapter is to study the financial literacy programme practised by ESAF, a small finance bank, and by AMCCSL, a multistate credit cooperative society, comparatively. In this context, the chapter tries to analyse the differences between these two MFIs and their contributions in terms of the profile of customers, products, financial literacy models, delivery processes of financial literacy, and which model is suitable for marginalised section of customers for financial inclusion. This study can be used for the successful implementation of financial literacy models by other MFIs.

3 Objectives and Methodology

The broad objective of the study is to explore the financial literacy initiatives of a cooperative society and an SFB in India. The specific objectives are as follows:

- To explore the financial literacy initiatives of ESAF Small Finance Bank.
- To explore the financial literacy initiatives of AMCCSL.
- To analyse the differences between AMCCSL and ESAF in providing financial literacy.

It is an explorative study, so qualitative research methodology is adopted. It helps to gain an in-depth understanding of the financial literacy initiatives of AMCCSL, a Credit Cooperative Society, and ESAF, a Small Finance Bank (SFB), the module used, the pedagogy employed to deliver the content, the processes in place for conducting financial literacy initiatives, the feedback from the customers, and their perception and retention of the concepts learned from these modules. The case study method is used to examine the holistic and meaningful characteristics of the financial literacy initiatives of these credit cooperative society and small finance bank to gain a deep insight into the objectives stated above in their entirety, covering every aspect from conceptualisation to delivery, feedback, and follow-up.

3.1 Data Collection and Analysis

The primary data was collected through in-depth physical and virtual interviews from the respondents of Nagpur (ESAF Small Finance Bank) and Pune (AMCCSL). Interviews were electronically recorded after obtaining permission from the respondents. In cases where participants were not given permission to record the interviews by the studied-organisation, the interviews were transcribed after the interview was conducted. All the interviews were carried out during the official working hours of AMCCSL and ESAF at their branch offices and field offices. Interviews were conducted in Hindi and English. The interviews were transcribed and coded. From the codes, themes were generated, and thematic analysis is presented in Sect. 5.

4 Case Studies of ESAF and AMCCSL

In this section, two case studies of a small finance bank, ESAF, and a cooperative society, Annapurna Mahila Multistate Cooperative Credit Society, are presented to understand their journey, the financial products offered by them, the profile of their customers, and their financial literacy programmes (Table 1).

4.1 Case Study 1: ESAF Small Finance Bank

4.1.1 About ESAF

ESAF Society was launched with a vision of sustainable holistic transformation of the poor and the marginalised in the year 1992, in a small house named 'Little' at Thrissur, Kerala. The exemplary success of Grameen Bank in Bangladesh had

Table 1 Financial profile of ESAF and AMCCSL as of 2023–24

Variable	ESAF (in Rs.)	AMCCSL (in Rs.)
Gross loan portfolio	1,96,593,560,000	1,35,25,13,432
Profit after tax	4,255,680,000	2,54,25,679
Total asset	2,60,868,820,000	2,51,39,43,749

Source Audited Financial Report of MCCSL and ESAF Small Finance Bank

reinforced the vision of K. Paul Thomas, the Founder and Managing Director of ESAF, of changing lives through micro finance. In 1995, he launched Micro Enterprises Development Services, which resulted in the formation of ESAF Microfinance and Investments Pvt. Ltd., in 2008. The increased focus on micro-finance was inevitable, as the founder was clear in his understanding of the importance of the financial component in the holistic economic development of the poor by fighting the partiality of prosperity.

In 2015, the Reserve Bank of India, the financial regulator in the country, granted an in-principle licence to ESAF to launch a Small Finance Bank. ESAF Small Finance Bank was one amongst the ten NBFCs to receive an 'in principle' approval from the Reserve Bank of India (RBI) to set up a Small Finance Bank in the private sector. ESAF Small Finance Bank was incorporated on May 05, 2016, with its registered office in Thrissur.

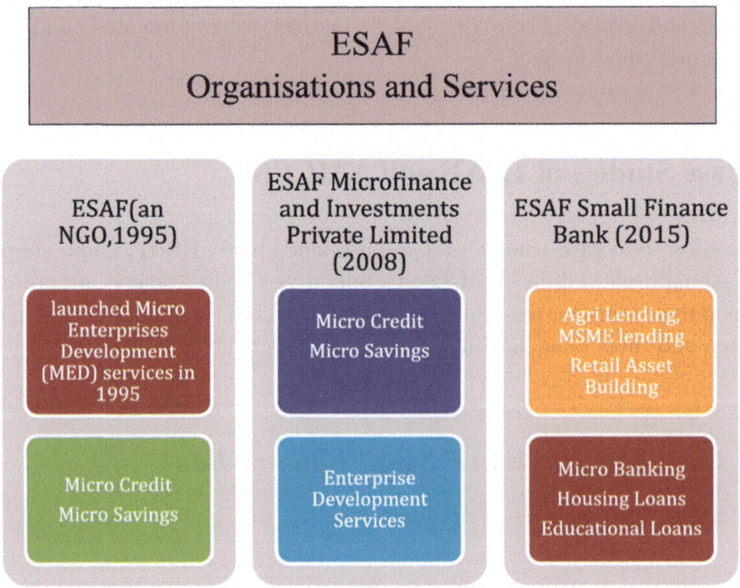

Source Primary Data collected by the Authors

4.1.2 Products and Services Offered

ESAF is offering several microfinance services to the marginalised sections of society. It provides a variety of savings accounts to suit the needs of different types of customers, such as senior citizens, women (mahila), and students. Pradhan Mantri Jan Dhan Yojana, along with regular and premium savings accounts, is also offered. The interest rate is 4%, calculated on the end-of-the-day balance and credited to the accounts on a quarterly basis. Tailor-made accounts for the business requirements of customers, such as basic, classic, premium, and diamond current accounts, are offered. Regular and tax-saver fixed deposit (FD) accounts are provided at the highest interest rate of 8.75% per annum, with an additional 0.5% for senior citizens. Under the Hrudaya Deposits scheme, any person can make a minimum investment of Rs.15 lakhs, which is then extended to benefit the lowest strata of society. ESAF also offers regular, flexible, and group-based recurring deposits (RD) to facilitate small savings, with the highest interest rate being 8.75% per annum and an additional 0.5% for senior citizens. Clean energy product loans are available for the purchase of solar-based power generators, biomass-based power generators, and non-conventional energy-based public utilities, such as lighting systems, solar inverters, etc. For all agricultural activities, including ancillary activities like the purchase of implements, developmental activities undertaken on farms, vermi-composting, and undertaking farm work for farmers on a contract basis, etc. ESAF Haritha loans are offered. It also provides loans against property as a mortgage. These loans are offered against property for various purposes, such as business, education, marriage, asset purchase, etc. Furthermore, ESAF offers business loans for various business purposes, including the purchase of assets, business expansion, working capital requirements, agriculture and allied agricultural products, and any other income-generating activities.

Also, ESAF offers loans for housing, i.e., for the purchase of a constructed house/flat, new house construction, renovation, and extensions—incremental/progressive constructions. Micro Banking—includes products and services for advancing financial inclusion through door step services. For customers who are to undertake any new or expanding lawful micro-enterprise activity conducted by self or by family members, income generation loans are offered. For current customers availing of micro banking services who require higher loans for their business, business loans are offered. Ultra-poor loans are designed for rural areas where the loan requirement is less than Rs. 10,000 for undertaking any micro business. Vidya Jyothi Loans are offered for meeting the education expenses of SHG members' children, including tuition fees, sponsoring laptops, and non-tuition fees. For meeting the costs of constructing hygienic toilets and for the cost of requisite material, construction, and labour, Nirmal Jeebandhara loans are offered. Micro energy loans are offered for accessing clean energy products like solar lamps, energy-efficient cooking stoves, water purifiers, etc., among members for a better, environmentally friendly life. Loans provided for any purpose or for top-up loans are broadly categorised under general loans. Under the PM Jan Dhan Yojana Account, BSBDA,[5] account with a debit card is issued to account openers with no requirement of keeping a minimum balance.

4.1.3 Profile of the Customers

A majority of the clientele consists of people who are deprived of the benefits of the formal banking system and require small loan amounts. These include vegetable sellers, SHG group members, and small-scale business owners. ESAF's client base comprises over 99% women. Around 85% of the clients hail from rural areas, of which 100% are women. Among them, 30% belong to religious minorities, 24% are from backward communities, 58% are from Other Backward Communities (OBCs), and 1% of the clients are physically challenged.

Currently, ESAF has Ultra Small Branches (i.e., existing MFI branches) in 93 districts across ten states in India, viz. Chhattisgarh, Jharkhand, Karnataka, Kerala, Madhya Pradesh, West Bengal, Maharashtra, Bihar, Tamil Nadu, and Puducherry.

4.1.4 Financial Literacy Initiatives

Customer Financial Capability Building Programme: During the year, the retail and Ultra Small Branches (USB) conduct several financial literacy sessions for their existing women customers. It is a 45-minute to 60-minute session where various concepts of basic financial literacy are covered. Each branch generally conducts one such session per month, which is attended by a minimum of 80 to a maximum of 200 members of the bank.

The Senior Citizen's Week: A get-together opportunity for senior citizens to socialise is used to educate the participants on the latest financial products and caution them about the importance of precautions and protections needed in financial dealings.

The Balajyothi-Children's Week: Under this initiative, lectures are conducted at schools near selected branches. The program, titled 'Money, Me and my Bank' provides financial education to children. Post the session, children open Balajyothi Accounts and are given a 'Savings Box' inscribed with the words ESAF SFB—My First Bank. ESAF also conducts different activities, such as drawing competitions and essay competitions for the children.

- More than 24,000 children participated in a financial education program.
- 2516 children participated in the essay competition.
- 7444 children participated in the drawing competition.

[5] It is defined as undertaking financial planning and a tendency to consume and save.

4.1.5 Details of the Financial Literacy Sessions

The major focus of financial literacy initiatives is on people needing small finances, such as vegetable sellers, SHG group members, and small-scale business owners, who are also the major customers of the banks. Giving loans is not the agenda of these sessions. The main agenda is to encourage customers to save at the bank instead of at home or other places. The session lasts for 45 minutes to one hour. The module used is prepared by the central branch and distributed across all the branches. The financial literacy sessions are attended by the existing members only, not their other family members, like spouses, as it is exclusively for their target segment, which is women. Each branch has approximately 2000 members or more. Thus, the branch decides on a venue, such as community meeting spaces like Baudh Vihar or Sanskritik Bhavan, where all the SHG groups of that area are invited to attend the session. The target of the branch is to organise one such session every month in the area based on need. The branch decides the time and place for the session, and then the awareness department conducts the session. The message for the upcoming sessions is communicated through the staff on the day of disbursement/collection to the clients. The session is attended by approximately a minimum of 80–100 members and a maximum of 200 members. The trainer is an employee of the organisation and thus is not paid separately. The trainer looks exclusively into the awareness sessions. Ex-bank employees or existing reputed bank employees from other branches are also invited to give detailed explanations based on their experience. Discussions on various government schemes, like Atal Pension Yojana (APY),[6] Pradhan Mantri Jeevan Jyoti Bima Yojana (PMJJBY),[7] etc., and other topics that are missed are covered by the visiting guests. The budget allocated for each session is Rs. 10,000, which is used to pay the rent for the community hall, speakers, refreshments, carpets/chairs on rent, and projectors. An entry is made in the register by the people attending it, and it is maintained at the branch office. No collaterals, like financial diaries or piggy banks, are given by the bank. If there are multiple questions after the sessions, the attendees are encouraged to ask the staff who meet them every week. A feedback form is given randomly to 20–25 women from the branch, which includes general questions. However, this is not being implemented everywhere. As of now, there is no follow-up after these sessions. From next year, with the use of unique client IDs, follow-ups would be pursued based on the ID. For example, if a client ID with No. 303 says in the financial literacy session that she wants to open an RD, it would then be checked in the system if she has opened the RD or not, and based on this, a follow-up would be taken. From next year, with the creation of the ID, the awareness department would also aid the branches in tracking improvements in repayment, increases in savings amounts, opening of RDs, etc., through the unique client ID

---

[6] A pension scheme for Indian citizens. It's designed to help workers in the unorganized sector.

[7] It is a life insurance scheme that was announced by the Government of India in the 2015–16 budget. The scheme offers a life insurance cover of Rs. 2 lakhs for any reason of death.

after the financial literacy sessions. All the women are offered savings products as well. The attitude of women is very positive towards these sessions. However, there is no way to ensure 100% attendance of the SHG members who are invited, as the session takes place in the afternoon, and thus, many women who leave in the morning for work miss out on the sessions. Other women attending the session are requested to share their learnings with the other members of the group. Various other programmes like skill development, entrepreneurship development, capacity building, etc., are also in the pipeline to help create sustainable livelihoods for their members.

4.1.6 Topics Covered in Financial Literacy Sessions

- KYC documents are required when opening a bank account
- Importance of making a budget, savings, and responsible loan-taking
- Details about fixed deposits, recurring deposits, pension accounts, the importance of a nominee, and other document details required for the same
- Importance of timely repayment of loans to maintain a good credit score
- Brief about online banking (NEFT, RTGS, IMPS) and its benefits
- Doorstep banking through business correspondent
- Grievance redressal options at the bank branch as well as at the Banking Lokpal (an RBI initiative)
- Caution measures while banking
- Smart and careful use of ATM card
- Caution measures while making investments

4.1.7 Customer's Perception of Financial Literacy Initiatives

The customers joined ESAF to support the financial needs of their families, such as children's education, marriage, and sometimes basic survival by starting a business. This was often due to various reasons like the loss of the husband's job, the husband's death, or to meet the growing financial needs of the family, including children's education and marriage. They made humble beginnings with loan amounts of Rs. 8000–Rs. 10000 and started businesses like tailoring, selling bangles and accessories, providing tiffin services, running grocery stores, and selling pickles and papads.[8] Tailoring was the most pursued business among the customers. Over the years, the loan amounts have increased significantly for most of the women, currently ranging from Rs. 100,000 to Rs. 250,000. Most of the women were middle-aged and had either passed 12th grade or completed graduation. All the women, except those who had joined recently, had attended the financial literacy programme. The most remembered concept from the financial

[8] Papadis a snack that originated in the Indian subcontinent.

literacy session was how to use an ATM card and the precautionary measures to be taken while using it. Younger women, compared to the older women in the sample, could use the ATM card by themselves without support from others, whereas older women often needed the assistance of a family member to withdraw money. However, it could not be clarified whether they were able to use the ATM card confidently after the financial literacy sessions or due to other reasons. The importance of saving with the bank was the second most remembered topic. Only two women maintained budget diaries to regularly note down household expenditures. Other women believed that it was all in their minds and well managed there, thus writing it in a diary was not considered essential. Some women preferred saving first before buying expensive items like a fridge, TV, sewing machine, mobile phone, or two-wheeler, while most of them preferred buying on instalments due to the deferred payment facility, despite paying an additional amount, as it did not hit their pockets all at once. Savings accounts and recurring deposits (RDs) are still the preferred modes of saving. However, they held these accounts with other banks, as these micro-lending branches are yet to be converted into SFBs. Thus, they maintained these accounts with other scheduled and cooperative banks that collected RD money from their doorstep. They preferred long-term RDs of three to five years and were unaware of the interest rates and the final amount due to be received by them. Financial decisions, in some cases, are made by the woman herself or jointly with her husband. If the children are grown up and settled, they are also included in decision-making. Most of the women demanded higher loans to expand their businesses and the provision of all services, like savings and RDs, under one roof.

4.2 *Case Study 2: Annapurna Mahila Multistate Cooperative Credit Society*

4.2.1 About AMCCSL

The oldest form of microfinance institutions is cooperative societies. Annapurna Mahila Multistate Cooperative Credit Society is one of them. It is a part of Annapurna Pariwar, a group of six non-profit organisations working for the empowerment of the poor with different services. Under the leadership of Dr. Medha Purao Samant, in 1986, Annapurna Cooperative Society was registered as the State Cooperative Society in Maharashtra. In 1997, it was renamed Annapurna Mahila Multi-State Co-operative Credit Society Limited (AMCCSL) and was registered under the Multi-State Cooperative Act, 1984. The main aim of AMCCSL was to empower the marginalised section of women. Most of the member-borrowers are from slums and are illiterate or semi-literate. Along with microfinance, capacity building of the members is the major focus of AMCCSL.

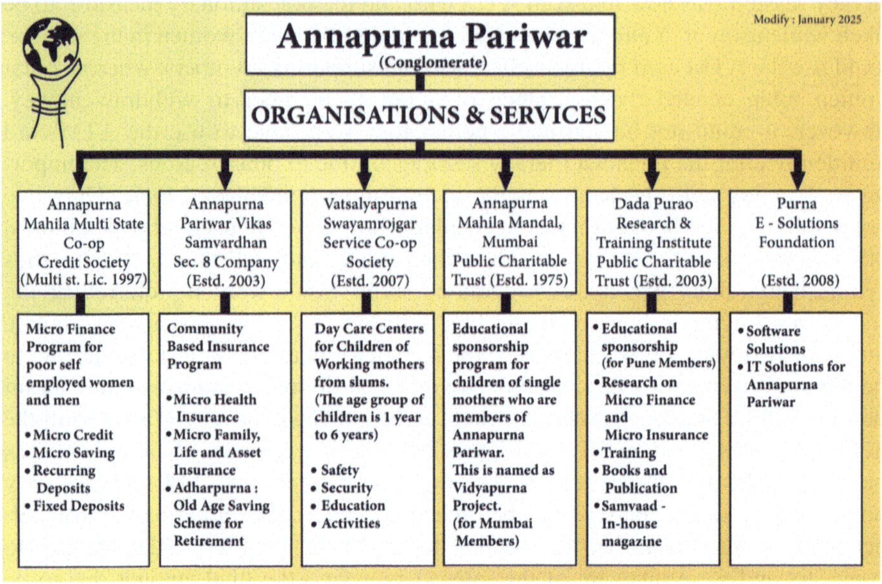

Source Organogram collected by the Authors from Dr. Medha Samant, CMD, Annapurna Pariwar.

Annapurna Pariwar consists of six sister organisations: Annapurna Mahila Multi State Co-op Credit Society, Annapurna Pariwar Vikas Samvardhan Section 8 Companies, Vatsalyapurna Swauamrojgar Service Co-op Society, Annapurna Mahila Mandal Charitable Trust, Dada Purao Research & Training Institute Public Charitable Trust, and Purna E-solutions Foundation. The authors, in their previous article, have analysed that Annapurna Pariwar adopted the approach of serial social entrepreneurship to address social problems. Each of the organisations under the Annapurna Pariwar was created to deal with the complex social issues of the urban slums in Pune and Mumbai (Guha et al., 2021).

Presently, AMCCSL is providing micro loans and micro savings to its members. Loans include productive loans, loans for housing, loans for repayment of past debts, loans for asset creation, education loans, etc. Savings include compulsory savings with every loan and voluntary savings such as recurring deposits and fixed deposits. AMCCSL has adopted innovative practices such as community meetings, financial literacy training, and an annual general meeting for the successful functioning of the organisation. Further, Adharpurna, a pension programme of Annapurna Pariwar, is a long-term recurring saving programme that provides a payout like a pension upon retirement. It was started by AMCCSL in 2016, and by 2024, member enrolment is 34,000. The accumulated fund is Rs. 26 crores.

4.2.2 Profile of the Member—Borrowers

The member-borrowers of AMCCSL are from the slums of Pune and Mumbai city. Most of them are illiterate or semi-literate. They are vegetable vendors, domestic help, piece-rate workers, and small business owners. Member-borrowers have taken loans repetitively. Over time, they graduated from basic loans to SME loans as well. Basic loans range between Rs. 55,000 and Rs. 2,00,000, and SME loans range between Rs0. 2,00,000 and Rs. 20,00,000. As of 2022–23, in Pune, 67,748 members saved Rs. 40,56,00,842, and in Mumbai, 56,795 members saved Rs. 28,53,57,943.

4.2.3 Financial Literacy Programme of AMCCSL

AMCCSL is serving the poor, marginalised section in the slums. Most of the customers are semi-literate. Since its inception, AMCCSL has been imparting financial literacy to its member-borrowers. They have innovatively developed processes and products for the members. It is observed that financial literacy has gained attention from every corner, such as government agencies, banking organisations, non-banking financial companies, non-governmental organisations (NGOs), and many other organisations such as cooperatives, community-based organisations, etc.

The staff of AMCCSL perceived that financial literacy is a part of their daily activities, as each member of AMCCSL makes financial decisions every day. It is their responsibility to make the members aware of the legitimate uses of the money they lend. The approach of AMCCSL is very focused, and they enable the members to make informed decisions. The financial literacy programme of AMCCSL aims at educating its member-borrowers. Through this programme they helped members in capacity building, which led to improvements in their credit worthiness and human values as well. It is important to study the innovative educational materials developed by AMCCSL for its member-borrowers and the process of training. To understand the role of AMCCSL, learning the delivery mechanism of financial literacy adopted by AMCCSL is essential.

Education Material

Dr. Medha Purao Samant, CMD of Annapurna Pariwar, is known for her innovative ideas in every sphere of microfinance delivery. She has designed innovative products and developed very simple financial literacy materials, as most of the member-borrowers belong to marginalised sections of society and have a lower level of education.

Flashcards for Member-Borrowers
As we know, for people with less education, pictorial representation of any concept is easily understandable. Initially, AMCCSL developed flash cards as educational tools to teach member-borrowers different concepts related to financial literacy, such as various financial products. These cards are self-explanatory. Field staff conduct literacy sessions where they show the photos on the flash cards, and the content on the opposite side is used by the staff to explain the concepts. These cards are spirally bound materials. Generally, they use these cards to teach concepts of savings, loans, insurance, and pensions. The staffs of AMCCSL have found that these cards are very useful and impactful. For every product, AMCCSL has created one card.

Flyers for Members
Flyers are designed to disseminate knowledge about the process of AMCCSL. They include guidelines for every activity, starting from group formation to the insurance claim. Each process is clearly outlined. Every time field executives meet members at their doorstep, they explain the updated information. AMCCSL has innovatively used different colour codes for each product's information in the flyer. Members are trained to file every document shared by AMCCSL in safe custody.

Manuals for Staff
In AMCCSL, every staff member has been going through a training programme. They are provided with manuals as per their job descriptions. These manuals contain guidelines about all the products and processes. Staff members use the manuals as a ready reference for any product or process-related queries. Manuals are updated regularly to include changes regarding the products and processes, if any. Other methods of training include posters or flexes on the wall, conducting drama, role play, and showing films.

Videos
AMCCSL has adopted digital technology for its training programmes and operations. It has started using audio-visual media for financial literacy training. They have installed LCD television sets in every branch, and video recordings are kept loaded on the LCD television sets. Since these video recordings are created by the senior staff members of AMCCSL, members easily relate to them while watching the videos. The length of the videos is never kept longer than 30 minutes, as the attention span of less literate members is low. It also varies according to the information being provided. Each video contains comprehensive content that covers all the related information about a particular product or process. Sometimes, documented success stories of fellow member-entrepreneurs are shown to the members. To make members aware about the fraudulent schemes of financial activities, awareness-based video clips, along with examples, are shown to them for better clarity (Bhandare, 2017).

4.2.4 Process and Protocols

With such exhaustive educational material, AMCCSL has the responsibility to educate its members in an effective manner. It has developed a process to facilitate financial literacy for its members. They have set certain protocols for the members. A researcher of microfinance, Bhandare (2017), mentioned that for loan disbursement, each member should be present at the branch along with a relative, adult family member, or spouse to act as the guarantor and witness of the loan disbursement. This is mandatory, and it is shown in a video played in the community office to all the members and their family members.

Like other MFIs, AMCCSL conducts monthly meetings for the group members both at their residences and at the branch. Community meetings are conducted at the branch for the review of group performances and health insurance claims, if any. Financial literacy training is also conducted at the branch for the respective groups one or two months before the closure of their loan. Every member of the respective group must attend this meeting personally, as the attendance for this meeting will be considered for the group review. It is important for the members to attend such meetings, as their next loan (higher amount) will be decided based on their attendance. Every member has been provided with a Radio-Frequency Identification (RFID)-enabled identity card, and attendance for every meeting is recorded in the system itself. Such protocols are designed by AMCCSL to automate the process. During the loan repayment recovery meeting, all the group members are required to be present at one of the members' homes.

4.2.5 Delivery of Financial Education

Financial literacy training programmes for the members are conducted at respective branches. Executives from the head office come and facilitate the programme at the branch. After the session, queries and questions from the members are discussed. This financial literacy meeting is conducted for the members who are taking a loan for the second time and onwards. Similarly, in community meetings, some officials from the head office visit the branch and address the member-customers. Along with these meetings at branches, field executives of each respective branch repeat counselling sessions at the member's residences as and when required. The branch manager also joins the team to speak to the members and counsel them on various financial issues if it is necessary. Auditors and service executive managers often visit the field to make the members aware of financial literacy on micro insurance and to counsel members on process-related matters.

5 Thematic Analysis

After the collection of the data, it was transcribed, and a manual coding method was adopted to generate the themes for thematic analysis. In this section, thematic analysis is presented, and a discussion based on the analysis is performed to address the objective.

5.1 Different Structures of Programme Implementation Adopted by ESAF and AMCCSL

ESAF and AMCCSL, both the organisations had the opportunity to transform into small finance banks as both started their journey in the 1990s, have a long history of providing micro-financial services, and both of them were approached by the banks to become SFBs. However, from the journey of both organisations, it is clear that the objective of choosing two legal forms respectively is different. Though both want to work for the marginalised section, ESAF opted for a small finance bank to serve a large number of clients, whereas AMCCSL opted for a multistate cooperative society to provide ownership to the member-borrowers. Ownership of the marginalised section is perceived as a tool for empowerment.

ESAF has undergone the transition from an NGO to an NBFC-MFI and then to a small finance bank between 1995 and 2015. The purpose is to serve a greater number of people from marginalised sections and provide focused financial literacy training. Whereas AMCCSL transitioned from a State Cooperative Society to a Multi-State Credit Cooperative Society between 1986 and 1997, as this organisation aimed to provide ownership along with financial literacy training to the marginalised sections in urban slums. Both organisations have different objectives:—ESAF worked on horizontal scaling up, whereas AMCCSL worked on vertical scaling up. Here, horizontal scaling up means increasing outreach in terms of the number of members, and vertical scaling up means increasing the number of services provided to the same number of members.

5.2 Innovative Training Programmes for Financial Literacy

Both the organisations designed very innovative training programmes for financial literacy; however, their processes are different. ESAF organises one financial literacy training session for all customers of the branch per month. In this programme, the family members of the customers are not allowed. In the case of AMCCSL, financial literacy training is part of everyday work. As the customers are semi-literate or illiterate, the staffs of AMCCSL think that financial literacy should be imparted every day, as these members have to make financial decisions daily. In the monthly meeting, family members are allowed to attend the financial literacy sessions. It can be concluded that AMCCSL implemented financial literacy training in a holistic way, where not only members but their family members are included in the training programme whereas ESAF is only concerned about its customers' financial literacy training.

ESAF designed financial literacy workshops for different age categories, such as women, children, and senior citizens, and each category has a different pedagogy. They have also used street plays, skits, and movies for the workshops on financial literacy. AMCCSL designed innovative educational materials as their members are semi-literate, they have used pictorial flashcards for financial literacy training. Additionally, they have used several videos of AMCCSL staff and members so that participants can accustom with the financial situations of the staff members who are from their community. Both the organisations used flyers of instructions regarding the processes. Due to the different backgrounds of the customers, both the organisations have adopted different methods.

5.3 *Trainers are Different for ESAF and AMCCSL*

In ESAF, the trainers are people from within the organisation who work in their CSR wing or are a part of the Awareness Departments, focusing on different training and capacity-building initiatives. Every trainer has a specified area assigned to him/her, and all the training conducted in that area is done by that particular employee. Guest speakers, who are retired employees of the organisation, banks, and other authorities, are invited to the sessions to cover topics other than the ones included in the module. In this case, one-to-one discussion is not possible. Listening to senior officials of the organisation would also motivate the customers to listen to the lecture carefully. The retired employees also put in their best efforts to provide relevant information in the session, as being invited to the session as a speaker is a symbol of respect and reverence by ESAF.

At AMCCSL, financial literacy training is conducted by field staff, and these staffs are trained by the managerial staff at the head office. They are equipped with audio visuals, flyers, posters, and flexes. As the field staffs are from the same communities as the member-borrowers, it is beneficial for them to understand the concepts from them. These staff also helps the member-borrowers in their everyday financial planning by giving examples from their context. AMCCSL prefers to depend on the internal staff as they engage in the daily activities of AMCCSL and know the customers well. This solves the problem of information asymmetry. Furthermore, it helps the staff to create tailor-made programmes for the member-borrowers.

It is observed that AMCCSL members are advised to maintain the reading materials on financial literacy, which they have received during the training. However, in ESAF, no information was gathered on the maintenance of a register to track the number of people attending the session. Maintaining a register would help in the follow-up exercise to understand if the customers have started using any of the products and services based on the financial knowledge and awareness created during the session.

5.4 Differences in Topics Chosen by AMCCSL and ESAF

It is found that two organisations during the pedagogy development, chose different topics for financial literacy training. In ESAF, topics include information on different government schemes, bank schemes, their experiences in the sector, etc. This helps the participants gain expert knowledge on these topics and opens them up to new information relevant to them. Whereas AMCCSL includes training on financial decision-making along with information about financial products, fraudulent financial products, financial processes, etc. AMCCSL staff mentioned that financial literacy training is part of their everyday work. As the members are from marginalised backgrounds, it is crucial to facilitate them in making financial decisions. Even auditors also conduct field visits to explain the importance of microinsurance products and their processes.

5.5 Development of Process and Tools for Impact Measurement of Financial Literacy Camps

There are no existing processes in place for the evaluation of the financial literacy sessions. There is an immediate question and answer round post the sessions to address the doubts of the participants and gather feedback for the session. However, a structured process and tools need to be developed and followed by ESAF to measure the impact of these initiatives and understand if the objective of conducting financial literacy camps is being met. Since the modules cover the concepts required to measure financial literacy levels, as discussed above, there is no mechanism to measure the level of financial literacy of participants either immediately after the sessions or after a certain interval. Measuring financial literacy levels before and after the sessions may enable quantifying the impact of these sessions on the financial literacy levels of the participants.

In the case of AMCCSL, financial literacy training is conducted in branch offices. After each session, members pose their questions, and executives discuss each of them. In the community meetings, a few executives from the head office attend, and they address the member-borrowers. Field officials also provide counselling at the doorstep whenever the members are facing financial challenges. So, staffs from the head office to the field office are engaged in financial literacy training, and there are several follow-ups happening at the community meetings and at the doorstep of the members. Higher officials like auditors and service managers visit the field to make the members aware of microinsurance and counsel them on the processes. Also, each of the members is given Radio-Frequency Identification (RFID)-enabled identity cards, which track their attendance in the financial literacy training meetings.

6 Discussion and Conclusions

In this study, the oldest form of MFIs, a multistate Credit Cooperative Society, AMCCSL, and the recent form of MFIs, a small finance bank, ESAF, have been considered to conduct a comparative study on the financial literacy programmes of these organisations. Financial literacy is a tool for financial inclusion. It is found that different structures of MFIs, such as SFB and cooperative society, have adopted different pedagogy and processes. For the dissemination of financial literacy, several methods and channels, such as basic education, social media, workshops, community meetings, etc., have been identified and are being used. This is supported by Kumari and Viz (2013). There is a distinct difference between these two institutions in perceiving the financial literacy programme. AMCCSL considers financial literacy as part of their day-to-day activity, whereas ESAF considers financial literacy to be delivered as per RBI norms once a month in each branch for all customers of the branch. They conceptualised different financial literacy programmes for different customers, such as senior citizens, micro-entrepreneurs, SHG members, etc. In this context, Srinivasan (2013) studied that the major aim behind the setting up of small finance banks is to promote financial inclusion through financial literacy, as there is theoretical evidence that they will be better able to transmit financial literacy among their clients. Further, Mohanty (2018) analysed that small financial banks have huge potential in unbanked and underserved areas and play a major role in the development of the micro, small, and medium enterprises sector. Ray (2016) acknowledged the potential of SFBs, but he analysed that the performance of these institutions has not been satisfactory. In our study, we have found that in AMCCSL, from the head office to the field staff, all are engaged in the delivery of financial literacy. However, in ESAF, some internal managers and retired bank managers are involved in it, and the time duration for the training is shorter in the case of ESAF. There are no follow-up sessions organised by ESAF, whereas in AMCCSL, after the training in branch offices, field staff conduct follow-ups at the doorsteps of the member-borrowers. It is recommended that ESAF requires a robust documentation and reporting system for the workshops conducted.

In AMCCSL, most of the members are from the marginalised sections of the urban slums. So, they adopted the tool of pictorial representation of the concepts of financial products and processes. This process helped the staff of AMCCSL to empower the community financially (Mitra, 2014). In ESAF, clients are from every income class. So, they considered several topics related to bank-products and banking norms rather than financial education about how to manage their financial resources and make financial decisions. One-to-one discussion was not considered. Perhaps the majority of the clients are from the middle-income class, who do not need basic financial education. It is discerned from the analysis that cooperative societies have more capability to work for the marginalised sections of society to empower them financially. This outcome of the research is similar to Anandaram and Dubhashi (1999). They recommended that the cooperative movement needs to be strengthened, as rural and urban areas both need to have a strong cooperative movement in the context of liberalisation where inequality is rising. AMCCSL also trained their officials to deliver financial literacy to the member borrowers. This is recommended by Aryal and Panta (2015) in their study, where they suggested a policy for financial literacy programmes for cooperative executives. These executives can then make business decisions efficiently for the cooperatives, which might lead to higher income for the cooperatives. This, in turn, will translate to the welfare of the cooperative members.

It is also found that ESAF has gone through several transitions, from NGO to NBFC-MFIs to SFB, whereas the structure of AMCCSL still remains a cooperative society. So, the pressure of transition was less in the case of AMCCSL. Though the rules and regulations under the Ministry of Cooperation have changed a lot, the main aim remains the same. In the case of ESAF, due to changes in the structure, the rules and regulations under each structure were different, and to settle under the SFB structure, ESAF is facing challenges in delivering the financial literacy programme to different segments of customers as per RBI norms. So, the transition from a non-regulatory structure to a highly regulatory structure requires more time to develop pedagogy and implement financial literacy programmes.

In a nutshell, both the organisations have different roles to play in financial inclusion. While the financial literacy model of AMCCSL has the potential to financially educate the marginalised sections of society, the financial literacy training of ESAF is beneficial for bank customers. This training helps customers understand various banking products, government schemes, KYC norms, banking fraud, etc., which enables them to make informed decisions. Their initiatives for children are noteworthy, as they help children understand the need of financial management at an early age.

Annexure

See Fig. 1.

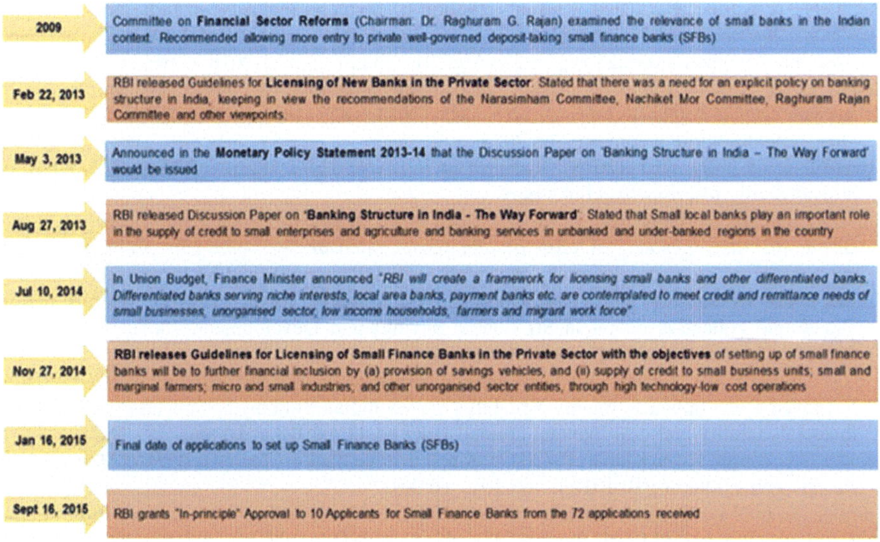

Fig. 1 Banking sector reforms and the creation of small finance banks. *Source* Reserve Bank of India

References

Abijith, S., & Raghavendra, N. (2018). An Empirical study on selected small finance bank in Mysuru with reference to micro, small and medium enterprises. *International Journal of Mechanical Engineering and Technology*, *9*(11), 723–731.

Agarwalla, S. K., Barua, S. K., Jacob, J., & Varma, J. R. (2013). Financial literacy among working young in Urban India. *IIM A, W.P. No. 2013-10-02*, 1–27.

Agarwalla, S. K., Barua, S. K., Jacob, J., & Varma, J. R. (2015). Financial literacy among working young in Urban India, development. *Elsevier*, *67*(C), 101–109.

Anandaram, K. S., & Dubhashi, M. (1999). Role of cooperatives in social development, *Indian Journal of Industrial Relations*, *35*(1), pp. 108–113, Published by Shri Ram Centre for Industrial Relations and Human Resources.

Aryal, N., & Panta, B. S. (2015). Financial literacy and co-operatives sustainability: A study among the executive members of the co-operatives, International Journal of Community and Cooperative Studies, 3(3), pp. 17–29, September 2015, Published by European Centre for Research Training and Development UK. http://www.eajournals.org

Bhandare, P. V. (2017). *Financial literacy models and status of financial literacy in India, mimeograph* (pp. 1–120). Tata Institute of Social Sciences.

Bhargava, N. R. (2016). A study on finacial literacy and fiancial education : An overview scenario in India. *Research Journal of Management Science*, *5*(9), 51–57.

Chakrabarty, K. C. (2012). Exploring the challenge of financial education across emerging economies. *RBI Monthly Bulletin*, *2012*, 1291–1294. Viewed at http://www.rbi.org.in on 12.6.2020.

Chakrabarty, K. C. (2013). Financial inclusion in India—journey so far and way forward, Keynote address by Dr. K C Chakrabarty, Deputy Governor of the Reserve Bank of India, at the Finance Inclusion Conclave, organised by CNBC TV 18, New Delhi, 6 September 2013, pp. 1–8. Viewed at http://www.bic.org on 2.10.2019.

Dangi, N., & Kumar, P. (2013). Current situation of financial inclusion in India and its future visions. *International Journal of Management and Social Sciences Research*, 2(8). Retrieved from http://www.irjcjournals.org/ijmssr/Aug2013/23.pdf on 12.1.2018 at 10 am.

Godar, D. B. (2024). Financial literacy and saving behaviour of co-operative employees in Butwal, *Global Scientific Journal*, 12(5), May 2024, 1453–1469, retrieved from http://www.globalscientificjournal.com on 22.8.2024.

Government of India. RBI. (2015). *Websites of Banks in India*. Retrieved from RBI Website: https://rbi.org.in/scripts/banklinks.aspx

Guha, S., Samant, M. P., & Reji, E. M. (2021). *Is serial social entrepreneurship leading towards sustainable development? A case of annapurna pariwar in social entrepreneurship and sustainable development*, edited by A. Singh & E. MReji, published by Routledge.

Hulme, D., & Montgomery, R. (1994). Cooperatives, credit and the poor: Private interest, public choice and collective action in Sri Lanka, Savings and Development, *18*(3), pp. 359–382 Published by: Giordano Dell-Amore Foundation.

Indian Economy.Net. (2016). *What is financial stability and development council (FSDC)*. Retrieved from Indian Economy.Net: https://www.indianeconomy.net/splclassroom/what-is-financial-stability-and-development-council-fsdc/ on 11.4.2018 at 10 am.

Jayadev, M., Singh, H., & Kumar, P. (2017). Small finance banks: Challenges, *IIMB Management Review*, https://doi.org/10.1016/j.iimb.2017.10.001

Kamboj, S. (2014). Current scenario of financial literacy in India. *International Journal for Entrepreneurship and Small Business Management*, *1*(1), 61–68.

Kumari, S., & Viz, P. (2013). Financial literacy—An overview of growing effort. *IOSR Journal of Economics and Finance*, 79–85.

Mitra, R. (2014). Cooperatives: A democratic instrument of human empowerment. Social Scientist *November–December*, *42*(11/12), 47–70. Published by Social Scientist

Mohanty, J. J. (2018). Leveraging small financial banks (SFB) in achieving financial inclusion in India. *International Journal of Business and Management Invention (IJBMI)*, *7*(2), 8–18. Ver. III.

National Centre for Financial Education. (2015). *About NCFE*. Retrieved from https://www.ncfe.org.in/about-us on 2.1.2019 at 1 pm.

Nayituliki, A., & Munene, P. (2022). Financial literacy and business capability of women members of cooperatives in Gasabo District, Global Scientific Journals, *10*(6), June 2022, retrieved from http://www.globalscientificjournal.com on 26.8.2024.

OECD (2011), Improving financial education efficiency: OECD-bank of Italy symposium on financial literacy, OECD publishing. https://doi.org/10.1787/10.1787/9789264108219-en on 13.6.2018, pp. 1–152.

OECD International Network on Financial Education. (2008). *OECD international gateway for financial education*. Retrieved from http://www.financial-education.org/join_infe.html on 12.6.2017 at 1 pm.

Ray, P. (2016). Proceeding of the first American academic research conference on global business, Economics, Finance and Social Sciences (AAR16 New York Conference) ISBN: 978-1943579-50-1 New York, USA. 25–28 May, 2016. Paper ID: N624.

Srinivasan, R. (2013). An introspection of the impact of Indian financial literacy programmes on financial inclusion. *IOSR Journal of Business and Management*, 1–6.

Viswan, M. G. (2017). A study on the awareness and perception about small finance bank with special reference to ESAF small finance bank, *6*(4), SSN-2277-1166.

Building Social Safety Nets: Community Based Micro-Insurance at Annapurna Pariwar

Kanish Debnath

Abstract This chapter provides an updated overview of the global landscape of micro-insurance with a focus on life and health micro-insurance. Micro-insurance, designed to serve low-income populations, plays a crucial role in providing financial protection to vulnerable communities, especially in developing countries. In particular, this chapter will delve into the beneficial features of Annapurna Pariwar's insurance model, which can be recognised as an exemplary case in the micro-insurance industry. Annapurna Pariwar's approach is unique in its ability to offer affordable and accessible health coverage to underserved populations, ensuring that even those with limited financial resources can receive the care they need. The chapter will highlight the key attributes of this program, such as its premium structures, including family members of the beneficiary, comprehensive coverage, and community-driven approach. These characteristics contribute to the sustainability and long-term success of Annapurna Pariwar's health insurance program, making it a valuable case study for other initiatives. Finally, the chapter concludes by drawing important lessons from Annapurna Pariwar's model, offering insights for future micro-insurance programs aiming to replicate its success. These lessons will serve as a guide for policymakers, insurance providers, and development organisations seeking to design and implement sustainable micro-insurance solutions that effectively address the healthcare needs of low-income populations.

This work represents an updated version of a chapter from my Doctoral Thesis (The role of community health insurance in perfecting financial inclusion, Indian Institute of Management Ahmedabad, 2016). Additionally, I authored a more detailed and accessible book intended for a broader audience (Community based health insurance: Planting a seed for tomorrow's need, Dada Purao Research & Training Institute, 2017).

K. Debnath (✉)
MYRA School of Business, Mysuru, Karnataka, India
e-mail: kanish.iimahd@gmail.com

J. D. Ranadive, S. Guha (eds.), *Building Pathways to Women's Empowerment*, India Studies in Business and Economics,
https://doi.org/10.1007/978-981-95-7159-8_8

1 Introduction

Explaining 'Insurance' in simple, non-technical terms presents a significant challenge. Nevertheless, such explanations are often necessary to persuade households in the lowest income bracket to adopt insurance coverage against the risks they encounter in their daily lives. Generally, insurance constitutes a legal agreement that provides financial protection against unforeseen losses to life, health, and other valuable assets over a specific period. Several studies show that it is often the economically disadvantaged who have the greatest need for insurance coverage (Osei Afriyie et al., 2022), but at the same time, these households do not demand it (Schneider, 2004). This inherent contradiction, coupled with other issues such as the heterogeneity of the population, the nature of risks, information asymmetry between the care providers and the insured, and the need for affordable premiums, prevents traditional and commercial insurance providers from offering insurance coverage to the poor. In this context, the significance of Annapurna Pariwar's community-based insurance programs can be properly understood. These insurance programs have not only served those who needed insurance the most, thereby filling a market gap, but have also managed to persuade households and create demand to become self-sustainable and have stood the test of time. This chapter will aim to cover Annapurna Pariwar's successful journey as a micro-insurance provider and draw out lessons for other Non-Governmental Organisations (NGOs), Governmental Organisations and Insurance Providers who wish to better understand this market.

The establishment of Annapurna Mahila Mandal in Mumbai in 1975 marked a significant milestone in the efforts to empower and support underprivileged women in India. Founded by Padmashree Prematai Purao and Comrade Dada Purao, this charitable trust coincided with the International Year for Women, highlighting its alignment with global initiatives for gender equality. Padmashree Prematai Purao's background as a Goan freedom fighter and her recognition as a prominent female activist in the 1960s lent credibility and experience to the organisation's mission. Her numerous national and international accolades further underscore the impact and importance of her work in advancing women's rights and welfare. Comrade Dada Purao was a well-known leader of the bank employees. He had a long term vision of connecting the poor masses to bank credit in order to bring financial stability. In furtherance of the same goal of empowerment of women in 1993, Dr. Medha Purao Samant established Annapurna Pariwar in Pune. This demonstrates the family's intergenerational commitment to social change and women's empowerment. Over the years, Annapurna Pariwar has evolved into a network of six sister development organisations, significantly broadening its reach and impact across the majority of slum areas in the Indian cities of Pune and Mumbai. This growth reflects the organisation's success in addressing the multifaceted challenges faced by impoverished women and their families in urban slums. By focusing on financial stability, educational opportunities, and health conditions, Annapurna Pariwar adopted a holistic approach to poverty alleviation and women's empowerment. This has led to tangible improvements in the lives of countless women and their families, fostering a sense of empowerment and self-reliance in these communities. Through various programmes and initiatives, Annapurna Pariwar has created a supportive ecosystem that enables women to break free from the cycle of poverty and pursue their aspirations.

At present, the diverse programs and projects at Annapurna Pariwar are managed by six sister organisations. This allocation of responsibilities has been implemented thoughtfully and strategically to ensure the efficient provision of all services. These sister organisations are enlisted below along with the vertical they handle.

1. **Micro-finance:** Annapurna Mahila Multi-State Co-operative Credit Society Limited
2. **Micro-insurance:** Annapurna Pariwar Vikas Samvardhan
3. **Children's Day Care Center:** Vatsalyapurna Service Coop Society
4. **Scholarships for education:** Dada Purao Research & Training Institute, Pune and Annapurna Mahila Mandal, Mumbai (Vidyapurna Project)
5. **Research and Training:** Dada Purao Research & Training Institute, Pune
6. **Software Solutions:** Purna E-Solutions Foundation

This chapter will further examine Annapurna Pariwar's micro-insurance programme, which is managed under the sister organisation Annapurna Pariwar Vikas Samvardhan (APVS). I shall not elaborate further on the other organisations within Annapurna Pariwar, as I am confident that other chapters in this book will comprehensively cover these entities in sufficient detail. From 2013 to 2015, as a Ph.D. scholar, I spent countless hours examining various aspects of Annapurna Pariwar's micro-insurance program and evaluating it from an academic perspective (Debnath, 2016). In this chapter, I present my analysis of the micro-insurance program updated from its earlier version in Debnath (2017). It should be noted that the objective herein is to present an evaluation of a micro-insurance programme after it achieved sustainability and inclusion by focusing on its 21-year trajectory since its inception in 2003, documenting the entire APVS experience up to 2024. The rest of the chapter is organised as follows. The subsequent section examines the differentiation between conventional insurance and micro-insurance. Section 3 explores various micro-insurance initiatives implemented in different regions over the last two decades, highlighting their unique features and target populations. Section 4 presents the study of the effectiveness of Annapurna Pariwar's micro-insurance program in providing financial protection to low-income individuals and communities. Finally, Sect. 5 concludes with lessons for MFIs, NGOs, and other institutions interested in the provision of health micro-insurance for low-income households and making the program beneficial for insured members and sustainable for all stakeholders.

2 Understanding Insurance and Micro-Insurance

Similar to credit loans, insurance is also provided through a contractual agreement between a provider and a beneficiary. This is illustrated in Fig. 1. The owner of any asset (for example, a car) approaches an insurer to obtain the insurance contract.

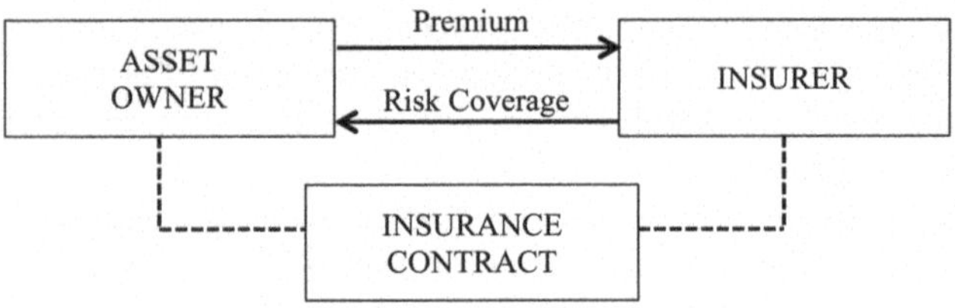

Fig. 1 An insurance contract between two parties

There are dedicated insurers for every asset. 'Health' and 'Life' of individuals are also considered as insurable assets such as a car, house or shop. The contract will state the premium, risk coverage, and duration of insurance, among others. The asset owner pays a small premium to obtain the desired risk cover for a time period. The time period is normally taken as one year for most insurance contracts.

On the surface, it may appear as a simple arrangement between the two parties. However, it is much more than that. Insurance contracts extend beyond simple agreements and encompass a complex interplay of risk assessment, financial planning, and legal obligations. Upon receiving a request from an asset owner, the insurer conducts a thorough evaluation of the asset's value, potential risks, and the asset owner's risk profile. This assessment forms the basis for determining the premium, which is essentially the price of transferring risk from the asset owner to the insurer. The premium is calculated using actuarial science, considering factors such as the likelihood of a claim being made, the potential cost of that claim, and the insurer's operational expenses. While risk assessment is also performed before the disbursement of credit loans, the liability and solvency requirements are much higher for insurers.

It is important to note that there are seven key principles of insurance that are applicable to any insurance contract. These principles form the foundation of insurance agreements and help ensure fairness and transparency between insurers and insured parties. I outline these principles below and explain them in the context of health insurance, which is arguably the most complex asset to be the insured.

1. **Principle of Utmost Good Faith:** In health insurance, both the insurer and the insured are expected to provide honest and complete information. The insured must disclose their medical history, existing health conditions, and lifestyle habits (e.g. smoking or drinking). Similarly, the insurer must clearly explain the terms, coverage, and exclusions of the policy.
2. **Principle of Insurable Interest:** This principle ensures that the policyholder has a legitimate interest in the health of the person being insured. For example, individuals can take health insurance for themselves, their spouse, children, or dependents, but not for unrelated third parties.
3. **Principle of Indemnity:** In health insurance, indemnity ensures that the policyholder is compensated only for the actual medical expenses incurred, subject to policy limits. The goal is to restore the insured to their financial position before the illness or injury without offering financial gain.

4. **Principle of Contribution:** If the policyholder has more than one health insurance policy, the principle of contribution ensures that the claims are shared proportionally among the insurers. For example, if an individual incurs medical expenses and submits claims to two insurers, both will share the liability in proportion to their coverage, preventing overcompensation.
5. **Principle of Subrogation:** After the insurer has paid the claim, they have the right to recover the expenses from a third party responsible for the insured's illness or injury. For instance, if the insured's injury was due to an accident caused by someone else's negligence, the insurer may recover costs from the at-fault party or their insurer.
6. **Principle of Loss Minimization:** The insured is expected to take reasonable steps to minimize medical expenses. For example, if someone is unwell, they should seek timely medical attention to prevent their condition from worsening. Neglecting a minor issue and allowing it to escalate may result in higher costs, which could affect coverage.
7. **Principle of Proximate Cause:** In health insurance, this principle helps determine whether a medical expense is covered under the policy by identifying the primary cause of the illness or injury. For instance, if the insured undergoes a surgery due to a pre-existing condition excluded in the policy, the claim may be denied, even if the immediate reason for the surgery appears unrelated.

These general principles hold good for both conventional insurance and micro-insurance. Insurance is used to manage unpredictable events, which other industries rarely deal with. In addition to the challenges posed by the uncertainty of the occurrence of various events, insurers have to further deal with information asymmetries and the unobserved quality of services provided to the claimant. Thus, from a for-profit insurer's perspective, there can be other requirements to be met before a health risk can be insured. These are the following:

- There must be a large number of similar individuals facing the same health risk who are willing to insure themselves and their family members.
- The health problem or illness must be accidental and not purposefully caused.
- The value of treatment and its financial compensation can be predetermined.
- The health issue should not affect multiple individuals simultaneously (i.e. it should not be catastrophic such as Covid-19).
- The demand for insurance is high, and the average loss can be managed from premium collections, leaving some room for operational expenses.
- It must be economically feasible for customers to pay the calculated premium.

In India, the economically disadvantaged population faces significant challenges in accessing health insurance (Planning Commission, 2009). This group is characterised by diverse risk profiles, often stemming from their living and working conditions, which are detrimental to their overall health. These individuals frequently reside in overcrowded, unsanitary environments and engage in physically demanding or hazardous occupations, which increases their susceptibility to various health issues. Consequently, insurance companies are hesitant to offer health coverage to this demographic because of the perceived high risk and potential financial losses. The combination of elevated health risks, limited financial resources, and the reluctance of insurers creates a significant barrier to healthcare access for India's economically disadvantaged population. This situation perpetuates a cycle of poor health outcomes and financial vulnerability, highlighting the need for innovative and inclusive health insurance solutions tailored to the unique needs of this population (Sarwal & Kumar, 2021). Community-based health micro-insurance models run by mutual insurers can address this gap in 'health risk protection' and bring in a large segment of the uninsured population under insurance coverage.[1] Table 1 highlights the distinctions in features between Micro-insurance and Conventional insurance.

Table 1 Difference of features between micro-insurance and conventional insurance

Features	Micro-insurance	Conventional insurance
Target market	For low-income households with limited insurance literacy	For medium- to high-income families possessing some awareness of insurance benefits
Product design	• Frequently characterised by single product design with rudimentary features and limited compensation coverage • Community based premium pricing on limited actuarial data	• More complex financial products are available with multiple features such as savings, investment, retirement planning, etc. • Risk based pricing driven by multiple parameters and data
Marketing	Usually sold as combined product with micro-credit through MFIs and NGOs	Employs conventional licensed channels—agents, banks, internet and other sources
Enrolment	• Simple processes with limited or no screening; fewer exclusions • Basic documents to ascertain identity of individuals	• Comprehensive process with multiple screenings and exclusions • Multiple documents to ascertain identity and age of persons
Policy manuals	• Simple policy language with minimal or no exclusions • May allow delayed or irregular premium payments	• Complex language with multiple exclusions, terms and conditions • Requires regular payment with penalties for any delays
Claims handling	• Simple and quick process • Small co-payments needed • Limited documentation	• Comprehensive process • Significant co-payments may be needed for some products • Detailed documentation
Administration	• Mostly restricted to small geographic areas • Mostly organized as a Not-for-Profit entity	• Encompassed large areas with high insured memberships • Mostly created as a For-Profit entity

[1] See more at https://nextbillion.net/insuring-india-mutual-insurance-model-path-to-scale/.

Micro-insurance, while adhering to the same fundamental insurance principles, generally refers to insurance products with modest premiums and limited coverage of risks. This concept shares a striking resemblance with micro-credit, which involves providing small loans to individuals or groups of borrowers. Further, much like micro-credit, micro-insurance is a specialised form of insurance designed to cater to low-income individuals who cannot afford conventional insurance. In addition to the seven core principles of insurance, it must have four key features: accessibility, affordability, flexibility, and simplicity. To be effective, micro-insurance must be accessible to all, administered cost-efficiently, and delivered on a large scale to benefit both insurers and the insured. Premiums must be kept low to match the paying capacity of low-income households. The products are customised to meet specific community requirements and are designed to be easily understood even by uneducated individuals, including clear explanations of covered risks, claim procedures, and indemnity timelines. Collectively, these features aim to make insurance accessible and comprehensible to the underserved population.

3 A Brief Coverage of the Landscape of Micro-Insurance Programs

The first comprehensive landscape survey on micro-insurance was likely conducted by Roth et al. (2007). The data for their report were collected through primary and secondary research conducted by a team of 11 micro-insurance experts who endeavoured to identify and include as many micro-insurers and their products as possible within the world's 100 poorest countries. In 2006, the survey identified 246 non-governmental micro-insurers, 357 micro-insurance products and 116 social security schemes covering about 78 million people in the 100 most economically backward countries globally. The report also identified many different micro-insurance providers such as commercial insurers, NGOs, Mutuals, Community Based Organizations and other informal insurers, Cooperatives, Governmental or Parastatal insurers, and Takafuls. Commercial insurers are increasingly interested in micro-insurance due to its profit potential, market expansion opportunities, and social benefits. Being regulated, they maintain reserves and have access to reinsurance, and their consumers are better protected. They prefer partnering with external delivery channels but face challenges in finding suitable partners in the low-income market. NGOs, including development organizations and microfinance institutions, are effective channels for delivering microinsurance, particularly health coverage, due to their proximity to low-income populations and donor support. Parastatal insurers are government-owned insurance companies, that often lack innovation and management quality and prioritize government policies over sustainable micro-insurance provision. Finally, Takaful insurers operate under Islamic financial principles, investing only in non-interest bearing assets and functioning similarly to non-profit mutuals by returning a portion of earnings to members.[2] The growing popularity of Takaful insurance in Muslim-majority countries has led to increased interest from conventional insurers seeking to tap into this market segment.

Notably, Roth et al. (2007) observed that health insurance was the most sought-after micro-insurance product, yet it exhibited a significantly low coverage rate among insured individuals. The authors additionally identify several limitations among the health insurance products offered by the majority of micro-insurers. Firstly, many are intrinsically linked to the public healthcare delivery system. In nations where the public health systems were inadequate, the efficacy of insurance also suffered. Secondly, most of the insurance products were donor-driven and only a few appeared to have achieved sustainability in their operations. Thirdly, most experienced the issue of low membership and adverse selection,[3] resulting in higher healthcare utilisation among the insured compared to the non-insured. While this is a positive outcome for policymakers as it reduces the burden of illness among the impoverished, it certainly can jeopardise an insurance programme. Fourthly, the indemnity cover is often quite low, rendering it less beneficial to individuals who face health shocks.

The latest landscape report on micro-insurance (Merry & Calderon, 2024) notes that in 2022, health micro-insurance was the second largest product category with 72 million people insured across 36 countries. Although this report encompasses a smaller number of countries and programs compared to Roth et al. (2007), the observations remain remarkably consistent even after one and a half decades. Merry and Calderon (2024) elucidate that health microinsurance, in the majority of regions, continues to comprise basic health products with limited benefit coverage and a low number of insured members in each program. Their report indicates that in terms of both 'total premiums collected' and 'median premium per person', health insurance ranked eighth, despite being among the top three product categories. In this context, understanding the success narrative of Annapurna Pariwar, a community-based health mutual that achieved self-sustainability with over 200,000 members distributed across multiple informal settlements in the cities of Mumbai and Pune becomes increasingly relevant.

Roth et al.'s (2007) landscape study demonstrated that economically disadvantaged countries have limited insurance regulations. In an unprecedented move in 2000 and further in 2002, the Insurance Regulatory and Development Authority of

---

[2] This profit-sharing model aligns with Islamic principles of fairness and community support. Takaful companies typically maintain separate funds for shareholders and policyholders, ensuring transparency and adherence to Sharia law.

[3] Adverse selection refers to a situation where individuals who are at higher risk of making insurance claims are more likely to purchase insurance. This occurs because people with greater health risks or higher likelihood of accidents have more incentive to buy insurance coverage. As a result, insurance companies may end up with a pool of higher-risk policyholders, leading to higher claim payouts than expected. To combat adverse selection, insurers often use strategies like medical underwriting, waiting periods for coverage, or charging higher premiums for riskier individuals. However, this can make insurance less accessible or affordable.

India (IRDAI) published the 'Obligation of insurers to rural or social sectors' that compelled insurers to have a certain quota of their customers from the underdevelopment regions and sectors. Roth et al. (2007) argues that this regulation would have certainly pushed commercial insurers to innovate and bring in micro-insurance products. Consequently, IRDAI has endeavoured to incorporate various informal insurance providers within the regulatory framework. This topic will be covered in greater depth in another chapter of this volume.

At about the same time, India also introduced the National Rural Health Mission (NRHM) in 2005 with the objective of enhancing public health services, particularly focusing on states with inadequate public health infrastructure and indicators (Bajpai et al., 2010). These states were called High Focus States. The NRHM endeavoured to implement diverse policies and sub-strategies to enhance both the quality and quantity of public healthcare systems; however, progress was notably slow and resulted in limited cost savings for healthcare amongst low-income groups. Subsequently, the Indian government implemented state-subsidised social health insurance schemes. The Rashtriya Swasthya Bima Yojana (RSBY), initiated in 2008, aimed to provide health insurance coverage for Below Poverty Line (BPL) families. In 2018, the RSBY was superseded by the Ayushman Bharat Pradhan Mantri Jan Arogya Yojana (AB-PMJAY). Sarwal and Kumar (2021) observe that despite government-subsidised schemes, social health insurance schemes, and private voluntary health insurance, a minimum of 30% of the population (approximately 40 crore individuals) lack any form of health insurance coverage, which they designate as 'India's missing middle'. In such scenarios, community-based organisations and mutuals can fill this void and save the poor from asset-depleting health shocks. Annapurna Pariwar's insurance program is a fitting example in this context.

4 Examining the Health Insurance Program of Annapurna Pariwar

In the following sub-sections, the performance of Annapurna Pariwar Vikas Samvardhan (APVS) is graphically analysed. APVS is a nonprofit company registered under Section 25 of the Indian Companies Act of 1956. It has been in operation since the year 2003 and is completely owned and run by members themselves. The company provides credit-linked health and life insurance to the borrower and her family members. As mentioned earlier, APVS is one among the sister organisations of Annapurna Pariwar, which offers financial as well as non-financial products. It must be noted here that although all six organisations under Annapurna Pariwar have independent boards and separate books of accounts, there are many complementarities across them. All six organisations together help in forming the Joint Liability Groups (JLGs) for loans provided by Annapurna Mahila Multi State Co-operative Credit Society Limited. Hence, an insurance product can ride on the popularity of its previous successful product. Along its journey, APVS has also made some big changes such as making the insurance product compulsory for loan-takers, diversifying its base from all slums in Pune to half of the slums in Mumbai, and also periodically increasing both the premiums and the list of covered diseases.

Annapurna Pariwar's Community Health Insurance Program under APVS started in 2003 with the actuarial guidance of Mr. François-Xavier HAY from MACIF, France and Inter Aide, a French NGO. It also received technical support, including underwriting of claims from Uplift (a non-profit company formed by eight NGOs including APVS). A few years later, APVS chose to develop its own software platform and have its own technical and medical team to assist the program. I was made aware of Annapurna Pariwar and APVS during a seminar at the National Insurance Academy in 2013. Subsequently, Dr Archana Singh, who is also an author of this book, accompanied my Thesis Advisor Dr. Samar K. Datta and me to meet Dr. Medha Purao Samant for an introduction to their Community Based Insurance Model. Following extensive deliberations, the decision was made to evaluate the APVS model and systematically extract lessons from their approach, with the aim of developing a template for replication by other NGOs. However, the initial objective was to demonstrate to the broader community that Community Based Health Insurance through mutual support can achieve sustainability. This section updates the evaluative exercise I undertook in 2015 with roughly 12 years of data.

It must be clearly noted that in this chapter, I present my evaluation of a micro-insurance program that achieved sustainability and inclusion within the timeframe between 2003 and 2014. In that, my objective is to demonstrate the success of the program in the 21 years since launch and to document the entire APVS journey till 2024. The APVS health insurance scheme as it is in 2014 is presented in Table 2. It has undergone a lot of changes during its 21-year journey from starting with a few branches across a few slums in Pune to now reaching out to members across all slums in Pune and fifty percent of slums in Mumbai. The major events that substantially impacted the Indian economy and potentially jeopardised the micro-insurance programme were the demonetisation initiative in November 2016 and the multiple waves of Covid-19 during 2020–21. A separate study can aim to understand how Annapurna Pariwar strategically averted these crises.

Annapurna Pariwar's health insurance plan's success stems from their dedicated medical doctors, who run client awareness programs at Annapurna Pariwar's branch offices, perform free health check-ups, and are available 24 × 7 on the phone. They also help sign Memorandums of Understanding (MOUs) with good private hospitals that form a network of healthcare providers and medical practitioners. This helps members to visit these hospitals and clinics at the time of need without having fears of being turned away or exploitatively charged. The same activity is performed for diagnostic centres, pathology laboratories and chemist shops for giving low-cost services to Annapurna Pariwar's members. Over time, Annapurna Pariwar has built its own software system to record every member's pre-existing illness, past claims and current claims. Annapurna Pariwar's success

Table 2 Features of APVS health insurance scheme

Client eligibility	There are no criteria for selection (or exclusion) of potential members The client who takes a loan (compulsory) from Annapurna Mahila Multi State Co-op Credit Society Ltd. Spouse and children of the client are encouraged to join Dependent parents and relatives of the member and spouse can also be added to the health insurance policy The client must not default on the loan There are no restrictions on age of insured persons	
Premium contribution	The premium amount is determined based on the loan amount and the number of people in the family (see Table 3); there is a separate contribution towards hospitalisation expenses	
	Destination	Paid to the fund of the branch Each branch has a separate fund
	Duration	For the duration of the loan and A period of 12 months
Renewal	Loan duration < 12 months	Even if loan is repaid, policyholders can still get coverage for the duration of 12 months
	Loan duration > 12 months	At the end of every 12 months until the loan is repaid, the policy is automatically renewed for the next 12 months or for the remaining months (if < 12) The corresponding amount (depending on the number of months left) is directly taken from the savings account. A new Health card (Nidhi card) is given to the member
Services offered besides claims	Health care support through a free 24 × 7 helpline that is trained to provide guidance on the next steps to follow Referrals to specialist OPD for concessional rates Information on facilities at Public or networked Private hospital Health card ensures proper treatment at concessional prices Laboratory investigations at concessional rates Medicine at concessional rates Regular client education on precautionary measures	
Coverage Rules	There is a complete list of covered diseases under a Policy document and the maximum claimable amounts under each bracket (see Table 4) Elected Community Representatives can add/modify diseases and their coverage rules to this document Elected Community Representatives also pass/reject the claims raised in a meeting diligently held every month. The group debates the reimbursement amount case by case and have the power to waive the above restrictions if the case so demands.	

also owes to its unique claim settlement process where elected community representatives, who are highly aware of their neighbour's illnesses and treatments availed, meet every month along with the facilitating senior team members to debate the reimbursement amount for every claim case. If a claim is rejected, it is also the responsibility of a representative to explain to her neighbour why it was rejected. This process removes the information gaps making the organisation better aware of the health of all members and also speeds up the settlement process.

Table 2 shows the current features of Annapurna Pariwar's health insurance plan such as the eligibility of clients for the insurance support, premium contribution, conditions for renewal of the insurance policy, the rules of insurance coverage, and the additional services offered to members. Over its 21-year journey, Annapurna Pariwar has implemented several modifications to its insurance features, consistently enhancing the benefits for all members. Over time, their micro health insurance program has expanded its coverage to encompass pre-existing chronic conditions as well as emerging health issues, including mental illnesses. Individuals who obtain insurance coverage for themselves and their family members are invariably issued a health card, referred to as the 'Nidhi' card. This card contains comprehensive information regarding the claims process and provides step-by-step guidance for any medical treatment or hospitalization requirements. The card also has the contacts of empanelled medical officers who can guide them on calls and also answers many commonly asked questions. Annapurna Pariwar's insurance plan has also evolved in complexity over time, particularly with regards to its premium structure (Table 3) and the maximum claimable amounts for the various diseases covered (Table 4). This information is available to everyone via the Nidhi cards.

Prior to addressing the risk management strategies implemented in Annapurna Pariwar's insurance program, it is pertinent to examine and discuss the premium structure and the maximum claimable amounts. The two—premiums and claims—are two sides of the same coin and therefore Tables 3 and 4 should be consulted simultaneously. Thus, while it may appear that members who take higher loans are

Table 3 Annual premium of APVS health insurance scheme

	Health insurance premium amount (in ₹)			
Loan Amount (in ₹)	One person in family	Two persons in family	Three persons in family	Four persons in family
35,000 to 55,000	530	960	1300	1660
60,000 to 1,00,000	720	1300	1780	2280
1,05,000 to 1,50,000	840	1540	2100	2710
1,55,000 to 2,00,000	970	1800	2470	3180
2,05,000 to 2,50,000	1080	2000	2780	3580
2,55,000 to 3,00,000	1130	2080	2850	3680
3,05,000 to 3,50,000	1150	2130	2950	3800
3,55,000 to 4,50,000	1180	2180	3030	3900
4,55,000 to 15,00,000	1200	2230	3100	4030
Hospitalization Annual Contribution (add-on for all loan amounts)	105	210	315	420

Table 4 Maximum claimable amounts under the APVS health insurance scheme

Loan amount (in ₹)	Maximum claimable amount based on the type of illness (in ₹)									
	One-Day illness	Two-three days illness	Normal illness	Less serious illness	Serious illness	Very serious illness	1st cesarean	2nd cesarean	Cataract	Primary infertility
35,000–55,000	3500	4000	7800	9900	30,000	40,000	30,000	7500	5200	15,000
60,000–1,00,000	4500	4500	8600	11,300	30,000	40,000	30,000	9000	5700	15,000
1,05,000–1,50,000	5500	5500	9400	12,700	30,000	40,000	30,000	10,500	6200	15,000
1,55,000–2,00,000	6500	6500	10,200	14,100	30,000	40,000	30,000	12,000	6700	15,000
2,05,000–2,50,000	7000	7000	10,600	14,800	30,000	40,000	30,000	12,750	6950	15,000
2,55,000–3,00,000	7500	7500	11,000	15,500	30,000	40,000	30,000	13,500	7200	15,000
3,05,000–3,50,000	8000	8000	11,400	16,200	30,000	40,000	30,000	14,250	7450	15,000
3,55,000–4,50,000	8500	8500	11,800	16,900	30,000	40,000	30,000	15,000	7700	15,000
4,55,000–15,00,000	9000	9000	12,200	17,600	30,000	40,000	30,000	15,750	7950	15,000
Hospitalization Benefit for all Loan Amounts: Rs. 500/- per day (as per admission days), applicable for all types of illnesses										

also bearing the burden of higher premiums from Tables 3, 4 shows that they are also given higher coverages for minor illnesses which occur more frequently. The insurance scheme also has a minor add-on for hospitalisation episodes thereby creating another fund pool for such expenses. It is also interesting to note that while specifying the premium amounts by the number of persons in a family, Table 3 stops at 4 members per family. This phenomenon represents an indication of the evolving societal dynamics, as family structures increasingly transition towards a nuclear model, even within slum areas. Another interesting observation is that for very serious illnesses, the 1st caesarean or C-section operation for safe delivery of babies, and for infertility treatments the maximum claimable amounts are the same irrespective of the loan amounts. This shows the strength of a community-based and community-driven health insurance program.

4.1 Risk Handling Measures Employed

The organisation, being community driven, is more informed about the health of members and their economic conditions. This information comes from two sources—first, the elected community representatives who keep a check on any moral[4] and morale hazard[5] from the households. The second are the trained staff who can be contacted through a 24 × 7 free helpline number and their in-house doctors who check every medical detail of each claim. These insights are used judiciously during settlement of claims.

The 24 × 7 free healthcare helpline and free health check-up at Annapurna premises are very important initiatives by the organisation. When medical advice is given to the sick family member promptly, it makes the treatment process more effective and manageable for the family. Here, the organisation not only guides the family on the correct diagnosis and treatment, but also on which nearby hospital or clinic to visit where the treatment facility is present and can be availed at a reasonable cost. The helpline service, however, is yet to be fully utilised by the community. Even among members who raised claims recently, the average usage of the helpline at different stages of their treatment has been 61%. APVS branches

[4] Moral hazard refers to the situation where one party engages in riskier behaviour because they do not bear the full consequences of that risk. This often occurs in financial and insurance markets when individuals or organizations take excessive risks, knowing that losses will be covered by another party, such as an insurer or the government. It can lead to inefficiencies and increased costs, requiring mechanisms like monitoring or incentives to mitigate its effects.

[5] Morale hazard, as used in insurance, describes an insured person's carelessness or indifference towards the potential for loss, often due to the belief that insurance will cover any damage or loss. Morale hazard is subtly different from Moral Hazard described above. Moral hazard refers to a deliberate shift in behaviour aimed at gaining from an event that takes place. In contrast, morale hazard pertains to an involuntary change in a person's actions when they have insurance coverage.

in the city of Mumbai have better average utilisation of the service at 65% than in the city of Pune having an average utilisation of 58%.

Notably, out of all members using the helpline, around 60% make the first call before getting admitted. The organisation's target must be to get more members to make the first call before getting admitted so that they can be appropriately guided to the nearest clinics and hospitals that can offer the same facilities at lower costs. Often this discount is bargained for by APVS for its members, which they are mostly unaware of. It is noteworthy to consider the advantages of being a group beneficiary of a health service provider as opposed to an individual beneficiary. As a collective, APVS members are able to access superior services at reduced rates compared to the costs they would incur if they were admitted as individual members.

Ultimately, one of the primary objectives of any insurance company is to diversify its risk portfolio. Since APVS too offers three insurance products—health insurance for self and family members, (called Health Mutual Fund), life insurance for self and family members (called Family and Life Mutual Fund) and for protection of assets of borrowers (called Asset Loss Mutual Fund), it too achieves some benefits of diversifying. If we look at the monthly Incurred Claims Ratio (ratio of incurred claim expenses to premium earnings) for the three insurance products—HMF, FLMF and ALMF, it can be noticed that HMF has the highest Incurred Claims Ratio and ALMF has a considerably low Claims Ratio. It is possible because HMF operates at a higher level with higher premiums and claim settlements. This also highlights the relative importance of health insurance (HMF) over other products. Moreover, as a community-based health insurance program serving economically disadvantaged populations, there exists a persistent risk of catastrophic events leading to the program's insolvency. While numerous organizations seek reinsurance from major insurance providers such as SwissRe, APVS has opted to mitigate risks by treating each branch as an independent insurer and obtaining reinsurance from other branches when necessary. In the event of significant shortfalls, AVPS secures loans or short-term transfers from Annapurna Mahila Multi-State Co-operative Credit Society Limited (AMCCS), Annapurna Pariwar's microfinance organization. Over the course of two decades since its inception, APVS has remained sustainable.

4.2 Clients Who Opt Out of the Program

Clients of APVS can easily discontinue their memberships with Annapurna Pariwar after completion of loan repayment. A discontinuation result in the entire family being removed from health and life insurance coverage and therefore it is not always in their best interests. However, an attrition rate of more than 30% is a standard observation by the organisation. This leads to a general question that if the dropout rate is as high as 30%, is it because there are households who are self-selecting themselves into the program just to get the benefit of insurance services?

Though the program specifically excludes pre-existing illness for new members, if this is found true, then this behaviour of clients may affect the sustainability of health insurance program. Overall APVS seems consistent in improving its balance sheet over the years. While this is a healthy sign from the point of view of the organisation, this performance may appear different from perspectives of the consumer. This is attempted next.

4.3 Annual Growth Trends

This section provides an overall understanding of how a community-based organisation can grow over time. Most charts in this section were sourced from the audited annual reports of Annapurna Pariwar Vikas Samvardhan (APVS) for the years 2003–2004 till 2013–2014 and the rest were obtained from their databases.

Foremost, the Fig. 2 shows the trend in number of people insured by APVS over the years. The chart shows an exponential growth curve with a sharp rise in membership from the year 2008–09. The rationale for this change was that health insurance participation was transformed from a voluntary to a compulsory requirement for all borrowers in 2007, with the aim of mitigating self-selection issues. This decision was a difficult one to make, as many households did not want to give away a part of their savings towards insurance premiums. It was a tough task for the organisation to convince their members that since they are not tied up with any commercial insurer, the premiums are not going to get wiped out once the term gets over. It would be preserved in a fund for future needs. The decision to make the Health Mutual Fund participation from being voluntary to compulsory was not imposed on Annapurna Pariwar's members but was taken in the Annual General Meeting in 2006 where thousands of members approved it by raising their hands in unison. Operations in Mumbai had also started in the year 2007–2008 and from the onset health insurance was marked compulsory with loans.

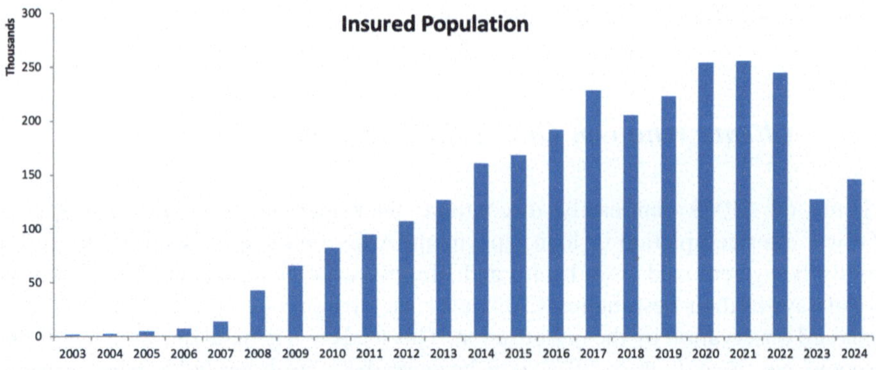

Fig. 2 Growth of insured members from inception till 2024

The program features, as delineated in Table 2, indicate that participation by immediate family members still remains voluntary. This may raise concerns towards program sustainability due to adverse selection. However, if the insured population of year 2024 is further examined (refer Fig. 3), then a healthy participation from young dependents is observed, putting these doubts to rests. Since any insurance program rests on the law of large numbers, having a large pool of young members ensures the stability and sustainability of the program as they are less likely to make claims compared to elderly members in the family.

The reserves and surplus of APVS (Fig. 4) have grown several times to be in excess of ₹70 million. Within it, the health fund has increased significantly from ₹0.1 million to ₹24 million. If we divide the health fund amount by the member base, we see that the available fund per member has increased from ₹49.96 to ₹167.37. This seems to be a significant improvement. There is also no sign of catastrophic loss to the health fund except during the period of the Covid-19 pandemic.

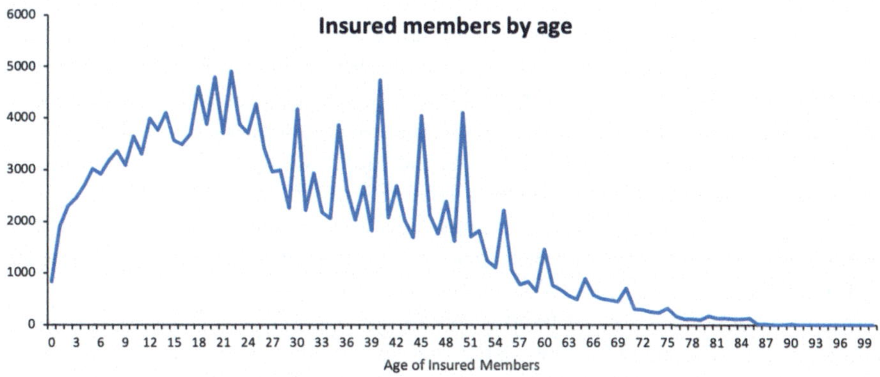

Fig. 3 Number of insured members age-wise in year 2024

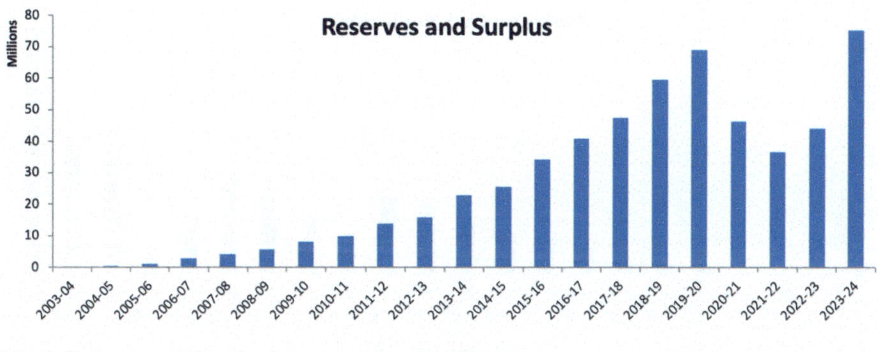

Fig. 4 Reserves and Surplus from inception till 2024

Fund management is an important aspect for any insurance operations. While in case of conventional insurance, the fund after paying claims adds to the profit of the company, in case of a mutual insurer, any additional money available after paying all claims goes towards a Reserve Fund, labelled here as the 'Past Reserve Fund'. This acts as a fall-back option whenever the current earned premiums become insufficient for meeting claims for the month. In APVS, the process of claim settlement is as follows. First, the earned premium is maintained as a liquid account at each branch level and the health fund is accumulated as a fixed account at the organisation level. This task is made easy through a software system that maintains the earned premium for each branch. For a month, any positive income after paying all claims is transferred to the Health Fund. If in any month the earned premium amount falls short of claims to disburse, then the branch-level claim disbursement committee follows these steps in a sequential manner—(a) reduce all claim reimbursement to a maximum of 75%, (b) check with the organisation if other branches have positive income that can cross-subsidise their claims, and finally, (c) make use of Past Reserve Fund deposit to meet the pending claims with the help of their own software system.

Now, after liabilities, assets come under consideration. Two major assets that affect the daily operations of any entity are cash equivalents and fixed assets. Figure 5 shows the growth in cash equivalents that include—short-term deposits, current account balances and cash in hand. The organisation can also deploy its funds across many banks depending on returns and convenience for obtaining loans against deposits. It is clearly evident that the major strength has been partnering with scheduled banks. Cash on hand is kept to a minimum, which reflects on the well-designed processes to handle claims and other expenditures. The cash with scheduled banks is so large that the other two components—cash on hand and cash with other banks, appear concealed in the following figure.

Figure 6 show the value of fixed assets minus depreciation. There was a sharp decline in assets in the FY 2009–2010, which was due to the shifting of office premises that was accompanied by a major sale of assets—furniture, computers, office equipment and others. The existing software was also written-off.

Fig. 5 Cash and cash equivalents from inception till 2024

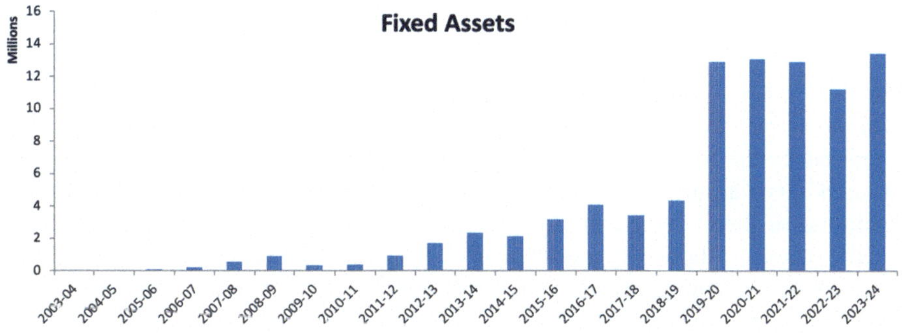

Fig. 6 Fixed assets from inception till 2024

Subsequently higher investments were made to improve the Management Information Systems (MIS). This addition of software, computers and peripherals (including normal depreciation) was made to improve managerial decision-making. The next significant investments came in the FY 2019–2020 as Annapurna Pariwar decided to design an integrated Micro Finance & Micro Insurance Management System (MFMIMS) under a new sister organisation called the Purna E-Solutions Foundation. This system effectively integrates various project-specific modules related to microfinance and microinsurance, which are managed by different group organizations within Annapurna Pariwar.

Apart from storing the premiums collected and outlay on claims, Annapurna Pariwar Vikas Samvardhan (APVS) utilises their MIS system to preserve information on their members' family details—(a) current age of each member, (b) stated or detected pre-existing illnesses, and (c) current education and income information. The system also stores the details of every claim settled including the illness faced, hospital visited, treatment given, date of hospital admission and discharge (if hospitalised). In addition, the in-house doctor also writes a short history of the ailment along with technical details. This storehouse of information is easily retrievable by APVS' managers and doctors in the form of reports and spreadsheets. This helps them to constantly monitor the program and propose changes if necessary.

Annapurna Pariwar is also focusing on integrating data exchange and synchronization between the MFMIMS software and a mobile application named AppPurna. This app facilitates the automation of loan disbursement, recovery, and insurance claim processes directly in the field. It communicates with the MFMIMS software at the Head Office, enabling senior management to oversee activities via their mobile devices, thus enhancing efficiency and the quality of loan documentation. The application is expected to significantly reduce turnaround times and costs by minimizing the need for staff and cutting down on stationery expenses.

4.4 Performance Indicators

The performance indicators presented in Table 4 were established during two workshops on "Performance Indicators in Microinsurance" in 2006 and 2007 organised by the Microinsurance Network (Wipf & Garand, 2010). These indicators can serve as universal benchmarks for assessing microinsurance providers, regardless of their specific product offerings, organizational structures, or operational contexts. These key performance indicators (KPIs) offer a standardized approach to evaluating the efficiency and effectiveness of microinsurance operations across diverse settings. However, it is crucial to recognize that these indicators, while valuable, provide only a partial view of an organization's overall performance. While these KPIs offer a rapid assessment of operational execution, they should not be considered a comprehensive evaluation tool. The complexity of microinsurance operations involves numerous factors that may not be fully captured by these indicators alone. Factors such as local market conditions, regulatory environments, socioeconomic contexts, and specific organizational goals can significantly impact performance outcomes. Therefore, a thorough analysis of a microinsurance provider's performance should incorporate these indicators alongside a more in-depth examination of qualitative factors, long-term sustainability measures, and the provider's ability to meet the unique needs of its target population. For instance, the claim rejection ratio indicates the proportion of rejected claims to total claims. While this serves as a valuable measure of social performance, a high claim rejection ratio may not necessarily indicate poor performance, as claims can be rejected for numerous valid reasons (such as pre-existing illness or cosmetic surgery). Given that valid rejections are often indistinguishable from invalid rejections in the majority of cases, this performance measure is omitted from consideration. Furthermore, as no indicator can be considered superior to others, certain indicators proposed by Wipf and Garand (2010) were modified based on data availability and to facilitate improved interpretation.

Another way of gauging performance can be through measures of efficiency. The conventional way of doing so is to look at the ratio of total outputs to total inputs (called technical efficiency) or at the ratio of total outputs to total costs (called cost efficiency). In case of non-profit organisations where the inputs and outputs are not easily parameterised, non-parametric approaches such as the Data Envelopment Analysis (DEA) or the Stochastic Frontier Analysis (SFA) are employed. In both of these approaches, performance is measured relative to the most efficient organisation or the efficient frontier. In case of microinsurance institutions, the lack of available market data has hindered such analysis. Therefore, one can finally argue that growth in member base is the only thing that helps an organisation sustain (Table 5).

These indicators are discussed in detail in the following sections along with the Figures for the APVS community health insurance scheme along with detailed discussions.

Table 5 List of key performance indicators

Indicator	Definition	Modified definition
Incurred expense ratio	= Incurred expenses/Earned premium	= Incurred expenses/ Earned income
Net income ratio	= Net income/Earned premium	= Net income/Earned income
Coverage ratio	= Number of active insured/Target population	Unmodified
Growth ratio	= (Number of insured t—Number of insured t-1)/ Number of insured t-1	Unmodified
Solvency ratio	= Admitted assets/Admitted liabilities	Unmodified

Source Wipf and Garand (2010), modified by author

4.4.1 Incurred Expense Ratio

The incurred expense ratio indicator is the share of incurred expenses to the earned premium within the same accounting period. It had to be modified slightly in this context as APVS has income from sources other than premiums. It is as shown below:

$$\text{Incurred Expense Ratio} = \text{Incurred expenses}/\text{Earned income}$$

The Incurred Expense Ratio is an indicator of efficiency. It explains the portion of income required for covering all marketing, sales, administration, claims settlement, and distribution costs of the microinsurance programme. The Incurred Expense Ratio provides valuable insights into the operational efficiency of microinsurance programs. By comparing expenses to income, it allows insurers to assess their cost management effectiveness and identify areas for potential improvement. This ratio is particularly crucial in the microinsurance sector, where maintaining low operational costs is essential for providing affordable coverage to low-income populations (Fig. 7).

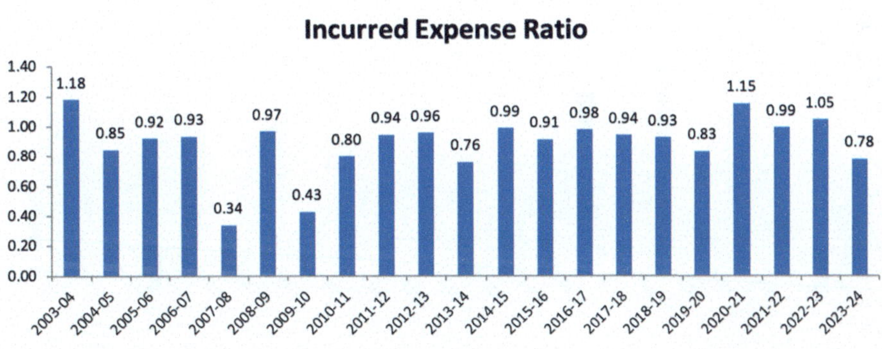

Fig. 7 Incurred expense ratio from inception till 2024

While a low incurred expense ratio reduces the cost burden to the insured, it may also lead to low client outreach. On the other hand, higher expenses can result in increased premiums causing client dissatisfaction. In case of APVS, the ratio is high for all years except two years. Since premiums have not increased year-on-year, the high ratio may reflect their investments into the community in the form of claim settlements, hospital tie-ups, medical guidance call-centre, etc. Since the ratio has never crossed unity, except at the start, the program seems to be under good managerial control. APVS also spends considerably on staff salary and welfare.

4.4.2 Net Income Ratio

The Net Income Ratio indicator is the share of net income to the earned premium within the same accounting period. Again, this had to be modified slightly in this context as APVS has income from sources other than premiums. It is as shown below:

$$\text{Net Income Ratio} = \text{Net income}/\text{Earned Income}$$

This indicator shows how profitable the programme is. Ideally the net income should be positive. Consistent negative values may suggest that the necessity to make changes to the program to achieve viability. Many microinsurance programs experience losses in their initial years until they reach a critical mass of insured and a level of efficiency. On the other hand, persistent highly positive values may indicate unwarranted high premiums and thus poor value to clients. Though a member-owned program may deliberately keep a high ratio for building surplus, consumers may start feeling disillusioned with the program and may either leave or switch over to a competitor with lower premiums. Either way, the ratio is an important decision-making tool for the micro-insurer.

Figure 8 shows the Net Income Ratios for APVS for 21 years of its operations. The initial negative value is well expected. Further, apart from the two spikes in

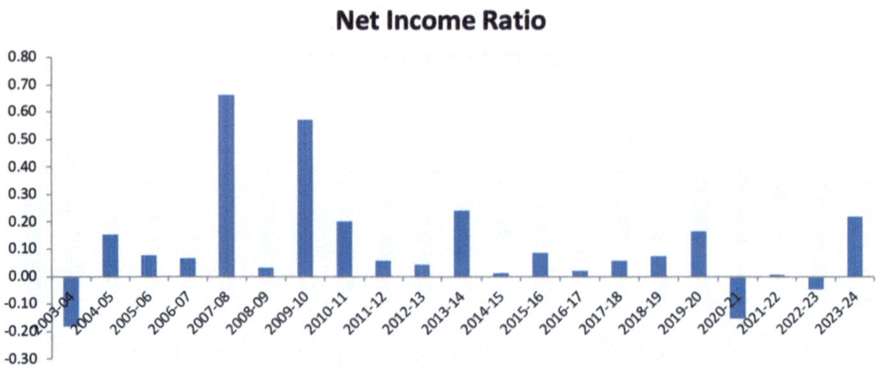

Fig. 8 Net income ratio from inception till 2024

2007–08 and 2009–10, it had modest net income ratios. The spikes can be attributed to a change in insurance product from being voluntary to compulsory in 2007 and an increase of premium amount from ₹60 to ₹100 in 2009 respectively.

4.4.3 Coverage Ratio

The Coverage Ratio indicator is the share of the number of people actively insured to the target population. Naturally the target population cannot be defined in an easy manner and is based on estimates of the organisation. The indicator is as shown below:

$$\text{Coverage Ratio} = \text{Number of active insured}/\text{Target population}$$

The Coverage Ratio can be also considered equivalent to Participation Ratio or Penetration Ratio. In a community-based health insurance program, potentially all members should be eligible for coverage. There could also be a defined target segment of the population such as old aged people, etc. This ratio is an important indicator of marketing and distribution effectiveness subject to the product being actuarially fair. It also shows the acceptance of the product among the community members. The calculated Coverage Ratio based on estimates of the target population of APVS shows an increasing trend. Assuming a target population of 100,000 in the year 2008, the target population is estimated to increase at a CAGR of 10% since inception and at 15% since then. A higher percentage was considered since 2008 because Annapurna Pariwar also started its operations in Mumbai alongside Pune. The trend is displayed in Fig. 9. The coverage shows a steep jump in 2008 because of the insurance product becoming compulsory with loans. As discussed earlier, this was a community-led joint decision to tackle the problem of adverse selection. It is quite evident that the coverage was healthy till the year 2016 and it has been on a decline ever since. I suspect this could be due to the adverse impacts

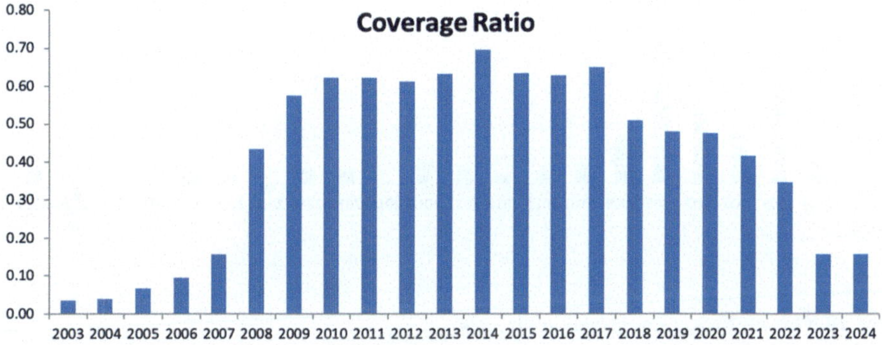

Fig. 9 Coverage RATIO from inception till 2024

of the demonetisation exercise in 2016 and the Covid-19 waves in the years 2020–2021 and also due to other competitors in Microfinance. The final coverage figure for 2024 is 16%, which is still adequate for the sustainability of the program.

4.4.4 Growth Ratio

The Growth Ratio indicator is defined as the ratio of the net addition of insured population between time *t* and *t-1* over the total insured population in time *t-1*. The ratio is as shown:

$$\text{Growth Ratio} = (\text{Number of insured}_t - \text{Number of insured}_{t-1})/\text{Total insured}_{t-1}$$

The Growth Ratio is an indicator of the program's success in achieving a critical mass of insured. Its importance is further emphasized for voluntary programs, in which case a positive trend of growth ratio often signifies marketing success, product value, and appeal. However, there are few things to be noted here. First, growth will usually be higher in the initial periods for the same net additions of insured because of the lower base. Second, the growth ratio may slowly stagnate over time as the entire target population gets covered. Then either the product must be innovated or newer markets need to be explored. The Growth Ratio for 21 years of APVS is presented in Fig. 10. Again, this has to be looked at together with the Coverage Ratio (Fig. 9) and the number of insured. Although the growth in the initial years appears to be large, with the highest growth (almost double) being registered in the year 2008, APVS is was still growing at a healthy rate of around 17% till the year 2017 (last five-year average). Subsequently the growth rate has declined and the organisation has witnessed two years of negative growth in the year 2022–2023, probably due to Covid-19.

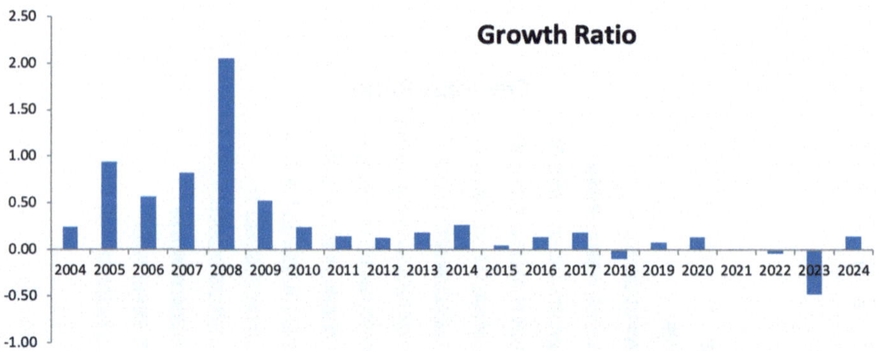

Fig. 10 Growth Ratio from inception till 2024

4.4.5 Solvency Ratio

Fiscal prudence of an organisation can be measured through the Solvency Ratio. This is defined as the ratio of Admitted Assets of the organisation to the Admitted Liabilities within the same accounting period. The indicator is as shown below:

$$\text{Solvency Ratio} = \text{Admitted assets}/\text{Admitted liabilities}$$

The overall Solvency Ratio portrays the financial strength of the microinsurance program and its ability to meet its obligations now and in the future. In the commercial market, regulators address solvency issues in various ways including prescription of minimum capital and surplus requirements, investment limitations, capital adequacy tests, accounting standards, risk-based capital methods, and disclosure (Wipf & Garand, 2010). An adequate Solvency Ratio should be in excess of 1. However, having an exorbitantly high ratio in the long run is also not good as it signifies an inefficient use of capital. In any insurance programme, long-term solvency ensures protection for the clients. A failure of a microinsurance programme would have a negative impact on clients' trust and interest in insurance protection services even though they have a need for them. APVS shows a steady rise in its solvency ratios post 2007 and also very low figures in the period 2016–2021 (Fig. 11). The last three-year average of its solvency ratio is 0.76, which though may not be the ideal, signify adequate churning of capital at the cost of moderate safeguards against any major catastrophe.

4.5 *Social Performance*

In this section, the social inclusion behaviour of the insurance programs of Annapurna Pariwar is reviewed. In this context, I draw on my qualitative experiences from visiting various branches of the organization and participating in many

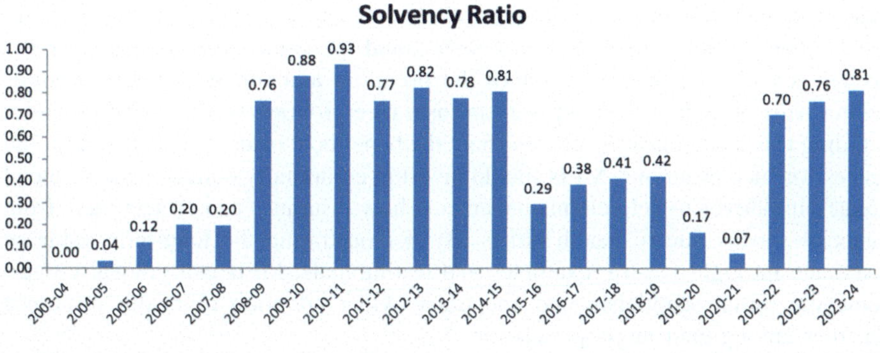

Fig. 11 Solvency ratio from inception till 2024

Annual General Meetings. The program is quite inclusive of both genders and also of community members belonging to all age groups. My findings also reveal that more than half of Annapurna Pariwar's members fall below the established poverty threshold, indicating that the program is quite inclusive of households that are close to the poverty line. This inclusivity suggests that the program's targeting mechanisms are effective in reaching its intended beneficiaries. The program's success in reaching a diverse range of beneficiaries indicates its robust design and implementation. It demonstrates a nuanced understanding of the varied needs within the target population, allowing for a more comprehensive and equitable distribution of resources. This approach not only enhances the program's overall impact but also contributes to its long-term sustainability by fostering broader community support and engagement. However, further research is required to determine if the program is equally successful in improving their poverty situation and helping them to come out of poverty.

5 Conclusion

In their recent book on India's social safety nets, Rahman and Pingali (2024) elucidate that in the context of low- and medium-income economies where markets are underdeveloped, it is a good *idea* for society as an *institution* to provide mutual social insurance to its members. In the true spirit of inclusive growth, Community Based Organisations, Mutuals, and Cooperatives that provide micro-insurance play a crucial role in India's social safety system. The success of Annapurna Pariwar's efforts must encourage non-profit and even some for-profit microfinance institutions to build strong network ties within the communities they are serving, and consequently diversify their product portfolios to include insurance of health.

Though many MFIs may fear losses when their target population belong to low socio-economic backgrounds, they must understand the cumulative benefits of positive network externalities. These externalities can be generated through (a) affordability of premiums, (b) proper coverage of illnesses including outpatient services, (c) transparency of scheme features, (d) proper guidance for suitable treatment, and (e) timely settlement of claims. At the outset, clients who are accustomed to taking loans may not understand the value of insurance since the insurer is under no burden to return the premium amount. It therefore requires greater trust building efforts to start an insurance program than a credit program. Building trust and educating clients about the benefits of insurance is crucial for the success of such programs. MFIs should invest in community outreach and financial literacy initiatives to help clients understand how insurance can protect them from financial shocks due to health issues. By demonstrating the long-term value of insurance through real-life examples and testimonials, MFIs can gradually overcome the initial scepticism and encourage wider adoption of health insurance schemes among their target population.

Regulation plays a pivotal role in expanding the participation of NGOs and Microfinance Institutions (MFIs) in the microinsurance sector, particularly in health insurance. By addressing systemic barriers, regulatory frameworks can create an enabling environment for these organizations to operate effectively. For instance, regulations can mandate insurers to extend their services to rural and underserved areas, ensuring inclusivity. Liberal entry norms for NGOs and MFIs as microinsurance agents further facilitate their involvement without requiring complex licensing procedures. Additionally, regulations can prescribe minimum coverage standards and allow composite products that combine life, health, and asset insurance to cater to the specific needs of low-income households. These measures not only enhance accessibility but also encourage innovative partnerships between insurers, NGOs, and MFIs, leveraging their local networks and trust within communities.

Moreover, regulatory oversight ensures sustainability and accountability in microinsurance operations. By monitoring compliance with rural and social sector obligations, regulators can prevent exploitation and promote equitable distribution of services. They can also address challenges such as limited financial capacity or management expertise among NGOs and MFIs by fostering capacity-building initiatives. For example, integrating health goals within microfinance programs has shown positive outcomes in Ghana, where decentralized credit associations partnered with local health systems to improve health literacy and service delivery. Real-time monitoring mechanisms further enhance transparency and efficiency in claims management, reducing fraud risks. Thus, robust regulations not only incentivize NGOs and MFIs to enter the microinsurance space but also ensure their operations are aligned with broader social protection goals.

Regulation in India has been instrumental in shaping microinsurance services, particularly in health, by establishing a framework that facilitates access for low-income populations. The Insurance Regulatory and Development Authority of India (IRDAI) plays a crucial role in this context through the introduction of specific regulations, such as the IRDA Microinsurance Regulations of 2005 and its subsequent amendments. A report of the Committee on Standalone Microinsurance Company authorised by the IRDAI notes that despite these advancements, regulatory challenges persist that impact the effectiveness of microinsurance services (IRDAI, 2020). Furthermore, while regulations allow for simplified insurance processes aimed at affordability, they also impose constraints such as capping coverage amounts and limiting agents to partnerships with only one life and one non-life insurer (IRDAI, 2020). This can hinder competition and innovation within the sector. To enhance the reach and effectiveness of microinsurance in health, ongoing regulatory reforms are necessary to adapt to emerging delivery channels, such as digital platforms, and to ensure that these services remain accessible and beneficial to those they are intended to protect. The Annapurna Pariwar model gives a useful framework to follow and implement for NGOs and MFIs who seek to financially secure the lives of their members and their families. This model emphasizes a holistic approach to poverty alleviation by addressing multiple aspects of financial security, including savings, credit, insurance, and pension schemes. By providing a comprehensive suite of financial services tailored to the needs of low-income individuals and families, the Annapurna Pariwar model aims to create a safety net that protects against various economic shocks and vulnerabilities. Its success in India demonstrates the potential for replication and adaptation in other developing regions, offering a promising pathway for sustainable poverty reduction and economic empowerment.

References

Bajpai, N., Sachs, J., & Dholakia, R. (2010). *Improving access and efficiency in public health services: Mid-term evaluation of India's national rural health mission*. SAGE Publications India Pvt Ltd. https://doi.org/10.4135/9788132107873

Debnath, K. (2016). *The role of community health insurance in perfecting financial inclusion* [Ph.D. Thesis, Indian Institute of Management Ahmedabad]. http://hdl.handle.net/11718/18186

Debnath, K. (2017). *Community based health insurance: Planting a seed for tomorrow's need*. Dada Purao Research & Training Institute, ISBN: 978-81-934834-1-1.

IRDAI. (2020). Report of the committee on standalone microinsurance company. https://sewainsurance.org/wp-content/uploads/2021/03/Report-of-the-SAMI-Committee-19.8.20.pdf

Merry, A., & Calderon, J. R. (2024). *The landscape of microinsurance 2023* (pp. 100). Microinsurance Network. https://microinsurancenetwork.org/resources/the-landscape-of-microinsurance-2023

Osei Afriyie, D., Krasniq, B., Hooley, B., Tediosi, F., & Fink, G. (2022). Equity in health insurance schemes enrollment in low and middle-income countries: A systematic review and meta-analysis. *International Journal for Equity in Health*, *21*(1), 21. https://doi.org/10.1186/s12939-021-01608-x

Planning Commission. (2009). *A hundred small steps: Report of the Committee on Financial Sector Reforms*. Sage.

Rahman, A., & Pingali, P. (2024). *The future of India's social safety nets: Focus, form, and scope*. Springer International Publishing. https://doi.org/10.1007/978-3-031-50747-2

Roth, J., McCord, M. J., & Liber, D. (2007). *The landscape of microinsurance in the World's 100 poorest countries*. MicroInsurance Centre. https://www.shareweb.ch/site/EI/Documents/FSD/The%20Landscape%20of%20Microinsurance%20in%20the%20World's%20100%20Poorest%20Countries%20-%202007(en).pdf

Sarwal, R., & Kumar, A. (2021). *Health insurance for India's missing middle*. NITI Aayog. https://osf.io/s2x8r

Schneider, P. (2004). Why should the poor insure? Theories of decision-making in the context of health insurance. *Health Policy and Planning*, *19*(6), 349–355. https://doi.org/10.1093/heapol/czh050

Wipf, J., & Garand, D. (2010). *Performance indicators for microinsurance: A handbook for microinsurance practitioners* (No. 2). Appui au Développement Autonome (ADA). https://www.indexinsuranceforum.org/sites/default/files/Handbook_Performance_Indicators_version_2%5B1%5D.pdf

Regulatory Space for Microinsurance in India: Challenges and Relevance for Annapurna Pariwar

Archana Singh

Abstract This chapter covers the evolution of the microinsurance regulation of Insurance Regulatory and Development Authority of India (IRDAI) and the corresponding journey of the microinsurance sector in India. The Regulation of Social and Rural Obligation 2002 and the Microinsurance Regulation of 2005 kickstarted a series of initiatives by insurance companies that were eager to collaborate with Non-Governmental Organizations (NGOs)/Microfinance Institutions (MFIs) to cover the space. Annapurna Pariwar (AP) faced challenges in these collaborations and started its sole journey of setting up mutual insurance to cover the health risks of its members. The chapter examines the position and contribution of Annapurna in offering risk management solutions and the challenges faced in this regulatory space. It also discusses how mutual insurance is placed in the current guidelines and its impact on organisations like Annapurna. It discusses other regulations like Point of Salespersons, IMF Regulation, and CPSC Regulation, which were intended to increase access to insurance for the masses. It touches upon the initiatives taken by the regulator to make insurance more inclusive for smaller organisations that are providing innovative alternatives to the low-income segment of society. It concludes with recommendations that will help AP upscale and handhold other community-based organisations in offering insurance. These changes will be important in achieving the 'Insurance for All by 2047' targets set by IRDAI.

A. Singh (✉)
National Insurance Academy, Pune, Maharashtra, India
e-mail: sarchana@niapune.org.in

J. D. Ranadive, S. Guha (eds.), *Building Pathways to Women's Empowerment*, India Studies in Business and Economics,
https://doi.org/10.1007/978-981-95-7159-8_9

1 Introduction

India is one of the fastest-growing insurance markets in the world, with an estimated 17% year-on-year (YoY) growth in the coming decade and forecasted to be the sixth largest by 2032 (Swiss Re, 2023b). One of the major challenges faced by India is the increasing protection gap, defined by Feinman (2019) as the extent to which significant losses are not covered by insurance. The government has launched social insurance schemes, namely Pradhan Mantri Jeevan Jyoti Bima Yojana, a term life insurance policy; Pradhan Mantri Suraksha Bima Yojana, a personal accident (PA) policy; and Pradhan Mantri Jan Arogya Yojana–Ayushman Bharat, a health scheme, to provide insurance coverage to the marginalised sections of society. The regulator has made efforts to promote insurance for low-income and rural populations by introducing separate regulations that encourage insurance companies to operate and explore unreached markets. However, there is increasing concern about the growing protection gap, especially after the COVID-19 pandemic. The natural catastrophe protection gap in India was 95%, or USD 2.61 billion, in 2021, one of the highest in the world (Geneva Association, 2023) and significantly above the emerging markets' average, the non-life insurance penetration is at 1% (Swiss Re, 2023a). Currently, less than 10% of people in rural India have life insurance coverage, while less than 20% of the rural population has health insurance coverage (Roy & Jain, 2023). The situation is equally bad or even worse in urban slums and semi-urban areas (Bhat et al., 2018). However, segregated data is not available about insurance coverage there. The problem is slightly better for microenterprises (micro and small enterprises), as found in the study conducted by NIA. The study found that the percentage of enterprise owners taking health insurance is 24%, and group insurance for their employees is 44% (Singh & Sathyakumar, 2023).

Access to social security is a fundamental human right. Insurance can provide financial protection and help reduce poverty, as it can prevent the gains from development initiatives from being lost when vulnerable households experience a loss or crisis. It is necessary to complement developmental efforts to boost productivity with corresponding efforts to bridge the protection gap (Churchill, 2006). The poor and marginalised are exposed to the greatest risks of natural disasters, pandemics, social unrest, and crime, which hit them harder. Vulnerability and poverty go hand in hand, but microinsurance can break a part of the vicious cycle that ties them together (Morduch, 2006). Studies conducted by Collins et al. (2009), Dercon (2005), and Cohen and Sebstad (2005) observe that microinsurance plays a protective role by helping manage financial risks that have commensurate setbacks. It also has a productive role by helping create assets and improving purchasing power. Together, it has the potential to break the cycle of poverty and usher in economic growth. Janzen and Carter (2019) noted that poor households with inadequate access to financial markets can sell assets to smooth consumption and reduce consumption to protect assets. An innovative microinsurance scheme reduces both these forms of costly coping. Microinsurance also helps meet the social objectives of governments, regulators, and non-governmental organisations (Churchill & Reinhard, 2012).

The availability and access to microinsurance are directly aligned with the Sustainable Development Goals (SDGs), as inclusive finance is an enabler of the developmental goals of the SDGs, 2030, where it impacts 8 of the 17 goals. These include SDG 1, on eradicating poverty; SDG 2, on ending hunger, achieving food security, and promoting sustainable agriculture; SDG 3, on promoting health and well-being; SDG 5, on achieving gender equality and economic empowerment of women; SDG 8, on promoting economic growth and jobs; SDG 9, on supporting industry, innovation, and infrastructure; SDG 10, on reducing inequality; and SDG 17, on partnerships for the goals (UNCDF, 2023).

Wiedmaier-Pfister and Chatterjee (2006) opine that an inclusive insurance market can be created if regulators have a mandate from policymakers to take their market development responsibilities seriously. However, they observe that creating an enabling environment for outreach and sustainability in the large low-income market is a challenge. Ensuring consumer protection alongside encouraging innovative solutions to cater to the insurance needs of low-income households is another challenge faced by regulators in emerging markets (Wiedmaier-Pfister & Chatterjee, 2006).

Insurance Regulatory and Development Authority of India (IRDAI), the regulator in India, has taken the path of forcing and incentivising the formal sector insurers to expand their activities to reach out to the low-income and rural markets, with limited success. On the other side are development institutions that are very resource-constrained but are working in this direction silently by innovating and educating the customers. However, they are not recognised by the regulator and get no incentive (Singh & Bihari, 2018) apart from the goodwill of the customers, who are equally resource-constrained. This chapter narrates the evolution of the regulatory space in India to create insurance inclusion and the story of an alternative form of organisation co-created by Annapurna Pariwar (AP), jointly with its members, to provide risk management services for women microentrepreneurs of Pune and Mumbai. AP is among the very few organisations that set up a community-based insurance model to care for the health, life, and asset risks of the members, following mutual/cooperative principles.

The chapter has six sections. The second section captures the evolution of microinsurance regulation in India. The third section discusses the mutual/cooperative model of insurance to understand the relevance of the community-based insurance model of AP. The fourth section discusses the Annapurna Model of Insurance, which focuses on customer centricity. The fifth section of the chapter provides a way forward by recommending the formalisation of the community model of insurance in India and provides evidence of formalisation in the literature. The last section is the conclusion.

2 Evolution of Microinsurance and Microinsurance Regulation of IRDAI

This section covers the evolution of the microinsurance regulation of IRDAI and the corresponding journey of the microinsurance sector in India. It also captures the initial journey of AP in setting up mutual insurance and its efforts to try to fit in through self-regulation.

3 Advent of Microinsurance in India: A Historical Account

India has had the presence of insurance companies for about 200 years now. It has seen many changes from time to time, evolving into the present form of regulatory regime. India had the presence of 245 private life insurance companies, provident societies, and 107 general insurance companies before it gained independence in 1947. The life insurance business was nationalised by the government in the year 1956, and Life Insurance Corporation (LIC) of India was formed by amalgamating these life companies. Similarly, general insurance companies were nationalised and merged to form four public-sector insurance companies in January 1973.

The most recent and major change that the insurance sector saw was when the government took the path of liberalisation in 1999, based on the recommendations of the Malhotra Committee report (1994). An independent regulator for the insurance sector, 'The Insurance Regulatory and Development Authority' (IRDA), was constituted in April 2000. Later, it was renamed 'The Insurance Regulatory and Development Authority of India' (IRDAI) in December 2014 (IRDAI, 2014). Private sector participation was allowed in August 2000 for the first time after nationalisation.

At this juncture, IRDAI notified the 'Regulation for Social and Rural Obligation' in 2000, intending to ensure inclusive growth of the insurance sector (Ilangovan & Chandramohan, 2010). This regulation echoed the practice of priority sector lending norms laid out by the banking regulator, Reserve Bank of India (RBI), for all Indian commercial banks to address concerns regarding the financial inclusion of rural and low-income populations in the country. The IRDAI regulation defined the rural and social sectors and placed an obligation on both life and nonlife insurers, as well as standalone health insurance companies, to write a certain percentage of business from both categories. The percentages and numbers were a proportion of the annual business underwritten and the number of lives covered by a company. The regulation was amended in 2002, 2004, 2005, and 2008.

As a result of these regulatory initiatives, insurance companies included small-ticket-size rural insurance products in their offerings. However, there was no attempt to understand the needs of the low-income market, and no innovations were observed in product development. The sum insured of conventional products was lowered, and accordingly, premiums were adjusted. Understandably, product development requires in-depth quantitative research based on historical or time-series data on mortality, morbidity, and risks. Market research is also required to understand the needs and behaviour of the target market. This was not possible because of a lack of time and resource commitment from stakeholders for continuous research.

The data from IRDAI indicates that LIC, a public sector insurance company, was keen to carry out the mandate of the government and to make its mark in inclusion. LIC adopted a partner-agent model for distribution. They worked with Non-Governmental Organizations (NGOs)/Microfinance Institutions (MFIs) to sell their products to minimise administrative costs. LIC sold about 90% of the life microinsurance policies during this period. However, the overall impact was not significant, considering the volume of the target population. They faced problems in distribution, and renewal rates were low. Most of the partnering NGOs/MFIs faced issues with documentation, servicing, and claim settlement, and they often dropped out from renewals. Only a few of them, namely 'Shri Kshetra Dharmasthala Rural Development Project (SKDRDP)' in Karnataka and 'Mandi Sakshartha Samiti' in Himachal Pradesh, were able to bring regular renewals of their members. The contribution of private sector companies was minimal in this direction.

The Government of India also contributed towards insurance inclusion by introducing a social insurance scheme named Janashree Bima through the LIC in August 2000. The scheme was intended to provide financial assistance to low-income and poor households in rural areas engaged in 48 specific occupations and social groups. The scheme covered natural and accidental death as well as accidental disability for a premium of Rs. 200. In October 2007, the government launched another scheme named Aam Aadmi Bima Yojana with similar features for rural landless households (Table 1).

While these schemes and products of LIC covered the risk of life and accidents, general insurance companies also launched products to cover risks of asset loss, health, and hospitalisation; however, they did not match the zeal of LIC in selling these products, and data on the sale of general microinsurance products was not reported by IRDAI.

4 Early Explorations by Annapurna Parivar for Insurance: An Untold Story

While the government and insurance companies were working towards insurance inclusion, Pune-based non-profit group AP was silently working in this direction to meet the felt needs of its members. AP was established in 1993, self-funded by the founder Dr Medha Purao Samant, to facilitate credit to women microentrepreneurs in the urban slums of Pune. The poor's heavy reliance on informal financial services like moneylenders is expensive and exacerbates poverty (Wiedmaier-Pfister & Chatterjee, 2006). Medha Tai saw vegetable vendors borrowing at high interest rates to sustain their businesses, which left no room for them to make a profit. This became the trigger point in 1993 to start this initiative with nine women borrowers and a capital of nine thousand. After working for more than three decades, AP now has about 2.5 lakh members.

After a few years, the sudden death of a few members and subsequent dialogue by the founder with members identified the need for financial security and risk management amongst the members, which emerged as a need for insurance. AP explored possibilities to collaborate with insurance companies to design suitable health insurance products for its members. However, they could not find a useful product to suit their requirements, and insurance companies were not flexible enough to customise their products. Medha Tai started thinking about managing the risks internally with the help of some international volunteers. AP also made a failed attempt to distribute the 'Janshree Bima Yojna' through LIC during this time. It started participating in the scheme in 1998; however, it faced difficulties due to delays in claim settlement. Group members would stop loan repayment in case of the death of a member, disheartened by a delay in the claim settlement. It also faced difficulty in managing documentation. Because of this, it stepped out of the scheme in 2009. This further strengthened its resolve to develop an alternative risk management model for its members.

This gap in demand and supply led to AP designing its first health insurance scheme for the 3000 members in 2003. AP took membership fees from the members and created a fund to take care of the emergency health needs of the members. One part of the fee was used for administrative expenses, and the rest was collected in the reimbursement fund. The starting premium was Rs. 50 per member. It provided health coverage to four members of the household. It initially reimbursed the cost of treatment up to Rs. 5000 in case of hospitalisation in government hospitals. There were different rates of reimbursements for network private hospitals and private hospitals outside the network (Leist & Radermacher, 2004; Singh, 2014).

The eligibility criteria and claim settlement process were meticulously laid out. The information regarding fund management was shared with the members monthly to maintain transparency. The fund worked well, and the incurred claim ratio (ICR)[1] was also under control (Table 2).

The fund became profitable after five years of operations in 2008. The claims ratio has remained positive throughout the years, barring the COVID-19 years (Annexure I). The renewal rate is more than 75%, which indicates high customer satisfaction.

[1] Incurred claim ratio (ICR) is a ratio of the total claim amount paid by the insurance company to the total premium amount collected in a financial year calculated as total claim / total premium.

Table 1 Microinsurance Industry Data from the first microinsurance regulation to the revised regulation (2007–2015)

Year	Individual category		Group category		Industry total		Share of LIC	
	Policies (No. in Lakh)	Premium (Rs Cr)	Lives Covered (No. in Lakh)	Premium (Cr)	Lives Covered (No. in Lakh)	Premium (Rs Cr)	Lives Covered * (%)	Premium (%)
2007–08	9.4	18.2	122.4	201.3	131.8	219.5	93	95
2008–09	21.5	36.6	125.5	206.0	147.0	242.5	86	84
2009–10	29.8	158.2	168.4	243.4	198.3	401.6	85	94
2010–11	36.5	130.4	152.6	155.2	189.1	285.6	86	91
2011–12	46.2	115.7	101.9	109.8	148.2	225.5	90	91
2012–13	50.4	109.7	139.8	218.0	190.2	327.7	92	95
2013–14	27.7	95.7	131.8	141.8	159.5	237.4	88	89
2014–15	8.2	28.9	231.5	315.6	239.7	344.5	88	87

Source IRDAI, analysis by the author (*individual number of policies considered as number of lives covered for aggregation)

Table 2 Incurred claim ratio of health mutual insurance since inception (2003–23)

Year	2003–04	2004–05	2005–06	2006–07	2007–08	2008–09	2009–10	2010–11	2011–12	2012–13	2013–14
ICR	1.18	0.85	0.92	0.93	0.34	0.97	0.43	0.80	0.94	0.96	0.76
Year	2014–15	2015–16	2016–17	2017–18	2018–19	2019–20	2020–21	2021–22	2022–23	2023–24	
ICR	1.13	0.87	1.04	1.11	0.85	0.86	1.26	1.49	0.97	0.74	

Source Debnath (2016) and Annapurna Pariwar

Awareness and active participation in the scheme by the beneficiaries enable higher utilisation rates and renewal in community-based microinsurance schemes (De Bock & Ontiveros, 2013; Hussien & Azage, 2021; Mesbah et al., 2022; Mirachet et al., 2019). Most of the members of SHGs and JLGs join the scheme through referrals, which again indicates high customer satisfaction. In some cases, wherein NGOs extended the insurance services of insurance companies in a partner-agent model, the premium rates increased at the time of renewal beyond the clients' affordability because of the high claim ratio, which NGOs could not sustain and subsequently dropped out of intermediation.

In 2006, Community-Based Family Insurance was introduced by AP to take care of emergency financial needs in case of the death of a family member of the borrower. It was based on a tie-up with LIC for extending the benefits of Janashree Bima Yojana, a central government scheme. The members were not required to pay separately for enrolment under the scheme, as it was subsidised by Health Mutual Fund (HMF) and Family Life Mutual Fund (FLMF). It also provided compensation for asset loss in accidents and disasters like fire and flood without any extra premium.

In 2009, Family and Life Mutual Fund, a community-based life insurance, was introduced to manage the financial shock of the members and provide financial assistance to their family members. The fund waived off the loan in case of the death of the member and paid a sum of Rs. 15,000–20,000 to the nominee. Every time, the product development was done in consultation with the members and addressed their immediate concerns triggered by certain events (Annexure II). The cost was affordable, and the reimbursement was sufficient to take care of emergency needs. Product designing and pricing were done by the French actuary and his team.

This was a timely intervention introduced by AP, as the government and the regulator were concerned with the limited reach of insurance and were taking steps to promote insurance inclusion. It was one of India's few examples of community-based mutual insurance after nationalisation. We can call it microinsurance, as it provides support to the low-income population in times of financial shock. It also aligns with the basic definition of insurance: 'contributions of many pay for the losses of few'.

The terms and conditions were also framed to take care of the procedural and financial convenience of the members. In other words, it was a scheme democratically designed 'by the members for the members'. Hence, it is either called Community-Based Insurance or Cooperative/Mutual Fund for Health, Life, Family, Asset, and Pension.

5 The First Microinsurance Regulation: Did it Solve Any Problems?

When AP was moving ahead from health mutual insurance funds to life and family insurance mutual funds, a separate microinsurance regulation was introduced by the regulator in 2005. This was a novel attempt by the regulator to encourage commercial insurance companies to develop products and promote distribution channels focused on low-income households. The new regulation complemented the cause of insurance inclusion. This was the first-of-its-kind regulation in the world in 2005, followed by the Philippines in 2006, Peru in 2007, Mexico in 2008, Taiwan in 2009, and Brazil in 2012 (Biener et al., 2014). The regulation defined microinsurance and microinsurance agents and specified the microinsurance channel. The coverage limit and terms for the various products, as well as the maximum commission (as a percentage of premium), were also clearly defined. The regulation allowed a memorandum of understanding (MoU) between life and nonlife companies to introduce a combination of life and nonlife products, which was not permitted in conventional insurance.

It intended to simplify the insurance offering for customers by producing hybrid products that covered various life and general risks in a single policy through a single window. However, the collaboration between life and general insurance companies did not happen, as both life and nonlife companies followed different systems and processes. The technologies and customer service portals used by insurance companies were also vastly different from each other. This kind of collaboration would have required the integration of these systems, which was not viable for the insurance companies, especially considering the low margins, lack of distribution channels, and limited revenue from this business.

This regulation generated interest among insurance companies to develop tie-ups with NGOs and MFIs to act as a distribution channel. Insurance companies took up microinsurance as an activity line and reorganised separate departments to look after rural, social, and microinsurance business. Da Costa (2013) observes it as a regulatory innovation that was intended to save the cost of distribution for insurance providers in building rural infrastructural reach, while the intermediaries were to gain revenue from commissions without having to shoulder any actuarial risk. The insurance companies followed the partner-agent distribution model, wherein NGOs/MFIs act as agents of insurance companies. The MFIs/NGOs collaborated with commercial insurers to cover their clients with insurance. They leveraged their customer/member/beneficiary base and provided group insurance and customer services on behalf of insurance companies. The insurance companies passed on the commission, which covered the administrative cost of the NGO/MFI. The MFIs/NGOs collaborated with commercial insurers to cover their clients in insurance.

However, the initiative could not be sustained because the intermediating NGOs/MFIs faced backlash from the members/clients as the repudiation rate (claim rejection) was extremely high, and the turnaround time (TAT) for claim settlement was long. The claim settlement process had high documentation requirements to prove eligibility and evidence, which were difficult and costly for the intermediating NGOs/MFIs. Insurance companies had no strategy to improve the claim experience through client education and access to health services. They had no strategy to handhold and guide the intermediating NGOs/MFIs in enrolment and claim settlement. The community and intermediaries had no role in the claim settlement apart from arranging the documents. The entire process of claim settlement lacked transparency. This made the intermediaries' job difficult, which involves answerability to customers. Lack of information and awareness of the claim process reduced the trust level among the clients. In some cases, the premium rates increased at the time of renewal beyond the affordability of the clients because of the high claim ratio, which NGOs could not sustain and dropped off from intermediation. These policies did not address the concerns of clients, 'who will get the benefit of no-claim/low-claim'. There were no arrangements for profit sharing with the customers in the current system of insurance companies in India. It went against the basic principles of the Bottom of the Pyramid market, framed by Prahlad and Hart (2002), who emphasised new product formulation and value pricing. The benefits of the Bottom of Pyramid (BoP) strategy taken up by business organisations and social businesses in the space of health, education, telecommunication, energy solutions, and food are well known (Prahalad, 2005). Gupta and Kanungo (2022) demonstrate that higher financial inclusion for the BoP segment is achieved by financial intermediaries adopting digitisation, which is emphasised in the BoP strategy. Value for money for clients was also emphasised by Kim and Mauborgne (2004) in their famous Blue Ocean Strategy of marketing. The **Blue Ocean Strategy** (Kim & Mauborgne, 2015) is a business approach that emphasises creating a new, uncontested market space (a 'Blue Ocean') rather than competing in an existing, overcrowded market (a 'Red Ocean'). The strategy focuses on innovation, differentiation, and creating demand in an area where competition is minimal or non-existent, rather than trying to outcompete rivals in a saturated market.

6 Revised Regulations: An Attempt to Expand the Horizon

Both regulations were subsequently revised and replaced after a decade by new regulations in 2015. The IRDAI (Obligations of Insurers to Rural and Social Sectors) Regulations, 2015, adopted a pragmatic definition of the 'rural sector' based on the Population Census of India and included new segments of the population in the social sector, defining what constitutes the unorganised sector, informal sector, and economically backward classes.

The new Microinsurance Regulation (2015) redefined general microinsurance products by adding microenterprises to its scope. It qualified (specifying) the policies issued to micro, small, and medium enterprises (MSMEs) up to an annual premium of Rs. 10,000 for each MSME. The prescribed maximum and minimum age of entry for both life and general insurance, as well as the terms of cover for life insurance, were removed in the new regulation of 2015. The regulation expanded the definition of microinsurance agents and included more entities in the distribution channel. Additionally, the regulation augmented the Rural and Social Obligation Regulation by incentivising the sale of microinsurance in rural areas. Accordingly, all microinsurance products sold in rural markets were regarded as businesses in both rural and social sectors for compliance.

The commission rates for microinsurance agencies were also revised. The 2005 regulation had specified only the upper limits of commission, whereas the new regulation detailed the specifications regarding the first premium commission and the subsequent commission. There were constant complaints from insurers that the microinsurance sum insured limits (Rs. 50,000) prescribed in the 2005 regulation were exceptionally low, which made it unattractive for customers who were willing to pay the premium. The other limitation was related to the limited distribution channel. These issues were addressed in the new regulation of 2015.

A series of other reforms and developments by other regulators complemented the steps taken by the IRDAI. India has come a long way in facilitating the market for alternate channels, as was desired by Chatterjee (2012) (Table 3).

Other regulations like Point of Salespersons,[2] IMF Regulation,[3] and CPSC-SPVs Regulation[4] were intended to increase access to insurance for the masses. However, the industry data indicates that the impact of these regulations was also limited. The growth rate of the number of lives covered under microinsurance and the micro-insurance premium was also meagre compared to the industry figures (Table 4).

This was also a time when the government announced the Jan Suraksha Schemes in 2015, which covered the risk of life through Pradhan Mantri Jeevan Jyoti Bima Yojana (PMJJBY) and PA through the Pradhan Mantri Suraksha Bima Yojana (PMSBY) scheme. Subsequently, the Rashtriya Swasthya Bima Yojana (RSBY) health scheme was replaced by Pradhan Mantri Jan Arogya Yojana (PMJAY), aka Ayushman Bharat scheme, and the National Agricultural Insurance Scheme (NAIS) crop insurance scheme was replaced by the Pradhan Mantri Fasal Bima Yojana (PMFBY) scheme.

The insurance companies covered their regulatory compliance through these schemes. Hence, microinsurance became less attractive for insurance companies. A study by the National Insurance Academy, Pune, India, in 2019 found that only 14 out of 58 insurance companies have microinsurance on their websites' product lists (Singh et. al., 2019).

India has been lagging behind in insurance density and penetration despite efforts by the regulator and the Government. By international standards, India is lagging in insurance protection compared to the global average. Global insurance penetration (ratio of premium to GDP) is 7, and density (per capita insurance premium) is Rs. 77,017 (889 USD). Meanwhile, India's insurance penetration is 3.7, and its density is Rs. 8230 (95 USD). The insurance density of China is

[2] IRDAI regulates and supervises PoS to ensure that the salespersons are adequately trained, follow ethical practices, and comply with regulatory guidelines to safeguard consumer interests.

[3] **IMF (Insurance Marketing Firm) Regulation** refers to the set of rules established by the IRDAI for entities that market and sell insurance products. These firms act as intermediaries between insurers and customers, helping to broaden the distribution of insurance products in India.

[4] The IRDAI (Insurance Services by Common Public Service Centres) Regulations, 2019, outline the framework for CPSC-SPVs (Common Public Service Centre—Special Purpose Vehicle) to provide insurance services, including allowing them to print policy documents on plain A4 Paper and encouraging insurers to hold e-policies with registered Insurance Repositories.

Table 3 Steps taken to facilitate insurance inclusion in India

Changes required to serve the small-ticket market with alternative distribution channels	Status in India
Low documentation	Requirements for photograph and address proof were waived off for premium up to Rs. 10,000
Technology for creating a financial identity	Aadhaar number and KYC norms, facilitating the way forward
Management of high volumes of small transactions	Robust technology platforms like UPI are present
Interbank and wholesale payment systems	Core banking solution facilitates fast transactions
Regulation for telecommunications players to participate	Present in market
Mobile banking	Highly developed
Tele- and mobile marketing	Present in market
e-contracts	Present (Section 10A of the Information Technology Act, 2000 [IT Act] & Section 85A of the Indian Evidence Act, 1872)
Virtual marketing through virtual kiosks	Present in the market, government promoted CSCs are good examples, apart from private players
Bancassurance	Heavily used for the distribution of social insurance schemes promoted by the government
Distribution of insurance through supermarkets and retail chains	MI regulation (IRDAI, 2015) has created space for it
Consumer protection regulation	In place
Investment in consumer education by the regulator	In place

Source Bester et al. (2009), compiled by author

Table 4 Growth of microinsurance in India after the 2015 regulation

Year	Policies (No. in lakh)	Policies (YoY) growth (%)	Premium (Cr)	Premium (YoY) growth (%)
2015–16	301.7	21	334.1	− 3
2016–17	332.0	9	498.6	33
2017–18	597.4	44	1433.4	65
2018–19	1221.7	51	3237.8	56
2019–20	1417.6	14	4653.1	30
2020–21	1023.7	− 38	4568.3	− 2
2021–22	1329.5	23	6346.0	28
2022–23	1631.3	19	8792.8	28

Table 5 Insurance density & penetration

	Insurance penetration	Insurance density
Global	7	Rs. 77,017 (889 USD)
India	3.7	Rs. 8230 (95 USD)
China	3.9	Rs. 33,267 (384 USD)

Source Swiss Re, 2024

Rs. 33,267 (384 USD), which is more than five times that of India, and the penetration is 3.9 (Swiss Re, 2024) (Table 5).

As per the latest data, 3.3 crore people are registered under PMJJBY, 45.9 crore individuals are covered in PMSBY, and 36.5 crore households are covered under Ayushman Bharat (NHA, 2025). Along with this, 19 crore individuals are covered under LIC policies, 54.4 crore are covered under PA, and the population covered under commercial health insurance is 57 crore (IRDAI, 2023–24). Together, these numbers show a progressive picture. However, the health insurance protection gap of about 40% and the adequacy of coverage in terms of under-insurance show a significant protection gap.

7 Annapurna Pariwar in Current Regulatory Space: An Act of Balancing

A wide gap exists between the rich and the poor regarding access to insurance in India. Access to insurance is better for people employed in the formal sector. The insurance uptake in the formal sector is also incentivised by taxation. The unorganised sector employees have limited resources, and access to insurance is also difficult due to high documentation requirements. The informal sector financial institutions, consisting of NGOs/MFIs, were exploring options to bridge this gap and manage the risk of their customers, who worked in the unorganised sector. Many of them came forward and played a significant role in innovating products and processes to protect the poor (Pinto, 2015). After the two regulations were announced, insurance companies also started looking for NGOs/MFIs to partner with as distribution channels. Organisations like BASIX and SEWA were successful in fostering tie-ups with insurance companies and extending insurance coverage to their members.

Annapurna Pariwar was one such organisation working to reduce the protection gap for the urban poor and microentrepreneurs. AP had covered the life and accident risks of its members through the JBY scheme of the Central Government. AP struggled to extend the benefits of this scheme to its members and found the claim process difficult and ambiguous. It also faced challenges in following documentation compliances of the partner insurance companies. They also struggled to get a suitable health insurance product or scheme through general insurance companies. They started searching for appropriate health insurance solutions for their microborrowers around the year 2000–2001. However, they experienced that insurance companies were not flexible in modifying their products and processes to suit the needs of members. This was the time when FX Hay, a French actuary working in India with InterAid (a French funding agency), offered to design a community-based health product following the principles of mutuality. The fundamental principles of mutualism are solidarity, democratic governance, sustainability, and value maximisation for members. AP developed its health insurance product with the French actuarial team and started its journey of setting up mutual health insurance in 2003. However, the insurance regulator had no provision to regulate this kind of community-based risk management initiative. Since MFIs, SHGs, and NGOs do not meet the capital requirements and hence do not get licences, they are not legally considered insurance providers (Da Costa, 2013). AP falls under Category 2 (organisations regulated and/or licenced under any other law—formal entities under laws other than the insurance law) according to the International Association of Insurance Supervisors (IAIS, 2007).

Wiedmaier-Pfister and Chatterjee (2006) observed that many informal micro-insurance schemes have emerged to fill the gap in protection. AP operates without an insurance licence. They maintain their existence and grow silently, working to solve the problems of their clients and self-regulating with the hope that supervisors will not react against them. The journey of AP is a good example of this. They aspire that the model will prove its worthiness, that someday their contribution will be recognised, and that an inclusive regulatory space will be created for them, opening a path for upscaling.

However, when industry experts look at it, they may not qualify it as insurance, as it does not fall under the purview of the regulator. However, this was the best possible solution, as Prahalad and Hart (2002) observe that the poor in developing countries operate in an informal or extra-legal economy to save the time and cost involved in securing incorporation of their enterprises. As per regulation, an entity shall register as an insurance company after fulfilling the capital adequacy requirement of Rs. 100 crores and obtaining a licence to become eligible to underwrite risks. The current guideline did not specify any distribution arrangement to take care of the risk management requirements of the underprivileged sections of society, to which AP was catering. The onlookers also questioned its sustainability and legitimacy, as it did not have the support of a formal insurer and was not following any regulatory guidelines. Such challenges were faced by AP in maintaining transparency and openness in its operations and fund management. The scheme was also fully supported by the members, as each decision was taken after several rounds of dialogue with them.

Wiedmaier-Pfister and Chatterjee (2006) also observe that, while there are some benefits to the absence of regulation, there are many associated disadvantages.

The advantages of not being a registered insurer are many, which translate to value for money for customers.

1. No burden of adherence to regulatory standards
2. No need to comply with the supervisory burden, such as comprehensive reporting, internal controls, and the cost of appointed actuaries

3. Flexibility and freedom to innovate
4. Low cost of operations
5. Scope to offer cheaper products

The adverse impacts of not having a licence are many:

1. Customer protection is a major concern. Customers have little recourse if the hospital does not keep its promises.
2. Long-term viability is another concern in the absence of actuarial pricing and the lack of adequately skilled management.
3. Another concern for long-term viability is the high exposure to greater covariant risk due to the geographical concentration of the risk pool and customer profile. Maintaining solvency can be a challenge during natural disasters and pandemics.
4. They do not have access to reinsurance, as it is not a licenced insurer.
5. If the insurance regulation prohibits the use of the word 'insurance', it impacts the branding and marketing of these products.
6. The growth can pose a threat to sustainability; as societies become larger, the effectiveness of the member-governance system is undermined, and a separation is required between management and ownership.
7. Accumulation of assets and funds increases the risk of fraud or theft, which is difficult for member governance to control.
8. Maintaining social orientation can be a challenge when microinsurers get formalised after they become licenced.

AP has developed such systems and processes that effectively mitigate these disadvantages (Table 6).

The customers of AP have remained loyal despite increasing competition in the market. The biggest competition is the government schemes, namely PMJJBY, PMSBY, and PMJAY. Apart from this, many fintech companies and MFIs/NBFCs have started operating in Maharashtra. The recent development of the Hospi Wage product by AP is an interesting example of how customers produce innovative ideas from the market, and AP responds to them with innovation. Under Hospi Wage, AP offers wage loss compensation of Rs. 500 per day to the members as well as family members in case of hospitalisation. This is over and above the hospital bills/expenses reimbursement. The customers of AP were approached by fintech companies who were selling hospi-cash products of insurance companies. The customers came with this demand to AP. AP saw it both as a challenge and an opportunity. Within a year, they collected information from the market and developed a new product in 2024, named HospiWage, offering many more benefits compared to the competitors. AP could do this because they have much more customer centrality.[5] Their unique selling proposition

[5] **Customer centrality** is a business philosophy or approach where the customer is at the heart of every decision, strategy, and operation within an organization. It means that a company prioritises the needs, preferences, and satisfaction of its customers in all aspects of its business. This customer-first mindset influences everything from product development to marketing strategies and customer service practices.

Table 6 How Annapurna Pariwar took care of the disadvantages of not being licenced for the insurance business

Sr No.	Disadvantage of informal setup	How Annapurna Pariwar effectively mitigated it
1	Customer protection	Annapurna Pariwar signs an MoU with hospitals. If services are not satisfactory, they remove the hospital from the list of network hospitals. Hospitals tend to comply with the service demands as AP provides bulk access to customers.
2	No access to actuaries and skilled manpower	Annapurna Pariwar has access to the voluntary services of a pool of actuaries guided by F. X. Hay[a]; hence, their products are actuarially priced. Recently, an actuary has joined the team.
3	Long-term viability and maintaining solvency	Annapurna addressed it by creating a reserve from unused funds or surplus generated by the fund. They also conduct a real-time assessment of the available funds and adjust the compensation accordingly.
4	No access to reinsurance	It remains a major limitation in upscaling the operations of Annapurna Pariwar. They managed covariant risks like COVID-19 by pooling extra premiums, reducing the limit of compensation, stopping new enrolments and utilising reserve funds. Within two years after COVID, all the past reserve funds were rebuilt again by following strict discipline.
5	Not being part of the formal sector impacts marketing and communication	Annapurna Pariwar participates directly and indirectly in policy advocacy and commands strong goodwill for the women's empowerment it has achieved over the years. It also commands strong customer loyalty. Wiedmaier-Pfister and Chatterjee (2006) observe that microinsurance providers often operate under other authorities, like banking regulators, and because of that, they escape regulatory oversight. This is also the case with Annapurna Pariwar. The insurance schemes of Annapurna Pariwar are not seen as part of the insurance sector, even though they provide insurance services.
6	Sustainability of governance, separation of management and community with an increase in size	Over a period, Annapurna Pariwar has evolved its system of decision-making and claim settlement to accommodate its growth. In the beginning, decisions were made in community meetings. Currently, these decisions are taken by community representatives. Experts are involved in these decisions to provide their technical inputs and guide them in sound decision-making. The in-house network of hospitals and telephonic guidance by in-house medical officers play a major role in the decision-making process of members.

(continued)

Table 6 (continued)

Sr No.	Disadvantage of informal setup	How Annapurna Pariwar effectively mitigated it
7	Increase in the risk of fraud or theft with the increase in funds and assets	Strong MIS, transparency regarding the availability and management of funds, timely internal and external audits, and close member scrutiny have helped manage funds and assets.
8	Maintaining social orientation	There are examples in the banking sector wherein MFIs/ NBFCs have obtained licenses for SFBs and are catering to the low-income market with a large customer base in urban slums, small towns, and rural areas. Annapurna Pariwar consciously decided not to pursue NBFC/SFB status and chose to remain a cooperative multi-state society to provide microfinance services, as well as to continue operating as a non-profit company in order to offer microinsurance services.

[a] FX Hay is based in France since 2008 but is a consultant and advisor for Annapurna Pariwar and has regular monthly meetings with Annapurna Pariwar's Senior Team dealing with Microinsurance. He has a team of young actuaries who design/modify Annapurna Pariwar's products, whenever required.

(USP) is bringing value to customers at a lower cost. Being a community-based model, they involve the members in the benefit design process and have a strong advantage in knowledge of clients' needs and willingness to pay (Radermacher & Dror, 2006). Mutual models follow the principles of self-help, self-administration, and self-responsibility. The members bear the actuarial risk and are liable for potential losses. Accordingly, profits remain in the system and are used for the advantage of members, aligning the interest of the individual with that of the group and strengthening social cohesion. Due to elevated levels of social cohesion, regular interactions bring social monitoring and traceability (Sobel, 2002). Because of this, this model lowers the costs emerging from fraud, moral hazard, and adverse selection.

8 Mutual Model of Insurance

This section examines the position and contribution of AP in offering risk management solutions and the challenges faced in the regulatory space. It also discusses how mutual insurance is positioned within the current guidelines and its impact on organisations like AP.

Mutual insurance companies are set up as an alternative risk management organisation to serve the members who are also their policyholders. Hence, the members, in addition to being customers, are also the owners. They are different from shareholding insurance companies, as policyholders are the owners of insurance mutuals/cooperatives. In other words, insurance mutuals/cooperatives are legal entities that do not have equity. The members possess distinct governance and other control rights in the company (Powell, 2017). A mutual insurance policyholder has the right to elect the management of the company, like the owners of a business enterprise (Hetherington, 1969). This ensures the interest of policyholders, as it maintains a balance between offering quality insurance products and services and generating profits.

9 Advantages of a Mutual Model

The principles of mutuality address the problem of the principal-agent issue prevalent in shareholding companies. The principal-agent problem is said to exist when the agent makes decisions on behalf of the principal (the owner). However, the decision is not aligned with the principal's best interests because the goals of the principal and the agent are not aligned (Smith et al., 1997). It exists in insurance companies because there is a conflict of interest between the insured and the insurer. Policyholders pay money to insurance companies expecting that the insurance company will compensate for their losses when they arise. The outgo towards compensation and services to policyholders is an expense to insurance companies, which impacts profitability; hence, insurance companies tend to reduce claims.

The mutual model also reduces adverse selection and moral hazard, common in stock companies, by reducing information asymmetry.[6] The products become cheaper as this arrangement removes the intermediation cost by eliminating the roles of agents/intermediaries and their commissions. It also reduces the cost of monitoring, information verification, and loss assessment because the system looks for value maximisation of the policyholder, and the trust level is high as there is no conflict of interest. The merits of mutual insurance allow the model to be

[6] **Adverse Selection** and **Moral Hazard** are two concepts that arise due to **information asymmetry**—a situation where one party in a transaction has more or better information than the other.

According to Stiglitz (1981), when information asymmetry exists in markets, it can lead to suboptimal outcomes where sellers and buyers behave in ways that harm both parties. Adverse selection in insurance occurs when one party has more information about the risk they carry, and they use that advantage to their benefit, potentially to the detriment of the other party. In the context of insurance, for example, individuals who know they are at higher risk of an event (like health issues or accidents) are more likely to purchase insurance, while those at lower risk may opt out. This leads to an imbalance where the insurer ends up with a pool of higher-risk clients than they anticipated, raising costs and premiums for everyone, which in turn becomes prohibitive for customers.

Moral hazard arises when one party to a transaction takes on more risk because they do not bear the full consequences of that risk. In insurance, for example, after purchasing a policy, a policyholder may be more likely to engage in risky behaviour (such as smoking or reckless driving) because they know their insurance will cover the potential costs.

Both adverse selection and moral hazard are direct consequences of **information asymmetry**. In both cases, **information asymmetry** distorts decision-making, often leading to inefficiencies or market failures.

cost-effective and responsive to the insured's needs. It also brings ownership by increasing trust in customers. It can serve as a good model for bringing insurance inclusion as it addresses the prime concerns of low-income and rural populations by bringing transparency, control by policyholders, and delivering value for money (Singh et al., 2022).

10 Mutual Insurance: How Popular is it Globally?

Mutual insurance is a well-developed and established form of insurance in developed economies and mature insurance markets like North America, Europe, and Japan. Mutual and cooperative insurers hold 27% of the global market share, and mutuals serve over a billion members and employ over a million people (ICMIF). About 80% of members/policyholders of mutual insurance are in Europe and North America.

Mutual insurance collectively shares the risks of members by creating a fund through contributions. This fund can be professionally managed by a commercial organisation or a community-based mutual organization (CBMO). The funds managed by commercial corporations are prevalent in North America, Canada, Europe, and Japan. The community-based mutuals are not-for-profit organisations that primarily exist in Asian, African, and Latin American developing or underdeveloped countries. CBMOs offer bottom-up financial intermediation in the form of health, life, or asset insurance, in which funds are pooled from members in an equitable manner (Dror et al., 2019).

Mutual health organisations were originally developed in Europe in the nineteenth century in the form of workers' organisations that set up mutual funds for healthcare. Mutual health organisations are based on a mechanism of risk-sharing and resource-pooling, improving access to healthcare through risk-sharing and resource-pooling and providing access to healthcare through solidarity (Fonteneau & Galland, 2006). The members belong to resource-poor families employed in the informal sector, which are commonly excluded from formal insurance. The membership fee/contribution to the fund depends on the willingness and ability to pay. Communities retain the risk and play a significant role in designing, developing, pricing, distributing, and managing the insurance programme for the members of their communities (Bhat et al., 2017). Thus, mutual insurance builds resilience in communities in developing and underdeveloped countries by providing financial education, risk reduction, and designing affordable need-based insurance products (ICMIF, 2017).

These organisations have a local presence and operate on a small scale. Because of this, their sustainability is questioned, as their risks are concentrated both geographically and demographically. Their ability to manage covariant risks is also limited, as their organisation-level risk management practices have not evolved to deal with large risks, and these organisations do not have access to professional financial management and reinsurance (Dror et al., 2019; Radermacher et al., 2009).

European countries have a long history of informal, friendly societies and mutuals, which are considered precursors of insurance mutuals. According to the National Association of Insurance Commissioners (NAIC), the first mutual insurer was established in England in 1696 to cover losses due to fire. The first American mutual insurance company, named the Philadelphia Contributionship, was founded in 1752 and covered householders' losses by fire.

11 Mutual Insurance in India: Past, Present, and Future

The history of mutual insurance in India is as old as the history of the current form of insurance companies. The first mutual insurance company, 'Bombay Mutual Life Insurance', was set up in the year 1870 (Desai, 1953). It was also the first Indian life insurance company established in India (https://licindia.in/history). The mutual insurance entities operated in the Indian market until the time of independence. The insurance legislation of 1938 defined mutual insurance organisations as 'an insurer having no share capital and all policyholders as members' (Bhat et al., 2017). However, the provisions referring to mutual insurance companies were deleted from the legislation in the 2015 amendments. This made the regulatory space restricted for mutual insurance companies.

The potential for establishing mutual and cooperative insurance in India is immense, with over 600,000 cooperatives and a membership of over 250 million. The cooperative movement is powerful in our country and is prevalent in producer-driven manufacturing industries. India has dairy cooperatives like Amul, Banas, and Dudhsagar, and agricultural cooperatives like the National Agricultural Cooperative Marketing Federation of India (NAFED), Indian Farmers Fertiliser Cooperative Ltd. (IFFCO), and Krishak Bharati Cooperative Ltd. (KRIBHCO). The cooperative sector has gained new impetus with government schemes like 10,000 FPO. India is one of the five emerging market countries selected by the International Cooperative and Mutual Insurance Federation (ICMIF) to grow mutuals and cooperatives community-based organisations (MCCOs) because of its large uninsured population, microinsurance focus, and the strong presence of ICMIF members on the ground within the region (ICMIF, 2017)

Numerous studies from the Indian market have identified a good number of mutual/cooperative insurers in India, covering more than two million underprivileged populations. AP, BimoSEWA, Dhan Foundation, SHEFERD, SERP-AP, and Uplift-India are a few of them. However, the current insurance law does not recognise these mutual insurers as insurers, as mentioned earlier. These organisations have manoeuvred their existence by maintaining compliance through the regulators they are registered with. These organisations cover the risks of their members by retaining their risks. They face difficulties in securing finance to upscale their activities. NBFCs do not enter tie-ups with them because they are not registered bodies with insurance regulators. They do not have reinsurance available to secure their risks. Reinsurers also find it difficult to reinsure their business for the same reason.

12 Insurance Mutual by Annapurna Parivar: Ingrained Customer Centricity

Insurance mutual was a natural and wise arrangement by AP, as Ahuja and Guha-Khasnobis (2005) observe that integrating insurance with microfinance activities helps by bringing economies of scale in financial management, providing a captive market, and enabling MFIs to use their existing network and distribution channels to sell insurance. Access to health insurance makes financial services cheaper for the borrower by reducing the interest rate charged on credit, as it improves the repayment rate by reducing disruption in income. Boutin et al. (2024) also posit that bundling health insurance with microcredit has meaningful outcomes for populations lacking formal coverage and employment, as well as institutions serving them. They observe that it controls health expenses and improves the financial protection of the clients by improving health-seeking behaviours, substituting seeking formal health centres for self-medication. It ensures a more resilient financial ecosystem and enhances the financial stability of microfinance institutions.

- Fonteneau and Galland (2006) have listed the basic features of community-based mutual insurance. They explain that these are not-for-profit and are based on groups sharing common characteristics. They are neutral regarding individual risk profiles in providing membership, and membership is voluntary. Since the members are both owners and beneficiaries at the same time, they have a high commitment to protecting the health and wellbeing of members of the communities. They adopt an approach of risk-sharing and resource-pooling through solidarity. They promote solidarity, democracy, and social cohesion among members. The decision-making is participatory and democratic. Often, the potential functions extend beyond insurance as they respond to the changing demands of the members.

Through their non-profit nature, their non-exclusion policy, and their low premiums, they guarantee access to some services, even if the coverage is limited. Participation contributes to the members' satisfaction, empowerment, and learning, and promotes health-seeking behaviour.

13 Features of Community-Based Mutual Insurance in Annapurna Pariwar Vikas Samvardhan (APVS)

These features can easily be identified in the systems, processes, and management functions of the insurance mutuals run by APVS. It is a not-for-profit Section 8 company, which houses microinsurance in AP. The key features of AP Health Mutual that differentiate it from the health products available in the market are listed below. The AP product addresses all the members' concerns and also addresses sustainability concerns.

Table 7 The revisions in health mutual policy in the last one decade

Features	2016	2019	2020	2021
Premium	Rs. 130 Pa per person	Rs. 155–265 Pa per person	Rs. 220–480 Pa per person	As per the loan amount & loan duration
Benefits	50–100% reimbursement for hospitalisation	No change	No change	
Reimbursement/ cover	Minimum Rs. 2500 maximum 18,000	Minimum Rs. 1700 maximum 28,000	Minimum Rs. 2000 maximum Rs. 28,000	Minimum Rs. 2000 maximum Rs. 40,000
Other services	24*7 call centre, client education, tie-ups with trust and private hospitals	Remains same	Remains same Additionally, tie-ups with pharmacies and pathology labs	Remains same

- Members receive education on health and hygiene so that their overall wellness improves.
- Members receive health guidance for the prevention and early detection of diseases.
- When private network hospitals that have a tie-up with VS are used, members receive concessions that reduce their out-of-pocket expenses.
- There is no age discrimination for inclusion in the scheme. Members can avail themselves of the same benefits from 0 to 100 years of age at the same price.
- The number of exclusions is fewer than those of any health insurance product in the market.
- Participation of community representatives, who are elected members, in the decision-making process.
- Claims sanctioned by an elected body of representatives

In the last 22 years, the premium was increased only four times by Rs. 50, to Rs. 100, Rs. 120, and Rs. 130, finally, as per the loan amount and loan duration. However, the benefits have been increased multiple times during this period (Table 7).

14 Governance in Annapurna Pariwar

Governance is the act of planning, influencing, and monitoring, through policy, the affairs and direction of an entity. It involves exercising power and decision-making that reflect stakeholders' interests (The Chartered Governance Institute UK & Ireland, 2022).

The uniqueness of AP is that it has ensured the social protection and development of its members while maintaining financial viability. After two decades of viable business and surviving natural disasters and challenges like COVID-19, we can safely assume that the model is sustainable as well.

As per ADB (1997), accountability, transparency, predictability, and participation are the four pillars of governance. AP has ensured accountability in its workforce by setting strict TAT for claim settlement. It has a system of levying penalties on the field force for delays in documentation. It maintains transparency by publishing monthly details of the availability of funds. They are also open to sharing their data with anyone interested in research. Data is also available on their website, which is regularly updated.

They maintain predictability by following all compliance requirements set by the banking regulator, RBI. They self-regulate their insurance operations by voluntarily adhering to the guidelines of the insurance regulator, IRDAI. AP is part of the network of MFIs, SA-DHAN, and they voluntarily disclose their data on this platform.

The rules and processes are documented in the form of standard operating processes/practices (SOPs), which are repeatedly explained to the field force. The members are also familiarised with the schemes and rules for membership, as well as the benefits of the schemes, from time to time, right from the time of joining the scheme. The board of AP has external directors as well as community leaders elected through a democratic process. This brings 'participation' to ensure access to reliable information and ensures timely redressal of grievances.

AP aligns with what The Chartered Governance Institute UK & Ireland (2022) observes: 'to govern a microinsurance effectively, one must devote time to understand insurance for the poor'. The directors are involved in activities directly and are the office bearers of AP, having grown from the ranks over the years. AP took the middle path of self-monitoring and self-regulating, ensuring compliance through constant dialogue with their members and maintaining transparency in the utilisation of the fund.

15 Self-Regulation by Annapurna Pariwar: How Regulatory Concerns are Taken Care

Annapurna Pariwar's management keenly follows the regulatory landscape of India and accordingly ensures self-compliance to take care of governance, sustainability, and consumer protection (Table 8). The data indicates that self-regulation by AP surpasses the mandate given by the regulator.

Informal insurance serves a valuable social and economic function, and its formalisation is in the public interest (Bester et al., 2009). This can be achieved by defining a clear path whereby informal providers can gradually and realistically

Table 8 Self-Compliance by Annapurna Pariwar

IRDAI regulatory requirements	Self-compliance by Annapunra Pariwar
The minimum tenure of health insurance products should be one year. Maximum tenure: three years.	The tenure of APVS' mutual health insurance product is one year.
Adequate dissemination of product details to clients.	APVS provides detailed information by way of wall charts, flipcharts, brochures, and membership cards to all its members. CRs regularly visit the clients and share/revisit the information.
Entry age should be at least 65 years.	APVS—entry age is 0–100 years.
All health policies shall provide for a nomination.	APVS provides a nomination facility to all its members.
A health insurance policy shall ordinarily be renewable, except on grounds of fraud.	APVS' community health mutual insurance policies are renewed every year.
Claim payment directly in the bank account.	All claims are credited to the member's account.
Commission structure/rate	Has no commission; staff gets a salary.
Mandatory disclosures: Terms of renewal Coverage and premium Maximum age of renewal Details of specific circumstances, if any, where a premium could be loaded. All exclusions	APVS discloses: Terms of renewal Coverage and premium Maximum age of renewal No practice of premium loading All exclusions
An insurer shall settle claims, including their rejection, within 30 days of the receipt of the last 'necessary document'.	APVS settles claims, including their rejection, within 15 days of the receipt of the 'document'. Post-COVID, claim section group meetings are conducted via WhatsApp calls. The claim amount is credited to the bank account of the claimant. The Community Representatives give post-pandemic approval for almost 98% of claims that have followed all the rules. Only 10% of claims are discussed by Community representatives in monthly meetings before approval, as some rules are not followed by the claimant.
Grievance redressal	Has a system of escalation through fieldworkers. Members can call the grievance number or step into the Annapurna Pariwar office and meet anyone they want.

meet regulatory requirements. He suggests that regulators need to increase their involvement with the informal sector as facilitators to support its transition to the formal sector by applying the principles of proportionality and materiality to ascertain the extent of informal insurance provision.

16 Future of Regulatory Space in India: Formalisation as an Agenda for Microinsurance to Thrive

This section touches upon the initiatives taken by the regulator to make insurance more inclusive for smaller organisations that are providing innovative alternatives to the low-income segment of society. It also discusses the advantages of the formalisation of community-based mutual insurance or other such forms. The section also evaluates how ready AP is for formalisation, given an opportunity.

The success of Annapurna Health Mutual was presented at many conferences and seminars. For the last 23 years, Medhatai has been running from pillar to post, convincing institutions like DS-Dhan, the finance ministry, and IRDAI to persuade them that this mutual model is good and that they should help it get registered and regulated, etc. However, the results have not been encouraging. The same views were presented by the SAMI committee formed by the regulators, and AP played an important role in drafting the report. The report recommended reducing capital requirements so that small entities dedicated to serving low-income populations could get registered and regulated as insurance companies. But even after five years of the SAMI committee report being published, things have not moved in this direction.

17 Recent Developments on Inclusion: Is There Any Silver Lining?

The regulator IRDAI took an essential step in this direction by forming a committee to suggest changes for the inclusion of stand-alone microinsurance institutions. In its report named 'Report of the Committee on the Standalone Microinsurance Company (2020)', the committee observed that India needs to improve access to insurance by introducing multiple players. The Insurance Act needs amendments to allow small players like community-based mutuals and microinsurance companies. Such changes will lead to a substantial increase in insurance penetration as they will focus on serving the underserved. This need became glaringly visible during and after the COVID-19 pandemic when millions of Indians, especially in the informal sector, lost their livelihoods. Experience from countries such as the Philippines, South Africa, and China shows that supportive regulatory frameworks and technology can help in increasing access to insurance (SAMI Report, IRDAI, 2020).

IRDAI introduced three tailor-made insurance policies for MSMEs in 2021, named Bharat Griha Raksha, Bharat Laghu Udyam Suraksha Policy, and Bharat Sookshma Udyam Suraksha Policy. The policies covered asset loss to the MSMEs due to fire, natural disasters, and other perils. IRDAI, in 2022, committed to enabling 'Insurance for All' by 2047, where every citizen has an appropriate life, health, and property insurance cover, and every enterprise is supported by appropriate insurance solutions. IRDAI introduced the concept of Bima Trinity in 2024 to meet the objective of 'Insurance for All by 2047'. The trinity includes the benefit-based product Bima Vistar, localised women-centric insurance field/sales force called Bima Vaahak, and an electronic marketplace to universalise insurance called Bima Sugam. In May 2024, IRDAI issued the Master Circular—Rural, Social Sector, and Motor Third Party Obligations, which requires the life and non-life players to do a certain percentage of business compulsorily towards meeting rural, social sector, and motor third-party obligations. The new regulation has taken Panchayat as the basic level for meeting the target (IRDAI, 2024).

There are also speculations about creating space for small microinsurance institutions along the lines of microfinance. However, the regulator is not willing to commit or comment on it.

18 Regulations to Increase Access to Insurance and Formalisation

Zingales (2009) notes that regulation plays a vital role in bolstering trust in insurance. It is imperative for establishing a strong and stable foundation for the healthy growth of the sector. The insurance legislation allows only Joint stock companies and cooperative societies to provide insurance services in the country. In the year 1999, when the insurance industry was privatised, the Insurance Act of 1938 was amended to include a cooperative society to provide insurance services. Biener et al. (2014) noted that high capital requirements can hinder the growth of the microinsurance industry, which is true for the Indian microinsurance sector. Because of the high entry barrier set by regulation, existing and potential microinsurance providers have remained excluded. It is a major barrier to the development of the market, resulting in a high protection gap. Da Costa (2013) posits that institutional investments are crucial for the development and upscaling of the agencies involved in the distribution of microinsurance. In the absence of a licence, the microinsurer is trapped in a vicious circle: lack of additional capital or reinsurance and no growth (Wiedmaier-Pfister & Chatterjee, 2006). Dror et al. (2019) noted that if community-based health microinsurance schemes perform well on five parameters—enrolments, premiums, operating costs, renewal rates, and claims ratio—capital will help them in sustaining their activity.

Many NGOs/MFIs are working on financial inclusion and are interested in starting their microinsurance vertical (Singh et al., 2019). If the regulatory space for these organisations is eased, they will have a high impact by venturing into the insurance business as dedicated players in the low-income market. The existing mutual/cooperative insurance entities will upscale by attracting investments and securing reinsurance arrangements.

Currently, the capital requirement for setting up an insurance company is Rs. 100 crore, which is prohibitive for small players. If the capital requirement can be made proportional to the liability carried by insurers across various business lines, it will take care of the interests of the insured as well as create space for small players who want to focus on the low-income market.

A long dialogue with regulators and experts in the field of insurance has indicated that governance and monitoring of insurance mutuals/cooperatives and small micro-insurance companies are foreseen as significant challenges (Singh et al., 2022). A simpler MIS-based monitoring system for small new entrants can address these concerns and may assist in starting operations by microfinance institutions in micro-insurance. Monitoring through IT-based solutions will help bring transparency and provide the opportunity for open public monitoring. Many community-based organisations already have processes in place that provide tech-based real-time data, ensuring periodic updates to members and transparency in operations. Promoting shared digital platforms can play a significant role in financial inclusion. The use of digital platforms in insurance distribution can bring ease and scale to operations and servicing.

A dedicated sandbox model[7] created for experimentation in microinsurance for three to five years for a membership base of up to 20–30 thousand members, will go a long way in encouraging innovators. This will facilitate the testing of innovative models and help in examining the model for viability and up-scaling. Re-insurers can be allowed to do business with these sand-box models so that a complete business environment can be simulated for experimentation. This will also help in reducing the gestation period for the development of new models.

Payment banks are successfully taking financial intermediation to the doorsteps of people. The role of payment banks in increasing access to microinsurance can become a game-changer.

A separate channel for insurance needs to be developed to bring focus to insurance. Select common service centres (CSCs) and Krishi Vigyan Kendras (KVKs) can be developed for this purpose. These institutions can be assigned to insurance companies for a specific duration to extend their services. Though CSCs are currently allowed to work with insurance companies, the heavy spread of services by them dilutes the focus on insurance. Specialisation in insurance will create the required focus.

Simplifying broking guidelines and reducing documentation to become a broker for microfinance institutions will help them contribute to the growth of microinsurance.

19 Formalisation of Community-Based Mutual Insurance: Annapurna, a Befitting Case

Annapurna Pariwar makes a good case for formalisation as per conditions by these standards. Chatterjee (2012) recommends that the process of formalisation should be complemented by efforts from regulators in terms of awareness campaigns,

[7] The **Sandbox Model** introduced by the **IRDAI** is an innovative regulatory approach designed to foster innovation in the insurance sector. It allows insurance companies, InsurTech firms, and other stakeholders to test new products, services, or technologies in a controlled environment, with some regulatory flexibility, before they are launched in the wider market.

Table 9 Formalisation of community-based mutual insurance by Annapurna Pariwar

Process to be part of formalisation	Current status of the regulatory environment and Annapurna Pariwar
Awareness campaigns	IRDA has a comprehensive advertising strategy for consumer awareness. Annapurna Pariwar is aware of the regulatory environment and utilises all opportunities to engage with various regulators and stakeholders
Amnesties or grace periods	To be considered by the regulator
Capacity-building	Annapurna Pariwar has access to training facilities and works diligently to build the capacity of all stakeholders
Consolidation of informal schemes	Has been doing it from time to time on its own
Developing partnerships with formal underwriters	Regulation has created scope for it. It was attempted in the past but was not sustainable. Open to doing it if the terms and conditions are favourable

amnesties or grace periods, capacity-building, consolidation of informal schemes, and developing partnerships with formal underwriters (Table 9).

Annapurna Pariwar has created systems to help and handhold other organisations in replicating the model. However, there can be challenges in upscaling and replication of the model, as it requires a higher commitment. The buy-in from the community can be another challenge. In the case of AP, microfinance and microinsurance moved hand in hand, and Medhatai's leadership played an important role in creating ownership, which may not be the case for other organisations. In case the capital requirements are reduced in the future, it will open flood gates for new registrations, as it happened in the microfinance space. It will create competition in the market. The big players may float their small companies, which may also play on price, funded by the deep pockets of promoters. Survival and growth of social entities with limited resources may be another challenge.

20 Conclusion

The success and impact of the socioeconomic intervention by AP are well documented by researchers. Krenz et al. (2014) note that it has resulted in changes in individual, household, and collective agency dynamics by facilitating pathways of individual and collective empowerment, directly impacting enhanced socioemotional well-being, increased economic assets, and improved household gender equity. AP developed people-centred systems right from the beginning (Leist & Radermacher, 2004). AP took the approach of inclusion, equity, access, self-reliance, and sustainability to economically empower the illiterate women of slums (Guha et al., 2020).

The benefits and features of a cooperative or mutual model can be summarised as follows: these models are **customer-centric** rather than focusing on stakeholders, ensuring that the needs and interests of the customers are prioritised. They also maintain a fine balance between **long-term** and **short-term** objectives, ensuring sustainable growth and profitability without compromising immediate customer needs. Additionally, cooperative or mutual models are based on **collective decision-making** and governance, fostering a democratic approach where all members have a say in the decision-making process. Finally, they emphasise **transparency**, ensuring that operations and financial matters are open and clear to all stakeholders, which builds trust and accountability within the organisation. In mutual societies, owners are also insurers; hence, these organisations enjoy a high level of trust from the policyholders. The social advancement and wellbeing of the poor is their guiding principle. Profit becomes surplus, which is retained for the sustainability of the society.

Chemouni (2018) posits that tax-financed health care is difficult with a limited tax base and suggests that innovative financing mechanisms are required to improve the quality of care. In a developing country like India, where most of the population is engaged in the informal sector and continues to depend on out-of-pocket expenditures, exploring alternatives that are superior to out-of-pocket expenditures is imperative (Mor & Ashraf, 2023).

International Association of Insurance Supervisors (IAIS, 2007) recommends specific legislation for not-for-profit institutions managing health insurance schemes that will set rules for such insurance activities, considering the special function and nature of those institutions. Hsiao and Yip (2024) posit that cooperative healthcare (CH), or the community-based model, is characterised by community-based risk-pooling and governance by leveraging communities' social capital. They argue that the community-based model can be seen as a solution to finance and deliver accessible and effective basic healthcare to low-income populations. They opine that for CH to be scalable, it needs to demonstrate that it can organise the delivery of accessible and reasonable-quality primary healthcare that people value, with management accountable to the communities themselves through structures that people trust, combined with government legitimacy. AP has gained people's trust by providing accessible healthcare financing and by building robust operational and management structures in the last two decades. What is needed is full government legitimacy.

The regulatory space must become more inclusive to provide a level playing field to organisations like AP and to upscale and handhold other community-based organisations in offering insurance. These changes will be important in achieving the 'Insurance for All by 2047' targets set by IRDAI.

Annexure I

Claim ratio of AVPS (claim = claim amount/premium)

Year	Premium (in Rs. Cr.)	Actual claim cost (in Rs. Cr.)	Claim ratio
2011	1.0	0.51	0.52
2012	1.3	0.60	0.45
2013	1.5	0.73	0.49
2014	2.1	1.01	0.48
2015	2.2	1.24	0.55
2016	2.7	1.10	0.41
2017	3.1	1.42	0.46
2018	3.0	1.29	0.44
2019	3.8	1.94	0.51
2020	4.02	2.24	0.56
2021	3.65	3.05	0.84
2022	4.55	3.35	0.74
2023	5.36	4.19	0.78

Annexure II

Insurance mutual	Year of launch	Trigger
Health insurance	2003	Death of a young member due to a cardiac ailment in 2000
Family insurance	2006	Death of five to six family members of Annapurna borrowers in a stampede in 2005
Life insurance	2009	Withdrawal from JBY due to a delay in claim
Asset insurance	2009	Two fire outbreaks in slums, 2005
Pension	2016	Discontinuation of the Swawlamban scheme by the Government and PFRDA has left members feeling confused and excluded.
Hospi-Cash (hospital wage insurance)	2024	COVID-19 and product offerings by competitors

References

Ahuja, R., & Guha-Khasnobis, B. (2005). *Micro-insurance in India: Trends and strategies for further extension* (No. 162). Working Paper.

Bester, H. J., Chamberlain, D., & Hougaard, C. (2009). *Making insurance markets work for the poor: Microinsurance policy, regulation, and supervision* (Bellville, South Africa, Cenfri). http://www.cenfri.org

Bhat, R., Holtz, J., & Avila, C. (2018). Reaching the missing middle: Ensuring health coverage for India's Urban poor. *Health Systems & Reform, 4*(2), 125–135. https://doi.org/10.1080/23288604.2018.1445425

Bhat, R., Menezes, L., & Avila, C. (2017). *Review of community/mutual-based health insurance schemes and their role in strengthening the financial protection system in India.* Published by USAID and Health Finance and Governance.

Biener, C., Eling, M., & Schmit, J. T. (2014). Regulation in microinsurance markets: Principles, practice, and directions for future development. *World Development, 58*, 21–40.

Boutin, D., Petifour, L., Allard, Y., Kontoubré, S., & Ridde, V. (2024). *Comprehensive Assessment of the Impact of Mandatory Community-Based Health Insurance in Burkina Faso JUNE 2024.*

Chatterjee, A. (2012). Access to insurance and financial-sector regulation. In C. Churchill & Reinhard, D. (Eds.), *Protecting the Poor: A Microinsurance Compendium* (Vol. 2, pp. 548–571). International Labour Organization.

Chemouni, B. (2018). The political path to universal health coverage: Power, ideas, and community-based health insurance in Rwanda. *World Development, 106*, 87–98.

Churchill, C. (2006). What is insurance for the poor? In C. Churchill (Ed.), *Protecting the Poor: A Microinsurance Compendium* (Vol. 1, pp. 12–22). International Labour Organization.

Churchill, C., & D. Reinhard (Eds.), (2012). *Protecting the Poor: A Microinsurance Compendium* (Vol. 2). International Labour Organization.

Cohen, M., & Sebstad, J. (2005). Reducing vulnerability: The demand for microinsurance. *Journal of International Development, 17*(3), 397–474.

Collins, D., Morduch, J., Rutherford, S., & Ruthven, O. (2009). *Portfolios of the Poor: How the World's Poor Live on $2 a Day*. Princeton University Press.

Da Costa, D. (2013). The 'rule of experts' in making a dynamic micro-insurance industry in India. *Journal of Peasant Studies, 40*(5), 845–865.

De Bock, O., & Ontiveros, D. U. (2013). *Literature review on the impact of microinsurance*. Microinsurance Innovation Facility, Research Paper, *35*.

Dercon, (ed.). (2005). *Insurance Against Poverty*. Oxford University Press.

Desai, U. (1953). The Bombay Mutual Life Assurance Society Ltd "Mutual Life Companies Should Be Exempted from Tax" Satisfactory Increase Over Last Year's Business (p. 1037). The Economic Weekly. Retrieved from the Economic Weekly website https://www.epw.in/system/files/pdf/1953_5/38/thebombaymutuallifeassurancesocietyltd_0.pdf

Dror, D. M., Majumdar, A., & Jangle, N. (2019). Estimating capital requirements to scale health microinsurance serving rural poor populations. *The Geneva Papers on Risk and Insurance-Issues and Practice, 44*, 410–444.

Feinman, J. M. (2019, *SSRN Electronic Journal*). The protection gap in homeowners insurance: An introduction. *Connecticut Insurance Law Journal, 27*, 82–115. https://doi.org/10.2139/ssrn.3452947

Fonteneau, B., & Galland, B. (2006). The community-based model: Mutual health organizations in Africa. In C. Churchill (Ed.), *Protecting the Poor: A Microinsurance Compendium* (Vol. 1, pp. 378–399). International Labour Organization.

Guha, S., Samant, M. P., & Reji, E. M. (2020). A case of Annapurna Pariwar. In *Social Entrepreneurship and Sustainable Development.*

Gupta, S., & Kanungo, R. P. (2022). Financial inclusion through digitalisation: Economic viability for the bottom of the pyramid (BOP) segment. *Journal of Business Research, 148*, 262–276. https://doi.org/10.1016/j.jbusres.2022.04.070

Hetherington, J. A. (1969). Fact v. fiction: Who owns mutual insurance companies. *Wisconsin Law Review*, 1068.

Hsiao, W. C., & Yip, W. (2024). Financing and provision of healthcare for two billion people in low-income nations: Is the cooperative healthcare model a solution? *Social Science & Medicine*, *345*, 115730.

Hussien, M., & Azage, M. (2021). Barriers and facilitators of community-based health insurance policy renewal in low- and middle-income countries: A systematic review. *Clinic Economics and Outcomes Research, 13*, 359–375. https://doi.org/10.2147/CEOR.S306855

Ilangovan, D., & Chandramohan, R. (2010). Monumental tasks ahead in micro-insurance in India. *CURIE Journal. CURIE Journal*, *2*(4), 58–63. Retrieved from https://web.p.ebscohost.com/ehost/detail/detail?vid=2&sid=78ad6fab-6840-4c41-8a4f-d210cd60cb3c%40redis&bdata=JnNpdGU9ZWhvc3QtbGl2ZQ%3d%3d#AN=48995956&db=bsh

Insurance Regulatory and Development Authority of India. (2014). Insurance Regulatory and Development Authority of India (IRDAI) – Change of name notification. https://irdai.gov.in

Insurance Regulatory and Development Authority of India. (2015). Insurance Regulatory and Development Authority of India (Micro Insurance) Regulations, 2015 (F. No. IRDA/Reg/2/92/2015). https://irdai.gov.in

International Association of Insurance Supervisors (IAIS) and CGAP Working Group on Microinsurance. (2007). *Issues in Regulation and Supervision of Microinsurance*. IAIS, Basel, Switzerland.

International Cooperative and Mutual Insurance Federation (ICMIF). (2017). *ICMIF country diagnostic on mutual and cooperative microinsurance in India.* The International Cooperative and Mutual Insurance Federation (ICMIF) in association with the Insurance Institute of India (III). Retrieved from https://icmiffoundation.org/wp-content/uploads/2021/06/India-diagnostic-complete-report.pdf

IRDAI. (2024). *Rural, social sector and motor third party obligations*. https://irdai.gov.in/document-detail?documentId=4858052

Janzen, S. A., & Carter, M. R. (2019). After the drought: The impact of microinsurance on consumption smoothing and asset protection. *American Journal of Agricultural Economics*, *101*(3), 651–671.

Kim, W. C., & Mauborgne, R. (2004). *Blue ocean strategy*. Harvard Business Review. https://hbr.org/2004/10/blue-ocean-strategy

Kim, W. C., & Mauborgne, R. (2015). *Blue Ocean Strategy: How to Create Uncontested Market Space and Make the Competition Irrelevant* (Expanded ed.). Harvard Business Review Press.

Krenz, K., Gilbert, D. J., & Mandayam, G. (2014). Exploring women's empowerment through "Credit-Plus" microfinance in India. *Affilia*, *29*(3), 310–325. https://doi.org/10.1177/0886109913516453

Leist, H., & Radermacher, R. (2004). *Brief technical report on Swasthyapurna mutual health fund*. Eschborn: Deutsche Gesellschaft für Technische Zusammenarbeit (GTZ).

Mesbah, A., Omidi Najafabadi, M., & Kianirad, A. (2022). SWOT analysis of agricultural microinsurance development in rural areas of Iran. *Agricultural Economics Research*, *14*(2), 191–203.

Mirach, T. H., Demissie, G. D., & Biks, G. A. (2019). Determinants of community-based health insurance implementation in west Gojjam zone, Northwest Ethiopia: A community based cross sectional study design. *BMC Health Services Research*, *19*, 544. https://doi.org/10.1186/s12913-019-4363-z

Mor, N., & Ashraf, H. (2023). Is contributory health insurance indeed an addiction to a bad idea? a comment on its relevance for low-and middle-income countries. *Social Science & Medicine*, *326*, 115918.

Morduch, J. (2006). *Microinsurance: The next revolution*. In A. Banerjee, R. Bénabou, & D. Mukherjee (Eds.), *Understanding Poverty*, (pp. 375–394). Oxford University Press, UK.
National Health Authority | GOI. (2025). https://nha.gov.in/
Pinto, V. (2015). Role of NGOs in Promoting Micro Health Insurance: A Study with Reference to "Sampoorna Suraksha" Health Insurance Scheme by SKDRDP, Mangalore (India). *South Asian Journal of Business and Management Cases*, *4*(2), 251–261. https://doi.org/10.1177/2277977915596268
Powell, L. S. (2017). *What it means to be mutual*. Alabama Center for Insurance Information and Research University of Alabama. Retrieved June, 2023, from https://www.namic.org/wp-content/uploads/legacy/publicpolicy/1703_WhatItMeansToBeMutual.pdf
Prahalad, C. K. (2005). *The Fortune at the Bottom of the Pyramid: Eradicating Poverty Through Profits*. Wharton School Publishing.
Prahalad, C. K., & Hart, S. L. (2002). *The Fortune at the Bottom of the Pyramid*. Strategy +Business. https://www.strategy-business.com/article/11518
Radermacher, R., & Dror, I. (2006). The community-based model: Mutual health organizations in Africa. In C. Churchill (Ed.), *A Microinsurance Compendium* (Vol. 1, pp. 401–422). International Labour Organization.
Radermacher, R., Roberts Singh, J., & Srivastava, S. (2009, September 23). Integrated Risk Management in Microinsurance. Papers.ssrn.com. http://ssrn.com/abstract=1477272
Report of the Committee on Standalone Microinsurance Company. (2020). IRDAI. https://irdai.gov.in/documentdetail?documentId=395546
Roy, A., & Jain, N. (2023). *Bridging gaps in the Indian insurance sector*. PwC. https://www.pwc.in/assets/pdfs/research-insights-hub/immersive-outlook-4/bridging-gaps-in-the-india-insurance-sector.pdf
Singh, A. (2014). Approach to health services for low-income households: Community based health insurance scheme. *Parvartak*, *VIII*(1).
Singh, A., & Bihari, N. (2018). A decade since the first microinsurance regulations in India. *Bimaquest*, *18*(1).
Singh, A., Shiv, P., & Srinivasan, G. (2019). 'Micro Insurance in India: Challenges and Solutions'. Study report by National Insurance Academy, Pune. https://doi.org/10.13140/RG.2.2.13195.31526
Singh, A., Uma, S., Sathyakumar, V., & Srinivasan, G. (2022). Study of Mutual Models in Insurance: A Background Paper by The National Insurance Academy, Pune. https://niapune.org.in/research-andpublication/research-reports
Singh, A., & Sathyakumar, V. (2023). *Examining Penetration of Insurance in Micro and Small Enterprises (MSEs). Financed by Micro Finance Institutions by National Insurance Academy, Pune*, Available on. https://niapune.org.in/research-and-publication/research-reportscompen dium Vol. 1 401–422 International Labour Organization.
Smith, P. C., Stepan, A., Valdmanis, V., & Verheyen, P. (1997). Principal-agent problems in health care systems: An international perspective. *Health Policy*, *41*(1), 37–60. https://doi.org/10.1016/s0168-8510(97)00012-2
Sobel, J. (2002). Can we trust social capital? *Journal of Economic Literature*, *40*, 139–154.
Stiglitz, J. E. (1981). The Economics of Information and the Information of Economics. *The Journal of Economic Perspectives*, *9*(3), 27–45. https://doi.org/10.1257/jep.9.3.27
Swiss Re Institute. (2023a). *India's insurance market: Poised for rapid growth*. Retrieved December, 2024, from https://www.swissre.com/dam/jcr:444d06a0-2f47-41e9-a1e0-59a112c88681/2022-11-expertise-publication-india-a-growth-engine.pdf
Swiss Re Institute. (2023b). *Sigma 3/2023—World insurance*. Retrieved December, 2024, from https://www.swissre.com/institute/research/sigma-research/sigma-2023-03.html#:~:text=China%20and%20the%20UK%20ranked,sixth%20largest%20market%20by%202032
Swiss Re. (2024, November 19). sigma 5/2024: Global economic and insurance market outlook 2025–26. Swiss Re Institute. https://www.swissre.com/institute/research/sigma-research/sigma-2024-05-global-economic-insurance-outlook-growth-geopolitics.html

The Chartered Governance Institute UK & Ireland. (2022). What Is Governance? Cgi.org.uk. https://www.cgi.org.uk/resources/factsheets/factsheets/what-is-governance/

The Geneva Association. (2023). The Global Insurance Protection Gap: Assessment and Recommendations 7 (2014). https://www.genevaassociation.org/sites/default/files/research-topics-document-type/pdf_public/understanding_and_addressing_global_insurance_protection_gaps.pdf. UNCDF. https://annualreport.uncdf.org/2023

United Nations Capital Development Fund. (2023). Sustainable Development Goals and UNCDF contributions. https://www.uncdf.org/sdgs

Wiedmaier-Pfister, M., & Chatterjee, A. (2006). An enabling regulatory environment for microinsurance. In C. Churchill (Ed.), *Protecting the Poor: A Microinsurance Compendium* (Vol. 1, pp. 488–504). International Labour Organization.

Zingales, L. (2009). The future of securities regulation. *Journal of Accounting Research*, *47*(2), 391–425. https://doi.org/10.1111/j.1475-679X.2009.00331.x

Digitalisation in Annapurna Pariwar

K. Naveen Kumar

Abstract Digital transformation in the microfinance sector is an evolving process, which creates value for both institutions and their clients. Annapurna Pariwar is a unique organisation that started digitisation across microfinance, micro-insurance, and human resources management. Established in 1993, Annapurna Pariwar has shifted from manual processes to digital systems. The organisation successfully created an internal technology called the 'microfinance management system' to facilitate customer identification and engagement, as well as collection and recovery processes. By leveraging technology, the organisation was able to enhance service delivery, reduce costs, perform real-time portfolio monitoring, and manage customers more efficiently to improve overall experiences. This chapter examines Annapurna Pariwar's digitalisation process, strategies, and its implications on business and customer management. The chapter provides important insights for policymakers, banks, and financial institutions aiming to utilise digitalisation for more equitable and scalable financial services.

1 Introduction

The microfinance sector has played a pivotal role in the last three and a half decades to narrow the financial inclusion gap by offering small loans and other financial services to underprivileged communities worldwide (Mader & Morvant-Roux, 2019; Mushtaq & Bruneau, 2019). At the outset, the primary objective of microfinance was to provide credit to low-income individuals in rural regions and, later on, in urban slums who had no access to formal financial institutions. Over time, the microfinance sector has

K. Naveen Kumar (✉)
National Institute of Bank Management, Pune, Maharashtra, India
e-mail: naveen@nibmindia.org

J. D. Ranadive, S. Guha (eds.), *Building Pathways to Women's Empowerment*, India Studies in Business and Economics,
https://doi.org/10.1007/978-981-95-7159-8_10

undergone extensive changes by adapting to new practices and technologies in order to operate in a more digitally advanced world. The transformation of microfinance institutions (MFIs) into digital finance entities has had a profound impact on their operations, client relationships, and product offerings (Dorfleitner et al., 2022).

In microfinance, the process of digitalisation involves incorporating various digital technologies, such as mobile banking, cloud computing, data analytics, and digital payment platforms, into its operations. These technologies help institutions improve operational efficiency, allow cost-cutting, and facilitate an enhanced customer experience (Dorfleitner et al., 2022). Furthermore, digitalisation presents the means by which outreach can be extended to remote and underserved areas in rural and urban pockets of the economy. Over 1.4 billion people worldwide, primarily in developing nations, are unbanked, as per the World Bank's findings (Ansar et al., 2025). With the rapid proliferation of mobile phones and internet connectivity, there is an unprecedented opportunity to close this gap in financial inclusion through digital microfinance solutions.

The Indian microfinance industry has seen substantial transformation over the last 20 years due to regulatory changes, product diversification, technological advancement, and newer geographical reach. As of September 2024, the microfinance business continues to grow rapidly, with a gross loan portfolio reaching INR 4080 billion and supporting over 81 million borrowers through 146 million active loan accounts (MFIN, 2024). However, the sector faces several problems, including high operating expenses, high interest rates, collection issues, and increased credit risks. Digitalisation has paved the way for MFIs to streamline their operations and make their businesses profitable and sustainable.

'M-Pesa' in Kenya and 'bKash' in Bangladesh are examples of how digital microfinance solutions can achieve global success. These platforms have made financial access in their respective regions more convenient, affordable, and scalable (Parvez et al., 2015; Thomas & Hedrick-Wong, 2019). Inspired by international best practices, the JAM trinity[1] and Digital Public Infrastructure (DPI), Indian MFIs have increasingly embraced digital technologies to enhance their processes and service delivery.

Digitalisation has a significant impact on microfinance and development services, as demonstrated by Annapurna Pariwar,[2] a renowned development

[1] JAM (Jan Dhan Yojana, Aadhaar and Mobile connectivity) is a National Mission on Financial Inclusion by Government of India, is an initiative to achieve complete financial inclusion for all households in the nation through an integrated financial services approach.

[2] Annapurna Pariwar is a group of six developmental organizations working over the last three decades to empower the urban poor through financial services, micro insurance as well as non-financial services like health, day-care centres and educational support for children of single mothers. Annapurna Pariwar offers more than credit services. It offers micro insurance, which include Health Mutual Fund (Community-Based Insurance Policy), LMF (CB IP), ALMF (CB Asset-less IP), FMF (CB Family IP), and Pension. All microfinance borrowers are shareholders of Annapurna Mahila Credit Cooperative Society (multistate), the biggest and most important organisation of the Annapurna Pariwar group. All microfinance borrowers re connected with microinsurance and pension which is housed in APVS, the second largest organisation in the group.

institution in India. Founded in 1986, the organisation has a long-standing commitment to providing financial assistance to marginalised groups, particularly women, through microcredit, microinsurance, and a bouquet of social welfare programmes. Due to the constraints of its traditional approach, Annapurna Pariwar embraced digitalisation as a strategic move to expand its reach, streamline operations, reduce operational expenses, and enhance customer satisfaction.

Digitalisation has provided Annapurna Pariwar with many benefits. On the operational side, digital tools have made it easier to reduce administrative costs, improve process efficiency, and increase data accuracy. The transition to digital platforms has brought about improved convenience, faster service delivery, and better financial literacy among clients. With digitisation in Annapurna Pariwar, every microfinance borrower's data, along with her family members' information, their education, health, and income is recorded in the in-house software system named Micro Finance Management System (MFMS). The MFMS data is accessible through a Tab-based technology named *AppPurna* to the field staff for their utilisation across the operational areas. Hence, loan disbursement, recovery, savings collections, as well as insurance claims, are all operated through *Mobile-Tabs* at the last mile. Annapurna Pariwar has enabled its clients to become more involved in economic activities, which has boosted household income and improved the welfare of the community.

The digitisation of MFIs like Annapurna Pariwar is a step towards achieving greater financial inclusion and poverty reduction. Digital microfinance's ability to democratise financial services could lead to the promotion of entrepreneurship, job creation, and better socio-economic outcomes for underprivileged communities. Studies indicate that the promotion of women's empowerment can enhance these advantages, as it has consistently been shown that their financial inclusion has a multiplier effect on household welfare and community development (Cheston & Kuhn, 2002; Gammage et al., 2017).

The process of digitalisation is not a simple one, but it does pose several obstacles during implementation. Some of the challenges faced by MFIs include lagging digital infrastructure in operational areas, low levels of digital literacy, and concerns about data privacy and security. The resolution of these challenges necessitates a combination of government aid, private sector collaboration, and community outreach. Annapurna Pariwar has been striving to overcome these obstacles through a continuous process of innovation, adaptability, and a focus on their clients.

The digital transformation undertaken by Annapurna Pariwar provides insights that can be gleaned by other MFIs and policymakers. The organisation's adoption of digital tools and emphasis on client empowerment have positioned it as one of the first major players in utilising technology to drive socio-economic development and enhance financial inclusion in India. The chapter highlights global benchmarks for microfinance digitalisation, with Annapurna Pariwar providing a comprehensive overview of various aspects of digitalisation, exploring the potential benefits and drawbacks of using technology in developing microfinance businesses. Through this investigation, it seeks to advance the conversation on how digitalisation can contribute to a more equitable and sustainable financial system.

2 Traditional Versus Modern (Digital) Microfinance

Microfinance has been a key instrument in the global efforts to reduce poverty and promote financial inclusion. The key goal of providing financial assistance to underprivileged and unbanked individuals has brought about positive changes in communities across developing and emerging economies (Mader & Morvant-Roux, 2019). Through their labour-intensive processes (doorstep credit assessment and delivery) and community-centric models, MFIs have traditionally provided credit, savings, and other financial products to individuals who were not able to access the traditional banking system. The microfinance sector is experiencing a digital revolution, which has created newer opportunities as well as challenges.

The use of digital technology in business operations is known as digitalisation, which enhances efficiency and accessibility while also enabling greater scale. In microfinance, digitalisation is not just a technological change; it's essentially the systemic transformation of how financial services are designed and delivered. The modern microfinance industry has the advantage of leveraging digital tools such as mobile technology, artificial intelligence (AI), blockchain, and big data analytics to reach a wider clientele group, reduce operational costs, and improve customer experience along the (financial and development) value chain.

The systemic technology transformation in MFIs will enhance financial services through appropriate product design and delivery approaches. The digitalisation in MFIs will transform from a branch-centric approach to a customer-centric approach, wherein microfinance services will be delivered through alternative digital channels with greater convenience and suitability. Digitalisation in MFIs also includes the business process transformation from manual to automated. The automation of KYC (Know Your Customer), loan application, disbursement, collection, and recovery processes in MFI businesses will enhance efficiency and lower operational costs for MFIs. The data-driven digital analysis of customer behaviour, financial needs, and preferences will enable MFIs to offer personalised financial products to both existing and new customers. Furthermore, digital channels will allow organisations to increase the width and depth of MFIs for sustainable financial inclusion.

2.1 Challenges in Traditional Microfinance Models

Recognising the impact of digitalisation requires a thorough understanding of the historical context of microfinance and its limitations. Microfinance has spread globally since its inception, originating from experiments like the Grameen Bank model introduced in Bangladesh during the mid-twentieth century, and now supports millions of people on their path to economic self-reliance. Nevertheless, the older models of microfinance have faced ongoing challenges (Kustin, 2017; Srivastava, 2010).

The microfinance industry faces several significant challenges, hindering its growth and effectiveness. High operational costs associated with client acquisition, loan disbursement, and debt recovery often necessitate manual processes, limiting scalability and profitability (Basu & Srivastava, 2005). While MFIs often have extensive physical networks, their geographic reach can sometimes be limited (Siwale & Godfroid, 2022). Furthermore, the scarcity of credit data for most microfinance clients poses a significant obstacle. The lack of adequate credit histories hampers accurate risk assessment, often resulting in higher interest rates and increased default rates (Fersi & Boujelbène, 2022).

The reliance on cash-based transactions and paper-based records exposes MFIs to fraud and operational inefficiencies (Lamichane, 2020). Finally, the customer experience can be negatively impacted by factors such as long wait times, inflexible loan structures, and limited product diversity, particularly among youth and urban microfinance clients (Lamrani Alaoui & Tkiouat, 2019). These challenges collectively impede the industry's ability to effectively serve its target population and achieve its social and financial objectives.

The high operational costs of acquiring, disbursing, and recovering clients have resulted in manual processes that limit the scalability or profitability of the microfinance industry (Basu & Srivastava, 2005). MFIs have limited geographic reach despite having strong physical branch networks and field agents (Siwale & Godfroid, 2022). Most microfinance clients lack adequate credit histories to accurately assess risk, which often leads to high rates of interest and higher default rates in the future (Fersi & Boujelbène, 2022). MFIs are exposed to fraud, errors, and inefficiencies due to the prevalence of cash-based transactions and paper-backed records (Lamichane, 2020). The customer experience has been negatively impacted by various factors, including long wait times, rigid loan structures, and limited product diversity among youth (and urban microfinance) customers (Lamrani Alaoui & Tkiouat, 2019).

These difficulties highlight the necessity of developing innovative solutions to improve the efficiency and inclusivity of microfinance operations. These barriers can be overcome through digitalisation, which will change the way financial services are delivered to the underserved (Omowole et al., 2024).

2.2 Advantages of Digitalisation in Microfinance Sector

Sustainable development hinges on financial inclusion, which provides access to a range of financial services that can enhance the quality of life for individuals and communities. Through digitalisation, the structural limitations of microfinance are addressed, and opportunities for innovation and growth are increased. Digitisation has made significant advancements in microfinance (Mpofu, 2023).

Mobile banking and digital wallets have made it possible for people in far-off places to access financial services without the need for physical establishments. This has helped bridge the last-mile gap. The use of digital platforms enables MFIs to reach previously neglected markets, such as rural and marginalised communities (Pazarbasioglu et al., 2020). Delivering financial products is cheaper through automated processes and digital platforms, making it possible to serve low-income customers sustainably. Automated process efficiency reduces administrative work and expedites loan processing, improving turnaround times across different levels of business operations (Jejeniwa et al., 2024).

MFIs can create personalised financial products using AI-driven analytics to meet their individual needs and behaviour patterns. The use of digital tools like mobile apps and interactive voice response systems enhances communication and fosters closer client relationships (Challoumis, 2024). The use of digital credit scoring models, which utilise alternative data such as mobile usage, social media activity, and utility payments, improves risk assessment accuracy for clients without traditional credit histories (Bello, 2023). Blockchain technology makes records secure and transparent, which reduces the risk of fraud and default (Zheng et al., 2022). Educational modules can be included in digital platforms to educate customers on financial literacy and the appropriate use of resources (Kuntze et al., 2019). Despite the constraints on physical interactions during crises, financial services were maintained through digital channels during COVID-19 (Mistrean, 2021).

2.3 Emerging Technologies in the Microfinance Sector

Numerous advanced technologies are essential for the digital transformation of microfinance. Having knowledge of these technologies allows us to explore their applications and implications. Mobile technology has transformed the way people interact with financial services, enabling them to make transactions, access credit, and manage savings through apps and SMS-based platforms (Sharma & Díaz Andrade, 2023).

By examining vast amounts of both structured and unstructured data, MFIs can gain insights into client behaviour, improve loan terms, and make predictions about repayment patterns (Rao & Mahalingam, 2025). AI and Machine learning enable the segmentation of customers, automation in loan origination, and the provision of chatbots for customer support, which enhance business operations (Mahapatra & Singh, 2021). Distributed ledger technology is a valuable tool for creating trust among microfinance clients due to its ability to guarantee secure, unalterable, and transparent transactions (Tasin et al., 2023). MFIs can use cloud computing platforms to manage financial data without sacrificing IT infrastructure, which is both affordable and scalable (Gasmelseid, 2015).

2.4 Challenges in Microfinance Digitalisation

Although digitalisation can bring about significant changes, microfinance still encounters obstacles. These include the following: (i) Inequality in access to digital infrastructure, such as internet connectivity and the use of smartphones, threatens to exclude certain segments; (ii) The importance of strong security measures for MFIs is increasing as they migrate to digital channels to secure data and cyber networks; (iii) The regulatory landscape in numerous nations may be technologically challenged, creating obstacles for MFIs; (iv) Clients and staff who are not familiar with digital tools may refuse to use them; (v) Credit scoring's use of alternative data raises ethical questions about privacy and potential biases in decision-making (Orlikowski & Gash, 1994; Pazarbasioglu et al., 2020).

The shift towards digital microfinance has significant implications for financial inclusion and poverty reduction. By incorporating cutting-edge technologies, MFIs can expand their customer base and deliver better value than before. The path to digital transformation is not a simple one and requires careful consideration. In the next section, the diverse international best practices in microfinance digitalisation are discussed.

3 Global Microfinance Business Experiences in Digitalisation

The microfinance sector has been transformed by the rise of digitalisation, which has enabled it to tackle problems such as high operational costs, limited outreach, and financial exclusion. The world has witnessed pioneering efforts to utilise digital solutions for expanding financial inclusion, improving operational efficiency, and promoting socio-economic development.

Kenya's Safaricom launched its *M-Pesa* mobile money platform in 2007, which is a notable example. The introduction of *M-Pesa* in rural areas with inadequate banking infrastructure paved the way for financial inclusion by enabling money transfers, savings, and access to microloans through mobile phones (Tuwei, 2018). M-Shwari and other similar products, created in collaboration with the Commercial Bank of Africa to offer savings and credit services, use digital scoring for credit. *M-Pesa*, reimagined as a unidirectional data network that facilitates access to users' cell phones via its USSD-based technology, has helped reduce operational costs for MFIs and increased the empowerment of women and small businesses (Ndung'u & Oguso, 2021).

The integration of mobile financial services with microfinance by *bKash* in Bangladesh has sought to increase financial inclusion for low-income and rural communities. The multilingual mobile apps of *bKash* are used to manage money transfers, bill payments, and microloan repayments (Rahman, 2020). By partnering with telecom operators through online channels, bKash has made improvements in loan origination rates, simplified microfinance procedures, and expanded outreach to underserved regions (Mujeri & Azam, 2018).

The Philippines' CARD—MRI[3] has transformed into a digital hub by adopting mobile banking, cloud-based systems, and e-learning technologies. By using these tools, customers can access financial services like savings deposits and loan repayments without the need to visit a branch in person. Through the use of digital literacy, CARD MRI has provided financial literacy and facilitated informed decision-making among rural communities through online learning modules. The cloud-based infrastructure has facilitated greater operational transparency and scalability (Dadios et al., 2018).

The Amartha system[4] in Indonesia merges conventional group lending methods with cutting-edge digital technologies, including AI-powered credit scoring and blockchain technology. Amartha's adoption of behavioural data for credit assessments and blockchain-based transparency in peer-to-peer lending has made it a powerful ecosystem (Saputra et al., 2019). Through this model, high repayment rates and accessible, affordable credit have made possible the success of rural entrepreneurs.

To simplify microfinance operations in Peru, MiBanco has incorporated mobile-enabled loan applications, geotagging, and digital wallets. Geotagging enables agents to be deployed in remote areas, while mobile platforms facilitate loan applications and financial products. Loan processing times have been reduced, rural entrepreneurs have improved, and local economic growth has been enhanced due to these advancements (Fernando, 2003).

In Rwanda, VisionFund[5] utilises mobile payment platforms to provide real-time dashboard information for loan monitoring and product customisation (Wang, 2021). VisionFund has aided in strengthening local economies by collaborating with telecom providers and utilising mobile technology to reduce cash-handling risks, while also improving service delivery for farmers and small business owners.

Small businesses in Mexico can secure loans through Konfio, an unsecured loan service, using artificial intelligence. The credit scoring system, powered by AI, assesses transactional and behavioural data to swiftly approve loans. By utilising its digital platform, Konfio helps SME businesses save money, create jobs, and strengthen the economy (Erturk & Zammit-Lucia, 2020).

To improve efficiency and transparency, Ensibuuko in Uganda provides cloud-based platforms to Savings and Credit Cooperative Organisations (Rahman & Fong, 2016). The ability to access savings and loans in rural areas is made easier

[3] Centre for Agriculture and Rural Development—Mutually Reinforcing Institutions.

[4] Amartha is an Indonesian digital microfinance platform that bridges female entrepreneurs, especially those in rural areas, with lenders who seek to invest in high-impact and profitable businesses. Technology enables it to streamline micro-lending and make it accessible, especially to those with no credit history. Amartha's platform has a self-learning algorithm to decide on risk levels and automate such crucial processes as application, information gathering, and credit scoring.

[5] VisionFund Rwanda is an owner-operated Christian mission-focused microfinance network partnering with caregivers in remote, impoverished areas to enable them to establish secure futures for their children. Driven by Christian belief, we believe it is imperative that we partner with the poorest of families and communities irrespective of religion, race, ethnicity, and gender to bring lasting transformation in their lives.

through mobile integration, and staff training programmes facilitate the transition to digital systems. Ensibuuko has enhanced operational effectiveness and financial inclusion in rural Uganda (Capital, 2019).

In Cambodia, AMK[6] Microfinance has integrated digital capabilities with agent banking to expand financial access. Mobile app-equipped agents are utilised to facilitate transactions and loan applications, while digital savings products promote financial inclusion in rural areas. Lower-tech users can easily navigate simplified digital interfaces, which enhances their adoption (Pimhidzai et al., 2019).

Lidya, headquartered in Nigeria, offers loan approval systems and credit scoring engines powered by artificial intelligence (AI) to assist small and medium-sized enterprises (Asante Boakye et al., 2023). By emphasising the digital approach, small businesses can experience faster processing times and more convenient transactions, resulting in improved productivity and economic growth.

Ethiopia's Kifiya Financial Technology has developed a unified digital platform integrating financial services such as utility bill payments, mobile banking, and microfinance operations, in addition to the above examples (Tenaw, 2019). The platform created by Kifiya has facilitated financial transactions and extended services to remote regions, in collaboration with banks and microfinance institutions. Integrating biometric verification into the system enables customers to be identified with confidence and security, solving problems related to identity fraud and financial protection (Timbula & Marvadi, 2023).

Jumo provides an integrated platform for financial institutions to offer microloans and savings products via mobile phones in South Africa (Pazarbasioglu et al., 2020). Jumo's machine learning algorithms analyse non-traditional data sources, such as mobile phone usage and transaction patterns, to determine creditworthiness. This approach has enabled financial institutions to extend credit to unbanked individuals and businesses, which has had a positive impact on the economy (Adeoye et al., 2024).

If these global practices are successful, it shows that digitalisation can transform microfinance (Pytkowska & Korynski, 2017). These programmes have demonstrated the potential to address financial inadequacy, improve access to resources, and promote social and economic development by utilising cutting-edge technologies, streamlining operations (and increasing outreach), among other measures. To address the challenges faced in microfinance, the use of digital tools should not only tackle existing issues but also contribute to creating a more inclusive and sustainable financial system (Omowole et al., 2024).

Digitalisation in microfinance has been demonstrated by success stories from around the world, providing valuable insights for India. The digital transformation that India is implementing in the sector can only be fully realised by improving rural digital infrastructure. Rural and semi-urban locations, which have a high

[6] AMK—'Angkor Mikroheranhvatho (Kampuchea) began its digital transformation in 2019 by upgrading its core banking system. It launched digital services like mobile banking, QR payments, and chatbot-based loan applications. AMK integrated with national platforms including Bakong and FAST, connected with over 300 billers, and expanded international transfers through partners like SWIFT and UnionPay'.

concentration of microfinance clients, still face connectivity gaps (Pal et al., 2023). These gaps can be bridged by working with telecom providers, leveraging government initiatives like Digital India, and promoting low-bandwidth solutions such as USSD-based mobile banking.

At the same time, microfinance institutions (MFIs) must improve their data-driven decision-making processes by utilising other forms of data, such as mobile usage patterns, payment behaviours, and social media activity, to ensure that credit profiling is accurate. By utilising AI and machine learning, they can improve the process of risk assessment and loan modification, and by working with data aggregators, they can aggregate more information on borrower interests (Bhatore et al., 2020).

Another important approach is to use training and digital tools to strengthen agent networks. Providing agents with secure, user-friendly digital devices can significantly enhance the service quality, and many clients consider them their primary touchpoints. Regular training on digital literacy, as well as customer service skills, can increase efficiency and trust. Real-time dashboards that track the performance of agents can provide accountability and transparency (Read & Atinc, 2017). Furthermore, MFIs must prioritise customer satisfaction by developing mobile applications that are simple to navigate and support multiple languages, catering to basic users. It is crucial to establish financial literacy programmes in rural areas to increase trust and awareness regarding the benefits of digital financial services. Specialised loan products, such as agricultural loans or women-oriented programmes, can also boost the adoption rate (Alam, 2023).

3.1 Developing Digital Ecosystems

There are other areas where innovation is relevant, such as building ecosystems around mobile money platforms. By partnering with services such as Paytm, PhonePe, and BharatPe, customers can access savings, loans, or other financial services through mobile wallets while making the process of digital transactions smooth. The adoption and familiarity of mobile money can be promoted through incentive schemes. How is this done? Secure and scalable digital architectures are essential for the growth of MFI-based systems. Strong cybersecurity measures are safeguarded by data protection, while cloud-based systems offer centralised storage and scalability. The adoption of blockchain can enhance the trustworthiness and transparency of financial systems, thereby providing greater assurance to the system (Daah et al., 2024).

The implementation of these innovations will require a significant public-private partnership. Technology can be propelled by partnerships with fintech startups, and interaction with government bodies can foster a supportive regulatory environment. The digital transition can be made faster by utilising public-private partnerships to share knowledge and resources. Similarly, financial inclusion must consider gender factors, as women in rural areas often do not have access to digital financial services. Women can be empowered by creating microfinance products that cater to their entrepreneurial needs, educating them as digital ambassadors, and developing shared savings and credit features on digital platforms.

Additionally, implementing the JAM (Jan Dhan, Aadhaar, and Mobile) trinity, digital public infrastructure (DPI), or other existing policy frameworks can facilitate faster client onboarding/access to services. Smaller MFIs can benefit from simplified regulatory processes and government-funded initiatives like Startup India, which can assist in technological upgrades. Social impact investment is a different funding option that considers the benefits of both financial returns and social impact (Brandstetter & Lehner, 2015). Scaling digital solutions can be achieved through the use of blended finance models, a combination of public and private funds, and collaboration with development organisations. Furthermore, APIs can also help MFIs in collection management and remittance services.

By implementing these approaches, the Indian microfinance sector can leverage digitalisation to address operational inefficiencies, expand outreach efforts, and promote financial inclusion (Santhosh Kumar & Aithal, 2024). Nevertheless, the advantages are not limited to individual institutions and clients and contribute significantly to overall economic development, financial stability, and social empowerment. By establishing an effective digital microfinance ecosystem, India can become a world leader in using financial technology to drive sustainable development (Birchall, 2003; Pal et al., 2023).

4 Digitalisation Journey of Annapurna Pariwar

Annapurna Pariwar was established in 1993 by Dr. Medha Purao Samant. Annapurna Pariwar was initially a small-scale microcredit initiative that sought to promote the financial inclusion of women. Based on the needs of its clients, Annapurna Pariwar kept on adding different services. It developed into a multifaceted institution that met various financial and social needs, including savings, loans, and insurance, over the years. Technological progress in microfinance, from manual bookkeeping to advanced digital solutions, is exemplified by Annapurna Pariwar's journey of software automation and digital transformation.

This section focuses on the different stages of Annapurna Pariwar's digitalisation, including its challenges, innovations, and effects. It offers an elaborate account of how a multistate cooperative society used technology to revolutionise microfinance and provide better services to underprivileged populations.

4.1 The Beginnings: Manual Operations (1993–1998)

Annapurna Pariwar's development was characterised by its manual nature. Ledgers were utilised to manage data, starting with only nine women and extending to 700 by the end of the first year. Medha-*tai*'s friends from the banking industry started coming once a month to help her with the book-keeping activity. It was a fully manual activity for the first five to six years, from 1993 to 1998.

After the first two or three years of the organisation's establishment, Medha-*tai* was able to appoint a part-time staff member to take care of the office work. She taught the staff how to manually enter data on loan disbursement, collection/recovery, and savings. Medha-*tai* developed a home visit form to capture the demographic profile of the clients. Furthermore, by this time, she had written the basic Operations Manual for the organisation. Using the manual, the disbursement of loans, collection of repayments, and savings of the clients were systematically recorded. With her innovative ideas, Medha-*tai* created basic operational manuals and home visit forms to guide both part-time workers and regular staff. Annapurna Pariwar's financial operations were built on a foundation of discipline and transparency, which became firmly established during this period. Additionally, these initial tools demonstrated the organisation's dedication to meticulous record-keeping, which would remain a fundamental aspect of its future digital initiatives.

It wasn't just manual data handling that posed challenges; it also involved building community trust. This phase was difficult. Annapurna Pariwar's success was largely due to the transparency promoted and Dr. Medha Purao Samant's personal connection with the members during this period. This trust was instrumental in the acceptance of technological advancements in later years.

4.2 Embracing the Digital Era: The FoxPro Program (1999–2001)

Manual book keeping proved to be a significant challenge due to the exponential increase in membership. By 1999 it was six years and Annapurna had crossed more than 2000 members. So daily manual book keeping was getting difficult. Acknowledging the necessity of automation, Dr. Medha Purao Samant collaborated with Mr. Ravi Joshi, a FoxPro software engineer, to create a personalised programme for the organisation. This was the first time the organisation had ventured into digital territory.

Although it was rudimentary, the FoxPro software was an excellent addition. It also simplified the data entry and record-keeping process, allowing Annapurna Pariwar to handle larger volumes of data with greater efficiency. The heart of this transformation was a computer given to them by Medha-*tai*'s husband's STEM Corporation, Nasan.[7] Staff training to use the software was designed to enhance their technical expertise and enable technology integration into daily life. It was the first step in demonstrating how digital tools could be used to simplify more complex processes and thus lay the foundation for future inventions.

[7] Nasan Medical Electronics is a private limited company set up by Mr. Y. B. Samant in the late eighties. His company manufactured medical electronic equipment to start with. In the last three to five decades they have ventured into many cardiac devices using technological and digital platforms including telemedicine.

Annapurna Pariwar was also shaped by embracing technology during this period. By implementing digitalisation and teaching the field staff to use the software, the organisation ensured that technology was integrated into its operations. This proactive attitude aided in mitigating resistance to change and established a standard for future technological advancements.

4.3 The Syslift Transition from 2003 to 2005: Overcoming Limits

Annapurna Pariwar's expansion into men's and women's loans under the Udyam Purna and Arthapurna exemplified the limitations of the FoxPro software. To cope with the increasing complexity, the organisation incorporated Syslift software developed by Interaid,[8] a French NGO supporting Annapurna Pariwar during that period. This programme was implemented in 2003.

The introduction of Syslift brought about necessary improvements but also created fresh challenges. The reconciliation of data from different software for Udyam Purna and Arthapurna was a time-consuming task that involved manual effort and frequent errors. The growing need for accurate financial information emphasised integration. Annapurna Pariwar initiated its research on global best practices in microfinance software, setting the stage for future advancements. During this period, Syslift's inauguration represented an essential turning point towards associating operational systems with the company's expanding size and complexity due to many financial services, loans, savings, insurance, etc.

This shift towards Syslift was also a demonstration that software had to be flexible. Although it resolved a few short-term issues, it stressed the need to anticipate future requirements and incorporate flexibility into the organisation's technological strategy. The experience influenced Annapurna Pariwar's decision to develop and use software's in the future.

4.4 The Use of a Loan Performer (2005–2009)

A crucial turning point was Annapurna Pariwar's adoption of Loan Performer[9] in 2005, which was developed by Crystal Technology in Uganda and recommended by the *Consultative Group to Assist the Poor* (CGAP). Enhanced microfinance

---

[8] Interaid is a French NGO that works in Indian slums, mainly in health and education. Interaid ventured into microfinance and micro insurance interventions with Annapurna Pariwar during the period 2001–2008. Later they moved out of microfinance and micro insurance. They are still active in health and education.

[9] Loan Performer is a CGAP recommended software for MFIs.

capabilities were available through Loan Performer, which included loans, savings, and share capital management, but not insurance products. Various financial operations were made more efficient and accurate with the help of this software.

Although Loan Performer experienced a significant increase in operational efficiency, it did not offer any modules for new needs like health insurance and voluntary savings. The software's lack of these attributes highlighted the significance of flexibility and marked the beginning of Annapurna Pariwar's specialised efforts to create customised systems. Despite its shortcomings, Loan Performer showcased the advantages of centralised data management, which was essential for meeting the organisation's expanding operational demands.

It also facilitated the sharing of knowledge and cooperation with other microfinance institutions through the adoption of Loan Performer. Annapurna Pariwar's involvement in international conferences on best practices established it as a leading player in the field. This period solidified the organisation's commitment to innovation and continuous improvement.

4.5 Software Customisation and Consolidation Programme in Association with Quantum (2009–2012)

In 2003, Annapurna Pariwar was faced with the task of managing a variety of offerings after the introduction of health insurance programmes and life, family, and asset need-based insurance products. A company called Quantum[10] responded by teaming up with Mr. Vinay Joshi to create specialised, tailor-made software to manage microfinance as well as micro insurance operations. The newer software included loan, savings, and share capital functions too. However, Syslift continued to handle insurance data separately for Annapurna.

Quantum's use of a free version of Oracle led to limitations, particularly as membership reached over 30,000 and insurance participants totalled to more than 100,000. It was not possible to handle all the data under one platform, and a strong, scalable solution was required. Moreover, the requirement for distinct systems for different services resulted in inefficiencies and necessitated a more unified approach. Notwithstanding the obstacles, Quantum's software was a crucial step in Annapurna Pariwar's journey towards full digital integration.

This stage also saw a change in the organisation's strategic approach to technology. It was evident that Annapurna Pariwar prioritised its members' individual needs and worked towards developing tailored solutions. Its technological advancement was marked by its emphasis on customisation.

[10] Quantum is a software company whose proprietor is Mr. Vinay Joshi. Quantum is an expert in developing ERP solutions and providing software systems to many pharma companies.

4.6 MFMS Software: In-House Digital Expertise (2011–2014)

Digitalisation became a priority for Annapurna Pariwar when the company chose to build its own software. Without any prior experience in software development, Nasan brought in skilled engineers. With Mr. Y.B. Samant as its head, Nasan requested its software team to select three software engineers to join Annapurna Pariwar. These experts went on to add another 10 software engineers, now making it an all-woman team of 12 in-house software engineers at Annapurna Pariwar. The MFMS, which was established to support Annapurna Pariwar's financial operations, was the outcome of this initiative.

MFMS was designed to handle loans, savings, insurance, and share capital with the added flexibility of in-house personnel. The system is also available for external use. The implementation of a unified platform by Microsoft (MFMS) replaced the software by Quantum in 2014, providing operational simplicity and data reduction efficiency. The emergence of MFMS signalled a shift towards technology independence for organisations. This move not only improved the organisation's operational efficiency, ease of operations, reduced TAP, enhanced client satisfaction, and lowered costs, but also connected its technological capabilities to growing services.

MFMS's achievement underscored the significance of investing in internal capacity building. By creating its own software, Annapurna Pariwar decreased its dependence on external vendors and gained more control over its technology. It was this experience that showed the importance of long-term planning and resource allocation in achieving digital transformation.

4.7 The Future of Advanced Automation: 2020 and Beyond

Annapurna Pariwar's digital evolution was expedited by the COVID-19 outbreak. The development of AppPurna, based on Tab technology, was carried out by Sahyadri,[11] Nasan's sister company. By digitising loan applications, KYC documents, and claim forms, field personnel were able to save time and improve data accuracy.

The integration of AppPurna with MFMS resulted in a feedback loop that enabled real-time data synchronisation. This innovation boosted the productivity of field personnel, decreased costs for members, and increased the decision-making power of the management. Parallelly, Annapurna Pariwar began to 'automate administrative and accounting functions', moving towards a paperless office. Shraddha InfoTech created APIs that facilitated the seamless exchange of data between MFMS and Tally accounting software, thereby decreasing manual labour and errors.

The potential of mobile technology in microfinance shines through with the success of AppPurna. The implementation of digital tools by Annapurna Pariwar's

[11] Sahyadri is an expert in Android app-based solutions. It also houses ERP systems which were useful in automating the admin department at Annapurna Pariwar.

field staff not only resulted in increased operational efficiency but also improved the overall experience for customers. Members experienced faster processing times and reduced administrative costs due to technological innovation. This had a significant impact on the overall economy.

This period also demonstrated the value of being able to respond to external circumstances. The use of technology to tackle the pandemic's operational disruptions allowed Annapurna Pariwar to demonstrate its resilience and adapt to changes. More specifically, Zoom and Whatsapp were used to communicate virtually during Covid. This further strengthened post-Covid communications through SMS and notifications to clients after each transaction. This experience enhanced the organisation's commitment to innovation and continuous improvement.

5 Learning from Annapurna Pariwar's Digitalisation Journey

The success of Annapurna Pariwar in implementing digital processes has provided valuable insights for microfinance institutions (MFIs) and other organisations looking to leverage technology to increase their impact. The organisation's experience demonstrates how digital solutions can be strategically invested in to overcome operational issues, enhance service quality, and promote financial inclusion. The digitalisation initiatives undertaken by Annapurna Pariwar are the focus of this section, which examines their relevance to microfinance as a whole.

5.1 Understanding the Importance of Change

The complexity of Annapurna Pariwar's operations led to the adoption of digitalisation. Initially, the organisation had to manually input data, but as its membership grew, it faced challenges. Eventually, the understanding that manual systems could not grow long-term led to technology being adopted. The key to effective scaling requires identifying operational bottlenecks and using technology to address them in an anticipatory manner. Organisations must periodically review their systems to identify areas where improvement is needed.

5.2 Customisation and Contextual Relevance

One of the most important milestones in Annapurna Pariwar's history was developing software internally for its specific needs. Loan Performer and other off-the-shelf solutions were initially successful, but their effectiveness was short-lived as new products like health and life insurance were introduced. Annapurna Pariwar invested in custom software to meet the needs of its members and operational requirements. It also facilitated designing products and services backed by software to suit the needs of different clients. Personalised solutions are necessary for an organisation's specific requirements. Although generic and quick fixes may provide solutions, custom-made systems are a better investment for long-term compatibility and efficiency.

5.3 Building Internal Capacity

The creation of an internal software development unit was a turning point for Annapurna Pariwar. Annapurna Pariwar utilised the expertise of team members who were well-versed in the organisation's operations to create solutions that seamlessly integrated with its processes. It also lowered dependence on third-party vendors, ensuring greater control over the organisation's internet infrastructure. Developing internal capacity for technological innovation allows organisations to quickly adapt and meet changing requirements. This process necessitates a combination of employee training and cross-functional collaboration.

5.4 Incremental Implementation

Annapurna Pariwar's digital transformation took place over several years, slowly but steadily. The organisation transitioned from using FoxPro systems to more advanced solutions like Interaid. Every transition was carefully planned to ensure uninterrupted operations and to minimise disruptions. A step-by-step approach to digital transformation is required. The process of phased implementation enables organisations to assess new systems, address issues, and refine processes before scaling.

5.5 Member-Centric Design

The adoption of AppPurna was a demonstration of Annapurna Pariwar's dedication to building solutions that accommodated members. The organisation's service delivery was enhanced, and administrative burdens were reduced by providing field staff with efficient tools to collect member data. Members enjoyed faster loan approval times and improved access to financial services. Technology is expected to improve the experience for members. Better outcomes are achieved when solutions that end-users can easily navigate and use are available.

5.6 Data Integration and Accuracy

Using multiple software systems to manipulate data was a persistent problem for Annapurna Pariwar. This problem was solved by the development of MFMS, which combined data into one platform to improve accuracy and reduce redundancy. Integrated data is essential for operational efficiency. Organisations must have systems in place that allow for seamless data exchange to maintain the integrity of data.

5.7 Leveraging Automation

Operations at Annapurna Pariwar were greatly enhanced by the automation of everyday functions like data entry and reporting. Integration with other accounting systems like Tally has also facilitated more efficient financial management, giving staff the opportunity to focus on strategic planning. The implementation of automation can decrease administrative burdens and increase productivity. Automated tasks that are repetitive should be identified by MFIs to maximise their resources.

5.8 Addressing Challenges Through Collaboration

Annapurna Pariwar enlisted the help of outside experts, software developers, and funding partners during its digital transformation. By means of these partnerships, the organisation was able to acquire both financial and technical expertise for implementation. Cooperation with outside parties can expedite digital transformation. Initiating partnerships with technology providers, donors, and industry experts can yield valuable insights.

5.9 Adapting to External Changes

Due to the Andhra crisis, Annapurna Pariwar had to update its systems because of new documentation and regulatory requirements for microfinance. The ability to adapt allowed for both compliance and operational continuity. In a constantly changing operating environment, flexibility is crucial. Organisations must adapt their systems and processes to keep up with regulatory changes and industry trends.

5.10 Sustaining Innovation

Annapurna Pariwar is committed to continuous improvement and digitisation of its administrative and accounting operations. Hence, the governing body of Annapurna Pariwar has adopted digital transformations. The organisation is committed to using technology to promote sustainable growth and has a vision of having offices without paper in the future. It further plans to digitise its operations wherein clients can log in from their smartphones to track loans and claims. Continuous change is occurring in the digital realm. It is essential for organisations to cultivate a culture of innovation and continuously seek out ways to improve their systems and processes, which will also have broader implications for the microfinance sector.

Learnings from Annapurna Pariwar's digitalisation experience are important for the wider field of microfinance. MFIs seek to expand their reach and influence through a strategic digitalisation process and approach. Therefore, some recommendations for implementing digitalisation in MFIs are discussed in the next paragraphs.

Optimising member services is the intended goal of technology adoption. Solutions that improve accessibility, affordability, and convenience are more likely to be successful. Building on internal knowledge of technology allows for greater control and reduces reliance on external vendors. Staff can benefit from digital transformation through the implementation of training programmes and knowledge-sharing initiatives. Continual implementation reduces risks and allows organisations to address challenges before scaling. The learning gained from pilot projects can be beneficial.

By consolidating information into common platforms, businesses can improve their operations and make more efficient decisions. System integration enables the achievement of regulatory requirements. Technology providers, funders, and industry peers can be connected to innovative solutions and resources. Joint ventures can also serve as a means of sharing knowledge and solving problems together. The microfinance sector operates in a fluid manner. It is essential for organisations to be flexible and adapt their systems and processes to accommodate changing needs and challenges. Digital transformation is a dynamic process to create value in the organisation. MFIs must cultivate a culture of innovation by regularly reviewing their systems and discovering fresh opportunities to enhance their impact.

These lessons can help Indian microfinance institutions expand their operations, reach a wider audience, and bring about financial inclusion through the use of technology. Besides addressing operational issues, these lessons also enable the sector to become an indispensable part of India's economic and social evolution.

6 Conclusion and the Road Ahead

Annapurna Pariwar's story highlights the impact of technology on the microfinance sector. Its unwavering dedication to continuous improvement and its ability to anticipate and adapt to changing needs have established it as a trailblazer in the industry. Advanced analytics and the continuous evolution of ERP systems are expected to contribute to improved efficiency and service delivery.

The Annapurna Pariwar programme is focused on utilising cutting-edge technologies like artificial intelligence, blockchains, and cloud computing to enhance financial inclusion and foster sustainable development. Blockchain can enhance transaction security and transparency, while loan applications can be approved with the help of insights derived from artificial intelligence. Cloud platforms can provide real-time data, resulting in improved decision-making and operational flexibility. The organisation's mission of empowering underprivileged groups has enabled it to establish new standards for microfinance innovation and impact.

The business of Annapurna Pariwar could also be extended in the future to other regions or states of the country with a wider range of products and services. The organisation may expand its reach to underprivileged communities in Indian slums and rural areas by utilising digital channels and collaborating with fintech firms. These efforts will be essential in achieving inclusive and sustainable development.

The tale of Annapurna Pariwar's transformation into a digital group is one marked by toughness, creativity, and vision. The company has exhibited the potential of technology to overcome obstacles and create new opportunities, using both traditional methods of managing financial transactions as well as newer technology, such as innovative apps. In its continuous journey towards progress, Annapurna Pariwar is a shining example of how grassroots organisations can use technology to their fullest advantage to facilitate social welfare by providing need-based solutions. By embracing innovation, Annapurna Pariwar has not only transformed its operations but also enhanced the quality of life for thousands of members, providing proof that digital transformation can be a potent catalyst for social change.

References

Adeoye, O. B., Addy, W. A., Ajayi-Nifise, A. O., Odeyemi, O., Okoye, C. C., & Ofodile, O. C. (2024). Leveraging AI and data analytics for enhancing financial inclusion in developing economies. *Finance and Accounting Research Journal*, *6*(3), 288–303.

Alam, M. R. (2023). *Microfinance and rural development: A service design plan for microfinance and women's outward mobility in rural households in the context of Bangladesh.*

Ansar, S., Klapper, L., & Singer, D. (2025), Financial inclusion and economic development: A review of the data and evidence. *Policy Research Working Paper*, 11021. World Bank.

Asante Boakye, E., Zhao, H., & Ahia, B. N. K. (2023). Blockchain technology prospects in transforming Ghana's economy: A phenomenon-based approach. *Information Technology for Development*, *29*(2–3), 348–377.

Basu, P., & Srivastava, P. (2005). Scaling-up microfinance for India's rural poor. *World Bank Policy Research Working Paper*, 3646.
Bello, O. A. (2023). Machine learning algorithms for credit risk assessment: An economic and financial analysis. *International Journal of Management, 10*(1), 109–133.
Bhatore, S., Mohan, L., & Reddy, Y. R. (2020). Machine learning techniques for credit risk evaluation: A systematic literature review. *Journal of Banking and Financial Technology, 4* (1), 111–138.
Birchall, J. (2003). *Rediscovering the cooperative advantage: Poverty reduction through self-help*. International Labour Organisation.
Brandstetter, L., & Lehner, O. M. (2015). Opening the market for impact investments: The need for adapted portfolio tools. *Entrepreneurship Research Journal, 5*(2), 87–107.
Capital, A. S. I. G. M. A. (2019). *Digitalisation for agriculture: The case of MUIIS.*
Challoumis, C. (2024). AI and the financial ecosystem: Understanding the cycles of money flow. In *XIX International Scientific Conference*, pp. 423–458.
Cheston, S., & Kuhn, L. (2002). Empowering women through microfinance. *Draft, Opportunity International, 64*, 1–64.
Daah, C., Qureshi, A., Awan, I., & Konur, S. (2024). Enhancing zero trust models in the financial industry through blockchain integration: A proposed framework. *Electronics, 13*(5), 865.
Dadios, E. P., Culaba, A. B., Albert, J. R. G., Paqueo, V. B., Orbeta, A. C., Serafica, R. B., Bairan, J. C. A. C., et al. (2018). *Preparing the Philippines for the fourth industrial revolution: A scoping study* (No. 2018–11). PIDS Discussion Paper Series.
Dorfleitner, G., Forcella, D., & Nguyen, Q. A. (2022). The digital transformation of microfinance institutions: An empirical analysis. *Journal of Applied Accounting Research, 23*(2), 454–479.
Erturk, I., & Zammit-Lucia, J. (2020). *Building digital finance in Europe: FinTech for social value.*
Fernando, N. A. (2003). *Mibanco, Peru: Profitable microfinance outreach, with lessons for Asia.* Asian Development Bank.
Fersi, M., & Boujelbène, M. (2022). Overconfidence and credit risk-taking in microfinance institutions: A cross-regional analysis. *International Journal of Organizational Analysis, 30* (6), 1672–1693.
Gammage, S., Kes, A., Winograd, L., Sultana, N., Hiller, S., & Bourgault, S. (2017). *Gender and digital financial inclusion: What do we know and what do we need to know.* International Center for Research on Women (ICRW).
Gasmelseid, T. M. (2015). Empowering microfinance processes through hybrid cloud based services. *International Journal of Systems and Service-Oriented Engineering (IJSSOE), 5* (3), 1–17.
Hossain, I. (2023). *Financial inclusion in Bangladesh through mobile financial services: A case study on marginal agricultural peoples of Bangladesh.*
Jejeniwa, T. O., Mhlongo, N. Z., & Jejeniwa, T. O. (2024). AI solutions for developmental economics: Opportunities and challenges in financial inclusion and poverty alleviation. *International Journal of Advanced Economics, 6*(4), 108–123.
Kuntze, R., Wu, C., Wooldridge, B. R., & Whang, Y. O. (2019). Improving financial literacy in college of business students: Modernizing delivery tools. *International Journal of Bank Marketing, 37*(4), 976–990.
Kustin, B. S. (2017). *Islamic (micro) finance and the possibility of social justice*. Doctoral dissertation, Johns Hopkins University.
Lamichane, B. (2020). Risks in Nepalese microfinance institutions (MFIs): A review of best practices. *Journal of Development Review*, 1–12.
Lamrani Alaoui, Y., & Tkiouat, M. (2019). Modeling customer satisfaction in microfinance sector: A fuzzy Bayesian networks approach. *International Journal of Engineering Business Management, 11*, 1847979019869533.
Mader, P., & Morvant-Roux, S. (2019). Financial inclusion and microfinance. In *Handbook of social policy and development* (pp. 411–430). Edward Elgar Publishing.

Mahapatra, P., & Singh, S. K. (2021). Artificial intelligence and machine learning: Discovering new ways of doing banking business. In *Artificial intelligence and machine learning in business management* (pp. 53–80). CRC Press.

MFIN. (2024). *Microfinance institutions network, Micrometer: Issue 51*. Retrieved from https://mfinindia.org/microfinance/industryOverview

Mistrean, L. (2021). Behavioural evolution of consumers of banking services in the COVID-19 pandemic situation. *The Journal of Corporate Governance, Insurance, and Risk Management, 8*(1), 84–100.

Mpofu, F. Y. (2023). Gender disparity and digital financial inclusion in advancing the attainment of sustainable development goals in developing countries. *International Journal of Innovation in Management, Economics and Social Sciences, 3*(3), 49–70.

Mujeri, M. K., & Azam, S. (2018). Role of digital financial services in promoting inclusive growth in Bangladesh: challenges and opportunities. *Institute for Inclusive Finance and Development, Working Paper, 55*.

Mushtaq, R., & Bruneau, C. (2019). Microfinance, financial inclusion and ICT: Implications for poverty and inequality. *Technology in Society, 59*, 101154.

Ndung'u, N., & Oguso, A. (2021). Fintech revolutionizing financial services: The case of virtual savings and credit supply technological platforms in Africa. *The Palgrave Handbook of Technological Finance*, 189–215.

Omowole, B. M., Urefe, O., Mokogwu, C., & Ewim, S. E. (2024). Integrating fintech and innovation in microfinance: Transforming credit accessibility for small businesses. *International Journal of Frontline Research and Reviews, 3*(1), 90–100.

Orlikowski, W. J., & Gash, D. C. (1994). Technological frames: Making sense of information technology in organizations. *ACM Transactions on Information Systems (TOIS), 12*(2), 174–207.

Pal, A., Dey, S., Nandy, A., Shahin, S., & Singh, P. K. (2023). Digital transformation in microfinance as a driver for sustainable development. In *Handbook of sustainability science in the future: Policies, technologies and education by 2050* (pp. 251–271). Springer International Publishing.

Parvez, J., Islam, A., & Woodard, J. (2015). Mobile financial services in Bangladesh. *USAID, mSTAR and fhi360*.

Pazarbasioglu, C., Mora, A. G., Uttamchandani, M., Natarajan, H., Feyen, E., & Saal, M. (2020). Digital financial services. *World Bank, 54*, 1–54.

Pimhidzai, O., Tong, K., Anantavrasilpa, R., Popovic, A., Mel, S., & Sanchez Martin, M. E. (2019). *Microfinance and household welfare: Cambodia policy note*. World Bank.

Pytkowska, J., & Korynski, P. (2017). Digitalizing microfinance in Europe. *Microfinance Centre*, 1–12.

Rahman, M. M. (2020). Financial inclusion for poverty alleviation: The role of Islamic finance in Bangladesh. *Enhancing Financial Inclusion Through Islamic Finance*, 2, 17–50.

Rahman, R., & Fong, J. (2016). Innovate for agriculture: Young ICT entrepreneurs overcoming challenges and transforming agriculture. *CTA Success Stories*.

Rao, D. N., & Mahalingam, M. (2025). AI and ML modeling and autonomous finance in microfinance: An overview. *Computational Intelligence for Autonomous Finance*, 167–197.

Read, L., & Atinc, T. M. (2017). *Information for accountability: Transparency and citizen engagement for improved service delivery in education systems*.

Santhosh Kumar, K., & Aithal, P. S. (2024). Influence of digital technology on microfinance sector: A study in Kerala. *International Journal of Applied Engineering and Management Letters, 8*(2), 186–197.

Saputra, A. D., Burnia, I. J., Shihab, M. R., Anggraini, R. S. A., Purnomo, P. H., & Azzahro, F. (2019). Empowering women through peer to peer lending: Case study of Amartha.com. In *2019 International Conference on Information Management and Technology (ICIMTech)* (Vol. 1, pp. 618–622). IEEE.

Sharma, H., & Díaz Andrade, A. (2023). Digital financial services and human development: Current landscape and research prospects. *Information Technology for Development*, *29*(4), 582–606.

Siwale, J., & Godfroid, C. (2022). Digitising microfinance: On the route to losing the traditional 'human face' of microfinance institutions. *Oxford Development Studies*, *50*(2), 177–191.

Srivastava, T. (2010). *Microfinance: A comparative analysis of varying contexts, current needs, and future prospects between developing and developed countries*. Master's thesis, Bowling Green State University.

Tasin, M. I., Hossain, M. R., Chowdhury, N., & Alam, S. M. (2023). *Revolutionizing microfinance: A blockchain-driven decentralized finance (DeFi) model for collateral-free loans*. Doctoral dissertation, BRAC University.

Tenaw, B. (2019). *The Role of e-payment on Productive safety net Program (PSNP) implementation performance in Ethiopia (The case of M-birr service in Tigray Region)*. Doctoral dissertation, St. Mary's University.

Thomas, H., & Hedrick-Wong, Y. (2019). How digital finance and fintech can improve financial inclusion. In *Inclusive growth: The global challenges of social inequality and financial inclusion* (pp. 27–41). Emerald Publishing Limited.

Timbula, M. A., & Marvadi, C. (2023). Digital transformation: Acceptance and use of technology among microfinance institutions in developing country: An application of UTAUT2 mode. *International Journal of Information Technology*, *15*(8), 4459–4468.

Tuwei, D. K. (2018). *Communication technology, capabilities and livelihoods: The role of mobile money in facilitating financial inclusion and development in rural Kenya*. Doctoral dissertation, University of Iowa.

Wang, Y. (2021). *Applying robotic process automation in the banking industry*. Doctoral dissertation, Massachusetts Institute of Technology.

Zheng, K., Zheng, L. J., Gauthier, J., Zhou, L., Xu, Y., Behl, A., & Zhang, J. Z. (2022). Blockchain technology for enterprise credit information sharing in supply chain finance. *Journal of Innovation and Knowledge*, *7*(4), 100256.

Augmenting the Value of Microfinance: The 'Plus' Services of Annapurna Pariwar

Tara Nair

Abstract The organisational growth and diversification of Annapurna Pariwar since the mid-1970s bears testimony to the vision of its leadership that access to credit, though is a foundational right of poor and resourceless women, they cannot move out of poverty just by availing credit. There are more acute constraints arising out the structure of societal institutions embedded as they are with gender norms and social norms rooted in patriarchy. They severely constrain women's capabilities to build a life of value for themselves and their families. Absence of affordable and reliable child care, access to children's education, and timely and affordable healthcare are the most critical human development deficits that burden poor households and push them back to chronic poverty. Annapurna Pariwar has systematically integrated services to address these constraints over the years and created a conglomeration of organisations consisting cooperatives (micro credit, early child care), non-profit companies (micro insurance/old age security, digital solutions), and public charitable trusts (education, research). Annapurna Pariwar's impact on the community and women, hence, needs to be assessed by analysing how these various value adding interventions have interacted with each other and with the larger systemic shifts occurred over a very critical phase in India's microcredit history. This chapter is an attempt to do such an analysis

T. Nair (✉)
Work Fair and Free Foundation, Bangalore, Karnataka, India
e-mail: tara01@gmail.com

J. D. Ranadive, S. Guha (eds.), *Building Pathways to Women's Empowerment*, India Studies in Business and Economics,
https://doi.org/10.1007/978-981-95-7159-8_11

1 Introduction

The inadequacy of minimalist credit programmes to address the complex interdependencies among the multiple dimensions of poverty has been recognised by development initiatives working with microfinance globally since the 1990s. As the microfinance programmes expanded across geographies, concerns were raised not only about its larger development outcomes but also about the operational and financial sustainability of the institutions delivering microfinance services (Sinha & Sinha, 2002). Many enquiries undertaken during the 2000s into the workings of microfinance emphasised its blended character. It was argued that microfinance represents a distinct institutional arrangement that combines the social and the economic objectives wherein resources are applied in clear pursuit of the simultaneous creation of both financial and social values, both profits and social wellbeing (Nair, 2010). Minimalist credit programmes were hence portrayed by many as inadequate, though essential, to address all types of deprivations that characterise multidimensional poverty (Reed, 2011). The bundling of financial and non-financial services has been considered the most desirable approach, especially for regions where poverty is entrenched and access to financial services is minimal. While evaluating credit-plus models from Mexico Biosca et al. (2011) found that non-financial services were used to enhance the likelihood of poverty reduction and to improve the returns to capital that borrowers availed from MFIs. It was also thought that plus services helped arrest default and diminish the risk of loans being diverted from productive to consumption activities due to external shocks.

Flores and Serres (2009) discuss three models of integration of non-financial services with microfinance: the linked, the parallel and the unified models. In the linked model, services are provided by two independent organisations. The MFI does not directly provide non-financial services but establishes a partnership with another entity to do so (for example, health services or technical assistance for agriculture). The parallel model is followed typically by multiservice organisations. In this case, financial and non-financial services are offered by the same organisation under different programmes that are managed by separate, specialised personnel who share the same brand. This way the MFI can retain direct control over all operations but with increased financial and administrative burden. The authors assume that the different programmes in the linked model target different clientele. The third model, the unified model is built on complementarity between financial and non-financial services by embedding them in a hybrid product to be provided by the same staff. In other words, non-financial services are blended with financial services in the unified model (for instance, the group training activities routinely carried out in meetings).

Despite such strong advocacy for the plus model, in the early 2000s, only a few players globally had tried to blend credit with non-credit services. For instance, the United States-based non-profit organisation, Freedom from Hunger (FFH) pioneered an integrated model of microcredit and education. By around the mid-1990s it had already implemented its Credit with Education programme through local partners in many countries in Asia, Africa and Latin America (Karlan & Valdivia, 2006). There are also examples wherein credit was added to poverty alleviation and empowerment-focused training approaches as it happened in the case of Pro Mujer set up in 1990 in Bolivia and expanded later to other Latin American countries including Nicaragua, Peru, Mexico and Argentina. The model was extended to Nicaragua in 1996, Peru in 1999, Mexico in 2001, and Argentina in 2005 (Pro Mujer, 2015). BRAC (the Bangladesh Rural Advancement Committee) has been offering non-credit support in the form of health training, agricultural extension services and legal awareness training (Garcia et al., 2021).

The microfinance plus services have followed a peculiar evolution trajectory in India. Self-Help Group (SHG) Bank linkage model was the dominant approach to microfinance in India almost until the end of the decade of the 1990s. It may be noted that in the early phase of microfinance development in the country (lasting up to the late 1990s) non-government organisations (NGOs) and cooperative institutions played a pivotal role as its promoters. The former adapted savings and credit activities as part of the broad bouquet of poverty reduction and women empowerment programmes they were already offering (Nair, 2015). The cooperative institutions like the Cooperative Development Foundation (CDF) in the undivided Andhra Pradesh promoted innovation within the cooperative system to develop mutually aided societies based on self-help (Ghate, 2007). Though the champions of financial sustainability principle critiqued the firm location of microfinance within the not-for-profit and nonfinancial institutions, these institutions driven as they are by the larger values of social equity and wellbeing have often demonstrated an alternative imagination of plus services. In the 1990s many of the NGO-MFIs were working on issues like nutrition, child care, gender violence, and natural resource conservation along with credit, often through associate entities.

As the commercial microfinance paradigm assumed greater salience in India through the 2000s, credit plus services came to be framed purely from the point of view of enhancing the efficiency of the credit operations. In the early part of the decade, about a third of the MFIs in India had plus services linked to their credit programmes (Sinha, 2005). Most of them offered commission-free insurance services, enterprise-related support or development programmes in the spheres of health and education. Such programmes, however, had either limited coverage or did not target microfinance clients. In many cases, the Indian MFIs started carefully and deliberately keeping the beneficiaries (of development programmes) and clients (of microfinance) apart to avoid an apparent moral hazard. In other cases, the management of non-financial services was separated from that of financial services. For instance, when Equitas, a large south India-based MFI was planning to launch a value-added service in the form of a series of stores selling goods to its customers who were small-scale vendors at wholesale prices, its major concern was the separation of management of both businesses (Mazer, 2011). The question of whether it was justified for a financial business to enter into an unrelated business like distribution was intriguing for the leadership.

The design and implementation of plus services of Annapurna Pariwar demonstrates that they have been shaped by a larger vision and philosophy of development rather than by a narrow agenda of efficient delivery of financial services to poor women. At the centre of Annapurna's imagination of development is a process of empowering poor women and their households. Such empowerment comes as much from provision of financial services as from other developmental services to cater to a range of needs and interests of women.

In this chapter we specifically discuss Annapurna's initiatives in early child care, old age social security, and educational scholarship services, the initiatives that have significant transformative potential for women's self-efficacy, agency, work participation and sense of security. The analysis in the chapter is based on secondary data, published reports, and detailed interviews with the Managing Director, heads of various programmes, and a selection of customers/shareholders. In depth interviews and field observation were also carried out in a few localities of Pune city to evaluate the working of the plus activities on ground.

2 'Plus' Services Annapurna: Through the Lens of Gender and Social Justice

Pulling women out of the confines of their homes to participate in economically remunerative employment requires more than sheer financial assistance. There are more acute constraints to their labour force participation. These are embedded deeply in the structure of societal institutions and shaped by the gender norms and social norms rooted in patriarchy. Studies have established that women bear a disproportionately larger burden of household care responsibilities—caring for children, the elderly and the sick—thanks to the cultural perception that they are innately inclined to be 'nurturers', a gender stereotype further reinforced by lack of opportunities for education and skill training (ILO, 2018). The latest estimates for 2023 show that 708 million women (aged 15 or older) are not in the labour force because of care responsibilities. Of the total working-age persons outside the labour force, women account for about a third (ILO, 2024). In the same year, the burdIndia had 53% of its women outside the labour force thanks to the burden of care (ibid). The gender gap in employment of families consisting of couples with young children (less than 6 years of age), as per the ILO estimates, is 38 percentage points. Disaggregated by income groups, the data quite interestingly reveal that single mothers with young children, irrespective of the overall economic status of the country, have a higher labour force participation as compared to women without young children. In other words, despite being burdened with childcare responsibilities, single mothers are compelled to work to provide for their families, often at the risk of the safety of children who are left alone at home.

The other issue that demands attention is the key demographic shift towards ageing due to fertility decline and increasing life expectancy. The elderly population constitutes about 10% of India's population (Niti Ayog, 2024). Some estimates show that this share will rise to about 19.5% by 2050 (IIPS, et al., 2020). Three-fourths of the elderly have some chronic illness while 78% have no pension coverage and 72% are not covered by health insurance. Workers in the unorganised sector also remain outside the pension system.

Further, it is important to note that the share of women among the elderly population has been on the rise in India. Research studies have highlighted the gendered vulnerabilities experienced by elderly women as a continuation of the neglect and discrimination they encounter throughout the entire life cycle (Giridhar et al., 2015). As the economic contribution of women to the family dwindles or stops completely with age their income insecurity increases along with dependence on other family members. The vulnerabilities arising from such a situation are starker for women in poor households. The social pension scheme for the elders has covered only a smaller percentage of old persons, often excluding poor women from its coverage (Rajasekhar et al., 2016).

Annapurna is one among a few women-led microfinance institutions spearheading an alternative movement in India to structure financial products and non-financial services to match the needs, priorities and constraints that every woman faces through her life cycle. The organisation has carefully crafted an institutional architecture incorporating child care support, savings, health insurance, and old age pension as critical programme pillars along with microfinance. Notwithstanding the conceptual divide between positions that support seamless integration of financial and other value-added services and clear ring-fencing of both, it has experimented with unique models of providing plus services.

3 Vatsalyapurna: The Early Child Care and Development Initiative

SDG Goal 4 has an important target to ensure that all girls and boys have access to quality early childhood care and development (ECCD) and preschool education (for children in the 3–6 age group) which is deemed essential for their future physical, cognitive, social and emotional development. Estimates show that about eight million out of the 36 million urban-resident children in the 0–6 age group reside in slums having poor housing and living conditions and access to basic facilities (PwC and Save the Children, 2015; NIUA, 2016). A study done in a slum in Delhi revealed that 37% of the children who never attended school cited financial issues as the reason for non-enrollment. India's National Policy for Children 2003 states that survival, health, nutrition, development, education, protection and participation are the undeniable rights of every child. Despite the existence of such glaring statistics and positive policy pronouncements, investing in children has never been a priority in the national development imagination. Especially, the country has not yet made early childhood development a fundamental right (Kapur et al., 2025). Pre-school education is one of the least invested sub-sectors within the education sector. As per the available estimates, expenditure on early childhood development has hovered around 0.7% of the total government expenditure and 0.1% of GDP between 2020–21 and 2024–25 (Save the Children and CBGA, 2022; Kapur et al., 2025). The per-child allocation of resources works out as Rs. 1993 (Kapur et al., 2025).

Further, the institutional architecture of ECE in the country has many paradoxes. For one, the Anganwadi Services (previously known as the Integrated Child Development Scheme or ICDS), the flagship ECCD programme in the government sector, is skewed in that it focuses almost singularly on nutrition, while it hardly gives attention to the preschool education aspect. The scheme's coverage too is limited to about a third of the children in the relevant age group (Save the Children and CBGA, 2022). The coverage is also biased towards rural areas. Though there are alternative channels run by the NGO and private sectors, the urban poor still face serious difficulties in accessing these facilities. The grossly underfunded ECE infrastructure in India not only increases the financial burden of low-income households but exacerbates the spatial and social imbalance in educational achievement too.

4 The Beginning

Annapurna forayed into daycare services in 2003. However, the motivation for adding such an atypical plus service did not come from the financial sustainability logic of the cooperative as it was typically believed. The savings and credit cooperative of Annapurna Pariwar was doing quite well by then. Most of its clients had established and expanded their petty businesses earning higher incomes. Many could invest in assets, including houses that they had been aspiring to have for a long time. They had started enjoying the freedom and power that economic self-sufficiency could bring about. But an unfortunate incident happened in a slum neighbourhood in Pune city that was being serviced by Annapurna laid bare the perilous and complex social milieu that has the potential to undo the economic and welfare gains achieved by women and their households. In the Karvenagar slum colony, a young girl was sexually abused by her neighbour while she was playing outside her home. That such a heinous incident took place within Annapurna's working area instilled a deep sense of fear and enormous guilt in the members of the cooperative. Many of them used to leave their young children back home under the care of older siblings or neighbours while they worked outside the colony. Several incidents of accidents and abuses were also coming to the fore through the media. It did not take much time for the leadership to identify that an appropriate solution to the problem was to create childcare facilities in the slums. However, it had to be ensured that the community felt the need for the service and shared the expenses of running the centres.

After months of campaigning and demand mapping the first day-care centre was set up in August 2003 in Karvenagar colony. Annapurna had been working in the slum for about a decade and gained trust and credibility among its members.

The finance to set up the centre was mobilised through a grant extended by the Times Foundation. This remained the only centre till 2005. Since then the number of centres started gradually increasing and by 2015 there were 21 *Vatsalya* centres—17 in Pune and four in Mumbai. The addition of each centre was preceded by a detailed mapping of the demand for childcare services in the area and the identification of potential partners with interest and basic resources to start it as a micro business venture. The programme also had to mobilise resources and develop operating procedures and standards in line with the national guidelines for creches regarding space, ambience, learning goals, training of tutors and child safety.

5 The Model

In 2007 when the number of centres reached five, the day-care activity was hived off under a separate cooperative—the Vatsalyapurna Swayamrozgar Seva Co-operative Society (VSSCS)—with women who run daycare centres as shareholders. The cooperative is managed by a management committee chaired by the Group Managing Director of the Annapurna Pariwar. The committee consists of representatives of day-care operators, the head of the Vatsalyapurna project, and a couple of senior shareholders of the cooperatives. The main educators and assistants were selected by the management committee.

Each operator enters into a memorandum of association (MoU) with the VSSCS secretary. The MoUs govern the relationship between the conductor and the cooperative and ensure a graded movement of every centre through time. The initial one month is considered the trial period. When a centre crosses the first month, it enters the probationary phase which lasts for six months. Centres that complete one year are subject to close monitoring and continuous evaluation.

Early childhood educators are required to develop a diverse set of skills and competencies by undergoing special education and training which is resource-intensive. Annapurna's Vatsalyapurna project, however, aimed at incubating a locally embedded model for the underprivileged and marginalised urban communities with locally available material and human power. This came as a major challenge facing Annapurna's leadership. Linkage with the Home Science College of SNDT University, Pune, has helped them overcome this constraint. The professors and students of the college work with the women most of whom are just matriculates to develop a methodology of education that suits the abilities already acquired by them and the material circumstances prevalent in their neighbourhoods. They are helped to develop skills in all activities—storytelling, games, creative artwork—but with the help of props and materials available at their homes and surroundings. They also receive a robust grounding in the conceptual aspects of child development. In short, an innovative, cost-efficient and locally relevant curriculum and pedagogy is the hallmark of the Vatsalyapurna project.

6 Method of Financing the Centres

The daycare centres are run as micro social enterprises set up by local promoters with the capital raised from VSSCS as debt. The loan thus to a woman promoter towards the building, expanding or modifying her house to set up a daycare centre as a micro business. The centre charges a monthly fee for their services. The fee amount covers a decent monthly return for the entrepreneur and the salary of the helper. It needs to be noted that the parent's willingness to pay for the services increased sharply from Rs. 25 to Rs. 900 over the past two decades validating the credibility of the model of childcare introduced by Annapurna. Unlike the other popular models financed entirely by public, private or philanthropic capital, Vatsalyapurna can sustain the child care and preschool education activity as a genuine business enterprise capable of generating a surplus for the promoter to service her loan regularly. The programme solicits grant support from corporations and individual donors too. Donors can adopt one or more centres in any area under the Adopt-A-Day Care Center project. Under the cooperative structure, the number of centres has increased by close to two centres per year since 2008. By the mid-2010s, the number of centres was the highest—17 in Pune and four in Mumbai. The number of centres came down to 12 in 2023 in the aftermath of the COVID-19 pandemic.

7 Learning and Sharing

Source Photo taken by the Author

All centres follow the same routine. Children are dropped off at the centres by their parents in the morning. They carry food and refreshments with them. For a working mother in the slum who is perennially income and time-poor, children's food often means packed snacks. The centres have worked hard to change this idea and educate parents about the significance of a balanced diet for the physical and cognitive development of children. Across the centres, parental attitudes towards nutrition have decisively changed due to this intervention. The children are made to share their food with their friends at the centre. This practice has helped them learn the importance of sharing and mutuality.

The daycare centres are financed through a blended model. The VSSCS contributes finances for the renting, upkeep and purchase of learning materials for the functional centres. The costs of supervision and accounting as well as the head office expenses are covered from the operational profits of AMCCS. The cooperative ploughs back five per cent of its profit for these purposes.

8 A Unique Model of Early Child Care and Education

Studies have discussed the characteristics of models being pursued in different parts of the global north and south ranging from government-funded ECCD programmes to CSR-funded schemes and partnership-based initiatives—between government, private sector, private investors and NGOs. These programmes use diverse financing mechanisms and partnerships like grants, direct funding, investments in infrastructure and operation, technical support, cash transfers, and social impact bonds (UNESCO, 2016). While all studies emphasise the significance of augmenting allocation of public resources to early childhood care and education there is an increasing realisation that the fiscal capacities of government have been on the decline. The external financial support by corporate or philanthropic partners more often than not is project-centric and hence unpredictable. In this scenario, the Vatsalyapurna programme presents a viable and sustainable alternative, especially for urban settings where income-generation opportunities are many for households, but regular and reliable institutional childcare arrangements are completely absent.

As depicted in Fig. 1, what makes the Vatsalyapurna model unique is its simultaneous attention to community ownership, deliberate location in low-income neighbourhoods, and the structuring of the intervention as an incubation of a micro-social business. While the model integrates three strategic objectives of child safety, child development and women's economic empowerment, as a micro business it blends different types of capital—loans, personal equity, knowledge capital and philanthropic capital. The early childhood educator and the parents of the children are the shareholders and owners of the Vatsalyapurna Cooperative Society while the AMCCS extends its goodwill by sharing a small portion of its profits to support operational expenses. The Vatsalyapurna initiative of Annapurna indeed is a distinct example of a plus activity in the world of microfinance. It demonstrates how microfinance institutions can deepen their social impact by designing solutions to address critical strategic development deficits without sacrificing their core objectives, values, and operational ethos.

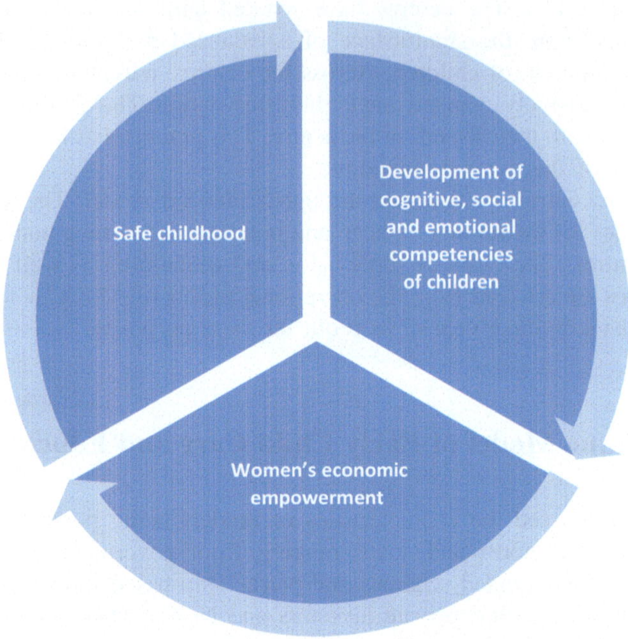

Fig. 1 Vatsalyapurna: blending child safety, development and women's empowerment

9 Adharpurna: The Savings-Linked Pension Scheme

A source of income at the old age was a felt need of the older members of the AMCCS for a long time. Most of them had either worked in the informal sector throughout their working life or spent their younger age doing unpaid housework. At the dusk of their lives, when the capacity to work and earn diminished, many of them found themselves dependent on family members financially. Most of them needed money regularly for medicines and meeting their personal needs. It may be noted that in the 1990s and early 2000s, the pension schemes prevalent in India were of two types—(1) the social security welfare schemes of the central and state governments, and (2) the occupation-based and earnings-linked pension schemes. The welfare pension schemes (like the Indira Gandhi National Old Age Pension Scheme) form part of the National Social Assistance Programme (NSAP) and are targeted at the elderly (above 60 years of age) population living below the poverty line. Such schemes have been in operation since the mid-1990s. Until the early 2000s, the occupation-based pension scheme benefit was an exclusive privilege enjoyed by the employees in the organised sector who form only about 10% of the total workforce (Ranadive, 2001).

Close to 90% of the population working in the informal or unorganised sectors have remained outside the purview of the pension system. In 2003 the central government established the Pension Fund Development and Regulatory Authority

(PFRDA) as the apex institution to regulate the pension sector. In the subsequent year, the National Pension Scheme (NPS) was launched. In 2009, NPS was extended to all citizens including unorganised sector workers and individuals from the weaker and economically disadvantaged sections. The NPS-Lite was launched in the same year by PFRDA to encourage marginal investors to accumulate savings during their productive lives to purchase an annuity for their old age. To reduce administration and transaction costs, the NPS-Lite model worked through aggregators like NGOs, MFIs and NBFCs who took on the responsibility of enrolment, collection, reconciliation and transfer of individual contributions along with ongoing services and information delivery.

10 The Genesis and Evolution

In the Union Budget 2010–11, the central government announced the launching of a co-contributory micro pension scheme called *Swavalamban*. The new pension scheme's objective was 'to encourage the people from the unorganised sector to voluntarily save for their retirement'.[1] The scheme's benefit was available to those who made a minimum contribution to their NPS accounts of Rs. 1000 and a maximum contribution of Rs. 12,000 per annum during the financial year 2010–11. The scheme was made available to all those NPS-Lite accounts that satisfied the necessary criteria. The government contributed a matching assistance of Rs. 1000 each to all such accounts for five consecutive years (2011–12 to 2015–16). An individual could join the scheme with as small a contribution as Rs. 100. The scheme was made voluntary for anyone in the 18–60 age group who could invest an amount of their choice every year through an aggregator. Once the subscriber reaches 60 years she would start getting a pension based on her accumulated savings.

A part of the contribution made by the account holders was to be invested in the equity market in fixed-income instruments like government securities (up to 55%) and corporate bonds (up to 40%). To reduce the risk to the contributor, stock market investment was capped at 15%. Every account holder was issued a PRAN (Permanent Retirement Account Number) which provided them access to the NPS account. Two types of accounts are available under the scheme—the Tier I which is a non-withdrawable account meant for savings for retirement and the Tier II account which is a voluntary savings facility. The subscriber is free to withdraw savings from this account whenever she wishes, though no tax benefit is available on this account. For Tier 1 account holders, the age of exit from the scheme is fixed as 60. Subscribers of Tier II accounts can opt to exit earlier. Overall, the Swavalamban scheme has been promoted as a voluntary, flexible, secure, and long-term

[1] Budget 2010–2011, Speech of Pranab Mukherjee, *Minister of Finance,* February 26, 2010. https://www.indiabudget.gov.in/budget_archive/ub2010-11/bs/speecha.htm.

contribution-based benefit scheme option for all those individuals whose incomes are low and unpredictable and are not covered by any other social security scheme.

Recognising the critical need for women to be income secure in their old age, Annapurna took the initiative in 2012 to discuss with its members the new pension facility launched by the government. It conducted several open discussions and a structured survey to understand the willingness of the members to enrol in the Swavalamban scheme as subscribers. Having received an enthusiastic response from them, on the foundation day of the organisation in August 2012 Annapurna announced that it would join the scheme. The *Annapurna Pariwar Vikas Samvardhan* (APVS), the non-profit Section 8 company set up in 2003 was designated as the implementing arm for the scheme. The responsibilities of APVS included facilitating registration, distributing PRAN Cards, following up on regular savings, and handling grievances. With the concerted efforts of the leadership and the branch offices of Annapurna about 12,000 of the cooperative members were enrolled in the scheme by 2014.

The members were encouraged to save or 'pay in' Rs. 100 every month rather than Rs. 1000 in lump sum. This practice, it was thought, would inculcate financial discipline of regular savings in them. The funds collected monthly were remitted by APVS to the Life Insurance Corporation (LIC) which was designated as the nodal agency by PFRDA. For every Rs. 1000 remitted, PFRDA spent Rs. 100 as service charges—APVS received Rs. 70, while Rs. 30 went to the LIC.

Even as Annapurna was striving to streamline the operations around the implementation and sustenance of the Swavalamban scheme, the Union Budget of 2015–16 proclaimed the introduction of another pension scheme, the Atal Pension Yojana (APY) to service all citizens in the 18–40 age group. The subscribers of APY are guaranteed a minimum monthly pension of Rs. 1000 to Rs. 5000 and co-contribution of 50% of the subscriber contribution or Rs. 1000 per annum, whichever is lower by the central government. All those who are not covered by any Statutory Social Security Scheme can enrol under APY. Here again, the government's contribution continues for five years.

Now with two similar pension schemes in operation, Annapurna started facing serious difficulties with implementation in the field. There was considerable ambiguity in the way both schemes would roll out. For instance, the Swavalamban scheme is meant for people aged between 18 and 60 while APY targets those in the 18–40 age group. There were no other guidelines from the government's side to enable a rational selection of the scheme by the younger age group. Moreover, the service charges paid to aggregators were suddenly stopped. The distribution of PRAN cards which were earlier done through Annapurna's branch network could not be carried out in the changed circumstances. There were delays in receipt of cards and many were lost in transit. All these complicated the work of the AVPS team. The leadership kept writing to the authorities citing these difficulties, but no redressal was in sight. It became amply clear that Annapurna had to structure its long-term saving for retirement product to create a viable and effective solution to the problem of income insecurity of its members in their old age. Amidst such confusion, Dr Medha Sawant, the Managing Director of Annapurna consulted Francois Xavier Hay, the actuarial and risk management consultant of the organisation, who helped design *Adharpurna* as a long-term savings-linked pension product which is designed on the same lines as the government schemes. The decisive difference is that Adharpurna is a community-based mutual model owned by members which is legally allowed to create reserves from the savings of the funds (National Insurance Academy, 2020).

11 The Adharpurna Product

Adharpurna was launched in May 2016 in Pune and Mumbai. All but two of the 12,000 members who were also borrowers of the AMMCCS willingly shifted to this in-house programme. Whatever amount they had saved under the Swavalamban scheme (totalling about Rs. 25 million) would remain with the PFRDA until the time the women become eligible for a pension or to withdraw the amount.

The new savings product is also delivered through APVS. It requires the members to 'pay-in small amounts monthly till the time when they receive payout in small amounts monthly'. The payout starts when the member turns 65. However, for a member to avail of the benefit of a pension she has to satisfy two conditions: (1) monthly saving ('pay-in') has to be regular, and (2) the minimum cumulative savings must be Rs. 40,000 at the time of maturity. If any one of these conditions is violated, the total amount saved is paid back to the member with 10% interest, but after deducting 0.5% administrative charges per year.

The amount of monthly savings collected from each member depends on her age at the time of enrolment, the number of years she has until she attains 65 years of age, and the expected pension payout after the age of 65. In case a member passes away before the maturity of the scheme, the cumulative pay-in money is paid back to the nominee with 10% interest on it and after deducting 0.5% administrative charges per year but without causing any pinch in the amount. If a member decides to withdraw the savings before maturity (described in the books as 'wilful withdrawal'), 10% interest is paid on the cumulative pay-in amount. However, along with administrative charges (0.5% per year of savings), a pinch of 15% is also deducted from the amount withdrawn.

The number of saving members under the scheme rose from about 12,000 to 36,000 during the eight years from 2016–17 to 2022–23 but declined marginally to 34,670 in the subsequent year. Over the same period, the amount of savings by members rose from Rs. 10.85 million to Rs. 38.85 million. As Table 1 and Fig. 2 show, members' contributions registered a decline of about 30% in 2020–21, the year when the livelihood shock of the COVID-19 pandemic was the most severe. However, the growth momentum picked up in the subsequent two years.

Table 1 Performance of Adharpurna

	Contribution of members (Rs. million)			No. of members (in '000)		
Year	Mumbai	Pune	Total	Mumbai	Pune	Total
2016–17	4.45	6.40	10.85	5.00	7.22	12.22
2017–18	6.59	9.66	16.25	6.31	8.92	15.23
2018–19	8.97	14.12	23.09	12.04	17.7	29.74
2019–20	13.08	21.24	34.32	13.45	19.32	32.77
2020–21	9.53	14.66	24.19	12.74	18.01	30.75
2021–22	13.27	19.34	32.61	14.77	19.83	34.60
2022–23	13.46	20.29	33.75	15.55	20.89	36.44
2023–24	14.36	24.49	38.85	14.74	19.93	34.66
CAGR (%)	15.77	18.26	17.29	14.47	13.53	13.92

Source MIS data, AMMCCS

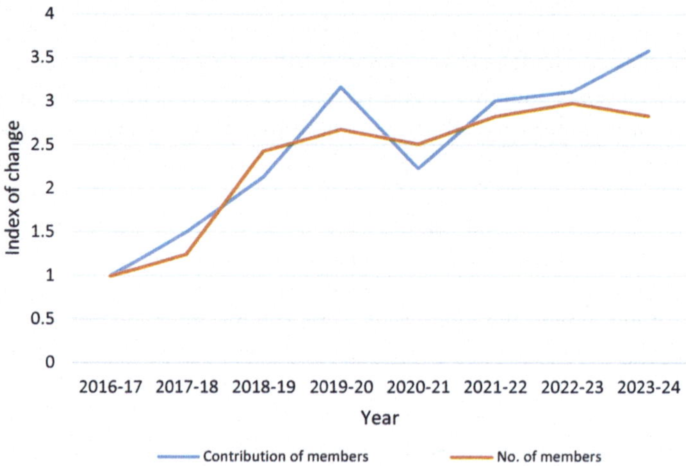

Fig. 2 Trend in members' savings. *Source* Same as Table 1

Thus at a compounded rate, the total member savings grew at 17.3% (15.8% in Mumbai and 18.3% in Pune) over the period 2016–17 to 2023–24. A look at the performance of the different savings products offered by AMMCCS reveals that the share of Adharpurna contributions in its total savings fund rose from 16.4% in 2018–19 to 22.5% in 2022–23. Adharpurna savings account for about 11% of all savings mobilised by AMCCS.

Between June 2016 and September 2024, 708 members of the scheme expired whose cumulative savings came to Rs. 40.20 million (average savings of Rs. 5691). The total number of members who withdrew their Adharpurna savings as they could not save regularly stood at 12,814. Importantly, 53% of them pulled out their savings during 2020–21, signifying the impact of the pandemic breakdowns of incomes and livelihoods. 23 members who saved till the age of maturity were not eligible for pension as their savings were below Rs. 40,000. As of September 2024, 34 members have started getting pension from their Adharpurna savings account. Importantly, about 10%–14% of the long-term saving members are single women.

The elderly population depends mainly on four sources for their income security, namely, family support, work participation, assets accumulated over their lifetimes, and benefits extended by employers or the state (The World Bank, 2024). In high-income countries, old people receive substantial income support in the form of pensions and public transfers. In contrast, elderly people in developing countries typically depend on their families in their old age or receive a meagre social pension which is non-contributory. Those who are employed in informal employment or unorganised enterprises are not eligible for social security benefits and employer-guaranteed pensions. Many continue to be part of the informal labour force even after they cross the working age. Given these realities, micro pensions can create 'an accessible, affordable all-inclusive pension system' (Nutsubidze & Nutsubidze, 2024). As we discussed in this section old age income security schemes in India have largely adopted the direct benefit (DB) approach with a specified schedule of contributions/benefits. However, a sizeable chunk of beneficiaries of these schemes find it difficult to maintain their regular contributions mainly due to fluctuations in income flow. For instance, it has been reported that within six months of instituting the *Pradhan Mantri Shram Yogi Maandhan* or PM-SYM (2019), the latest state-run old age security initiative, 21% of workers left it owing to rising inflation and increasing cost of living.[2] The scheme was launched to specifically address the issue of income insecurity of the unorganised sector workers or the workers employed in activities outside the formal sector who are in the 18–40 age group.[3] The subscribers of the scheme are required to make a monthly contribution ranging from Rs. 55 to Rs. 200 until the age of 60 after which they are assured of a minimum pension of Rs. 3000 per month. In case the beneficiary dies before the age of maturity, their spouse would receive a minimum family pension of Rs. 1500. Though the PM-SYM has features very similar to Adharpurna, in the case of the latter the monthly deposits are collected by AMCCS out of which further credit is created. The subscribers earn interest on their long-term savings and pay the stipulated interest for the loans availed. This ensures the long-term sustainability of Adharpurna.

---

[2] '21% Informal Workers Leave PM Pension Scheme, Inflation, Cost of Living Main Factors', https://thewire.in/labour/21-informal-workers-leave-pm-pension-scheme-inflation-cost-of-living-main-factors, 14 July 2023.

[3] The unorganised sector workers include home based workers, street vendors, mid-day meal workers, head loaders, brick kiln workers, cobblers, rag pickers, domestic workers, washermen, rickshaw pullers, landless labourers, own account workers, agricultural workers, construction workers, beedi workers, handloom workers, leather workers, and audio-visual workers, and the like.

12 Vidyapurna: The Educational Scholarship Programme

The third important ‘plus’ service offered by Annapurna Pariwar is the educational scholarship for school children. Scholarship schemes both in the central and state sectors have been in operation in India since 1961 (Sharma & Singh, 2020). Most of these are merit-based or merit-cum-means based scholarships, while a few are means-based scholarships. These are offered to high-performance students from top-class schools usually for classes 9 to 12. There are special scholarship schemes for children belonging to SC, ST, OBC, DNT and minority communities. Vidyapurna, the educational scholarship programme of Annapurna Pariwar covers children of single mothers in the age group of 6–18 years (that is, from *balwadi* to 12th grade). The programme’s mandate is to help children studying across classes and belonging to single-parent households from among cooperative members to complete school education without dropping out. The scheme also benefits children who are under the guardianship of widowed grandmothers who are borrowers of AMCCS. Named Vidyapurna, the scholarship programme was launched in Pune in 2002 as a response to a request for financial assistance from a widowed mother of three children. A child who enrols in the programme at any stage continues to receive financial support till they finish the 12th class. The programme was extended to Mumbai in 2015.

Over the last 17 years since 2007–08, the programme has mobilised grant support of close to 25 million and extended 10,792 scholarships. The number of scholarships in the late 2000s was around 50–60, which rose to around 300 in the first half of the 2010s. There was a sharp rise in the number of scholarship recipients in the latter half of the 2010s to more than 900 on average. We have presented in Table 2 the total number and amount of scholarships granted over successive triennia since 2007–08. The data clearly shows the steady expansion of the scheme coverage over the years. The average amount of scholarship has doubled over the years from Rs. 1200 to Rs. 2500. The mothers find the support very helpful especially in the months of June–July when they have to incur extra expenditure on books and school supplies for the new academic year.

Table 2 Progress of the Vidyapurna programme

Time period	Amount (Rs. million)	No. of children sponsored	Average sponsorship
2007–10	0.21	161	1267
2010–13	1.07	827	1300
2013–16	4.10	1640	2500
2016–19	4.59	2802	2500
2019–22	7.00	2798	2500
2022–25	6.41	2564	2500

The Pune component of the Vidyapurna programme is managed by the Dada Purao Research and Training Institute (DPR&TI), the research and training arm of Annapurna Pariwar. The implementation of the scholarship programme in Mumbai is taken care of by Annapurna Mahila Mandal, a registered charitable trust within Annapurna Pariwar. The financial resources for running the programme come out of the operational profits of AMCCS. As in the case of the Vatsalyapurna programme, AMCCS ploughs back five per cent of its profits to meet the running cost of the Vidyapurna programme.

Though there have been many examples of MFIs in India offering credit products to finance the education of clients' children, there are not many models where children are granted scholarship support. In a study done in 2014 to identify the responsible microfinance practices followed by MFIs in India, MicroSave found only two such cases out of a sample of 10 (MicroSave, 2014). Their number seems to have dwindled further in subsequent decades as the microfinance industry became more commercialised and profit-oriented focusing almost exclusively on wealth maximisation of investors. Annapurna Pariwar stands as a rare exception to this trend.

13 Health, Life and Asset Mutuals

Apart from the initiatives that we discussed in detail in this chapter, Annapurna operates a community-based insurance programme for its members and their families. The health, life and asset insurance coverage is offered through three community-based mutuals managed by the APVS. As per the National Insurance Academy (2020), a mutual society is a 'low claim-low fraud model which focuses on health care rather than hospitalisation (in case of health insurance)' where 'owners are also insurers, hence these organisations enjoy a high level of trust of policyholders. Social upliftment and wellbeing of the poor is their guiding principle. Profit becomes surplus which is retained for the sustainability of the society' (pp. 36–37).

Membership in the Health Mutual benefits women in accessing reliable healthcare-related advice from Annapurna's in-house medical officers, continuous client education, affordable and good quality hospital care thanks to the Health Care Providers' Network set up by the organisation, and a refund of 50–100% hospitalisation expenses (ranging from Rs. 2000 to Rs. 40,000). The average annual contribution per member ranges between Rs. 220 and Rs. 480.

The Family and Life Mutual has borrowers of loans as its members who make an annual contribution based on the size of loans availed. The insurance cover is extended through the tenure of the loan. In the unfortunate event of the borrower passing away while the loan is still being repaid, the entire outstanding amount is written off. Additionally, financial assistance is extended to the family. Financial assistance is also extended to borrowers if spouses or other family members pass away or when the family suffers from accidental loss of assets.

Chapter 8 of this volume presents in-depth analyses of the mutual societies promoted by Annapurna Pariwar.

14 Conclusion

The structural barriers that constrain women's opportunities and agency are hardly addressed by commercial microfinance institutions. Their mental models are anchored on the perception that exclusion is a manifestation of market failure and poverty is a simple 'cash flow' problem (Goetz and Sen Gupta, 1996). While Credit and, to a limited extent, savings were seen sufficient to ameliorate the cash flow situation of poor households effectively, provision of 'market-like' alternatives would take care of exclusion (Kabeer, 2005). The organisational growth and diversification of Annapurna Pariwar since the mid-1970s bears testimony to the vision of its leadership that though credit is a foundational right of poor and resourceless women accessing it alone cannot move women out of poverty. There are more acute barriers arising out of the structure of societal institutions embedded as they are with gender norms and social norms rooted in patriarchy. These factors severely constrain women's capabilities ('the ability to do and to be') to craft a life of value for themselves and their families and the realisation of those capabilities ('functionings', as described by Amartya Sen) (Nussbaum, 2003). The absence of affordable and reliable child care, access to children's education, access to timely and affordable healthcare, and lack of income security and dignity in old age are the most critical human development deficits that burden the poor, especially women, and push them into chronic and intergenerational poverty.

Annapurna Pariwar, over the years, has systematically integrated multiple financial and non-financial services within a linked model (Folores & Serres, 2009) with a range of organisations consisting of cooperatives (microcredit, early child care), non-profit companies (micro insurance/old age security, digital solutions), and public charitable trusts (education, research) to address such deficits. The organisation has not hesitated to tread unconventional pathways to remain relevant to its members and to the larger society. For instance, the day care programme of Annapurna has ushered a social innovation in the sphere of early childhood care and education. This unique initiative has not only helped fill a gap that is deep and long-standing in a sector plagued with fragmented institutional arrangements unaffordable and inaccessible to the urban poor, but has transformed the ways in which women exercise their agency, The multi-faceted social security programme—consisting of health, life, accident and asset insurance—of Annapurna helps its members effectively protect themselves against unexpected risks and shocks.

Cross-subsidising social programmes using profits from microfinance operations is considered bad economics and even dangerously unviable in the current scenario. However, Annapurna Pariwar continues to nurture programmes like Vidyapurna and Vatsalyapurna by carefully ploughing back a part of the wealth that the cooperative creates for the thousands of small shareholders, thereby investing in their wellbeing—in the true spirit of solidarity and cooperation. The individual and compounded impact of these initiatives on the community at large and women and children, in particular, has been deep and enduring.

References

Biosca, O., Lenton, P., & Mosley, P. (2011, October). Microfinance non-financial services: A key for poverty alleviation? Lessons from Mexico. In *Sheffield Economic Research Paper Series SERP Number: 2011021*. University of Sheffield, The United Kingdom.

Flores, I. L., & Serres, P. (2009). Microfinance and non-financial services: An impossible marriage? *Private Sector and Development, 3*, 3–6.

Garcia, A., Cecchi, F., Eriksen, S., & Lensink, R. (2021). The plus in credit-plus-technical assistance: Evidence from a rural microcredit programme in Bolivia. *The Journal of Development Studies, 58*(2), 275–291.

Ghate, P. (2007). Consumer protection in Indian microfinance: Lessons from Andhra Pradesh and the microfinance bill. *Economic and Political Weekly, 42*(13), 1176–1184.

Giridhar, G., Subaiya, L., & Verma, S. (2015). Older women in India: Economic, social and health concerns. In *Building knowledge base on ageing in India: Increased awareness, access and quality of elderly services, thematic paper 2*. Institute for Social and Economic Change, Bangalore; United Nations Population Fund, New Delhi; Institute of Economic Growth, Delhi; and Tata Institute of Social Sciences, Mumbai.

Goetz, A. M., & Sen Gupta, R. (1996). Who takes the credit? Gender, power, and control over loan use in rural credit programs in Bangladesh. *World Development, 24*(1), 45–63.

Goswami, R. (2001, June 5–7). Indian pension system: Problems and prognosis. In *Paper presented at the International Actuarial Association (IAA) pensions seminar*, The Grand Hotel, Brighton.

International Institute for Population Sciences (IIPS), National Programme for Health Care of Elderly (NPHCE), Ministry of Health and Family Welfare (MoHFW), Harvard T. H. Chan School of Public Health (HSPH), & University of Southern California (USC). (2020). *Longitudinal ageing study in India (LASI) wave 1*, 2017–18: India report. International Institute for Population Sciences. Mumbai.

International Labour Office. (2018). *Care work and care jobs for the future of decent work*. International Labour Office.

International Labour Office. (2024). *The impact of care responsibilities on women's labour force participation*. International Labour Office.

Kabeer, N. (2005). Is microfinance a 'magic bullet' for women's empowerment? Analysis of findings from South Asia. *Economic and Political Weekly, 40*(44/45), 4709–4718.

Kapur, A., Pandey, S., & Sharma, A. (2025). *Investing in India's children: A look at child budgets*. The Hindu Centre for Politics and Public Policy.

Karlan, D. S., & Valdivia, M. (2006). Teaching entrepreneurship: Impact of business training on microfinance clients and institutions. In *Center discussion paper no. 941*. Yale University.

Mazer, R. (2011). How many "plus-es" can we add to "microfinance ++?". Available at https://www.cgap.org/blog/how-many-plus-es-can-we-add-to-microfinance. Accessed September 28, 2024.

MicroSave. (2014, December). *Responsible microfinance practices by microfinance institutions in India*. MicroSave.

Mujer, P. (2015). *25 years empowering women in Latin America*. Pro Mujer two-year report, 2014–2015.

Nair, T. S. (2010). Commercial microfinance and social responsibility: A critique. *Economic and Political Weekly, 45*(31), 32–38.

Nair, T. (2015). Vignettes in transformation. In T. Nair (Ed.), *Indian microfinance since the 1990s* (pp. 1–41). Routledge India.

National Insurance Academy. (2020). *Micro insurance in India: Challenges and solutions*. NIA.

National Institute of Urban Affairs (NIUA). (2016). *Status of children in urban India: Baseline study 2016*. Delhi.

NITI Aayog. (2024). *Senior care reforms in India: Reimagining the senior care paradigm: A position paper*. New Delhi.

Nussbaum, M. (2003). Capabilities as fundamental entitlements: Sen and social justice. *Feminist Economics*, *9*(2–3), 33–59.
Nutsubidze, T., & Nutsubidze, K. (2024). Micro pensions in developing countries: Implications and policy relevance. *CRR WP 2024-7*, July. Center for Retirement Research at Boston College.
Rajasekhar, D., Kesavan, S., & Manjula, R. (2016). Contributory pension schemes for the poor: Issues and ways forward. *Working Paper No. 377*. ISEC.
Reed, L. R. (2011). *State of the microcredit summit campaign report 2011*. Microcredit Summit Campaign.
Save the Children and Centre for Budget and Governance Accountability. (2022). *Cost of universalising early childhood education in India: A policy brief*. Save the Children.
Save the Children and PwC. (2015). *Forgotten voices: The world of urban children in India*. Save the Children.
Sinha, S., & Sinha, F. (2002). Rising to the challenge of scale in India: Growing the micro-finance sector. In T. Fisher & M. S. Sriram (Eds.), *Beyond micro-credit: Putting development back into micro-finance* (pp. 263–299). Vistaar Publications. New Delhi.
Sinha, F. (2005). Access, use and contribution of microfinance in India: Findings from a national study. *Economic and Political Weekly*, *40*(17), 1714–1719.
Sharma, S., & Singh, A. (2020). *Importance of scholarship scheme in higher education for students from the deprived sections* (IEG Working Paper No. 395). Institute of Economic Growth. Delhi.
The World Bank. (2024). *Understanding income security for older adults*. The World Bank.
United National Educational Scientific and Cultural Organization. (2016). *Financing for Early Childhood Care and Education (ECCE)*. UNESCO, Asia and Pacific Regional Bureau for Education.

Entrepreneurial Orientation, Effectuation, and the Social and Solidarity Economy: How 'Medha Tai' Co-Created Annapurna Pariwar

Monica Nandan, Marissa Kaloga, and Gokul Mandayam

Abstract This chapter situates the *founder Medha Purao Samant* within the evolving cultural, political, social, and economic contexts since 1993, demonstrating her social entrepreneurial characteristics and transformational perspectives over the course of 30 years as an entrepreneur. It describes the various leading social entrepreneurial perspectives, orientations, and frameworks that explain the journey that the founder, the leadership team, and the organisation travelled. Finally, the chapter concludes by illuminating the community-oriented practices that forms the core of the empowerment-based cooperative management model.

1 Introduction

The concept of social enterprise has evolved over the past several decades. A term initially used to describe hybrid organisations that earn income and serve a social purpose has developed into a complex set of definitions. These definitions range from 'organizations that combine entrepreneurial dynamics to provide goods or

M. Nandan (✉)
Strategic Partnership and Social Impact, Department of Social Work and Human Services, Wellstar College of Health and Human Services, Kennesaw State University, Kennesaw, GA, USA
e-mail: mnandan@kennesaw.edu

M. Kaloga
Management & International Business, University of Auckland, Auckland, New Zealand
e-mail: marissa.kaloga@auckland.ac.nz

G. Mandayam
School of Social Work, Rhode Island College, Providence, RI, USA
e-mail: gmandayam@ric.edu

J. D. Ranadive, S. Guha (eds.), *Building Pathways to Women's Empowerment*, India Studies in Business and Economics,
https://doi.org/10.1007/978-981-95-7159-8_12

services with a primacy of social aims and constraints to redistribute profits in the interest of the community' (Defourny & Nyssens, 2010) to 'any business venture created for a social purpose—mitigating/reducing a social problem or a market failure—and to generate social value while operating with the financial discipline, innovation, and determination of a private sector business' (Peredo & McLean, 2006). While the debate continues regarding what is and what is not a social enterprise, the growing attention to these new kinds of organisations is also a signal of a larger-scale movement to shift thinking away from conceptualising social enterprises as combining 'capitalism + impact' to a different type of economic approach that prioritises the social and environmental good that organisations can generate, both in processes and outcomes: the social and solidarity economy (SSE). Far from being a new idea, it has diverse origins, from nineteenth-century European mutualist movements to Mahatma Gandhi's Swadeshi movement. The interest in exploring SSE as a meaningful alternative economic arrangement was influenced in recent years by acknowledging SSE as a pathway to reaching the Sustainable Development Goals. In 2023, the United Nations recognised this burgeoning wave of economic theory and practice in its resolution 'Promoting the Social and Solidarity Economy for Sustainable Development' (United Nations, 2023), defining it as:

> Enterprises, organisations and other entities that are engaged in economic, social and environmental activities to serve the collective and/or general interest, which are based on the principles of voluntary cooperation and mutual aid, democratic and/or participatory governance, autonomy and independence and the primacy of people and social purpose over capital in the distribution and use of surpluses and/or profits, as well as assets, that SSE entities aspire to long-term viability and sustainability and to the transition from the informal to the formal economy and operate in all sectors of the economy, that they put into practice a set of values which are intrinsic to their functioning and consistent with care for people and planet, equality and fairness, interdependence, self-governance, transparency and accountability and the attainment of decent work and livelihoods and that, according to national circumstances, the social and solidarity economy includes cooperatives, associations, mutual societies, foundations, social enterprises, self-help groups and other entities operating in accordance with the values and principles of the social and solidarity economy ...

Beyond the definition, this resolution encourages UN member states to promote and implement SSE approaches with novel financial mechanisms and structures. Growing acknowledgment of SSE has provided a third lens beyond the binary Capitalism or Socialism orientation of organisations and economies. However, visualising a shift to a global economy based on social and environmental impact can be daunting. Consequently, case studies or illustrations of how organisations can be co-created to facilitate a different kind of value proposition in line with the SSE can be helpful for readers.

Established in 1993, *Annapurna Pariwar* (AP) provides an exemplary model for SSE organisational development, community activation, and program implementation through the eyes of a community-based social entrepreneur. This chapter explores key insights from Dr. Samant's (also known as Medha Tai) development of *Annapurna Pariwar*, showcasing how community-based social entrepreneurs can apply entrepreneurial orientation and effectuation principles[1] to build successful SSE organisations. Through Medha Tai's journey, it highlights the strategic ways in which local entrepreneurs can drive social impact by leveraging these frameworks to foster sustainable and resilient community-based enterprises.

The chapter begins with highlighting key principles of effectuation, SSE, and social entrepreneurship orientation. Following this, we establish Medha Tai's orientation as a community social entrepreneur, sharing her unique journey from a socialist upbringing to a career in corporate banking to founding and scaling an impactful social entrepreneurial venture. Her strategic approach is explored through the effectuation lens (Sarasvathy, 2001) with examples from *Annapurna Pariwar*'s long history of financial and social programs. We explore how Medha Tai exhibited critical characteristics of entrepreneurial orientation, namely opportunity creation, innovative solution design, taking affordable risks, and proactive problem-solving. The chapter concludes with a discussion on how Medha Tai's social entrepreneurial approach fostered a fully independent SSE organisation with well-integrated principles of democratic governance, solidarity and cooperation, and impact-focused economic activity.

2 Theoretical and Conceptual Framework

This section establishes the conceptual framework for analyzing *Annapurna Pariwar (AP)* by drawing on three key areas: SSE, entrepreneurial orientation and effectuation. These theories provide a robust lens through which to understand AP's approach as a community based social entrepreneurial venture operating within the SSE founded on democratic governance principles. Entrepreneurial orientation emphasises opportunity recognition, innovation, and calculated risk-taking, which are essential for social enterprises, or social entrepreneurial ventures, navigating complex community needs. Effectuation complements this by focusing on how entrepreneurs start with available resources, adapt to uncertainty, and co-create solutions with stakeholders rather than following predetermined plans. Together, these theories form a comprehensive framework that captures how Medha Tai effectively leverages entrepreneurial thinking to address social challenges, demonstrating a strategic and iterative approach to building sustainable, inclusive community-driven initiatives. These frameworks provide a pathway to articulate the dynamic processes at play within AP, positioning it as a model of an effective community social entrepreneurial venture.

[1] Effectuation principle refers to a decision-making approach in entrepreneurship where the focus is on utilising available resources and taking action to create opportunities in uncertain environments, rather than gathering needed resources for a predetermined goal.

2.1 The Social and Solidarity Economy

An autonomous sector independent of the government, the SSE is grounded in three principles: democratic governance, solidarity and cooperation, and impact-focused economic activity. Democratic governance emphasises collective decision-making, ensuring all stakeholders, particularly marginalised groups, actively shape the organisation's direction and activities (Utting, 2015). This participatory approach ensures that power is distributed, and decisions reflect the community's needs. Solidarity and cooperation are likewise central to SSE, with organisations promoting collaboration over competition, focusing on shared goals, fostering social cohesion, and building networks of mutual support (Laville, 2010). Finally, the value proposition of economic activity in the SSE is focused on generating social impact rather than maximising profit. Organisations committed to community well-being often reinvest their profits to advance social and environmental objectives, as noted by Defourny and Nyssens (2010). This practice aligns with the broader goals of the SSE, which emphasises sustainability, equity, and inclusivity. Within this framework, economic activities are seen not merely as profit-generating endeavors but as powerful tools for empowering communities and addressing pressing societal challenges (Fig. 1).

The SSE has roots in the cooperative and mutualist movements of nineteenth-century Europe, which sought to counter the exploitative effects of industrial capitalism. Pioneers like Robert Owen and Charles Fourier advocated for cooperatives

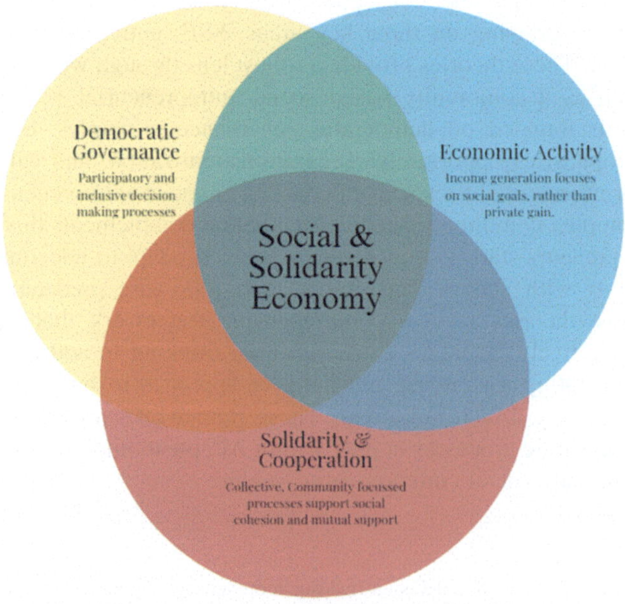

Fig. 1 Characteristics of Social and Solidarity Economy Organisations

and mutual aid societies, emphasising collective ownership and democratic governance (Fairbairn, 1994). Building on these foundations, the social economy tradition emerged in the late nineteenth and early twentieth centuries, characterised by cooperatives and mutual organisations that balanced economic activity with social goals, embodying fundamental SSE principles such as solidarity and inclusivity (Defourny & Develtere, 1999). In the late twentieth century, the solidarity economy concept gained momentum, particularly in Latin America and Europe, as a response to neoliberal policies and market-led economic exclusion. Countries like Brazil and Argentina spearheaded grassroots solidarity movements that prioritised cooperation and community-led development (Singer, 2009). By the twenty-first century, SSE had gained global recognition, with the International Labour Organization (ILO) and the United Nations highlighting its role in sustainable development, particularly in promoting social and environmental goals (Utting, 2015). These global movements laid the groundwork for formalising SSE structures and principles. Today, social and solidarity economies (SSE) present a compelling alternative to traditional economic models, including state-run, voluntary sector, and market-driven approaches. SSE emphasises community engagement, social justice, and sustainable development, offering innovative solutions that prioritise people over profit. This model fosters cooperation, enhances local resilience, and addresses societal needs more effectively than conventional economic frameworks (Laville, 2010).

2.2 The Social and Solidarity Economy in India

While early European collectives influenced today's SSE model, this organisational approach also draws from global roots. India has a history of strong cooperative models emphasising self-reliance, cooperation, and solidarity. Famously, Mahatma Gandhi's Swadeshi movement in the early twentieth century advocated for local production and self-sufficiency, laying the groundwork for economic decentralization and collective ownership (Gandhi, 1938). His vision of economic trusteeship, where wealth is managed for the community's welfare, aligns with the SSE's principles of social and environmental impact and democratic governance. Building on Gandhi's ideas, India's cooperative movement, also known as the *Amul Cooperative*, was founded in 1946, which empowered rural dairy farmers through collective action, providing a successful model of inclusive economic activity and solidarity (Kurien, 2005). Elaben Bhatt is an example of a pioneering social reformer who founded the Self-Employed Women's Association (SEWA) Bank in 1974 to provide financial services to self-employed women who often lived in poverty in India. Her work with SEWA Bank enabled thousands of women to save and access credit for business growth while simultaneously strengthening women's voices in economic and social decision-making. Her efforts were embedded in the Gandhian principles of self-reliance (*Swavalamban*), decentralization and local empowerment (*Gram Swaraj*), nonviolence and constructive action (*Ahimsa & Nayi Talim*), dignity of labor and non-exploitative work that uplifted the vulnerable (*Sarvodaya*) and grassroots empowerment through a trust-based lending and cooperative model (Bhatt, 2005).

In the 1980s and 1990s, Self-Help Groups (SHGs), which originated as social support groups, sometimes operated as cooperative savings and credit, where marginalised women pooled their resources to gain financial independence (NABARD, 1995). Their historical context in India can be traced to grassroots movements, government initiatives, and international influences. Early foundations include a combination of the prevalence of Gandhian Philosophy and the establishment of rural cooperatives that led to organised efforts to promote SHGs in India. An example of the earliest organised efforts to promote SHGs in India came through the non-governmental organisation called MYRADA (*Mysore Resettlement and Development Agency*) in the 1980s. MYRADA staff observed that informal groups of rural women were saving and lending money among themselves. Recognising the potential of this model, MYRADA began organising these informal savings groups into formal SHGs and linking them with banks.

The SHG concept gained momentum when the *National Bank for Agriculture and Rural Development* (NABARD) launched the *SHG-Bank Linkage Programme* (SBLP) in 1992. This program aimed to provide formal credit access to the rural poor by linking SHGs with banks. Eventually, it became one of the most extensive microfinance programs in the world, providing low-cost credit to millions of rural women. By 1999, the Government of India launched the *Swarnjayanti Gram Swarozgar Yojana* (SGSY). SGSY aimed to promote self-employment in rural areas, mainly targeting women and marginalised groups. SHGs were the central focus of this program, which aimed to provide them with capacity-building support, access to credit, and market linkages. In 2011, the SGSY was restructured into the *National Rural Livelihoods Mission* (NRLM) to reach out to the poorest households through SHGs. This mission aimed to promote sustainable livelihoods, reduce poverty, and foster financial inclusion. It further formalised the role of SHGs in India's rural development policies.

The **Self-Help Group-Bank Linkage Program (SBLP)** is a flagship financial inclusion initiative pioneered by the **National Bank for Agriculture and Rural Development (NABARD)** in India. Introduced in **1992** as a pilot project, this program has since evolved into the world's largest microfinance program, facilitating access to formal financial services for individuals living in poverty, particularly women. The pilot project was a partnership between SHGs, banks, and non-governmental organisations in which the Reserve Bank of India (RBI) allowed banks to lend directly to SHGs and NABARD committed to providing re-finance and promotional support (Kumar et al., 2020).

The socio-economic and cultural impact that SHGs has in rural areas mainly includes women's empowerment through gaining financial independence, collective bargaining power, and social capital. SHGs have also served as a forum for addressing issues such as domestic violence, education, and health care. SHGs were crucial in promoting microfinance in India, allowing women and marginalised communities to access small loans, build savings, and invest in income-generating activities. This has impacted underserved areas in the country, specifically regarding greater financial inclusion. From a social capital perspective, many SHGs have taken on broader social roles, such as improving local governance, promoting health awareness, and participating in environmental conservation activities. For example, in Kerala, the Kudumbashree Mission is a prominent example of SHGs taking on broader social roles. This initiative not only focuses on financial inclusion and livelihood generation but also actively participates in local governance by involving women in decision-making processes at the grassroots level. Additionally, Kudumbashree SHGs promote health awareness through various campaigns and workshops, and they engage in environmental conservation activities such as waste management and organic farming (Tabassum, 2024).

This history of SHGs provides a landscape from which *Annapurna Pariwar's* collective model grew, addressing criticisms and demonstrating how SSE principles—democratic governance, economic independence, and solidarity—can be effectively integrated into community-based social entrepreneurial organisations for creating sustainable and inclusive economic practices. By building on established mutual aid models (SHGs) and developing new approaches that embedded principles of trust, social capital, and empowerment, Annapurna Pariwar strengthens women's financial security, social standing, and overall well-being, thereby fostering sustainable development in marginalised communities.

2.3 Entrepreneurial Orientation and Community Social Entrepreneurs

Many social entrepreneurs (SEs) exhibit an entrepreneurial orientation during the formation of their ventures. This orientation encompasses several key elements, including the creation or identification of opportunities, the design of innovative solutions, the willingness to assume affordable risks and endure potential losses, and a proactive approach to problem-solving (Helm & Andersson, 2010).

A fundamental aspect of the entrepreneurial orientation is the ability to recognise or create opportunities where others may see challenges or limitations. SEs possess a keen awareness of social needs and gaps in existing solutions, which drives their quest to address these issues. This proactive identification of opportunities is often rooted in their personal experiences, professional expertise, and observations of unmet needs within their communities.

SEs are sensitive to the entrepreneurial 'window of opportunity' (Shane & Venkataraman, 2000), an important component of a larger process of systemic change. This concept refers to the optimal moment when environmental and circumstantial factors align to make the pursuit of an innovative solution both viable and impactful. SE's operate within a broader social innovation system—a network of practitioners and institutions collaboratively tackling social challenges while influencing both societal development and innovation (Guo & Bielefeld, 2014; Phillips et al., 2015). As Guclu et al. (2002) elucidate, changes in external conditions can significantly influence receptivity to new ideas, thereby either expanding or constricting the window of opportunity. For SEs, the window of opportunity is not merely about timing but also about aligning external conditions with their innovative aspirations. Shifts in societal, economic, or political environments can create favourable conditions for introducing new solutions, thus enhancing the potential for impact. Conversely, unfavourable conditions can close these windows, necessitating adaptability by SEs to navigate such fluctuations. SEs often identify/create a range of innovative solutions that are responsive to complex social problems (Phillips et al., 2015).

The pursuit of opportunities is profoundly influenced by how well they align with the social entrepreneur's personal identity and overarching goals. Effective social entrepreneurship involves ensuring that the innovative solution resonates with the entrepreneur's core values, mission, and long-term vision. This alignment ensures not only the personal commitment to the cause but also the authenticity and sustainability of the solution.

Several personal factors shape a SE's readiness and ability to capitalise on opportunities. Their level of commitment to the cause is crucial, as it drives persistence and resilience in the face of challenges. Additionally, the entrepreneur's qualifications and abilities—encompassing their skills, experience, and knowledge—determine their capacity to develop and implement the solution effectively. Moreover, the stage of life in which entrepreneurs find themselves—such as their career phase or personal circumstances—can impact their willingness and ability to seize and act upon opportunities.

Essentially, sensitivity to the window of opportunity is a key characteristic of SEs. It involves recognising and acting upon the optimal moments when external conditions are favorable for innovative solutions, aligning these opportunities with personal values and goals, and considering the impact of personal commitment, qualifications, and life stage. This multifaceted approach enables SEs to effectively leverage opportunities for creating meaningful social impact.

The field of social entrepreneurship is dynamic, encompassing various academic disciplines and evolving definitions. Peredo and McClean (2006) and Mort et al. (2003) highlight that SEs work by prioritising the objective of creating and diffusing any social value, using innovation, and taking calculated risks to bring social well-being into the community. Many SEs also focus on deep transformations and large-scale societal changes and seek to generate revenue by obtaining social results. Studies by Thompson et al. (2000) and Mort et al. (2003) underscore that SEs possess a high level of commitment, immense strength in the face of adversity, the capacity to assume risks, and the ability to generate trust and credibility in third parties. Other studies, such as those by Martin and Osberg (2007) and Koe Hwee Nga and Shamuganathan (2010), identify traits like sensitivity to exclusion, kindness, openness to new ideas, and strong self-discipline as crucial for success. Jiao (2011) points to charisma and unwavering belief in the social enterprise as defining characteristics. Notwithstanding the diversity in definitions, SEs share a strong sense of purpose and dedication to addressing 'wicked' problems.[2]

Sometimes, community practitioners operate as social entrepreneurs to address community-based 'wicked' problems. Boehm and Cnaan (2012) describe community practice as a democratic, grassroots approach to social work rooted in community members' perspectives and preferences. This approach involves discussing and debating core issues from various viewpoints, enriching the dialogue, and fostering collaborative problem-solving. Community practice extends beyond cultural humility to address structural oppression and support collective liberation (Carruthers, 2018). Nandan et al. (2016) explain how community practitioners serve as social entrepreneurs in their efforts to address recalcitrant community-based challenges experienced by residents. Community social entrepreneurs exemplify critical community practice skills, demonstrating flexibility within structured phases such as engagement, assessment, intervention, and evaluation of their intervention/programs) (Hardina, 2012). Their interventions may include locality development, social planning, and social action (Rothman, 1968). Community social entrepreneurs (CSEs) are characterised by their commitment to solving complex issues alongside those directly affected by these challenges, i.e., co-creating solutions with residents impacted by the challenge, i.e., co-creating solutions with residents impacted by the challenge. They operate across different sectors and may engage as transformational or global social entrepreneurs, depending on the context and nature of the problem they are addressing.

CSEs focusing on local issues within a specific geographical area leverage their deep connections and networks within the community, including relationships with corporations, organisations, partners, and alliances. Their approach involves several vital strategies: soliciting community participation at various stages of planning and implementation; forming coalitions with activists in the social, business, and government sectors to foster innovative change; utilising resources such as volunteers and material support; and employing media and social networks to raise awareness and influence policymakers (Nouman & Cnaan, 2023). Their work aims to enhance social awareness and strengthen community engagement to improve quality of life (Sadan, 2012).

As local change agents, CSEs identify problems, navigate political and cultural environments, and possess a unique ability to spot opportunities, devise solutions, and build organisations. Their commitment to their work often spans decades, placing those impacted by the challenges at the centre of problem-solving and decision-making processes (Bornstein, 2004). CSEs often move away from traditional models in favour of approaches that engage ordinary citizens to address underserved markets

---

[2] A wicked problem is a complex social or policy issue that is difficult to define, has no clear solution, and is interwoven with other problems. Solutions to wicked problems are often incomplete, contradictory, and context-dependent, with no definitive stopping point. The concept was first introduced by Rittel and Webber (1973) in their paper *'Dilemmas in a General Theory of Planning.'* They described wicked problems as issues that lack a single, optimal solution and require iterative, participatory approaches to address.

at scale (Bornstein, 2004). Fundamentally, CSEs are driven by a vision to enhance the well-being of the most marginalised members of society, demonstrating a broad range of qualities and skills that enable them to tackle complex social challenges effectively.

Given the diversity of issues tackled by CSEs and SEs, the field continues to evolve and encompasses varied academic disciplines and professions. CSEs and SEs who operate within SSE tend to add value to the social, financial and environmental well-being of marginalised communities. To sum it up, social entrepreneurs focus their vision on activities that add value to the well-being of the most vulnerable sections of the community.

2.4 Designing Innovative Solutions

Once an opportunity is identified, SEs design innovative solutions tailored to address the specific social issues they have uncovered. This involves developing novel approaches or adapting existing methods to create effective and sustainable solutions. The innovation process is characterised by a blend of creativity and practicality, ensuring that the solutions are both impactful and feasible within the given context.

Social innovation, akin to social entrepreneurship, encompasses a range of definitions reflecting its complex and multifaceted nature. According to the Stanford Social Innovation Review, social innovation is described as 'a novel solution to a social problem that is more effective, efficient, sustainable, or just than existing solutions and for which the value created accrues primarily to society as a whole rather than private individuals' (Phills et al., 2008). This definition highlights the transformative potential of social innovation, emphasising its capacity to enhance societal well-being and address social challenges in a manner that transcends conventional approaches.

The Organization for Economic Co–operation and Development (OECD) provides an alternative perspective, defining social innovation as 'the design and implementation of new solutions that imply conceptual, process, product, or organisational change, which ultimately aim to improve the welfare and well-being of individuals and communities' (OECD). This definition underscores the diverse dimensions of social innovation, encompassing changes in concepts, processes, products, or organisational structures. The OECD also notes that numerous initiatives within the social economy and civil society have demonstrated innovation in addressing socio-economic and environmental issues while contributing to economic development.

Both definitions underscore the essence of social innovation as a mechanism for creating meaningful and sustainable societal impact. By fostering novel approaches that improve upon existing solutions, social innovation plays a crucial role in advancing the welfare of communities and addressing pressing global challenges. Ultimately, it is the innovation that helps social entrepreneurs create social value.

2.5 *Taking Affordable Risks*

SEs are prepared to take calculated risks as part of their pursuit of social impact (McGregor, 2024). This involves assessing and managing potential losses in a manner that aligns with their overall mission and capacity. Adopting a risk-tolerant mindset allows them to explore uncharted territories and experiment with new approaches that may lead to significant social advancements. The willingness to face and manage known and unknown risks is crucial for driving innovation and achieving meaningful outcomes (Klein, 2025).

In social entrepreneurship, navigating risk is a multifaceted challenge beyond mere financial considerations. SEs grapple with a spectrum of risks described below, that are often inherent in identifying and addressing complex social issues, necessitating a careful balance of foresight, strategy, and adaptability.

2.5.1 Financial Risks

Financial risks are perhaps the most palpable and immediate concern for SEs. These risks encompass the costs associated with launching and sustaining new initiatives, including but not limited to startup capital, operational expenses, and funding shortfalls. SEs must meticulously calculate the costs and benefits of their proposed actions to ensure that they can secure and effectively manage financial resources. This often involves developing detailed financial projections, creating robust funding strategies, and maintaining rigorous financial oversight to mitigate the risk of insolvency or financial instability (Popkova & Sergi, 2021).

2.5.2 Social Capital Risks

Social capital risks pertain to the relationships and networks that SEs depend upon to execute their initiatives. These relationships include connections with community members, partners, donors, and other stakeholders. Risks in this area involve potential conflicts of interest, stakeholder support shifts, or community erosion of trust. For instance, a SEs might face backlash from community members if a proposed solution does not align with their needs or values. Managing these risks requires building and maintaining strong, transparent relationships, fostering open communication, and demonstrating a consistent commitment to the community's welfare (Crowley & Barlow, 2022).

2.5.3 Emotional Risks

The emotional risks SEs face are often underestimated but can be profoundly impactful. These risks include the personal stress and emotional strain associated with the high-stakes nature of social entrepreneurship. SEs frequently encounter setbacks, failures, and the emotional toll of working with marginalised populations. Navigating these emotional challenges requires resilience, self-care, and support systems. SEs must also be prepared to manage their emotional responses to criticism, failure, and the slow pace of change while remaining motivated and focused on their mission (Zimmer & Pearson, 2018).

2.5.4 Political Risks

Political risks involve navigating the complexities of regulatory environments, political climates, and policy changes that can impact social entrepreneurship initiatives. SEs may face challenges related to compliance with local laws, shifts in political support, or changes in government policies that affect their work. For example, new regulations or political instability could disrupt program implementation or alter funding landscapes. Effective social entrepreneurs anticipate these risks by engaging with policymakers, staying informed about relevant legislation, and advocating for supportive policies (Dutta et al., 2013; Goldsby et al., 2024).

2.6 Navigating Risks Through Strategic Processes

To effectively navigate these risks, SEs employ a variety of strategic processes. The initial phase of understanding the social problem involves comprehensive research and stakeholder consultations to identify and assess potential risks. Brainstorming and designing prototypes necessitate careful consideration of the possible implications and unintended consequences of proposed solutions.

During implementation, SEs must be vigilant in monitoring and evaluating their initiatives to identify emerging risks and make necessary adjustments. Being vigilant includes gathering feedback from beneficiaries and stakeholders, adapting strategies based on real-world data, and being responsive to changing circumstances. A strategic and comprehensive approach to risk management supports the sustainability of their initiatives and contributes to the broader effectiveness and resilience of social entrepreneurship as a field (Helm & Andersson, 2010).

2.6.1 Proactive Approach to Problem-Solving

A proactive orientation is another hallmark of social entrepreneurship orientation. SEs actively seek to address challenges before they escalate, employing a forward-thinking approach that anticipates potential issues and devises strategies to mitigate them. This proactive stance enables them to navigate uncertainties and adapt to changing circumstances effectively, thereby enhancing the likelihood of their ventures' success (Singh, 2024).

In social entrepreneurship, the role of the SE extends beyond merely responding to immediate needs; it involves proactively designing and implementing innovative services, programs, policies, or processes that anticipate future challenges and opportunities. Leadership, empathy, resilience, critical thinking, and financial acumen enable SEs to tap or create opportunities (Sherman, 2011) This pioneering approach is characterised by introducing novel solutions and administrative techniques that can influence the trajectory of change, even if the impact is not immediately evident. Social entrepreneurs leverage their deep understanding of social issues and a forward-thinking mindset to design and deploy services or products that address these anticipated needs. By aligning their innovations with environmental shifts, SE introduce solutions that are timely and resilient to future changes.

2.7 Leading the Sectors

SE often emerge as leaders within their respective sectors or industries through their innovative ventures, acting as network orchestrators across diverse sectors. Their role as pioneers involves creating and implementing new solutions and influencing the broader discourse and practices within their fields. By demonstrating the effectiveness of their approaches, they can inspire other organisations to explore similar strategies and contribute to a collective effort to address social challenges (Busch & Barkema, 2019; Delventhal, 2024; Thorgen & Omorede, 2015).

2.8 Creating a Legacy of Change

The innovations introduced by SE often lay the groundwork for long-term change. While the immediate impact of their solutions may be modest, their influence on future developments can be substantial. By setting new precedents and demonstrating the effectiveness of their approaches, SEs contribute to a legacy of change that continues to evolve and expand over time (Drayton, 2006; Sotikare, 2023).

In conclusion, SE play a crucial role in shaping the future direction of social change. Through their proactive approach to designing innovative services, exploiting environmental changes, and leading their sectors, they set new benchmarks and inspire broader adoption of transformative solutions. Their efforts address current needs and pave the way for sustained progress and improvement within their fields.

2.9 Effectuation in Community Social Entrepreneurship

The effectuation framework offers a distinctive approach to entrepreneurship and community social entrepreneurship, emphasising the iterative process of problem-solving and opportunity creation, beginning with the available resources and expanding to include resources identifiable within the extensive network. Unlike a causal entrepreneurship approach that begins with goal setting and planning before acquiring resources, effectuation describes a more adaptive and resourceful approach.

Effectuation, as defined by Sarasvathy (2001), is a decision-making logic entrepreneurs use in uncertain environments, where the future is unpredictable and shaped by human action. Rather than using a linear predictive approach, entrepreneurs use effectuation work with available means and adjust their goals based on emerging opportunities. The five fundamental principles of effectuation are (1) the bird-in-hand principle, which emphasises starting with what one has; (2) the affordable loss principle, which encourages investing only what one can afford to lose; (3) the crazy quilt principle, which highlights forming partnerships to co-create the future; (4) the lemonade principle, which focuses on leveraging surprises as opportunities; and (5) the pilot-in-the-plane principle, which stresses that entrepreneurs can control and shape the future through their actions (See Appedix for details and examples).

Pragmatically, if a SE addresses a community's lack of access to education, they might start by utilising their knowledge and networks to identify immediate needs and resources. They engage with community members to understand their specific educational challenges, explore potential solutions collaboratively with people in their network, engage with new stakeholders outside their traditional network, and adjust their approach based on real-time feedback and emerging opportunities. Weerakoon et al. (2019) highlight that SEs motivated by a deep passion for specific causes may conduct competitor analysis before developing solutions to meet perceived needs.

This framework is particularly valuable in environments characterised by uncertainty and limited resources, where linear traditional planning methods may be less effective. SEs can create tailored and practical solutions that evolve as they gain more insight and experience by focusing on available resources and engaging with the community and tapping people in extended networks. Essentially, the effectuation framework highlights a pragmatic and iterative approach to entrepreneurship: Entrepreneurs begin with the resources at their disposal—be it skills, knowledge, or relationships—and seek to leverage these to address the challenges they encounter, engage deeply with individuals who are directly affected by the issues they aim to resolve, and discuss 'What can we do together?' rather than imposing pre-defined solutions; explore various possibilities in partnership with the people they serve and adapt their strategies based on feedback, emerging opportunities, and resource availability; involve a diverse range of perspectives and expertise to uncover innovative approaches and refine their strategies.

This adaptive and inclusive method fosters innovation and responsiveness, making it a powerful tool for social entrepreneurs seeking to create meaningful and sustainable impact (Sarasvathy, 2001). SEs intuitively answer the following questions during this inclusive and iterative process.

- Who am I? This involves understanding one's skills, experiences, and resources.
- Whom do I know? This includes recognising the value of existing relationships and networks.
- What do I know? This pertains to leveraging knowledge and expertise.
- What can I do? This focuses on identifying actionable steps that can be taken with the available resources and insights.

Against the backdrop of social entrepreneurship and the effectuation framework guiding community social entrepreneurs, the following case study details the 30-year journey of Medha Tai. Through *Annapurna Pariwar* she exemplifies key concepts and principles from these frameworks, illustrating how entrepreneurial orientation and adaptive decision-making have driven the organisation's success and social impact, balancing community engagement, empowerment of women, profit-making, and democratic governance principles.

3 Case Study: Annapurna Pariwar

3.1 Medha Tai as Community Social Entrepreneur

Annapurna Pariwar was established in 1993 by Medha Tai, upon her relocation to Pune with her family. Juggling roles as a banker, mother, and wife, she engaged with local vendors, frequently purchasing vegetables from them. Through these interactions, she became acutely aware of the significant challenges faced by the women vendors: financial, physical, social, and emotional difficulties. For instance, many women were held hostage financially by local money lenders; others had to experience loss of a husband or a child to unexpected death; still others were victims of domestic violence. Driven by a desire to understand and address these issues, Medha Tai invested considerable time in engaging with the vendors while continuing her career in banking. She found that existing solutions, like self-help groups (SHGs), primarily catered to women in rural areas, where strong social connections fostered a supportive environment for mutual aid. Urban vegetable vendors operate in dynamic and fast-paced environments, often dealing with transient populations and weaker social ties. To thrive, they require stronger social cohesion, trust, and empowerment and a robust social support infrastructure. Self-Help Groups (SHGs) could play a crucial role by uniting individuals facing similar challenges, fostering mutual support, solidarity, and a sense of community based on shared experiences. Typically, these groups had membership ranging from 10 to 20 women. Sometimes SHGs also provided micro-loan support. Unfortunately, these SHGs often failed to ensure equitable access by member women to financial resources/loans, with influential members receiving loans while others acted as guarantors, undermining fairness.

Recognising the shortcomings of traditional financial models in granting access to low-income women vendors, Medha Tai, leveraging her experience and insights, co-created innovative solutions tailored to the unique challenges faced by these women. Discerning that the conventional banking industry, money lenders, and existing SHGs were inadequate for the needs of often illiterate women vendors, she shifted from her banking career to scale the microfinance product she co-created with the women. After almost 10 years of launching the micro-finance vertical–*Annapurna Mahila Multi State Co–op Credit Society Ltd*—she co-created and launched micro-insurance products–*Annapurna Pariwar Vikas Samvardhan*–and affordable child care services–*Vatsalyapurna Service Coop Society*. Today, for instance, *Annapurna Mahila Multi State Co–op Credit Society Ltd.* operates across states, giving small repetitive loans to self-employed women and men living at or below the poverty line, by forming their Joint Liability Groups (JLG); these individuals receive micro-loans without any security or guarantee and the cooperative enjoys a 100% recovery rate. Medha Tai's entrepreneurial approach led to the development of micro-insurance, childcare, educational scholarships, research, and training initiatives as verticals within *Annapurna Pariwar*. By addressing the challenges faced by women receiving micro-loans, she expanded her focus to other areas impacting women's lives.

The verticals (See Table 1) within *Annapurna Pariwar* provide compelling examples of an SSE organisation. As we describe the social entrepreneurship process employed by Medha Tai, we selectively refer to different facets of the verticals that illuminate Medha Tai's journey as a social entrepreneur.

Since its founding in 1993, Annapurna Pariwar (AP) has evolved from modest beginnings into a significant force for economic and social impact in Maharashtra and beyond, inspiring cooperative movements worldwide. Following the establishment of its core initiatives, Medha Tai focused on enhancing operational efficiency and launched *Purna E-Solutions Foundation*, a digital platform aimed at improving service delivery. Her community social entrepreneurship is reflected in her practical implementation of innovative models, responsiveness to feedback, and commitment to social equity, guided by five key principles of community engagement: trust, transparency, communication, and commitment (Morrel-Samuels et al., 2016).

Medha Tai's grassroots work with vegetable vendors highlights her role as a community practitioner (Boehm & Cnaan, 2012). She engaged with women in Pune and Mumbai's densely populated slums, where they face inadequate infrastructure, limited job opportunities, and poor access to education and health services. These environments, marked by evolving social norms and power dynamics, present unique challenges and opportunities. The programs she co-created with AP reflect community practice principles, showcasing cultural humility, evidence-based microcredit models, and efforts to build women's capacity and social capital to address socio-economic challenges (Van Wormer & Link, 2018). Her leadership emphasises flexibility and responsiveness to participant needs, ensuring that interventions respect local values and cultural contexts while fostering innovation (Mandayam et al., 2023).

As a community social entrepreneur, Medha Tai effectively utilised an entrepreneurial orientation to create impactful solutions addressing complex social issues.

Table 1 Annapurna Pariwar explanation of services provided

Service provided	Program detail
Direct microcredit	Annapurna Mahila Cooperative Credit Society (AMCCS) provides microcredit and savings programs to women and men in low-income groups for business creation or expansion, education, housing, asset creation, and repayment of old debts.
Microfinance franchises	Smaller semi-urban and rural microfinance institutions are franchise partners of AMCCS. They provide credit to SHGs and individual borrowers in agricultural and allied activities.
Community based insurance	Annapurna Pariwar Vikas Samvardhan is a comprehensive and borrower-owned health, life, family, and asset insurance program with additional provisions for pensions.
Child care	Vatsalyapurna Swayamrojgar Seva Cooperative Society daycare centers provide safe, developmentally enriching childcare for young children of poor working parents so that they are safe while their parents are working.
Program management software	Purna E Solutions Foundation is a Microfinance and Micro Insurance Management System (MFMIMS) that links the project modules of microfinance and microinsurance run by the different group organisations within Annapurna Pariwar
Educational scholarships	Vidyapurna gives educational scholarships to children of single mothers who are members of AMCCS
Learning and development	Dada Purao Research and Training Institute focuses on research in various areas such as microfinance and micro insurance. This includes internships, opportunities for students and scholars, academic publications, and providing industry training

Her work demonstrates a commitment to transforming marginalised communities by adopting innovative business models to solve persistent social problems (Dees, 1998; Zahra et al., 2009). She created meaningful change by designing and leveraging creative solutions following a deep understanding of community needs.

4 Capitalising on Contextual Changes: Medha Tai's Strategic Response to Emerging Opportunities and Community Social Entrepreneurial Orientation

Medha Tai's career exemplifies how keen awareness of contextual changes can lead to impactful social ventures. Witnessing the privatization of India's banking sector and the subsequent financial exclusion of marginalised women, she leveraged her decade of experience in a public sector bank to drive social and financial reforms, advocating for a more equitable financial system in Pune and Mumbai.

4.1 Expanding Horizons: From Microfinance to Comprehensive Solutions

In response to unmet needs, Medha Tai expanded AP's offerings beyond microfinance. Initially providing collateral-free loans, she recognised the necessity for educational scholarships, childcare services, e-solutions, and a research and training institute. Her appointment to a regulatory committee between 2003 and 2007 enabled her to influence policy, facilitating the introduction of micro-insurance products to better serve impoverished communities. Furthermore, she streamlined insurance claims processing through software development, enhancing operational efficiency.

Medha Tai's initiative to create affordable childcare addressed both developmental needs for children and economic opportunities for women caregivers, reinforcing her commitment to economic empowerment. Her background as a statistician and economist also informed the establishment of a research institute that evaluates AP's impact and trains future social entrepreneurs.

4.2 Designing Innovative Solutions

Once opportunities are identified, social entrepreneurs like Medha Tai design innovative solutions to address specific issues effectively. Her approach to microfinance and childcare services showcases groundbreaking innovations tailored to underserved populations. Medha Tai's pioneered microfinance products for women in slums, offering collateral-free loans and subsequently expanding to include micro-insurance. Her innovative products addressed health, life, and asset protection needs, setting a precedent for financial inclusion. In response to societal needs, such as the tragic rape incident in the slums, she established childcare services to create safe environments for children while enabling some mothers to work or assume the role of entrepreneurs. This initiative not only fulfilled immediate needs but also generated economic opportunities for local women. Her proactive adaptation to emerging needs further exemplifies Medha Tai's commitment to innovation. For instance, the introduction of a software vertical to streamline the processing of loans and insurance claims marked a significant advancement in modernising the administrative aspects of her initiatives. This move reflects her openness to technological innovation to enhance the efficiency and scalability of AP's services.

Medha Tai's community-based approach, characterised by engagement with women vendors, facilitated the development of relevant solutions to complex issues. Her initiatives have significantly improved the overall well-being of women, created social value and contributed to systemic change. As she aptly put it, 'I am not planning anything on my own, but if the need arises we may have to cover some other risks . . . . I think we have mostly developed all the social security programs based on the needs of urban poor' (M. Samant, personal communication, July 15, 2024). This openness and adaptability illustrate her innovative approach's essence and enduring impact on the communities she serves.

4.3 *Navigating Risks*

Medha Tai's entrepreneurial journey over the past three decades has been marked by her willingness to assume and navigate various risks, reflecting a deep commitment to addressing pressing and complex social issues. Her approach illustrates a comprehensive understanding of the multifaceted risks in social entrepreneurship, encompassing financial, social, and sector-specific challenges. Initially, she invested her own funds to support micro-loans, demonstrating her confidence in the beneficiaries' potential to repay. This financial risk was critical for scaling her operations. Social and political risks were inherent in her advocacy for inclusive policies within the financial sector, challenging established norms and positioning herself as a key voice in the movement for financial inclusion. Additionally, her foray into unfamiliar sectors like insurance and childcare required collaboration with experts, enabling her to navigate these challenges effectively. External challenges, such as the COVID-19 pandemic, tested her adaptability. Medha Tai pivoted operations, reopening childcare centers with health measures and developing digital solutions to streamline insurance claims, exemplifying her innovative response to unforeseen circumstances. By assuming financial, social, and sector-specific risks and responding to external challenges with innovative solutions, she has demonstrated a profound capacity for resilience and adaptability.

4.4 *Proactiveness*

Medha Tai exemplifies proactiveness through her unique approaches to microfinance, micro-insurance, and child-care services. Her approach diverged from traditional models, pioneering equitable and sustainable solutions for underserved communities and embodying her commitment to transformative change. A social entrepreneur might introduce a groundbreaking microfinance model in a region where traditional financial institutions have failed to reach underserved populations. This innovation, though initially serving a relatively small group, has the potential to reshape the financial landscape by demonstrating the viability of inclusive financial services and inspiring other organisations to adopt similar approaches. Medha Tai's approach to microfinance diverged from the conventional 'self-help group' (SHG) model pioneered by organisations such as the Grameen Bank. While SHGs typically involved groups of 10–20 women who pooled their savings to secure loans from banks, she introduced the Common Goals Group (CGG) model, also known as '*Samuddisht Gat.*' This model redefined group lending by structuring smaller, more manageable groups of five women each. In the CGG model, members collectively set goals and provided mutual support, ensuring each member benefited equitably from the group's resources. Unlike the traditional SHG model, where the most influential members often dominated loan distribution, the CGG model emphasised fairness and equal access. Medha Tai's innovation proactively addressed the inequities of the existing system, fostering a more balanced distribution of financial resources.

In micro-insurance, Medha Tai faced the challenge of creating affordable health, life, and asset insurance products for impoverished women and their families. In this area, no viable model existed at the time. The *Insurance Regulatory Development Authority* (IRDA) began addressing micro-insurance concepts around 2003, but Tai's initiatives predated the widespread adoption of these products.

More specifically, understanding the financial constraints of her members, Medha Tai conducted extensive consultations with the 3000 women in her micro-finance vertical to determine their ability to pay insurance premiums. She spent two years educating these women about the mutual insurance model, addressing their concerns about traditional insurance agencies and their desire for a more community-centric approach. Collaborating with a French actuary, Mr. F. X. Hay, she co-developed a mutual insurance model tailored to her members' needs. Initially introduced as a voluntary program, it became mandatory to ensure widespread coverage and affordability. The mutual insurance model allowed members to self-insure, pooling resources to cover health, life, and asset losses. This non-profit model proved highly effective in providing affordable insurance within the constraints of the local context.

4.4.1 Proactive Non-Financial Solutions

The rise of digital technology and the increasing demand for remote services have provided SEs with opportunities to create online platforms for delivering education, health care, or financial services. Medha Tai integrated these technologies into AP's models early on, not only to address needs during the COVID pandemic but also to prepare their ventures to adapt to future developments, setting a precedent for others in the sector. She established child-care services designed explicitly for non-school-aged children, which was crucial for enabling mothers to work outside the home while ensuring their children's safety. The introduction of this model in slums provided an example to the child-care industry in Pune and Mumbai, and demonstrated to other providers that affordable, developmentally appropriate, and safe care is possible for children living in slums. Further, the child-care self-sustaining model provided essential services for working women and created entrepreneurial opportunities for women in the community to become child-care providers. This dual approach advanced both women's economic empowerment and their children's welfare, showcasing Medha Tai's proactive strategies to address complex social challenges through sustainable solutions.

5 Effectuation Approaches in Medha Tai's Leadership of Annapurna Pariwar

In the following section, we illuminate how Medha Tai answered these four effectuation related questions during her social entrepreneurship journey.

5.1 *Who Am I?*

According to Guclu et al. (2002), the 'personal experience' of a social entrepreneur serves as a crucial motivator in their pursuit of a cause and in their drive to develop effective solutions. SEs are often inspired by their work experiences, family values, educational backgrounds, and personal interests. Their motivation frequently stems from direct encounters with the challenges they aim to address—whether through personal experiences or observations within their immediate circles, such as family, friends, colleagues, or regular community interactions.

This proximity to the issue—either through direct experience or through witnessing its impact on those around them—fuels their desire to seek out and create alternative solutions. Their dissatisfaction with existing approaches often propels them to explore and innovate beyond conventional methods, drawing on their insights and identities.

As the Zen monk Shunryu Suzuki famously remarked, 'In the beginner's mind, there are many possibilities, but in the expert's, there are few' (1970). This notion underscores the importance of understanding the background and context of a SE. By appreciating their experiences and perspectives, one can gain deeper insight into the solutions they design and the underlying motivations that drive their innovations.

Medha Tai's motivations as a social entrepreneur stem from her personal experiences and values rooted in equity, fairness, and empowerment. Growing up in a family of freedom fighters, she was deeply influenced by a Marxist ideology that emphasised social justice. Her father, a bank officer, demonstrated how small loans could empower poor women, shaping Tai's commitment to financial independence for marginalised communities (Times of India, 2009).

Her interactions with women vegetable vendors during her commutes highlighted the financial struggles and exploitation they faced. These experiences drove her to seek innovative solutions, utilising her banking background to create alternative microfinance options. Embracing a 'beginner's mind' approach, she fostered mutual dialogue among women, recognising the importance of peer support and community empowerment.

Hattab (2023) underscores that effectuation could assist SE in their decision-making process to improve their enterprises' performance. Medha Tai's commitment to education and research was inspired by her father, leading her to establish the *Dada Purao Research and Training Institute*. This institute has been crucial in scaling Annapurna Pariwar's impact, reflecting her belief that documentation and education are vital for social institutions. Her involvement with local universities further demonstrates this dedication.

Medha Tai did not view herself as an expert in financial problem-solving. Instead, she embraced the concept of 'mutual dialogue and interactions', believing that women could learn from and support one another as peer mentors. Moreover, all the verticals were built on the premise that the listening sessions with the women would inform and educate Medha Tai in her leadership and decision making She was confident that fostering interactions among women from different slums would build solidarity and facilitate mutual support across communities in Pune.

5.2 What Do I Know & Whom Do I Know

According to the effectuation framework, successful entrepreneurs leverage their existing resources, knowledge, and networks rather than relying on predetermined goals (Sarasvathy, 2001). Medha Tai exemplified this principle by utilising her educational background—a bachelor's in Statistics and master's and doctoral degrees in Social Work—to address the financial challenges faced by disenfranchised women. Through her professional network, Medha Tai gained support from senior bankers, which was instrumental in establishing Annapurna Pariwar's microfinance operations. This collaborative approach allowed her to enhance the organisation's foundation and secure essential funding.

As the organisation grew, Medha Tai recognised additional needs among micro-loan recipients, particularly in health and asset protection. Collaborating with an actuary, she co-designed affordable micro-insurance products, demonstrating her adaptability and responsiveness to community needs. Her empathetic engagement with women facilitated the development of a child-care model in response to a tragic local event. By co-designing solutions with community members, she fostered a cooperative spirit and ensured that services aligned with their financial capacities.

5.3 What Can I Do

Social entrepreneurs address societal challenges, particularly those gaps between socially desirable conditions and prevailing realities. This gap, often termed the 'social need', represents a significant opportunity for intervention and improvement. SEs, driven by a strong moral compass, are motivated to bridge this gap by leveraging tangible and intangible resources from a network of key stakeholders (Guclu et al., 2002).

6 Translating Personal Experience Into Broad Social Impact

One of the core questions SEs grapple with is how to translate their personal experiences into broader social impact. These experiences, which may include direct encounters with social issues or observations of systemic deficiencies, often shape their vision for change. SEs use their insights to design solutions that address their identified challenges. This process involves translating individual experiences into scalable interventions that benefit a wider community.

6.1 Leveraging Social Assets and Opportunities

Social entrepreneurs continually seek to maximise the impact of existing social assets to address social needs. They evaluate how best to utilise available financial, human, and intellectual resources to enhance societal well-being. This involves harnessing existing strengths, forming strategic partnerships, and using community resources to develop and implement effective solutions.

In addition to leveraging current resources, SEs are adept at capitalising on recent changes and emerging trends to create new opportunities for social impact. They are vigilant in identifying shifts in the social, economic, and technological landscapes that can be used to advance their goals. By staying attuned to these changes, they can adapt their strategies and innovate new solutions that respond to evolving social needs.

7 Continuous Innovation and Learning

Effective SEs engage in a dynamic process of innovation, adaptation, and learning. This iterative approach allows them to refine their strategies and solutions based on ongoing feedback and evaluation. Continuous innovation is crucial as it enables SEs to address new challenges, adapt to changing contexts, and improve the effectiveness of their interventions.

Medha Tai's journey exemplifies how **personal experiences** can translate into significant social initiatives that address societal gaps. Her commitment to **continuous innovation** and learning enabled her to refine strategies based on community feedback, establishing a robust framework for social impact. Initiatives in financial services, childcare, and education reflect her adaptability in responding to evolving community needs. Medha Tai's efforts underscore the importance of leveraging personal values and competencies in social entrepreneurship. The cooperative structure of Annapurna Pariwar fosters pro-social attitudes and community connectivity, empowering individuals to create opportunities that meet their needs (Sacchetti & Campbell, 2014).

8 Core Competencies and Moral Compass

With a background in economics, statistics, and social work, alongside extensive banking experience, Medha Tai possesses a profound understanding of social and financial systems, particularly regarding the inclusion of marginalised populations. Her commitment to addressing social needs is rooted in her Marxist and egalitarian values, guiding her decision to fully dedicate herself to her social enterprise once it reached a sufficient scale.

Medha Tai's approach involves critical questions regarding the translation of personal experience into broader social impact and leveraging existing social assets. Her experiences as a mother provided her with empathy for the childcare and educational needs of working women, leading to the co-design of impactful solutions.

9 Financial Services and Microfinance Innovation

Recognising the lack of affordable financial products for the impoverished, Medha Tai co-founded the *Annapurna Mahila Co-Op Credit Society* to provide collateral-free credit to women in Pune. Operating initially with limited resources, she personally ensured loan repayment from early recipients. As the organisation expanded, she faced challenges such as obtaining credit ratings and navigating audits, but she successfully created a microfinance model that served those excluded from traditional banking (Phills et al., 2008). Additionally, she established a micro-insurance mutual fund in collaboration with actuary Mr. F. X. Hay, which became sustainable by 2008.

9.1 Expanding Services and Community Engagement

Beyond financial services, Medha Tai identified and addressed critical community needs, such as affordable childcare and educational scholarships for children of single mothers. The 'mother-daughter empowerment' model for day-care centers, funded by *The Times of India Foundation*, exemplifies her innovative approach. By training caregivers and fostering a cooperative structure, these centers provided essential services while strengthening community support. The *Dada Purao Research and Training Institute* further demonstrates Tai's commitment to education and research, producing publications that keep community members informed about social issues and engage them in advocacy.

In summary, Medha Tai's journey as a social entrepreneur illustrates how personal experiences, core competencies, and a strong moral compass drive meaningful social impact. Her innovative solutions and collaborative partnerships highlight the essence of effective social entrepreneurship. By addressing financial, social, and economic challenges, she has created transformative outcomes for underserved communities. The cooperative values underlying AP promote flexibility and responsiveness to evolving community needs, positioning it as a vital space for empowerment and opportunity development.

10 Discussion

Medha Tai's journey as a SE empowered marginalised women in low-income communities by fostering collective action and self-reliance, principles central to the SSE (Laville, 2010; Utting, 2015). From the outset, democratic governance was foundational in AP's operations. By ensuring that the women who benefited from the organisation were also involved in decision-making processes, Medha Tai implemented participatory structures that mirrored the SSE's commitment to inclusive and community-driven governance (Fonteneau et al., 2011). The principle of solidarity and cooperation was equally essential, as Medha Tai fostered a strong sense of mutual aid and collective responsibility among the women involved, encouraging them to work together, pool resources, and support one another through microfinance and savings programs (Laville, 2010). Finally, economic activity was a critical component of the organisation's sustainable model, with profits from microloans being reinvested to provide essential social services like healthcare, insurance, and education, reflecting the SSE's emphasis on using economic activity to achieve social goals (Defourny & Nyssens, 2010). Medha Tai operationalised these principles through her leadership, demonstrating how SSE organisations can create inclusive, community-centered economic systems that prioritise social impact over profit (Moulaert & Ailenei, 2005).

Figure 2 illustrates how Annapurna Pariwar's processes and services are purposefully designed to embody the core characteristics of the SSE. As shown, the organisation integrates democratic governance, economic activity, and solidarity and cooperation, creating a holistic framework that aligns with SSE principles. Democratic governance in AP is grounded in participatory decision-making, emphasising inclusivity and women's empowerment through governance structures that actively involve members in shaping economic activities. This aligns with the SSE ethos of fostering grassroots involvement and local control, where decision-making power is redistributed away from traditional hierarchies and toward community members themselves (Defourny & Nyssens, 2010; Laville, 2010).

Economic activity within AP extends beyond mere financial transactions; it is an engine for social transformation. Through its microloans, social insurance, and savings programs, the organisation generates income while adhering to a circular economic model where profits are reinvested into community services. This approach reflects the SSE's commitment to sustainable development and the redistribution of economic benefits, ensuring that financial gains are directed toward enhancing community well-being rather than solely accumulating wealth

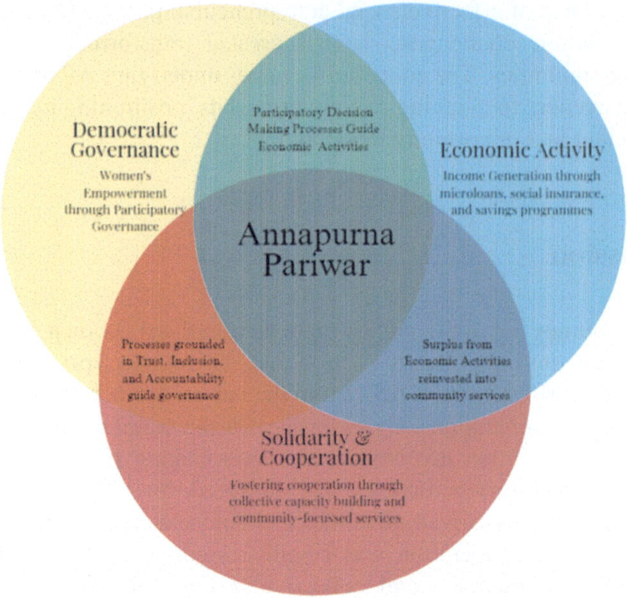

Fig. 2 Annapurna Pariwar as an example of SSE principles in action

(Utting, 2015). By intertwining economic activities with participatory governance, Annapurna Pariwar exemplifies how social enterprises can utilise economic tools to achieve broader social objectives.

Solidarity and cooperation are woven into the fabric of Annapurna Pariwar's operations, highlighting the importance of collective capacity building and mutual support. The organisation's focus on fostering trust, inclusion, and accountability within its processes resonates with SSE's value of solidarity, where cooperation among community members strengthens social bonds and resilience (Allard et al., 2008). This cooperative ethos ensures that AP's initiatives are not just top-down interventions but are co-created with and by the community, enhancing the legitimacy and sustainability of its impact.

The intersection of these three characteristics—democratic governance, economic activity, and solidarity—creates a dynamic and integrated model that can guide social entrepreneurs in designing SSE ventures. Annapurna Pariwar's framework demonstrates that the combination of inclusive governance, economically regenerative practices, and strong community solidarity can lead to more sustainable and equitable social enterprises. This holistic approach challenges conventional business models by prioritising social impact and community empowerment, setting a precedent for how SSE ventures can be structured to address both economic and social challenges simultaneously.

Medha Tai's journey with Annapurna Pariwar highlights how community social entrepreneurs can harness entrepreneurial orientation and effectuation to develop

SSE organisations that are both impactful and sustainable. By engaging deeply with her community, Medha Tai exemplified the principles of community organising, planning, and development, fostering collaborative problem-solving and co-creating solutions tailored to the specific needs of marginalised women. Her strategic approach emphasised empathy, iterative learning, and the courage to challenge conventional models, demonstrating that an inclusive and proactive mindset is crucial for driving meaningful social change.

The SSE framework provided a foundation for AP's operations, emphasising democratic governance, solidarity, and economic activity. Medha Tai's ability to mobilise these principles—by involving community members in decision-making, reinvesting economic gains into social services, and fostering cooperation—ensured that AP not only met immediate needs but also strengthened the community's capacity for self-reliance and mutual support. This approach underscores the importance of creating community-centered, participatory governance structures that empower stakeholders and drive sustainable impact.

Furthermore, Medha Tai's reliance on effectuation—using available resources, adapting to change, and co-creating solutions with stakeholders—illustrates a flexible and resourceful pathway for other social entrepreneurs. Her commitment to starting small, taking affordable risks, and scaling solutions based on community feedback allowed AP to remain responsive and relevant to the evolving needs of its beneficiaries. This effectual approach enabled AP to navigate complex challenges and continuously innovate, reinforcing the organisation's resilience and effectiveness.

The intersection of SSE and social entrepreneurship offers a powerful model for addressing complex societal issues, particularly in disadvantaged communities. By combining values-driven governance with entrepreneurial agility and opportunity recognition, SE can cultivate inclusive, equitable, and sustainable systems that prioritise people and the planet. Medha Tai's example demonstrates that the synergy of these approaches can lead to transformative outcomes, paving the way for other community social entrepreneurs to reimagine economic and social arrangements.

11 Conclusion

The case of *Annapurna Pariwar* under Medha Tai's leadership offers valuable lessons for community social entrepreneurs on building effective SSE organisations. By recognising opportunities, leveraging available resources, and engaging deeply with community members, social entrepreneurs can co-create innovative and sustainable solutions. Medha Tai's journey illustrates that embracing an entrepreneurial mindset, guided by the principles of effectuation and SSE, fosters resilient, inclusive, and community-driven enterprises. These lessons provide a practical framework for other social entrepreneurs seeking to address complex social challenges and build more equitable futures.

Appendix: Effectuation Principles and Examples

The Bird-in-Hand Principle

Instead of waiting for the perfect opportunity or ideal resources, entrepreneurs start with what they already have. This includes their existing knowledge, skills, networks, and available resources. By leveraging these elements, they create opportunities rather than searching for pre-defined ones. For example, a chef who wants to start a food business but lacks funding for a restaurant may launch a pop-up dining experience using their home kitchen and social media connections to attract customers.

The Affordable Loss Principle

Traditional business planning often focuses on maximising expected returns, but effectual entrepreneurs take a different approach by determining what they are willing to lose in pursuit of an opportunity. Rather than making large, risky bets, they invest only what they can afford to lose—whether in terms of money, time, or effort. This approach reduces risk and allows for iterative learning, making it easier to pivot or abandon an idea if necessary without devastating consequences. For instance, an entrepreneur testing a new product idea might invest a small amount in a prototype instead of mass production, ensuring they don't overcommit resources before validating demand.

The Crazy Quilt Principle

Entrepreneurs do not go it alone; they build partnerships and co-create opportunities with others. This principle emphasises the role of collaboration in shaping ventures, as stakeholders bring in their own resources, expertise, and insights. These partnerships create a patchwork—or 'crazy quilt'—of committed stakeholders who share risks and contribute to the venture's success. Effectual entrepreneurs focus on who is willing to join them rather than who they need to persuade, fostering an organic and evolving entrepreneurial journey. For example, a sustainable fashion startup might partner with a local textile manufacturer who shares their values, gaining access to materials in exchange for visibility and collaboration on marketing efforts.

The Lemonade Principle

Rather than viewing unexpected events as obstacles, effectual entrepreneurs embrace surprises and turn them into advantages. Whether it's a market shift, unforeseen challenge, or serendipitous encounter, these events are seen as opportunities to adapt and innovate. The ability to stay flexible and make the most of changing circumstances allows entrepreneurs to pivot in ways that a rigid, predictive approach might not permit. For instance, a coffee shop experiencing a sudden supplier shortage of a key ingredient might introduce a limited-edition alternative, which unexpectedly becomes a customer favorite and a permanent menu item.

The Pilot-in-the-Plane Principle

This principle underscores that entrepreneurs are not passive actors subject to market forces but active agents who shape the future through their decisions and actions. Instead of trying to predict the future, they recognise that their choices directly influence outcomes. By focusing on activities within their control—such as forging partnerships, experimenting with new approaches, and responding to real-world feedback—entrepreneurs drive the trajectory of their ventures rather than being driven by external conditions. For example, rather than waiting for perfect economic conditions, a tech entrepreneur might launch a beta version of their software, gathering real user feedback to refine and scale their product iteratively.

References

Allard, J., Davidson, C., & Matthaei, J. (Eds.). (2008). *Solidarity economy: Building alternatives for people and planet*. Changemaker Publications.

Bhatt, E. R. (2005). *We are poor but so many: The story of self-employed women in India*. Oxford University Press.

Boehm, A., & Cnaan, R. A. (2012). Towards a practice-based model for community practice: Linking theory and practice. *Journal of Sociology and Social Welfare*, *39*(1), 141–168. https://doi.org/10.15453/0191-5096.3653

Bornstein, D. (2004). *How to change the world: Social entrepreneurs and the power of new ideas*. Oxford University Press.

Busch, C., & Barkema, H. (2019). Social entrepreneurs as network orchestrators: A framework and research agenda on networks and leadership in the context of social innovation. *Handbook of Inclusive Innovation*, 464–485.

Carruthers, C. A. (2018). *Unapologetic: A black, queer, and feminist mandate for radical movements*. Beacon Press.

Crowley, F., & Barlow, P. (2022). Entrepreneurship and social capital: A multi-level analysis. *International Journal of Entrepreneurial Behavior and Research*. https://doi.org/10.1108/IJEBR-12-2022-ISSN1355-2554

Dees, J. G. (1998). *The meaning of social entrepreneurship*. Kauffman Foundation.

Defourny, J., & Develtere, P. (1999). The social economy: The worldwide making of a third sector.

Defourny, J., & Nyssens, M. (2010). Conceptions of social enterprise and social entrepreneurship in Europe and the United States: Convergences and divergences. *Journal of Social Entrepreneurship, 1*(1), 32–53. https://doi.org/10.1080/19420670903442053

Delventhal, S. (2024, June 7). The 10 most successful social entrepreneurs. Investopedia. https://www.investopedia.com/articles/investing/092515/10-most-successful-social-entrepreneurs.asp

Drayton, B. (2006). Everyone a changemaker: Social entrepreneurship's ultimate goal. *Innovations, 1*(1), 80–96.

Dutta, N., Sobel, R. S., & Roy, S. (2013). Entrepreneurship and political risk. *Journal of Entrepreneurship and Public Policy*. https://doi.org/10.1108/20452101311318683

Fairbairn, B. (1994). *The meaning of Rochdale: The Rochdale Pioneers and the cooperative principles*. Occasional Paper Series, Centre for Study of the Co-operatives, University of Saskatchewan, Canada.

Fonteneau, B., Neamtan, N., Wanyama, F., Pereira Morais, L., de Poorter, M., & Borzaga, C. (2011). *Social and solidarity economy: Building a common understanding*. International Labour Organization.

Gandhi, M. (1938). *The collected works of Mahatma Gandhi*. Publications Division.

Goldsby, M. G., Kuratko, D. F., Nelson, T. E., & Neck, C. P. (2024). Entrepreneurial Innovation Responsibility (EIR): Mitigating the political risks of disruptive innovation. *Journal of Small Business Strategy, 34*(2), 26–41. https://doi.org/10.53703/001c.92174

Guclu, A., Dees, J., & Anderson, B. (2002). The process of social entrepreneurship: Creating opportunities worthy of serious pursuit. https://centers.fuqua.duke.edu/case/wp-content/uploads/sites/7/2015/02/Article_Dees_TheProcessOfSocialEntrepreneurshipCreatingOppWorthyOfSeriousPursuit_2002.pdf

Guo, C., & Bielefeld, W. (2014). *Social entrepreneurship: An evidence-bsed approach to creating social value*. John Wiley & Sons.

Hardina, D. (2012). *Interpersonal social work skills for community practice*. Springer Publishing.

Hattab, H. W. (2023). Effectuation and the social entrepreneurship: An empirical study of the relationship between adopting the principles of effectual logic and social enterprises' performance in Egypt. *Business Administration, 174*.

Helm, S. T., & Andersson, F. O. (2010). Beyond taxonomy: An empirical validation of social entrepreneurship in the nonprofit sector. *Nonprofit Management and Leadership, 20*(3), 259–276. https://doi.org/10.1002/nml.253

Jiao, H. (2011). A conceptual model for social entrepreneurship directed toward social impact on society. *Social Enterprise Journal, 7*(2), 130–149. https://doi.org/10.1108/17508611111156600

Klein, P. (2025, February 28). A year of business lessons from social impact leaders. *Forbes*. https://www.forbes.com/sites/pklein/2025/02/28/a-year-of-business-lessons-from-social-impact-leaders/

Koe Hwee Nga, K., & Shamuganathan, G. (2010). The influence of personality traits and demographic factors on social entrepreneurship start up intentions. *Journal of Business Ethics, 95*(2), 259–282. https://doi.org/10.1007/s10551-009-0358-8

Kumar, S., Pinto, A. R., Arora, A., & Roy, S. (2020). SHG-Bank linkage: A success story. In *South Asia agriculture and rural growth discussion note series; no. 3*. © World Bank. http://hdl.handle.net/10986/34725 License: CC BY 3.0 IGO, Report to be retrieved from https://openknowledge.worldbank.org/server/api/core/bitstreams/35e1872c-79c8-588e-b372-ccdecacf625d/conten

Kurien, V. (2005). *I too had a dream*. Roli Books.

Laville, J. L. (2010). *Solidarity economy I: Building alternatives for people and planet*. Zed Books.

Mandayam, G., Nandan, M., & Bowen, E. (2023). Convergence of community social work practice, collective impact, and design thinking: What, why, and how? *Journal of Social Work, 23*(5), 916–938. https://doi.org/10.1177/14680173231166112

Martin, R. L., & Osberg, S. (2007). Social entrepreneurship: The case for definition. *Stanford Social Innovation Review*, *5*(2), 29–39. https://doi.org/10.48558/TSAV-FG11

McGregor, J. (2024, December 3). Under 30 2025 social impact: Meet the young leaders building new businesses for a better world. Forbes. https://www.forbes.com/sites/jenamcgregor/2024/12/03/under-30-2025-social-impact-meet-the-young-leaders-building-new-businesses-for-a-better-world/

Morrel-Samuels, S., Bacallao, M., Brown, S., Bower, M., & Zimmerman, M. (2016). Community engagement in youth violence prevention: Crafting methods to context. *The Journal of Primary Prevention*, *37*(2), 189–207. https://doi.org/10.1007/s10935-016-0428-5

Mort, G. S., Weerawardena, J., & Carnegie, K. (2003). Social entrepreneurship: Towards conceptualization. *International Journal of Nonprofit and Voluntary Sector Marketing*, *8*(1), 76–88. https://doi.org/10.1002/nvsm.202

Moulaert, F., & Ailenei, O. (2005). Social economy, third sector, and solidarity relations: A conceptual synthesis from history to present. *Urban Studies*, *42*(11), 2037–2053.

NABARD. (1995). Self-Help groups in India: A study of the issues and challenges.

Nandan, M., Mandayam, G., Collard, C., & Tchouta, R. (2016). An examination of community practice social workers as social intrapreneurs or social entrepreneurs. *International Journal of Social Entrepreneurship and Innovation*, *4*(2). https://doi.org/10.1504/IJSEI.2016.076686

Nouman, H., & Cnaan, R. A. (2023). Community social workers as social entrepreneurs: Lessons from Israel. *International Social Work*, *67*(2), 397–410. https://doi.org/10.1177/00208728221149283

Peredo, A. M., & McLean, M. (2006). Social entrepreneurship: A critical review of the concept. *Journal of World Business*, *41*(1), 56–65. https://doi.org/10.1016/j.jwb.2005.10.007

Phillips, W., Lee, H., Ghobadian, A., O'regan, N., & James, P. (2015). Social innovation and social entrepreneurship: A systematic review. *Group and Organization Management*, *40*(3), 428–461.

Phills Jr., J. A., Deiglmeier, K., & Miller, D. T. (2008). Rediscovering social innovation. Stanford Social Innovation Review. https://ssir.org/articles/entry/rediscovering_social_innovation

Popkova, E. G., & Sergi, B. S. (2021). Dataset modelling of the financial risk management of social entrepreneurship in emerging economies. *Risks*, *9*(12), 211. https://doi.org/10.3390/risks9120211

Rittel, H. W. J., & Webber, M. M. (1973). Dilemmas in a general theory of planning. *Policy Sciences*, *4*(2), 155–169.

Rothman, J. (1968). *Three models of community organization practice*. Columbia University Press.

Sacchetti, S., & Campbell, C. (2014). Creating space for communities: Social enterprise and the bright side of social capital. *Journal of Entrepreneurial and Organizational Diversity*, *3*(2), 32–48. https://doi.org/10.5947/jeod.2014.012

Sadan, A. (2012). *Community work: Methods for social change (in Hebrew)*. United Kibbutz Publishing House.

Samant, M. (2024, July 15). Personal communication.

Sarasvathy, S. D. (2001). Causation and effectuation: Toward a theoretical shift from economic inevitability to entrepreneurial contingency. *Academy of Management Review*, *26*(2), 243–263. https://doi.org/10.2307/259121

Shane, S., & Venkataraman, S. (2000). The promise of entrepreneurship as a field of research. *The Academy of Management Review*, *25*(1), 217–226. https://doi.org/10.2307/259271

Sherman, S. (2011, 28 February 2025). Teaching the key skills of successful social entrepreneurs. *Stanford Social Innovation Review*. https://ssir.org/articles/entry/teaching_the_key_skills_of_successful_social_entrepreneurs

Singer, P. (2009). *Introdução à economia solidária [Introduction to the solidarity economy]*. Fundação Perseu Abramo.

Singh, A. (2024). Problem mapping: Implications for social work education and practice. *Human Service Organizations: Management Leadership and Governance*, 1–14. https://doi.org/10.1080/23303131.2024.2431080

Sotikare, T. (2023, August 1). *How social entrepreneurs are changing the world*. Entrepreneur. https://www.entrepreneur.com/leadership/how-social-entrepreneurs-are-changing-the-world/456407

Suzuki, S. (1970). *Zen mind, beginner's mind*. Shambhala Publications.

Tabassum, K. (2024). Comparative roles and functioning of SHGs in different states of India. *Journal of Social Research*, 7(2). https://doi.org/10.33545/26179210.2024.v7.i2.413

Thompson, J., Alvy, G., & Lees, A. (2000). Social entrepreneurship—A new look at the people and the potential. *Management Decision*, *38*(5), 328–338. https://doi.org/10.1108/00251740010340517

Thorgren, S., & Omorede, A. (2015). Passionate leaders in social entrepreneurship: Exploring an African context. *Business and Society*, *57*(3), 481–524.

Times of India. (2009). https://timesofindia.indiatimes.com/city/pune/nurturing-entrepreneurship/articleshow/4419030.cms

United Nations. (2023). https://unsse.org/wp-content/uploads/2023/05/A_RES_77_281-EN.pdf

Utting, P. (2015). *Social and solidarity economy: Beyond the Fringe*. Zed Books.

Van Wormer, K., & Link, R. J. (2018). *Social work and social welfare: A human rights foundation*. Oxford University Press.

Weerakoon, C., Gales, B., & McMurray, A. J. (2019). Embracing entrepreneurial action through effectuation in social enterprise. *Social Enterprise Journal*. doi: https://doi.org/10.1108/SEJ-08-2018-0053

Zahra, S. A., Gedajlovic, E., Neubam, D. O., & Shulman, J. M. (2009). A typology of social entrepreneurs: Motives, search processes and ethical challenges. *Journal of Business Venturing*, *24*, 519–532. https://doi.org/10.1016/j.jbusvent.2008.04.007

Zimmer, K., & Pearson, K. (2018, August 2). Social entrepreneurs can change the world—But these 6 things are holding us back. World Economic Forum. https://www.weforum.org/stories/2018/08/six-challenges-social-entrepreneurs-need-to-overcome

The manufacturer's authorised representative in the EU is Springer Nature Customer Service Centre GmbH, Europaplatz 3, 69115 Heidelberg, Germany. If you have any concerns regarding our products, please contact ProductSafety@springernature.com

Printed and bound by CPI Group (UK) Ltd, Croydon, CR0 4YY
21/09/2026
02220008-0012